Undoing Human Supremacy

Undoing Human Supremacy

Anarchist Political Ecology in the Face of Anthroparchy

Edited by Simon Springer, Jennifer Mateer,
Martin Locret-Collet, and Maleea Acker

ROWMAN & LITTLEFIELD
Lanham • Boulder • New York • London

Published by Rowman & Littlefield
An imprint of The Rowman & Littlefield Publishing Group, Inc.
4501 Forbes Boulevard, Suite 200, Lanham, Maryland 20706
www.rowman.com

6 Tinworth Street, London SE11 5AL, United Kingdom

British Library Cataloguing in Publication Information Available

Library of Congress Cataloging-in-Publication Data
Names: Springer, Simon, editor. | Mateer, Jennifer, editor. | Locret-Collet, Martin, editor. | Acker, Maleea, 1975– editor.
Title: Undoing human supremacy : anarchist political ecology in the face of anthroparchy / edited by Simon Springer, Jennifer Mateer, Martin Locret-Collet, and Maleea Acker.
Description: Lanham, Maryland : Rowman and Littlefield, 2021. | Includes bibliographical references and index. | Summary: "This volume encourages us to move towards a renewed understanding of humanity as firmly located within the biosphere"— Provided by publisher.
Identifiers: LCCN 2021020645 (print) | LCCN 2021020646 (ebook) | ISBN 9781538159125 (cloth) | ISBN 9781538159132 (ebook) | ISBN 9781538161791 (paperback)
Subjects: LCSH: Human ecology. | Human-animal relationships. | Nature—Effect of human beings on.
Classification: LCC GF41 .U64 2021 (print) | LCC GF41 (ebook) | DDC 304.2—dc23
LC record available at https://lccn.loc.gov/2021020645
LC ebook record available at https://lccn.loc.gov/2021020646

Contents

Preface

An Anarchist Political Ecology

John P. Clark

WHAT IS TO BE UNDONE?

The title of this book is a very apt one. It tells us immediately that it is not merely about knowing, but above all about *doing*, and specifically about doing by *undoing*. It also tells us exactly what must be undone. It is "human supremacy" and "anthroparchy," by which is meant both the ideology and the institutionalized practice of human domination. Furthermore, it challenges us to face the reality of this domination. There could be no more urgent entreaty than this one at the present decisive moment in the history of the Earth.

One indicator of the extent to which human domination of the biosphere has become an overwhelming reality is the fact that "Human Appropriation of Net Primary Production" doubled over the past century to 25%. This means that a huge proportion of the planet's biomass is now being appropriated by humans. This proportion continues to grow and is projected to reach up to 44% by the middle of this century (Krausmann et al. 2013). While such statistics may seem disquieting, the process is perhaps more profoundly disturbing when one looks at the more concrete meaning of such appropriation. The mammalian world is now overwhelming dominated by humans. Human beings and their domesticated animals now constitute 96% of the biomass of all mammals on the planet, while mammals in the wild constitute a mere 4% of the total. Moreover, 70% of the biomass of all birds is that of farmed poultry alone, twice as much as that of all the other birds on Earth (Bar-On, Phillips, and Milo 2018).

The vast majority of the land has also succumbed to human domination. Humans have significantly transformed over three-fourths of the non-polar land area of the planet, thereby subverting the Earth's regenerative processes, and leaving less than one-fourth in a condition of relative wildness

(Watson et al. 2018). Finally, and most ominously, this ecologically devastating activity has culminated in the greatest, though most self-defeating, form of domination, the power of annihilation of life and life-forms. We have entered into the era of the Sixth Mass Extinction of life on Earth, in which extinction rates are perhaps 1,000 times the background rate and moving toward 10,000 times that rate (De Vos et al. 2015). At the same time, we are facing not only developing climate catastrophe but, according to sober scientific analysis, six other areas in which transgression of "planetary boundaries" threatens to produce disastrous state changes in the biosphere. (Rockström et al. 2009).

Much thought has recently been given to the concept of *biopower*. Perhaps it is time to give more thought to the concept of *biodomination*. The ecoanarchist sense of urgency that comes from an awareness of the depth of the crisis that results from this domination is expressed by the editors of this volume when they describe "the pursuit of an anarchist political ecology" as "an attempt to reestablish balance in our world before the end of all human beings becomes a certainty" (Introduction). In short, we now face the specter of an end to the history of human domination through a global ecological collapse that brings with it the fall of humanity itself. This is the ultimate significance of anthroparchy, or human domination. When Simon Springer argues near the end of this book that "anarchism must focus its energies on undermining anthroparchy as much as it does on any other system of oppression" (chapter 10), he is in no way overstating the importance of this world historical project.

CREATING ANARCHIST POLITICAL ECOLOGY

What then, is an anarchist political ecology? The three volumes of this work constitute a major step toward defining it, and demonstrate through their thirty wide-ranging chapters both its unity and its multiplicity. However, to begin with, we might look to the etymology of the term for guidance, since it reveals very well the fundamental nature of the field as a theory and practice. The term "anarchist" derives from the root *arche* and from the privative *a*, signifying negation. *Arche* in its political sense means "ruling," and denotes constituting a separate power over those who are ruled. But, in a larger sense, it refers to all systemic forms of domination, which anarchists oppose and seek to abolish. There is a second relevant sense of *arche* that is even more primordial than the political one. *Arche* initially had the connotation of "origin," and evolved into the ontological and epistemological concept of the "first principle." Thus, in its underlying philosophical sense, *anarche* means opposition to the imposition of abstract principles on a changing, developing, living reality. This anti-essentialist, anti-dogmatic, anti-ideological perspective underlies the ethics and politics of anarchism, and indeed anarchist epistemology, its way of knowing the world.

So much for "anarchist." We come next to "political ecology." The term "political" derives from the Greek *polis*, which refers to the political community. Anarchism espouses "the political" in the very strong sense in which *polis* denotes a local, place-based political community on a scale that makes it capable of communal self-determination. For anarchists, "the political" can be realized only if such a community is the basis for any political association on a larger scale. Next, we come to "ecology." The "eco" in ecology comes from the Greek word *oikos*, which refers to the home or household. For eco-anarchism, this means that our community is not only the basic political one, but rather a community of communities, made up of all the concentric local, regional, and planetary ecological communities of life, both human and non-human, in which we participate. Finally, the "logy" of ecology comes from the Greek word *logos*, a deeply resonant term that extends back in the history of thought to the ancient philosopher Heraclitus, who said that the logos is something that we should *follow*, and something that is *common* rather than merely individual. The logos is the way of nature that guides the path of all beings and all communities of beings, and which allows the good of each being to be attuned to the good of all beings.

For over a century, anarchist theorists and activists had been engaged in developing such a political ecology before it emerged in mainstream academia. A few examples of the tradition include the groundbreaking work of anarcho-communist geographers Reclus and Kropotkin in the late 19th and early 20th century, the Gandhian Sarvodaya Movement in India (inspired both by Indian local traditions and by Ruskin, Thoreau, and Tolstoy), Ralph Borsodi and the School of Living, beginning in the 1930s, and Bookchin and social ecology, beginning in the 1960s.

Building on this background, anarchist political ecology emerged in the past few decades as a broadly interdisciplinary field, encompassing many areas of the social sciences, the physical sciences, and the humanities. Some of the many related fields that are important to it are social ontology, value theory, environmental ethics, social ethics, normative political theory, sociological theory, cultural history, landscape history, cultural anthropology, political anthropology, ecopsychology, mass psychology, political psychology, political geography, cultural geography, social geography, environmental studies, human ecology, community ecology, social ecology, and evolutionary biology. What ties these together as a coherent project is a common critique of the dominant world system as unjust, oppressive, genocidal, and ecocide, and a common commitment to the development of a personal and social practice capable of overcoming that system and establishing a liberated Earth community.

THE EVOLUTION OF POLITICAL ECOLOGY

The crucial significance of such an anarchist political ecology becomes clear if it is seen in the context of the evolution of the larger field of political ecology. One sometimes sees within the academic world a kind of "institutionalization of charisma" in which a new, seemingly radical discipline or field emerges and threatens to challenge the status quo in the society, but then gradually becomes incorporated into the dominant system. In the end, it may even perform a legitimating function on behalf of that system, and create new opportunities for academic, professional and technical workers to operate within it.

Political ecology has, to a certain degree, gone through such a transformation, and this is one reason why a vibrant anarchist political ecology is so necessary. Some might say that it is necessary to help keep political ecology honest. In fact, it is necessary to help keep it sane (that is, in touch with geohistorical reality). As a field of study and research, political ecology has emerged and evolved in large part in response to developments within the larger society, as the global ecological crisis has slowly become more of a psychosocial reality. The potentiality for a developed political ecology was implicit in many tendencies within such fields as geography, ecology, anthropology, sociology, political theory, and social ethics, but it remained largely latent until engaged political ecologies began to develop within the global ecology movement.

During the 1980s, the radical environmental movement (or "radical ecology") and the global Green Movement both began to grow rapidly. The Earth First! "radical environmental" organization was founded in 1980, as part of a growing movement of direct action and eco-defense. *Die Grünen* (the German Green Party) entered the *Bundestag* (German Federal Assembly) in 1983, and both the green parties and the larger Green Movement soon spread internationally. The book *Deep Ecology* (Devall and Sessions) was published in 1985, and quickly became a kind of manifesto of the Deep Ecology Movement, which had a significant (albeit ambiguously) radicalizing influence on green politics and the environmental movement. In 1988, *Capitalism Nature Socialism*, the most important theoretical journal of radical ecology was founded in the United States, followed soon by similar publications in several other countries.

One of the first academic works to focus heavily on radical political ecology was *Environmental Philosophy: From Animal Rights to Radical Ecology*, published in 1993. Almost two-thirds of the text of the first edition was devoted to major radical political ecologies, specifically deep ecology, ecofeminism, and social ecology (Zimmerman et al. 1993). In subsequent editions (1998, 2001, and 2005), these perspectives were still represented, though increasingly less so, as the focus on more radical forms of ecology and environmentalism waned in the academic world. The "environmental humanities" and corresponding areas of the social sciences were becoming increasingly normalized, and political ecology reflected this drift.

Geographer Paul Robbins's *Political Ecology: A Critical Introduction* (2012), one of the leading works in the field, demonstrates this evolution. Robbins observes that while some political ecologists are physical scientists or "methodological technicians," most come from the social and behavioral sciences. The direction of development of political ecology is revealed in Robbins's comment that political ecologists "advocate fundamental changes in the management of nature and the rights of people, directly or indirectly working with state and non-governmental organizations (NGOs) to challenge current conditions" (13). The focus on the "management" of nature and the use of rights discourse are symptomatic of the increasing orientation toward working within state bureaucracies and NGOs.

What disappears from political ecology in this depiction is not only its relationship to radical philosophy and political theory but also its role as a theoretical dimension of radical and transformative social movements. A certain critical dimension remains, and the field is described as being concerned with phenomena as "winners and losers, hidden costs, and the differential power that produces social and environmental outcomes" (20). However, these topics have long been grist for the academic mill of mainstream, adaptive social science.

Interestingly, Robbins recognizes the importance of Kropotkin's (and to a lesser degree Reclus's) groundbreaking work in political ecology, which he calls a "critical social ecology" (29). He observes that it "sets a precedent" for the political ecology of a century later, through "its focus on production, its archival and field-based empirical approach, its concern for marginalized and disenfranchised people, its interest in local environmental knowledge, and its concentration on the landscape as an object of explanation" (28). While political ecology will certainly benefit from emulating all these aspects of Kropotkin's work, it is noteworthy that what is omitted is everything about Kropotkin's problematic that fundamentally challenges the existence of an exploitative and ecocidal system of domination.

QUESTIONS OF VALUE

As many of the chapters in this book demonstrate, anarchist political ecology is a fundamentally normative field, and one of its most important dimensions is the exploration of the most basic normative issues. None of these is more basic than the question of the nature of value. An answer to it requires a developed ecoanarchist theory of value that includes the critique of major existing value theories. Anarchist political ecology must not only engage in the traditional leftist critique of exchange value but must also uncover the implicit instrumentalist and anthropocentric presuppositions of concepts of use value. It must also show how the concept of intrinsic value can play a role in a developed ecological theory of value. And beyond this, it must show the limitations even of intrinsic value (as something having simple location within individual beings or their experience), and it must explore more radically ecological and holistic accounts of value, such as the theory of systemic value (Rolston, 1988).

Another key normative issue for anarchist political ecology, as is clear from many discussions in this volume, is that of moral standing or moral consideration. It is important to consider the various alternative criteria for moral consideration, such as life, consciousness, sentience, experience of pain and pleasure, personhood, level of complexity, being a subject of a life, self-consciousness, rationality, and moral agency (to mention some of the most important). Ecoanarchism obviously rejects the morally indefensible speciesist, anthropocentric position that moral standing can be based on membership in the species *Homo sapiens*. However, the assessment of the merits of various non-speciesist criteria remains a challenging undertaking.

Furthermore, anarchist political ecology needs to overcome the flaws of normative theories that are one-sidedly individualistic and focus excessively on individual organisms, beings, or persons, and those that are one-sidedly holistic theories and focus excessively on the group, the community, the whole, or the system. Instead, it must continue to develop a more dialectically holistic analysis that recognizes the integrity of both part and whole, and of singularity, particularity, and universality, without absolutizing, hypostatizing, or reifying any of these dimensions. Such a perspective is often epitomized in anarchist thought as the recognition of the value of "unity-in-diversity."

Anarchist political ecology is critical of individualistic theories such as utilitarianism that base moral value on the experience of sentient beings (Singer 1975) and rights theories that base it on moral personhood (Regan 1983). Because of their moral individualism, many animal rights theorists devote inadequate attention to how treatment of domesticated animals is part of systematic ecological devastation. For example, as Springer notes, they may fail to appreciate "how factory farming plays a key role in environmental ruination" (chapter 10). Similarly, Shane Mc Donnell points out problems that arise out of a failure to grasp the complexity of multi-level moral problems, for example, those that involve issues regarding the ethical treatment of animals, rights of human communities, and larger ecological values. He notes that "some equate Indigenous tribes hunting, animal agriculture, and super trawlers, seeing no ethical difference between these activities" (chapter 6).

For similar reasons, ecoanarchism rejects the limitations of biocentric theories that base moral value on the realization of the good of individual living beings (Taylor 1986). One might refer to this as the limitations of a "flat axiology." As Marcelo Lopes de Souza explains, the more consistent ecological ethic espoused by ecoanarchism "stresses the importance of whole ecosystems rather than just of Earth's living beings," and thus goes beyond biocentrism, which is "specifically concerned with the well-being of organisms" (chapter 5). Anarchist political ecology is in general agreement with ecocentric and holistic ethical theories that focus on the realization of good and value in relation not only to individual beings (organisms, sentient beings, persons) but also to species, ecosystems, and a larger "nature," including the biosphere and the whole Earth (Rolston 1988).

More complex self-realization theories show greater promise from an eco-anarchist perspective. Though they are often formulated in a human-centered manner, as exemplified by Martha Nussbaum's "human capabilities theory" (Nussbaum 2006) such theories can be expanded into a more ecological form. This the case to a certain degree for Arne Naess's interpretation of self-realization in terms of a transpersonal ecological "selfhood" (Naess 1989). Even more significantly, the ecofeminist ethics of care (Salleh 2017) has made some of the most important contributions to the development of an ecological ethics that recognizes the importance of value at all significant levels: that of human persons, of other living beings, of human communities, and of larger ecological ones. It is in many ways closest to the most developed ecoanarchist positions.

A fundamental challenge to the project of developing an ecoanarchist normative theory is the need to break definitively with the objectifying, reifying, and hierarchically dualistic language and concepts that we have inherited from the long history of domination. Thus, as Benjamin O'Heran points out, there is a need to replace the language of atomism and possessive individualism with forms that express more adequately the relatedness, interconnection, interbeing, and communality that eco-anarchism values. He suggests, inspired by Margulis and Haraway, that this might be achieved through reconceptualizing and reimagining "beings" as they, in fact, really are: as "holobionts," that is, "assemblages of different species that form complex ecological units," and as "symbionts," that is, "organisms in symbiotic relationships with each other trying to navigate heterogeneous relationships of mutuality and competition" (chapter 8).

Perhaps the greatest source of wisdom and inspiration in this area is Indigenous societies, which often have a relational ontology that is embodied in cultural practices and language, and which implies an ethic of reciprocity that encompasses all beings, as R.D. points out in relation to Mi'kmaq society (chapter 4). Perhaps the most illuminating discussion of how Indigenous language and culture can inspire and shape radically transformative politics is Dylan Fitzwater's study of the relationship between the Tsotsil language, Indigenous culture, and the Zapatista Revolution (Fitzwater 2019).

THE DIALECTIC OF DOMINATION

The approach of anarchist political ecology to all of the value issues that have been mentioned must be understood within the context of the ecoanarchist view of geohistory as the story of the struggle between freedom and domination. This ecoanarchist interpretation of the Earth Story was first developed in Élisée Reclus's 3,500-page work of social geography *L'Homme et al Terre* or *Humanity and the Earth* (Reclus 1905–1908), and is carried on in contemporary ecoanarchism. As is illustrated in a number of chapters in this volume, ecoanarchism tends to interpret freedom in terms of the flourishing of beings, and domination as that which blocks that flourishing. This analysis is applied to individual beings, communities of beings, species, ecosystems, the biosphere, and the whole Earth community.

Anarchist political ecology has a comprehensive critique of the system of domination that explores the dialectical interaction and mutual determination of all specific forms of domination. R.D. notes that "race, class, gender, sexuality, ethnicity, nation, ability, and age operate not as unitary, mutually exclusive entities, but as reciprocally constructing phenomena that in turn shape complex social inequalities" (chapter 4). The need for a deeply dialectical analysis of all forms of domination is also expressed in Ophélie Véron and Richard White's observation that "different systems of power and injustice . . . do not act independently of each other and, to be understood more properly, should be examined as interrelated forms of discrimination" (chapter 3). To carry out this project fully, anarchist political ecology must engage in a critical-dialectical analysis not only of all *forms of domination* but also of all *the spheres of social determination* that perpetuate these forms and which also might make possible the emergence of a new realm of freedom. These spheres include the social institutional structure, the social ideology, the social imaginary, and the social ethos (a sphere that includes the affective dimension and is the sphere of desire).

While there is a popular misconception (to which theorists also fall prey) that anarchist critique is fixated on the state, this is far from being the case. Anarchist political ecology engages in the most incisive simultaneous critique of all forms of domination. This includes the critical analysis of the relationship between capital and the state, and is expressed in distinctive theories of both the capitalist state and state capitalism. It examines the foundations not only of the state and law but also of capital and the market, in overt violence and the threat of violence. R.D. (following Harvey) cites the concept of "accumulation by dispossession" as an "accurate descriptor of capitalist violence" (chapter 4). This theme of the primary appropriation of power and property through forms of violence, force, and coercion (classically expressed in Marx's concept of primitive accumulation) is one of the most central themes of anarchist political theory.

Anarchist critique reveals the society of domination to be a system of ongoing violent expropriation of communal wealth and the wealth of nature. This is exhibited not only in the origins of the state and private property in conquest and subjugation, and in periodical regression to brutal coercive appropriation in periods of war and terror, but, above all, in the ongoing dependence of both state and capitalist power in explicit and implicit violence at every moment of their existence. In effect, what is sometimes described as a "state of exception" is only a more brutal and less mystified form of the ordinary, unexceptional operation of a violent and coercive system of domination.

FREEDOM AS MUTUAL FLOURISHING

Though this might seem self-evident, it might be worth reminding ourselves that despite the etymology of the term the ultimate concern of "anarchists" is not domination but freedom, that which lies beyond domination. If we are anarchists, we are anarchists only because we are libertarians, because we value freedom in the most expansive sense, as the full development of beings in relation to all other beings. Anarchists oppose domination because domination is what stands in the way of that freedom. We might also remember that the term "libertarian" (originally the French term *libertaire*) was invented by the great anarcho-communist and utopian writer Joseph Déjacque, who first used it to make the point that one could not be a true libertarian if one supported any form of domination, whether capitalism, the state, or (as he then pointed out of Proudhon) patriarchy. So, it is apt that Springer concludes this volume with a call for a "total liberation ecology." Anarchism seeks to liberate all beings in the entire Earth community from all forms of domination, so that their greatest potentialities may be liberated and they may flourish mutually.

Springer makes the important point that a "total liberation" perspective is one that "avoids the limited morality of the animal rights discourse" that grants a few favored species "ethical parity with humans" and thus continues to view the liberation of nature "through an anthropocentric lens" (chapter 10). There are almost 60,000 species of vertebrates and several million species of invertebrates. Ecoanarchism and anarchist political ecology are both theoretically and practically concerned with the flourishing of all of these interconnected life forms and with that of the whole Earth community of which they are members. Several of the chapters focus on this eco-anarchist conception of mutual flourishing of all beings. O'Heran, for example, pertinently cites Haraway's "ethic of co-flourishing" that is based on a practice of responding to all beings "we are in relation with" (chapter 8). Whether we are "anarcho-communists," "communitarian anarchists," or "communalists" (to mention several popular alternatives) our ultimate communal concern must be the good of this whole community of beings with whom we are in relation. Our community must be, as Martin Buber said, a community of communities, and the good we pursue must be a good of goods.

It is important, moreover, that we understand that to be "in relation" the Earth community is to have a relationship of participation in it, not merely in a political sense but in an ontological one. We must realize that we are not merely externally related to nature, but are, rather, creative expressions of nature, nature giving birth to itself. As Amster suggests, we must go beyond the static ideal of merely being "in harmony with" nature. As he says (quoting Purchase) we must also "actively enhance and improve upon the beauty, generosity and creative potentiality of organic life and nature" (chapter 7). Of course, we must admit that most previous human efforts to "improve on" nature have been a disaster. They have been based on the illusions of the civilized ego and on the idea that we act as beings that are ontologically separate from one another and separate from the Earth.

However, we are also capable of attaining a participatory consciousness of our integral role in the process of mutual flourishing, the liberation of life. If we are capable of achieving a good, whether for ourselves or for other beings, it is nature, and specifically the Earth, that is achieving this good through us. "We are nature becoming self-caring." To do this caring well, we must pay careful attention to how the Earth achieves the good of all terrestrial beings through the action of this multitude of beings, through the "Ten Thousand Things," as they were called by the Daoist sages. Following the dao, "the way of nature," means participating in what ecological processes have done throughout geohistory, that is, promote mutual flourishing.

To do this, we must become the kind of beings who are capable of doing it. In this connection, Friederike Schmitz pertinently cites Marti Kheel's call for a "unity of reason and emotion" (chapter 1). The aspirations of anarchist political ecology can be fulfilled only through the development of a culture and community of persons who both think and feel in a mutualistic and non-dominating way. This is also the implication of Gelderloos's statement (cited by Amster) that what is "most importantly" required for "an ecologically sustainable world" is "a common ecological ethos" (chapter 7). Anarchist political ecology is part of the quest for such an ethos, in which each person and community practices an ecological mode not only of thinking and feeling but also of being and acting.

BEYOND THE ANTHROPOCENE

Guldi and Armitage in *The History Manifesto* (Guldi and Armitage 2014) point out the crucial importance of situating historical phenomena in "Big History" (the history of the cosmos and the planet) and in "Deep History" (the long-term history of our species). Anarchist political ecology does precisely this, and more, in interpreting its subject-matter in the context of our place in Deep Geohistory. Bioregionalist Peter Berg used to do a wonderful bioregional mapping exercise called "Where you at?" in which participants mapped the key bioregional features of their local area. Anarchist political ecology is a project of waking us up to "Where you at?" at every level, from the very local to the broadly geohistorical. The latter is the level at which things often seem too big to notice, but are actually too big to ignore.

So, how should we describe our present point in geohistory? Anarchist political ecology questions the use of the flawed concept of "Anthropocene" to describe our present period. Randall Amster points out, quoting Ahuja, that this concept "generalizes to all humans the effects of particular environmental practices that have benefited only some humans at the expense of others" (chapter 7). It is for this reason that some have opted for the more critical concept of "Capitalocene," as has been proposed by Jason Moore (Moore 2015), and which focuses on the economic system that has been largely responsible for the severe ecological disturbances that are usually associated with the Anthropocene.

Such an approach is an advance. However, an adequate characterization of the major dimensions of the system of domination would require a collection of terms such as Androcene, Imperiocene, and Technocene, in addition to Capitalocene. From an ecoanarchist perspective, which is at the same time the perspective of the whole of terrestrial life, it might more simply be called the "Necrocene," that is, the new era of death on Earth, conceived of as the successor to the Cenozoic era, the previous new era of life on Earth (more literally, "of animal life").

Some have also given thought to a new regenerative geological era that might succeed out present period of ecocidal domination. Amster aptly envisions an "Anarchocene," one variation on the concept of a new era of non-domination (chapter 7). I have suggested that we might imagine the coming of a "Poetocene," a new era of creative flourishing. We might even call it the "Eleutherocene," the new era of a liberated Earth.

REFERENCES

Bar-On, Y., Phillips, R., and Milo, R. 2018. "The Biomass Distribution on Earth." *Proceedings of the National Academy of Sciences (PNAS)* 115 (25), 6506–6511.

Devall, B., and Sessions, G. 1985. *Deep Ecology: Living as If Nature Mattered.* Layton, UT: Gibbs Smith Publisher.

De Vos, J. et al. 2015. "Estimating the Normal Background Rate of Species Extinction." *Conservation Biology* 29 (2), 452–462.

Fitzwater, D. 2019. *Autonomy Is in Our Hearts: Zapatista Autonomous Government through the Lens of the Tsotsil Language.* Oakland, CA: PM Press.

Guldi, J., and Armitage, D. 2014. *The History Manifesto.* Cambridge: Cambridge University Press.

Kovel, J. 2007. *The Enemy of Nature: The End of Capitalism or the End of the World?* London: Zed Books.

Krausmann, F. et al. 2013. "Global Human Appropriation of Net Primary Production Doubled in the 20th Century." *Proceedings of the National Academy of Sciences (PNAS)*, 110 (25), 10324–10329.

Moore, J. 2015. *Capitalism in the Web of Life: Ecology and the Accumulation of Capital.* London: Verso.

Naess, A. 1989. *Ecology, Community and Lifestyle.* Cambridge: Cambridge University Press.

Nussbaum, M. 2006. *Frontiers of Justice: Disability, Nationality, Species Membership.* Cambridge, MA: The Belknap Press of Harvard University Press.

Reclus, E. 1905–1908. *L'Homme et la Terre.* 6 vol. Paris: Librairie Universelle.

Regan, T. 1983. *The Case for Animal Rights.* Berkeley: University of California Press.

Robbins. P. 2012. *Political Ecology: A Critical Introduction.* Malden, MA: Wiley-Blackwell.

Rockström, J. et al. 2009. "A Safe Operating Space for Humanity." *Nature* 461, 472–475.

Rolston, H. 1988. *Environmental Ethics: Duties to and Values in the Natural World.* Philadelphia, PA: Temple University Press.

Salleh, A. 2017. *Ecofeminism as Politics: Nature, Marx and the Postmodern.* London: Zed Books.

Singer, P. 1975. *Animal Liberation: A New Ethics for Our Treatment of Animals.* New York: Random House.

Taylor, P. 1986. *Respect for Nature: A Theory of Environmental Ethics*. Princeton, NJ: Princeton University Press.

Watson, J. et al. 2018. "Protect the Last of the Wild." *Nature* 563, 27–30.

Zimmerman, M., Callicott, J., Sessions, Warren, K., and Clark, J., eds. 1993. *Environmental Philosophy: From Animal Rights to Radical Ecology*, Englewood Cliffs, NJ: Prentice-Hall.

Introduction: The Political Ecology of Human Supremacy

Simon Springer, Jennifer Mateer,
and Martin Locret-Collet

Whether the example is a slaughterhouse, a petrochemical facility, industrial agriculture, a hydroelectric dam, or a mining operation, each reveals
the ways in which humans exploit and produce harm among other humans,
nonhuman animals, and ecosystems. While these forms of hierarchy and
violence are uniquely experienced across species and space, they are
inseparable and interrelated. They necessarily begin and end with human
actors imagining and giving meaning to these behaviors.

—David Pellow (2014, 9)

By its fields, its roads, its dwellings, and its buildings of every kind, by
the grouping of its trees and the general arrangement of the landscape,
each nation will display the extent of its own taste. If it really possesses a
sense of beauty, it will render nature more beautiful; if on the contrary, the
great mass of mankind should remain such as it is today, coarse, egotisti-
cal, and false, it will continue to imprint its sad qualities upon the world.
Then would the poet's cry of despair become truth—"Whither shall I fly?
Nature increases in hideousness."

—Élisée Reclus (1881, 193)

ANARCHISM, POLITICAL ECOLOGY, AND MORE-THAN-HUMAN GEOGRAPHY

The Earth is in crisis. We know this. We have known this for a long time. In
the throes of the unfolding nightmare we call "capitalism," it is not hard to
see and hear the violence that is being enacted against the planet. Our planet.
The only planet in the known universe to harbor life, and yet we are openly
flirting with the prospect of eradicating the flora and fauna that populate our

1

world. Pause for a moment and look out your window. Almost every reader will be able to see the deep scars of human arrogance on the landscape. Parking lots and roads that have paved over the soil, buildings of all sizes that have been erected in place of trees, telephone wires crisscrossing across your line of sight, and infrastructures of various forms that lay hidden just beneath the surface. Now close your eyes and listen. The incessant thrum of motors, the sound of steel being cut, a car alarm going off, and the irritating beeping of a loader backing up. Now think of the extractive activities that went into creating the landscapes we occupy. Consider the destruction of the habitats and homes of other species to make way for our own material comforts and conveniences. Think of what enables our lifestyles: the sewage plants, the garbage dumps, the manufacturing facilities, the oil refineries, the transportation networks, the mining sites, the factory farms, and the list goes on. In almost all instances the landscapes we occupy have been devised with only one concern in mind: ourselves. Very little thought is given to the ecosystems we inhabit, or to the biosphere as a whole and our place within it. Such is the nature of anthropocentrism. Although many of us are now sounding the alarm, we can't be heard over the pervasive noise of our industries or seen by the visionless politicians that lead us as lemmings. Our ecological condition is undeniably a political one, but it is never going to be solved through the protocols of electoral politics or the procedures of the state. We have tried those solutions. When they inevitably proved futile, we tried them again. All they have ever shown us is how miserable they fail. The refusal of the idea that these formal institutional mechanisms can ever save us from climate catastrophe, environmental collapse, and a hideous version of nature is to demand an anarchist political ecology.

Political ecology is a loosely defined area of study encompassing a large number of approaches (Clark 2012). Paul Robbins (2012, 20) points out that, more than a strictly defined academic field, it is "a term that describes a community of practices united around a certain kind of text." Despite this rich plurality, the genealogy of political ecology is quite easy to trace: two major intellectual figures of the 19th century, Peter Kropotkin and Élisée Reclus, are widely accepted as its founding fathers. Both men were of course anarchists and geographers, and yet in spite of their early influence on the field, a contemporary anarchist political ecology has been slow to emerge. This absence is particularly surprising given the recent (re)turn toward anarchist geographies and the vast potential such a lens offers on insisting that environmental challenges be politicized in such a way that questions the role of the state, capitalism, and other hierarchical orderings embedded within human societies (Clough and Blumberg 2012; Souza, White, and Springer 2016; Springer et al. 2012; Springer, White, and Souza 2016; White, Springer, and Souza 2016). It is hard to deny the role that anarchist theory had in breaking the prevailing tradition of environmental determinism in geography, where Kropotkin (1885) and Reclus (1894) refused to be complacent in seeing the physical attributes of a territory as determining the moral and corporeal traits of the people inhabiting that land, as well as their social organization. Their anarchism was defined as much by a rebuke of capitalism as it was by challenging deeply ingrained imperialist views on race and social domination (Clark and Martin 2013; MacLaughlin 2016). Their intellectual departure was a broadened understanding of geography that insisted the social, the political, the economic and indeed the environmental were all integral considerations in writing about the earth. Such theoretical insurgency was an outgrowth of the amalgamation of their philosophical and political thinking in concert with a deeply held concern for social justice and environmental advocacy (Mullenite 2016). As anarchists they rejected the concept of centrality, refused the legitimacy of all forms of domination, and drawing from evolutionary theory, they insisted on an ecological perspective that did more than reduce human systems and ecosystems to mere competition, arguing instead that cooperation and symbiotic living, or "mutual aid," were absolutely essential for any species to thrive (Dugatin 2011; Ferretti 2011). Humans were accordingly placed within nature as but a single component of it, rather than a distinct outside. Their version of geography was, consequently, always a hybridized and more-than-human one (Whatmore 2002, 2004), predating the contemporary flourishing of this theoretical development by over a century.

Recent efforts among anarchist geographers to re-investigate foundational concepts like "space" (Springer 2016) and "territory" (Ince 2012) have helped cast a new light on the flows and regulations that shape contemporary life and spatial organization, both in and outside of neoliberal and consumerist developments. Political ecology, as a very diverse body of work that tries to articulate the ever-changing dialectic between society and environmental resources, and further, between the various classes, communities and groups constituting society itself (Heynen, Perkins, and Roy 2006), offers considerable latitude for the deployment and development of anarchist thought and critique (Morris 2014). It is peculiar then that most political ecologists seem to shy away from further engagement with anarchist theory (see Death 2014; Perreault, Bridge, and McCarthy 2015), falling back on Marxism and neo-Marxism, which remain the dominant political ideologies in the field. Given that the State is an institution inextricably bound to capitalism (McKay 2014), and thus undeniably one of the primary perpetrators of environmental ruination, this is a curious crutch, worthy of our suspicion and doubt. While Murray Bookchin (1971, 1982) critiqued anti-ecological trends under the banner of "social ecology" in the 1970s and 1980s, the remerging field of anarchist geography in the 2010s has yet to advance an "ecology of freedom" that demonstrates a sustained engagement with important domains like environmental justice, resource security, and equitable ecological governance. Kropotkin and Reclus never actually characterized their work as "political ecology," as the use of the term did not become widespread until the 1970s, yet their thought unquestionably helped to lay its foundations (Purchase 1997). Their conceptions of interdependent human–environment interactions were supported by extensive and rigorous fieldwork, and decidedly non-centrist approaches to politics and ecology (Kropotkin 1892, 1902, 1912), which included a decentering of the human figure (Reclus 1901), as well as anticipating deep ecology perspectives, critiques of anthropocentricism, and the eventual arrival of more-than-human geographies over a century later. In sum, anarchism is inseparable from an ecological perspective (Carter 2007). Anarchist geography and political ecology consequently have much in common and much to offer to each other, philosophically, theoretically and methodologically. An obvious point of departure is Reclus's notion that "humanity is nature becoming self-conscious," which starts to erode the justifications for selfishness and superiority that underpin the contemporary understandings of what it means to be "human."

NATURE BECOMING SELF-CONSCIOUS

Becoming implies a process. It signifies an unfolding, a state of growing, or a transformation. Humans are not self-conscious nature, but rather a step toward that. We are but a single flowering of understanding in the greater mystery of existence. But we would do well to also recognize that we will never arrive in full bloom, for nature can never fully know itself. Think of your own consciousness, how you were born into this world, and how a sense of self came to be. Others knew you before you knew yourself. That idea alone, perhaps unexpectedly, implies a sense of external constitution to the internal. What you have come to understand as "self" was being defined before you even knew there was a "self" to know. So as enlightened and in touch with yourself as you may be, it is only ever a partial representation, and not the "true" or "essential" you. It can't be. Your understanding of your own consciousness is limited by that very consciousness. It is a bounded understanding. The same can be said of nature. The very existence of existence is indicative of an unknowable boundary, an event horizon through which the only passage is death. This threshold of knowledge might lead us to ask, "What exists outside the boundary of existence?" but the question itself reveals the limitations. It is a paradox to even ask because we are reframing an understanding of nonexistence as existence, as something that is knowable. To be human is to be alive, and to be alive is to know only that experience. In passing out of existence all knowledge of the self is lost, and there is no spacetime from which to make our perceptions. The nature of nature is therefore not something that nature itself can ever fully comprehend, precisely because it is bounded within itself and there is no juncture at which it can step outside or beyond its own parameters to gain an omniscient perspective.

The hubris of humanity often suggests there is a path to knowing, which is typically framed as the role of either philosophy or science. We often see the media report on our progress toward a "theory of everything." But while science reveals insights based on observations that bring us closer to understanding, it is a common misconception that our knowledge can ever be complete. Our perspective on the nature of existence and the existence of nature, including the types of questions we think to ask, are constrained by the limitations of our human frame of understanding. Knowledge, as Donna Haraway (1988) contends, is always situated. What this limit speaks to then is the need for a more-than-human geography that attends to the interconnectivity and complexity of life. If we are to try and move closer to understanding the world, in order to gain some perspective, we need to accept a certain sense of humility that recognizes that the vantage point of being human is not to have a monopoly on either consciousness or knowledge. We are increasingly aware that other species use tools, communicate with sounds in ways that approximate language, exhibit a range of emotions including joy and grief, demonstrate cognition and self-awareness, and have complex societies where individual members are recognized. All of these patterns of behavior have previously been regarded as exclusively the domain of human experience. In appreciating these other expressions of consciousness what is needed is an *embodied disembodiment*, where on the one hand we are cognizant of our positionality and are self-reflexive about both our struggles and privileges, but on the other hand are willing to recognize the connection we have to the entirety of existence. Our bodies are a mere shell of understanding, a collection of cells that order consciousness in a particular way. But there are other arrangements of cells that can order consciousness in ways that are every bit as important as our own. Things other than human exist, and therefore on that basis alone, they *matter* in the double sense of the word.

But what does it mean to become self-conscious when consciousness itself is an elusive concept? Definitions range from awareness and sentience to the ability to feel, wakefulness, or possessing a sense of self. The prospect of achieving a single, mutually agreed-upon definition of consciousness seems unlikely, and perhaps that should be part of the definition. Consciousness is meant to be subjective because we all experience life differently. "Anything that we are aware of at a given moment forms part of our consciousness," which in turn makes conscious experience "at once the most familiar and most mysterious aspect of our lives" (Schneide and Velmans 2008, 1). Consciousness then is perhaps best defined very simply as *being*. So just as there are human *beings*, so too are there monarch butterfly *beings*, cow *beings*, salamander *beings*, eagle *beings*, and dolphin *beings*. Each is unique and beautiful in its own way, and each is pluralized in the same sense that there is not a single human experience of existence. These are individuals. But like human individuals, they are intimately and intrinsically woven into the fabric of existence. Each is essential to the experience of nature. So is it really humanity that is nature becoming self-conscious as Reclus mused, or is every living thing a part of that movement toward self-consciousness? Is the experience of human *being* any more important than any other manifestation of *being*? We might answer yes to this question. But an affirmative response is only a reflection of the subjective experience of being human and what we choose and are conditioned to place value on. It is, in other words, an indication of our anthropocentrism, where we assume our own experiences as humans, are somehow greater than those of say a pig or a grasshopper. This measure of importance has come to form the basis of what Erika Cudworth (1998) has called "anthroparchy," or human domination of the environment. It also betrays a certain form of "anthroprivilege" that guides human morality in ways where we enjoy and maintain advantages that other species do not benefit from (Springer Forthcoming). If we are to move beyond the idea that humanity is tasked with expressing our dominion over nature and toward a renewed integral understanding of humanity as firmly located within the biosphere, as an anarchist political ecology demands, then we have to start interrogating the privileges, hierarchies, and human-centric frames that guide our ways of knowing and being in the world.

ANTHROPOCENTRISM, ANTHROPARCHY, AND ANTHROPRIVILEGE

The problem with discussing nature and its potential for becoming self-conscious is that "nature" itself is a human construct (Castree and Braun 2001). We take the idea of nature for granted and conceive of it in our own anthropocentric terms as something distinct from human creation. This is the beginning of our collective delusion that we are in some way unique and more intelligent than those who share the world we inhabit. But what if intelligence is redefined in terms of a species ability to adhere to and fit within the biophysical parameters of its environment? Adaptability to a particular habitat means that the ecosystem continues to function in a delicate balance with all of the flora and fauna that reside there. It requires an intuitive recognition that the lifecycle of any given species is entirely contingent on the web of other species that support it. There are always ebbs and flows to any ecosystem. Certain species may become too successful, whereby that very "success" comes to foreshadow demise. But no other species have disrupted the ecology in the ways that humans have. The realization of this exceptionalism, one that does not prioritize human ability but simply acknowledges its capacity for destruction, is precisely why we need political ecology. Yet political ecology to date has largely limited itself to human-centered concerns. The environment is viewed as something to be managed and negotiated by society, where the bulk of political ecology seeks to call into question how various communities and classes have differential power when it comes to the utilization and realization of resources. The damage, devastation, and destruction of the natural world are lamented largely for the impacts on human societies. When other species are considered, it is usually with a view toward the emotional value or utility that they provide to human life, rather than the recognition of those "other" lives themselves. Is a tree valuable only because of its potential to be turned into timber? Should we leave it standing so that we can sit under its shade? Or perhaps it is seen as a mechanism that produces oxygen and thus enables us to breathe. All of these responses center the experience of humans. Can't a tree just be a tree for its own sake?

We might consider such anthropocentrism itself as "natural," but it is in fact, and quite obviously, a social construct. The prioritization of humans is a reflection of our values and the story we have told ourselves as a society about nature. For those of us who are male, is it "natural" for us to think first and foremost of other males and to entrench our concerns for the privileging of males in the structure of our societies? We recognize this process as one of gender domination resulting in patriarchy. What about with regard to caring only, or at least first and foremost, about the lives of our national brethren? We can acknowledge this problematic form of nationalism as a process of othering that dehumanizes peoples who we deem to be not like "us." But what about this de-*humanizing* process? What does it mean to *de*-humanize? The underlying sentiment is that some people are relegated to a status where it is somehow acceptable not to care. They are rendered somehow non-human, and because of the lack of humanness, our empathy evaporates. A critical perspective on gender or nationalism demands that we care about all humans, regardless of their place of birth, their gender, their sexuality, their race, their class, or any other category of difference. Dehumanization thus betrays a deep-seeded and foundational sense of the importance of humans that goes beyond mere anthropocentrism. It is an expression of anthroparchy, a hierarchy that is constructed with humans at the apex, unapologetically affirming that this is our rightful place. As critical scholars and activists, we recognize and question the ways that difference is mobilized for a politics of hatred, separation, and violence when it comes to the human experience. And while large segments of any given society fall prey to these divisive narratives, even the most reactionary among us is loath to see themselves fall victim to prejudice. Nobody wants to be debased in such a way that they are treated *like an animal.* This analogy is the foundation of all our othering. Colonialism, racism, sexism, childism, homophobia, and transphobia are all mobilized through a view of the "other" as somehow less than human. What we don't seem to appreciate is that the human supremacy is the originary preconception. It is a foundational understanding that is entirely taken for granted (Jensen 2016; Lupinacci 2015).

The seed of all our arborescent violence is anthroparchy, and it is anthroprivilege that fertilizes the soil. Think of all the ways in which your own life is made easier through the exploitation of other forms of life. We are not meaning interdependence here, but actual misuse, manipulation, and mistreatment. As humans, at least under capitalism, we have moved beyond the idea that our exchanges with the natural world should be reciprocal. Kropotkin's (1902) notion of mutual aid has been abandoned in favor of clear-cutting forests, dumping toxic waste on coral reefs, and carving open vast craters in the Earth so that we can extract tar from the sand to fuel our insatiable appetite for more. More cars. More cell phones. More computers. More toys. More plastic bottles. More home renovations. More furniture. More appliances. More power tools. More weapons. More gadgets. More trinkets. More knickknacks. More packaging. More paper. More cheese. More hamburgers. Do you want fries with that? More garbage. More rivers of shit. More mountains of rubber tires. More melting of permafrost. More climate change. More of everything. More. More. More! And who cares? Political ecologists will tell you that they do. We don't question their sincerity, but so long as political ecology remains content to unpack and critique the implications of the colossal mess that we have made of the world in such a way that prioritizes fixing things for humans, it is a field of study that is merely pissing in the wind. This is why the reinsertion of an anarchist perspective is long overdue in contemporary understandings of political ecology (Clark 1990). Anarchism encourages us to contend with the multiple lines of difference, the various iterations of privilege, and the manifold set of *archies* that undergird our understandings of the world, and crucially, our place within it. It demands that we take non-human "others" seriously, where their domination is seen as every bit as vile as the forms of oppression that humans have devised and inflicted upon one another. If there is a world to be won, victory will only be achieved when we start to refuse the idea that we are its saviors, and instead begin to humble ourselves, allowing the will of the Gaia to guide us back into its loving embrace.

STRUCTURE OF THE BOOK

In reflecting on the broad implications of human supremacy, we want to start things off with a powerful chapter from Frederike Schmitz, titled very simply

"Animals in Anarchist Political Ecology." The global animal industry uses and kills over 60 billion land animals every year, who otherwise lead lives of misery and immense suffering. Schmitz argues that when confronted with the issue, most anarchists agree that the current practice of industrial animal farming is problematic insofar as it causes pain and suffering, not to mention environmental destruction and climate change. Nevertheless, the topic of human treatment of animals is often not regarded as being very important. She also identifies the controversy about what sort of change is required from an anarchist perspective: do we need to change the way animals are treated and move to more "humane" small-scale farms; should we stop animal husbandry but resort to hunting and fishing; or should we end the use of animals for food altogether, as demanded by the animal liberation movement? The chapter draws on the work of anarchist writers who address our relation to animals, namely Kropotkin, Reclus, and several contemporary authors who argue for or against animal liberation. Schmitz begins to help us unpack the ethical argument from commonalities which claims that characteristics we share with animals speak for an end to us using and killing them, or the argument from oppression which compares and relates the use of animals with the oppression of certain human groups. Ultimately, the chapter aims to show that there are strong reasons for anarchists to embrace the demand for animal liberation, and that an anarchist political ecology should incorporate that demand.

Partrik Gažo raises similar concerns in his chapter "Political Ecology of Animal Liberation: Emancipating Non-Humans from a Leftist Anti-Capitalist Perspective." He argues that a political ecology framework benefits from incorporating an animal liberation perspective. Gažo's main objective is to analyze and compare the approaches of members of the anti-authoritative, anarchist movement on the basis of their responses toward and relationship with the rights and liberation of nonhuman animals. The first part of the chapter reveals a historical perspective using the writings of anarchist geographers such as Peter Kropotkin and Élisée Reclus. It demonstrates the historical relevance of linking ideas of the rights and liberation of nonhuman animals with anti-authoritative thinking. In the second part of his chapter, Gažo looks at the approaches in the current anti-authoritarian movement. The movement is divided into two camps. The first camp holds a vegan position, while the other camp does not consider veganism to be important. The chapter shows that the two camps have different opinions in relation to the issue of non-humans and that their attitudes are diverse (historically and currently). Both groups of radicals emphasize direct action as an effort to directly confront hierarchical structures that they consider to be exploitative—whether humans, nonhuman animals, or nature. They also strive for holistic thinking, but each group defines it through unique arguments, using different ideas of consistent anti-authoritarian thinking. Finally, Gažo examines how this discussion contributes to political ecological knowledge or rather to the development of an anarchist political ecology.

Our next chapter, "Anarchism, Feminism, and Veganism: A Convergence of Struggles," comes from Ophélie Véron and Richard J. White. Changing gears a little, Véron and White want to place their central emphasis on the intersectional dimensions of human supremacy, contending that anarchism is key to this view. They argue that in contrast to other "radical approaches," which artificially uncouple and privilege particular forms of oppression and exploitation (e.g., class or gender), anarchist praxis recognizes an intersectional approach toward social and environmental justice. Given this understanding they contend that it should be logical to assume that an intersectional anarchist praxis would recognize and reject two (interlocking) forms of oppression, namely patriarchy (the institutionalized domination of men over women) and anthroparchy (the human exploitation of other species). However, despite important new visibilities of anarcha-feminism and veganarchism, these violent systems of archy continue to be overlooked, or their validity contested within mainstream anarchist theories and practice. Reflecting on the emancipatory grounds upon which anarchism stands, notably non-violence, freedom, and autonomy, the chapter explores the possibility of fighting against both patriarchal and paternalistic forms of social domination while (1) actively supporting forms of anthroparchy (e.g., the consumption of non-human animal corpses (meat, dairy, and eggs) and (2) fighting against sexist and speciesist forms of social domination while acting in ways that uphold statist and capitalist forms of exploitation and domination.

R.D. comes at the political ecology of human supremacy in a slightly different way again. In his chapter, "Vegan-Washing Genocide: Animal Advocacy on Stolen Land and Re-imagining Animal Liberation as Anti-colonial Praxis," he examines animal liberation movements in settler colonial contexts. He specifically focuses on movements primarily composed of and largely led by white settlers, and questions their potential to both reify and challenge the structure of the settler state. The chapter problematizes the understandings of animal advocacy that appeal to state sovereignty and erase Indigenous cosmologies of nonhuman relations and obligations. He is much more sceptical of intersectional approaches to animal advocacy, arguing that its attempts to bridge gaps in theory and practice have been little more than hollow moves to innocence. Rather than recognizing the strategic centrality of settler colonization to challenging mass animal enterprise, he contends that mainstream animal advocacy frameworks reify the logics of colonization and white supremacy. As animality is produced as a site of white supremacy, settler animal advocacy is positioned as an instrument of dispossession and colonization. For R.D., Indigenous resurgence is intrinsically committed to returning non-hierarchical interspecies relations, while anthropocentric logic operates as a pillar of white supremacy. Dispossession and colonization can be traced to the invasion of European animal agriculture, epistemologies, and cosmologies onto Indigenous land. Yet R.D. is critical of settler animal advocacy movements, and specifically their failure to name and challenge settler colonialism as it upholds colonial relations and the politics of recognition. The chapter fosters a praxis that figures animals as both colonial subjects and weapons of colonization, while prefiguring an animal liberation movement on stolen land that centers Indigenous decolonization, repatriation of land and relations, and anti-colonial solidarity.

For Marcelo Lopes de Souza, in his chapter, "Whose Environment? Epistemic-Political Disputes over a Concept and Its Uses," the label "environmental scientists" covers the professional identity of many geographers and biologists. *Environment* then is a key concept for many scholars, but it has also been a key concept for political activists around the world since the 1960s. However, the contents behind the term are far from being undisputed, and Souza seeks to unpack this idea. The trouble with the concept, he argues, lies in the fact that in spite of variations due to linguistic differences, a common ground at the international level seems to be the existence of two trends: on the one side, a naturalizing bias (which has been hegemonic both in academia and in the realm of common sense) on the basis of which "environment" is primarily understood as synonymous with "natural environment"; on the other side, a non-naturalizing approach that emphasizes a broader meaning according to which "environment" should *not* be primarily understood as non-anthropogenic processes, landforms, and so on. Such a disagreement, Souza convincingly demonstrates, is not restricted to academic debate, and its relevance is by no means only a theoretical one. Different approaches to environment have different implications for "environmental protection" and more generally for the questions and discussions regarding rights—from human rights to animal rights. The concept of environment and its uses are at the core of crucial epistemic-political disputes, which accordingly sheds significant light on the supremacy that humans have claimed for ourselves.

Next up is a chapter by Shane Mc Donnell, which bears a straightforward title "A Future Eco-Anarchic Society and the Means to Achieving It." Mc Donnell does not mince words and explores two key issues: (1) what might a future eco-anarchic world/society look like, and (2) what strategies and tactics can achieve this idyllic aim. As part of this eco-anarchic world, Mc Donnell promotes veganism as a means of improving one's personal health, reducing carbon emissions and slowing down climate change. He also critiques animal agriculture as an ecologically unsound enterprise. Hemp as a crop to replace trees in paper production is also explored, as are notions of "the commons," hydroponics, and vertical farming, with a view toward achieving better food production, control overproduction, and use of available land. Mc Donnell also discusses the strategies and tactics. He is aware that one necessarily encounters state and supra-state forces, along with various state-supporting institutions like non-governmental bodies. There is no advice for working through this uncomfortable pragmatism, however Mc Donnell maintains that using the state, its institutions and laws against itself to disrupt and dismantle ecocidal and oppressive forces can be useful. To make his case, Mc Donnell draws his examples from a variety of communities across the world including Mexico, Rojava, Denmark, and France.

In "Beyond the Anthropocene, toward the Anarchocene?" Randall Amster argues that the recent recommendation to formally designate the present epoch as the Anthropocene has raised as many questions as it purported to answer. On one hand, he suggests it offers a sobering assessment of human impact on the planet and its systems—perhaps with a political subtext to foster awareness of climate change and related forms of degradation. However, for Amster, the construct of the Anthropocene potentially reifies the human–environment dichotomy that many cite as part of the problem in the first place, and further inscribes an eponymous anthropocentrism that reflects the hubris underscoring myriad contemporary crises. Equally potent but less discussed are the justice implications, which Amster brings into view, by questioning the implication that *all* humans are responsible, since both the contributions and impacts of the so-called Anthropocene are demonstrably skewed along lines of power and privilege. Amster further questions the Anthropocene on the grounds that it follows a pattern of titling something after that which has been displaced. As an antidote to this tendency toward spatio-temporal delimitation, he suggests we might consider an approach that seeks prospectively to engage the next epoch, since the proposed one may already be nearing its coda. Thus, for Amster, the *Anarchocene* may be at hand—replete with possibilities for emergence, spontaneity, horizontalism, scalability, and other patterns of socio-ecological reflexivity that could become significant.

Next up in a chapter from Benjamin O'Heran creatively titled "Chthulucene Compacts: An Anarchist Guide to Multispecies Troublemaking." When examining the theoretical horizons of anarchist political ecologies, O'Heran notices that there is a startling lack of thought on how humans can create forms of politics *with* non-humans, as opposed to *for* them. This chapter reorients these theoretical horizons by speculating what a multispecies form of anarchism might look like in theory and in practice. Such forms of anarchism are, O'Heran argues, dependent on co-creating contingent cosmopolitical worlds based on interdependency/solidarity and flourishing/ mutual aid where these contingent cosmopolitical worlds can potentially be linked through practices of multispecies mutual aid and solidarity between humans and non-humans. Peter Kropotkin's theory of mutual aid and Élisée Reclus's notion of multispecies kinship are used by O'Heran to help plant the seeds for a posthumanist reading of classical anarchist political ecologies. These ideas are composted with Isabelle Stengers's notion of cosmopolitics and Donna Haraway's idea of flourishing to create forms of *response-ability* between humans and non-humans caught in relationships of reciprocal possession. For O'Heran, this new form of anarchist political ecology can be considered a "Chthulucene Compact," an agreement embodying the tentacular and interdependent nature of human/non-human relations, which itself makes life possible. By situating human/non-human relations and politics as a co-constructed process dependent on practicing multispecies mutual aid and solidarity, O'Heran demonstrates that human and non-human communities can conduct anti-hierarchical and mutualistic politics with each other, thereby expanding the theoretical horizons of anarchist political ecologies.

The next chapter " 'Street Dogs' of Istanbul: An Exemplary Case for the Construction and Contestation of Human Domination over Urban Animals" comes to us from Ali Bilgin and Kiraz Özdoğan who reflect on "Interspecies' Common Life Experiences through the Case of the 'Street Dogs' in Istanbul." The chapter focuses on the construction of anthroparchal domination over street dogs in Istanbul, displaying the discourse and practice it produces and the resistance it evokes. Bilgin and Özdoğan base their study on participant observation combined with bibliographical data. For centuries dogs in Istanbul could live without specific owners and establish independent links with humans. The authors remind us that dogs used to be socialized beings living in the urban habitat, fulfilling certain functions within urban social life. This relation became subject to administrative measures and interventions by the mid-19th century. Thanks to the collaboration of the modern medical discourse and a new governmental approach over the urban space, street dogs emerged as a public health issue and became a "hygienic" problem of concern for the municipality. They were allowed to live only as pets. This policy brought along numerous attempts to exterminate all the "unowned" dogs living in the urban space, which evoked various local resistances throughout a century. But Bilgin and Özdoğan argue that this policy did not entirely succeed, and a new approach called "Dog Population Management" emerged. The WHO, who adopted it during the neoliberal turn in Turkey, supported this new management scheme. It involves intervening in the lives of street dogs, taming their bodies, and shaping their behaviors within a conceptual-operational apparatus based on statistical data and ethological knowledge. Instead of annihilating the life, it aims to reshape it, to govern to, and to create a market around the issue. Today the street dogs are still part of the urban life in Istanbul thanks to the resistance led by both dog and human inhabitants of the city. Bilgin and Özdoğan's chapter presents this struggle for liberty of the dogs to live without "masters" as an inspiration for the anarchist imagination of non-speciesist common life. They argue that it displays spontaneous, creative interspecies cooperation and the creation of discourse and practice of a "here and now" politics.

Our final chapter by Simon Springer is called "Total Liberation Ecology: Integral Anarchism, Anthroparchy, and the Violence of Indifference." Few political ecologists have taken anarchism seriously, says Springer, while many anarchists have ignored the question of the animal other, treating anthroparchy, or the supremacy of the human species, as somehow different than other forms of hierarchy. Yet for him the relationship between the state, capitalism, and the subjugation of non-human animals should be clear in light of Ag-gag laws and the targeting of animal liberation activists as "terrorists." Building on the idea of an integral anarchism, which considers speciesism as forming the same violent genus as racism, classism, sexism, childism, ableism, transphobia, and homophobia, Springer argues that these ostensibly separate pieces are in fact interlocking systems of domination. He maintains that such an intersectional view leads us toward one inevitable ethical conclusion in the pursuit of an anarchist political ecology: veganism. Consequently the chapter questions the indifference that anarchists, political ecologists, and critical geographers alike have assigned to the unintelligible violence that is meted out against non-human animals, primarily through euphemizing their dismembered, decapitated, and disemboweled bodies as "meat." For Springer, the liberation ecology proposed by geographers Richard Peet and Michael Watts (1996) appears facile in the face of pervasive anthroparchy, which although every bit as vile as gender domination and white supremacy, barely registers within the current literature. Given the extraordinary depletion of water resources, widespread deforestation, intensified climate change, pervasive pollution, and mass murder that all flow from contemporary animal agriculture, Springer considers our current food practices as a form of ecocide. As an antidote to this shameful apathy and horrendous violence, he proposes "Total Liberation Ecology."

THE END OF HUMAN SUPREMACY

In the epigraph that opens this introduction, Élisée Reclus speaks of the necessity of possessing a sense of beauty, warning against a hideous nature. By this he seems to mean our nature as human beings, something his faith in anarchism leads him to believe could be changed. But how does one arrive at such a position of finding beauty when our current systems of organizing life through governments and capitalism are marked by the grotesque perversions of human supremacy? How do we make such transformations toward becoming beautiful when the scars on the face of the planet are almost every-where to be seen? How can we gain some perspective to not only see that the violence we do to the Earth is a cruelty to ourselves but also recognize that the Earth and our existence are one and the same? How do we overcome the false separation that pits humans against the planet, and views life as a Hobbesian nightmare of being solitary, poor, nasty, brutish, and short? There are no easy answers to these questions, particularly given how far we have come in our desecration of the planet. Anarchists were already lamenting the devastation over a century ago, and things have only gotten considerably worse since then. The destruction witnessed by early anarchists in the form of the indus-trial revolution and its ensuing pollution has not only spread geographically, but it has also intensified technologically. Developments like microplastics and nuclear reactors have significantly upped the ante in terms of the ability to do harm to life on Earth. The pace of ruin has increased as well, in large part owing to the human population exploding over the past 100 years. There are now over 7 billion human beings. But it gets worse. Vaclav Smil (2011) argues that the "human species has evolved to dominate the biosphere," so much so that "global anthropomass is now an order of magnitude greater than the mass of all wild terrestrial mammals." Wildlife now represents 1% or less of the total mass of all terrestrial vertebrate animals, with humans making up approximately 32%, and the remaining 67% being dedicated to livestock to feed ourselves. Meanwhile global terrestrial plant mass has been reduced by as much as 45 percent over the past two millennia, with the past 100 years amounting to more than 15 percent of that loss. The planet is on its knees. If submission to human whims is our objective, then clearly we have succeeded. But it is a hollow victory, and one that will—with absolute certainty—be our collective undoing. All ecosystems function in such a way as to ensure a sense of balance. No single species can become too successful, precisely because of the principle of mutual aid. That is to say, all living things are reliant on other living things to exist. It is life itself that breathes life into the world. On an extended timescale, the biosphere's equilibrium plays itself out through natural selection and the process of evolution. On shorter timescales, when ecosystems are disrupted, corrections come through pestilence and mass die-offs.

In this way, the Earth is intelligent. Its primary function is the preservation of life at large. It does not concern itself with preserving particular lives, of particular species. We might not think of the planet as being conscious, but of course it is. It is aware of imbalances, it has the ability to feel when things are not quite right, and in this wakefulness we can suggest that it possesses a sense of self. The Earth is very much alive. It is a single living organism in a vast cosmic sea. When the photo *The Blue Marble*, taken at a distance of 29,000 kilometers, was sent back by Apollo 17 in 1972, the beauty of our world became immediately apparent. People began to see the Earth for what it actually is and gain a new understanding of the human situation. We as humans are "a self-conscious biological species entirely dependent upon the health of a living planet around a small star in a universe without boundary or center" (Purchase 1997, 1–2). Less than two decades later, when Voyager 1 sent back an image of the Earth from 6.4 billion kilometers away, it demanded an existential reappraisal. Astronomer Carl Sagan (1994, n.p.) was mesmerized. "Look again at that dot," he said, "That's here. That's home. That's us. On it everyone you love, everyone you know, everyone you ever heard of, every human being who ever was, lived out their lives. The aggregate of our joy and suffering. . . . There is perhaps no better demonstration of the folly of human conceits than this distant image of our tiny world." Human supremacy at this distance seems utterly absurd. This "mote of dust suspended in a sunbeam" is unquestionably everything to us (Sagan 1994, n.p.). There could be nothing more beautiful than this pale blue dot. But to possess a sense of beauty, one must let that beauty possess your senses. To avert an impending collision with ecocide we must begin to look for the beautiful. To actively seek it in our modes of organizing, to desire its production in the things we create, and to work to create it in our views of the non-human world. The Earth is not for us to dominate. It never was. By thinking these oppressive thoughts, and worse still, by putting them into practice in our relations with other species and the natural world, we reveal just how sick and soulless our contemporary culture has become. We have lost our reverence, and thus the glory of the world has passed. Or has it? The pursuit of an anarchist political ecology is an attempt to reestablish the balance in our world before the end of all human *beings* becomes a certainty.

Anarchism is a politics of the *here* and *now* (Springer 2016), recognizing that any sense of change or awakening begins at *this precise moment*, in *this exact location* in which we find ourselves. If there is glory still to be found, then there is no room for procrastination. There is no politics of waiting for a revolution. Not when there is so much at stake. It begins by awakening to the present, for it is only right *here* and right *now* that our *being* actually exists. The past is a politics of either depression or nostalgia, and both are unwarranted for they do not address what we need right now. We can learn from our past, but learning must be applied to the context of our lived experience for it to be meaningful, and its application is possible only in the present moment. The future is similarly a path marked by our hopes and anxieties, but neither of those is certain. To ensure that it is our dreams that are realized and not our fears, we have to take action in the *here* and *now*. If your life is a boat, the experience of being shipwrecked tells you that there are many reefs that you will want to avoid. You may be anxious about those obstacles and hope to circumvent them. But your past and your future do not steer the ship. You must move the rudder to evade disaster. Consequently, the present is the key not only to ensuring our happiness but also to our very existence. The present moment is all that actually exists. Ralph Waldo Emerson once said, "To find the beautiful, we must carry it with us." It is in the present that we can find the stillness to look inside and find something we thought we might have lost. Mindfulness and connection to the thrum of life come into being when we awaken to the possibility of right *now*. It is in each moment of life that beauty arises, and we can very consciously choose to pick it up and embrace it in the form of love. Love for each other. Love for ourselves. Love for the Earth, which so long as we breathe, loves us still. So be still and breathe. Allow yourselves to feel the breeze of redemption in your hair. Breathe. Feel the warmth of the sun on your face. Breathe. Feel the laughter of childhood innocence in your belly. Breathe. Feel your union with this world. Allow nature to become conscious of your presence through your *being*. Being humble. Being awake. Being attentive. Being thoughtful. Being human in ways that respect, acknowledge, and celebrate all the other ways that *being* alive is expressed by this beautiful planet we call home. All beauty is integral, and so it is that the end of human supremacy can only be marked by a pale blue dot.

REFERENCES

Bookchin, M. 1971. *Post-Scarcity Anarchism*. Berkeley: Ramparts Press.

Bookchin, M. 1982. *The Ecology of Freedom: The Emergence and Dissolution of Hierarchy*. Palo Alto: Cheshire Books.

Carter, N. ed. 2007. *The Politics of the Environment: Ideas, Activism, Policy*, 2nd Ed. Cambridge: Cambridge University Press.

Castree, C., and Braun, B. eds. 2001. *Social Nature: Theory, Practice, and Politics*. Oxford: Wiley-Blackwell.

Clark, J. ed. 1990. *Renewing the Earth: The Promise of Social Ecology—A Celebration of the Work of Murray Bookchin*. Green Print.

Clark, J. P. 2012. "Political Ecology." In *Encyclopedia of Applied Ethics*, 2nd Ed., Vol. 3. San Diego: Academic Press, 505–516.

Clark, J. P., and Martin, C. 2013. *Anarchy, Geography, Modernity: Selected Writings of Elisée Reclus*. Oakland: PM Press.

Clough, N., and Blumberg, R. 2012. "Toward Anarchist and Autonomist Marxist Geographies." *ACME: An International E-Journal for Critical Geographies*, *11*(3), 335–351.

Cudworth, E. 1998. "Gender, Nature and Dominance: An Analysis of Interconnections between Patriarchy and Anthroparchy, Using Examples of Meat and Pornography." PhD thesis, University of Leeds.

Death, C. ed. 2014. *Critical Environmental Politics*. New York: Routledge.

Dugatin L. A. 2011. *The Prince of Evolution: Peter Kropotkin's Adventures in Science and Politics.* New York: CreateSpace.

Ferretti, F. 2011. "The Correspondence between Élisée Reclus and Pëtr Kropotkin as a Source for the History of Geography." *Journal of Historical Geography, 37*(2), 216–222.

Haraway, D. 1988. "Situated Knowledges: The Science Question in Feminism and the Privilege of Partial Perspective." *Feminist Studies, 14*(3), 575–599.

Heynen, N., Perkins, H. A., and Roy, P. 2006. "The Political Ecology of Uneven Urban Green Space: The Impact of Political Economy on Race and Ethnicity in Producing Environmental Inequality in Milwaukee." *Urban Affairs Review, 42*(1), 3–25.

Ince, A. 2012. "In the Shell of the Old: Anarchist Geographies of Territorialisation." *Antipode, 44*(5), 1645–1666.

Jensen, D. 2016. *The Myth of Human Supremacy.* New York: Seven Stories Press.

Kropotkin, P. 1885. "What Geography Ought to Be." *The Nineteenth Century CXXVI, 18* (December), 940–956.

Kropotkin, P. 1892 (2011). *The Conquest of Bread.* New York: Dover.

Kropotkin, P. 1902 (2008). *Mutual Aid: A Factor in Evolution.* Charleston, SC: Forgotten.

Kropotkin, P. 1912 (1994). *Fields, Factories, and Workshops.* Montreal: Black Rose.

Lupinacci, J. 2015. "Recognizing Human Supremacy: Interrupt, Inspire and Expose." In *Anarchism and Animal Liberation: Essays on Contemporary Elements of Total Liberation.* Nocella II, A. J., White, R. J., and Cudworth, E. eds. Jefferson, NC: McFarland & Company.

MacLaughlin, J. 2016. *Kropotkin and the Anarchist Intellectual Tradition.* London: Pluto.

McKay, I. ed. 2014. *Direct Struggle against Capital: A Peter Kropotkin Anthology.* Oakland: AK Press.

Morris, B. *Anthropology, Ecology, and Anarchism: A Brian Morris Reader.* Oakland: PM Press.

Mullenite, J. 2016. "Resilience, Political Ecology, and Power: Convergences, Divergences, and the Potential for a Postanarchist Geographical Imagination." *Geography Compass, 10*(9), 378–388.

Peet, R., and Watts, M. eds. 1996. *Liberation Ecologies: Environment, Development, Social Movements.* London: Routledge.

Pellow, D. N. 2014. *Total Liberation: The Power and Promise of Animal Rights and the Radical Earth Movement.* Minneapolis: University of Minnesota Press.

Perreault, T., Bridge, G., and McCarthy, J. eds. 2015. *Routledge Handbook of Political Ecology.* London: Routledge.

Purchase, G. 1997. *Anarchism and Ecology.* Montreal: Black Rose Books.

Reclus, E. 1881. *The History of a Mountain.* New York: Harper & Brothers.

Reclus, E. 1894. *The Earth and Its Inhabitants: e Universal Geography.* London: J. S. Virtue.

Reclus, E. 1901. "On Vegetarianism." *Humane Review.* http://dwardmac.pitzer.edu/Anarchist_Archives/bright/reclus/onvegetarianism.html.

Robbins, P. 2012. *Political Ecology: A Critical Introduction.* Malden: Wiley Blackwell.

Sagan, C. 1994. *A Pale Blue Dot.* http://www.planetary.org/explore/space-topics/earth/pale-blue-dot.html.

Schneide, S., and Velmans, M. 2008. "Introduction." *The Blackwell Companion to Consciousness.* Oxford: Blackwell Publishing Ltd.

Smil, V. 2011. "Harvesting the Biosphere: The Human Impact." *Population and Development Review*, 37(4): 613–636.

Souza, M. L. de, White, R. J., and Springer, S. Eds. 2016. *Theories of Resistance: Anarchism, Geography and the Spirit of Revolt.* London: Rowman & Littlefield.

Springer, S. 2016. *The Anarchist Roots of Geography: Toward Spatial Emancipation.* Minneapolis: University of Minnesota Press.

Springer, S. Forthcoming. "Check Your Anthroprivilege!" *Vegan Geographies.*

Springer, S., Ince, A., Pickerill, J., Brown, G., and Barker, A. 2012. "Reanimating Anarchist Geographies: A New Burst of Colour." *Antipode: A Radical Journal of Geography*, 44(5), 1591–1604.

Springer, S., White, R. J., and Souza, M. L. de. Eds. 2016. *The Radicalization of Pedagogy: Anarchism, Geography and the Spirit of Revolt.* London: Rowman & Littlefield.

Whatmore, S. 2002. *Hybrid Geographies: Natures Cultures Spaces.* London: Sage.

Whatmore, S. 2004. "Humanism's Excess: Some Thoughts on the 'Post-Human/ist' Agenda." *Environment and Planning A*, 36, 1360–1363.

White, R. J., Springer, S., and Souza, M. L. de. Eds. 2016. *The Practice of Freedom: Anarchism, Geography and the Spirit of Revolt.* London: Roman & Littlefield.

Chapter 1

Animals in Anarchist Political Ecology

Friederike Schmitz

INTRODUCTION

Over 60 billion land animals worldwide are killed for food every year. Most had miserable lives, mutilated and confined in crammed stalls, mothers separated from their young, suffering from overbreeding and living in appalling conditions. In the global animal industry, sentient beings are forced to take on the role of resources, commodities or means of production, and their own needs and interests are hardly taken into account. They suffer immensely and are killed in staggering numbers.

The animal liberation movement demands not that animals are treated better within this industry or that less animals are killed. Rather, people advocating animal liberation, as I will discuss it in this chapter, demand that we stop using animals for the production of meat, milk, eggs, and other animal products altogether. The concept also demands an end to hunting animals for food or fur.

In this chapter, I will argue that there are strong reasons for anarchists to embrace animal liberation, and that an anarchist political ecology accordingly needs to seriously address human–animal relations in order to challenge the current practice and outline future relations based on respect and cooperation rather than exploitation and oppression.

In the past, well-known anarchist thinkers have not shown much interest in the life and fate of animals, but there are some notable exceptions. Peter Kropotkin studied the behavior of animals extensively and highlighted the similarities between humans and animals, but he did so without objecting to meat-eating or the use of animals. His contemporary Élisée Reclus, however, made far-reaching criticisms of the way animals were treated in food production and argued for vegetarianism.

In recent decades several texts have connected anarchism and animal liberation, starting with the classic manifesto "Animal Liberation and Social Revolution" published in 1997 by Brian Dominick, where he explains how his anarchism and his veganism hang together (Dominick 1997). The social anarchist Bob Torres published a book called *Making a Killing* in 2007, and there are several zines and papers on the topic, not to mention the recently published *Anarchism and Animal Liberation* (Torres 2007; Nocella II, White, and Cudworth 2015).

Most authors elaborate on the central claim that there is a web of interconnected forms of oppressions, the exploitation of animals being one of them. It is not uncontroversial, however, among anarchists generally that the ultimate aim should be animal liberation—with its consequence of veganism. While most anarchists who comment on the subject agree that the treatment of animals in industrial capitalism is gruesome and needs to change, the demand for an end of all animal use, namely the demand for animal liberation, is not universally acknowledged.

There are at least three points of disagreement. The first concerns whether all forms of animal farming, including small-scale and "humane" farming, are problematic. The second is on the acceptability of hunting for one's own consumption within a lifestyle that strives for sustainability. And third is a disagreement about how important the issue actually is. Furthermore, even among those who favor animal liberation, there is disagreement over how, in an ideal society, humans should relate to animals—especially whether close relations with animals can continue, and whether domesticated animals may still live within human society.

In my view, existing texts on anarchism and animal liberation haven't been able to adequately settle these disputes. One reason for this is that they don't clearly distinguish between different ways of relating to and using animals and, further, because they don't distinguish between different reasons for criticizing the current practices and, connected to that, different arguments for animal liberation.

So in this chapter, I will draw from the work of Kropotkin, Reclus as well as contemporary anarchists in order to identify and discuss different arguments that can be put forward for ending the use of animals for production of food and other products. After explaining a premise of my discussion, I go on to examine arguments from aesthetic revulsion, arguments from emotions such as compassion, an argument from commonalities, and arguments from oppression and domination. In an excursion I will deal with the problem of unavoidable harm. In each section, I will discuss objections to these arguments related to the points of disagreement mentioned earlier. Also, I will show their relation to anarchist thought and evaluate their plausibility. Even though some of the arguments are purely ethical in nature, these, along with the other points I raise, have direct bearing on questions of political theory and practice and should therefore be taken into account from the perspective of anarchist political ecology.

USING ANIMALS AND HARMING ANIMALS

Before I look at the arguments, I need to explain one central premise of my discussion. I will assume in what follows that the productive use of animals necessarily implies seriously harming them in the process. Why is that? For one thing, in order to obtain meat, practically speaking, animals have to be killed, which is arguably a harm in itself. Also, in practice, killing typically involves stress, fear, and often extreme pain. Even in conditions different to the usual slaughterhouse—for example, when animals are shot in their normal surroundings, such as on pasture—it is impossible to do this routinely without at least sometimes causing animals to suffer. Similarly, in hunting, animals are often wounded instead of being immediately killed. Apart from the killing, animals used for food production are typically confined in small spaces, they undergo forced breeding in order to have more productive offspring, and they are routinely separated from their family. Even though it is not entirely theoretically impossible to use animals differently, that is, to not kill or harm them and still obtain some milk or eggs, it is a scenario that is utterly unrealistic and a scenario in which we could produce only a miniscule fraction of the current consumption of animal products, and at great cost.[1] Also, it is not what critics of animal liberation suggest—so in my discussion, I will dismiss this purely hypothetical scenario and focus on realistic scenarios.

DIFFERENT GROUNDS FOR CRITICISM, DIFFERENT GROUNDS FOR LIBERATION

Anarchists past and present have put forward a range of considerations that are used to argue for a change in the way we relate to animals. In what follows, I will identify different ideas and arguments and discuss how they bear on the question at hand: why should anarchists embrace animal liberation?

AESTHETIC REVULSION

Élisée Reclus expresses an idea that may appear, at first sight, a little peculiar, namely that violence toward animals, especially the butchering of animals, has to stop because such actions are ugly and go against an ideal of beauty. He writes:

> We look forward to the day when we will no longer have to rush quickly past hideous sites of killing to see as little as possible of the rivulets of blood, the rows of cadavers hanging from sharp hooks, and the blood-stained workers armed with gruesome knives. . . . We want to be surrounded by an environment that pleases the eye and is an expression of beauty. (Reclus 2013, 161)

Furthermore, Reclus criticizes an important aspect of domestication, namely the selective breeding of animals for certain purposes of production. Although humans' true mission, in Reclus's view, would be to improve and educate animals, we prefer "to increase the bulk of meat and fat on four legs to provide walking storehouses of flesh that hobble from the manure pile to the slaughterhouse" (Reclus 2013, 134). As a result, "The animals sacrificed to man's appetite have been systematically made ugly, weakened, deformed, and degraded in intelligence and moral worth" (Reclus 2013, 158). Here also, Reclus's criticism seems to be at least in part based on aesthetic revulsion.

Even though today few people would argue against industrial farming on explicitly aesthetic grounds, I think that Reclus captures something of importance, something that can be witnessed when people are confronted with facts or images of modern animal breeding and conditions in factory farms. The existence of chickens hardly able to walk or of slaughterhouses killing 200,000 chickens in a single day is something that many people immediately recognize, without the need for further reflection, as wrong. This recognition does not seem to be only about the animal suffering involved, but rather, it may be the reaction to practices that show a marked disrespect for animals and nature generally. In this way, the aesthetic judgement at the same time entails a moral evaluation. Other examples Reclus gives for "ugliness" also confirm this interpretation: "We turn with repugnance from the engineer who defaces nature by imprisoning a waterfall in cast-iron pipes, and from the logger in California who cuts down a tree that is four thousand years old and three hundred feet high in order to show its rings at fairs and exhibitions" (Reclus 2013, 162).

There are some problems with the argument of aesthetic revulsion however. On the one hand, this revulsion is a subjective response. While many people are indeed disgusted by industrial farming, some people are fascinated by it. On the other hand, even for people who share this revulsion, it is not obvious what follows from it. Is the problem merely one of industrial over-breeding and the sheer extent of animal production, or is it the confinement or the killing of animals which is "ugly"? Reclus does not object to keeping and using animals for work, he even advocates the consumption of eggs. For him, it is the deforming of animals and the killing that violate his sense of beauty. In contrast to that, Peter Gelderloos (2011, n.p.) claims: "Killing can be a beautiful thing." The two have contrasting reactions, and there is no way to prioritize between the two. Also, many people adhere to a bucolic vision of small farms with some livestock. Cows and sheep are part of their idea of a beautiful landscape, and the fact that they are eventually killed does not seem to undermine it. So after all, even though aesthetic revulsion can be a good starting point to engage with modern agriculture, it does not deliver conclusive arguments for animal liberation.

COMPASSION, LOVE, AND THE FEELING
OF SOLIDARITY

In his defense of vegetarianism, Reclus does not only refer to the supposed ugliness of slaughter. The "real concern" for him is "to recognize the bonds of affection and kindness that link man to animals" (Reclus 2013, 160). Emotions play a significant role in his philosophy—foreshadowing later anarchist thoughts on the revolutionary nature of passion and emotion. Reclus (2013, 33) talks about the "fervent love of the justice that extends to all that lives" and says, "I also include animals in my feeling of socialist solidarity" (Reclus 2013, 32).

For Kropotkin, feelings of compassion and sympathy between humans are an important basis of his vision of an anarchist society. In his famous work *Mutual Aid* he describes how widespread altruistic and cooperative behavior is in nature and different human societies. In his view, it is a given trait of human nature to be social and to care for others, which can and should be further cultivated in society (Kropotkin 1902/2006). Kropotkin himself does not apply this morality to animals, or only inconsistently.[2]

For Brian Dominick (1997, 6), compassion is the basis for his twofold position: "I am vegan because I have compassion for animals. . . . I am an anarchist because I have that same compassion for humans." The authors of the zine *from anarchism to animals*, Kevin Watkinson and Donal O'Driscoll (2014), talk about a "basic emotional reaction" of "being shocked by some form of animal cruelty," which for many people is the starting point for some sort of animal activism. It is also accompanied, the authors write, with an ethical belief that does not seem to be in need of further argument: "We recognize that, for whatever reason, the abuse of animals is wrong."

So emotions like these play an important role for people challenging animal exploitation. In philosophy generally, many people emphasize the importance of emotions for ethics, and especially in animal ethics, there is a rich tradition of approaches based in feminist care ethics.[3] But in what way do these emotions actually serve to justify the demand for animal liberation? Reclus uses them primarily to explain the actual motives of vegetarians. Dominick (1997) can be read as directly inferring from his compassion his demand for "total freedom for all," but he also makes clear in that paragraph that he identifies as a radical who refuses to "settle for compromised perspectives, half-assed strategies and sold-out objectives" (1997, 6), and so his demands have to be seen in that context. Watkinson and O'Driscoll (2014, 4) note that many people who have an emotional reaction to cruelty "never progress past the 'bigger cages' position, as the welfarist approach is characterised."

There are indeed several problems with approaches based mainly on feelings of compassion, love or solidarity. Nevertheless, they should not be dismissed too quickly. The first problem is, as Watkinson and O'Driscoll remark, that an emotional response to cruelty based on compassion often does not lead people to question the system of animal exploitation as such. In fact, many people shocked by footage from animal factories think the conditions are better on small-scale farms. Often, in reality this is not the case. On small-scale farms, many animals suffer from limited space and physical mutilation, where the young are routinely separated from their mothers and the animals are brutally transported and then killed. Whether this treatment is recognized as cruel or elicits compassion depends very much on the context and the way in which the information is presented, as well as on the receiver. But for many people, learning about these conditions can make them oppose the current use of animals generally. On the other hand, the same people might think that a benign form of husbandry is at least possible, maybe in a future society after capitalism where small farms are no longer driven by a profit motive and animals do not have to serve primarily as commodities.

Again, some people will feel that breeding or confining animals is in itself cruel, and have compassion with animals such that they do not want them to be killed. But other people will not have the same response—after all, there are many people who have no objections to confining and killing animals. We might say that this is only because they are alienated and shut out from their own emotions by oppressive social ideologies, but even if we consider that to be a plausible explanation, especially in current society,[4] using it to discount particular opinions seems patronizing. We cannot just assume our own response is the right response.

Apart from that, even for people sharing the same response—for example, resistance to killing an animal out of sympathy and compassion—it is not clear what that means for action. That is because a feeling does not automatically translate into a principle for action or for society. If you think, for example, as Peter Gelderloos does, that it is right and natural to use and kill animals, then you are prepared to do it even if it causes you emotional conflict. In fact, Gelderloos sees it as an advantage of his position that he actively engages with this emotional conflict (Gelderloos 2011). So emotions in themselves do not tell us what to do or which general goal to pursue.

From all of this, it does not follow that feelings are not important. Rather, they can be a trigger for a more thorough engagement with an issue. Especially for anarchists, feelings of compassion and solidarity should be respected and fostered, and there is so far no reason why we should not feel solidarity and compassion for animals too. But in order to come up with a reasoned critique of current society and a well-sustained vision for the future, we need to complement our feeling with rational examination, or, as Marti Kheel (2007, 48) calls it, we need a "unity of reason and emotion."

THE ARGUMENT FROM COMMONALITIES

The argument from commonalities is well known in philosophical animal ethics. Famous authors like the utilitarian Peter Singer and the animal rights advocate Tom Regan use it in order to show that animals deserve the same respect and consideration as humans. So for Regan, animals and humans do not differ in terms of morally relevant capacities since all capacities that have been referred to as constituting a difference—such as reason, self-awareness or moral agency—are not possessed by all humans. Infants and some humans with disabilities also lack them. What all humans have in common and what therefore must be the reason for having fundamental rights is that they are sentient and aware of their surroundings.[5] And since animals share this quality, he argues, animals are due the same fundamental rights as humans, namely rights to life, integrity, and freedom (Regan 2005).

Anarchists put analogous arguments forward even though they typically do not operate with the concept of fundamental rights. In this section, I will discuss the ethical idea that humans and animals are due the same amount of respect to disadvantage them because they are not human is wrong.

Again, a good starting point is Kropotkin, even though he does not endorse such normative claims about animals. What he does, however, is challenge a very prevalent worldview of his time: famous philosophers of the early modern and enlightenment period, like Kant, assume a fundamental divide between humans and animals based on certain capacities such as reason or rationality that supposedly only humans have. In connection with this, Kant is able to claim that whereas humans are ends-in-themselves, animals are to be regarded as mere objects, or means to human ends. Kropotkin on the other hand argues in his work—just like Darwin, in this respect—that humans and animals are closely related not only in sharing the same natural history but also in sharing a natural sociability that serves as the basis for our morality.

So even though the ethical implications of Kropotkin's studies in natural history are not straightforward, by showing the commonalities of humans and animals, he effectively challenges the ideology of human superiority.

Reclus (2013, 158) also emphasizes our commonalities with animals, and he does so in an ethical context, for example, when criticizing how the "character of the child [is hardened] in relation to this 'meat on feet,' which nevertheless, loves as we do, feels as we do." Again when explaining the grounds for his vegetarianism, he depicts the disregard for animals as unfounded. He writes:

> [The real concern for vegetarians is] to extend to our brothers who have been dismissed as inferior the feelings that have already put an end to cannibalism within the human species. The arguments that cannibals once gave against the elimination of human flesh from their daily diet have the same merit as those that the typical meat-eater employs today. (Reclus 2013, 160)

So while as a historical claim about the end of cannibalism this is probably false, Reclus's (2013, 136) main point is the comparability of the two causes. As a result, he hopes to live with animals on equal terms: "We seek to make of [the animals] neither our servants nor our machines, but rather our true companions."

Recent authors on animal liberation and anarchism also deal with the question of differences and commonalities between humans and animals. For Dominick,

> the dichotomy between human and animal is more arbitrary than scientific. It is no different than the one posed between "whites" and "blacks" or "reds" or "yellows"; between adult and child; between man and woman; between heterosexual and homosexual; local and foreigner. Lines are drawn without care but with devious intent, and we are engineered by the institutions which raise us to believe that we are on one side of the line, and that the line is rational to begin with. (Dominick 1997, 6)

Torres reproduces an argument made by animal rights advocate Gary Francione when he writes,

> we need to treat like cases alike. Though animals and humans are clearly different, they are alike in the sense that they both suffer and are both sentient. For this reason, we should extend the principle of equal consideration to animals. (Torres 2007, 23)

So does this line of argument support the demand for animal liberation? There are at least four possible objections. First, one can argue that even if animals are due equal consideration, this does not rule out using them for our purposes. Singer, for example, has questioned whether certain animals have an interest in continued life. If they don't, it does not make sense to think they have a moral claim to life. Killing them would not harm them and therefore not be a problem. Since several people have argued convincingly against this position, I will not discuss it further here.[6]

Another version of this objection goes back to Alasdair Cochrane (2012) who argues that whereas animals have interests in life and in not suffering, they do not have a genuine interest in freedom as such. Of course, he agrees that confinement can seriously harm animals. But he says that is only the case insofar as the confinement causes the animals to suffer. If they have enough space and can satisfy all their natural desires, it does not matter to them if they are under the control of humans. So he thinks that it would be legitimate to keep and use animals for the production of milk and eggs as long as we don't make them suffer and don't kill them.

I will come back to the question of freedom and control later. At this point however, I want to refer back to what I said about animal use and animal liberation in the introduction. It is very hard to imagine livestock farming without killing. Even if you wish to only produce eggs and milk, you would need to deal with the male offspring that is nowadays used for meat production, and you would need to care for all the animals that have grown to be unproductive which would make the whole business extremely ineffective. Livestock farming without serious harm for the animals involved is, in my view, impossible. In any case, since this concept of no-harm farming is so markedly different from (and incompatible with) what defenders of small-scale farming have in mind, Cochrane's highly hypothetical scenario loses its relevancy to the discussion at hand.

The second objection is put forward by Peter Gelderloos. He makes a number of points meant to show that veganism and the political project of animal liberation are not worth practicing or striving for. I will talk about the ecological argument and the anti-capitalist argument later. What concerns me now is the following idea:

> There is no coherent morality or ethics rooted in nature that can view the killing and eating of animals as wrong. In nature, killing and eating something is a respectful, intimate activity, and a necessary part of natural cycles. Viewing this as wrong is nothing but a shockingly alienated, civilized view that domesticates animals at a metaphysical level by reducing them to quasi-citizens in need of rights. Fuck that shit. Humans and all other animals are much more free and full outside of legal frameworks, without rights, only needs and desires. (Gelderloos 2008, n.p.)

He does not directly engage with the argument from commonalities, but his idea seems to be that such arguments cannot be relevant since killing and eating others are both natural and healthy in all ecosystems, and therefore it cannot be wrong. In a way, he does not seem to see the point of ethical considerations at all. He takes the talk of "animal rights" to necessarily be about legal rights and criticizes it for being reformist and uncritical of the state (Gelderloos 2011).

So the idea seems to be that killing is natural and, therefore, it cannot be bad. The obvious way to respond to this argument is to say that it is committing a textbook case of a naturalistic fallacy—just because in nature, things are such and such, we do not have to act this way. There are many things common in nature that we do not want to see as regular practices in an anarchist society, like rape or killing of weak species' members. In a way, Gelderloos (2011, n.p.) seems to acknowledge that we need better reasons than a reference to nature since he gives further reasons against the idea that killing is bad: "Killing need not be an act of negation, either. It can also be the foundation of a relationship. . . . Killing can be a beautiful thing."

Not only is it somewhat unclear what sort of relationship there can be with a dead animal—Gelderloos might have something in mind like Derrick Jensen (2006, 653) who thinks that by killing animals we take on responsibility for their species or their ecosystem—but this reasoning completely ignores the subjective perspective of the individual animal killed. Animals don't enjoy being killed, just as humans don't enjoy it. They all try to avoid it.

Apart from that, this reasoning also ignores the argument from commonalities. If killing animals is unproblematic, why should not the same hold for killing humans? In fact, Gelderloos seems to think that when he says that we should all "look forward to the day when we will also be killed and eaten." This sentiment, however, in my view, is either hypocritical nonsense—I assume that Gelderloos does not generally approve of humans killing other humans for food. Or, if he does, I would consider this inconsistent with basic anarchist values of mutual respect and solidarity within human society. I think it is safe to say that most people would not agree to being killed, so to do so for food would entail ignoring their own preferences in favor of our own. It seems strange to even argue this point.

There is a follow-up objection, which is brought up by Val Plumwood and further discussed by Ian Werkheiser. The idea is that when we judge that killing is wrong we assume a problematic separation between humans and animals. Reflecting on Plumwood, Werkheiser writes,

> This separation becomes clear, for Plumwood, when we consider the case of predation in nature. How are we to judge a wolf killing and eating a deer? If the ontological vegan says that the wolf is wrong to do so but doesn't know any better, then she is saying that humanity is special because humans have recognized a profound truth about nature of which no other animal is aware. Such a position also commits us to a strong moral realism and the claim that carnivores ought to

become scavengers, which we might not want to hold. If the ontological vegan instead says that it is not wrong for the wolf to eat the deer, then she is saying that humanity has a special duty to others that no other species has, and depending on how this is cashed out, it will most likely come down to another kind of human exceptionalism. (Werkheiser 2013, 176)

The response to this objection is that humans do indeed have capacities many other animals do not have: Not only the capacity to thrive on a plant-based diet but also the capacity to engage in ethical argument and to make decisions about one's food choices based on ethical feelings and beliefs. Because of this capacity, we have a corresponding responsibility that we cannot cast off by embracing our closeness to animals. Recognizing the special capacities is not a problematic exceptionalism insofar as it does not come with value claims. To deny that humans have special capacities would be somewhat absurd, given that this denial is written in a philosophical paper published in a magazine or online. To write papers and to engage in ethical argument are just things we humans do, just as other species do other things.

The third objection would be that if the argument from commonalities is accepted, it would have to be accepted also for plants, which would then mean that in most parts of the planet we would not have any unproblematic food choices left, and as a consequence me might as well eat animals. Something on these lines is also put forward by Gelderloos, but his argument is twofold. On the one hand, he argues that if we accept the ability to feel pain as the relevant criterion in the argument from commonalities, then plants might qualify for equal consideration as well since it is well possible that plants feel. On the other hand, he criticizes a supposed vegan obsession with pain, arguing that "pain is natural, necessary, and good" and says that just as in killing there is "an element of the beautiful in" inflicting pain on others (Gelderloos 2011). Again, he ignores the perspective of the victim and commits a naturalistic fallacy. Apart from that, he misunderstands the role of pain in the argument. Of course, one consequence of the argument is that inflicting pain on animals is as bad as inflicting pain on humans. But to identify the capacity to feel pain as the relevant criterion is not because pain is bad but because the capacity to feel pain is taken to be identical with being a conscious subject, a some*one* rather than a some*thing*, a being with a perspective of its own. It is these kinds of perspectives that require our consideration.

Now Gelderloos is certainly right that we don't and can't know if plants are sentient as well. However, there are good reasons to believe that they do not have a perspective in any way comparable to that of many animals and humans, which we understand very well. Of course, it is somewhat problematic to value similarity to ourselves in this way. On the other hand, we have to base our actions on something, and it seems to be better to base them on something we understand rather than something we don't understand—after all, even if we knew that plants feel, we wouldn't know exactly what would hurt them. So in my view it makes a lot of sense to respect plants as living beings and harm them as little as possible, but it does not make sense to use an argument from commonalities to show that we should not eat them.

The last objection is the following: If we take the argument from commonalities seriously, then we have to oppose the killing of animals just as much as we oppose the killing of humans. Even the most fervent animal liberationists are not prepared to do that—they just don't feel that accidentally running over a rat is as bad as accidentally running over a child, or that evicting a mouse from your—and their—home in the middle of winter is as bad as evicting a human family from their home in the middle of winter. But if we are not willing to accept the real consequences of the argument, so the objection goes, there must be something wrong with the argument.

In response, I want to distinguish between two things. First, emotional reactions. Being raised in an utterly speciesist society, we have learnt to feel differently about the deaths of humans and animals. This fact does not invalidate the argument. Second, practicalities. There are differences in how we can relate to animals and to how we can relate to humans. Whereas it is only a matter of economic and power structures that prevent us from providing a safe home for every human family, the case is different for mice. You cannot make an agreement with them that they'll stay in the cellar and use a toilet, nor can you stop them reproducing rapidly. So if you plan to continue living in your house—and after all, we need shelter to survive—you must in some way keep the mice out. Of course, you should do that in the way least harmful to them. However, once you've attempted to stop up every crack and hole they may gain entry by, and they've still managed to come in then you'll still have to take action. So even though as a consequence, you do to mice what you would not do to humans (eviction in winter), it does not invalidate the argument. For every ethical demand, it is true that "ought implies can," and there is only so much consideration you can give in such cases.

Still, one might feel that these responses don't really refute the objection. And I agree that humans have a place in our lives and our culture that we may find it hard to open up to animals. So maybe the argument from commonalities does not succeed in convincing us of equality between humans and animals. But that does not imply that it is flawed. It gives us very good reasons to question the common disregard of animals, urging us to give more consideration to animals—and even if we do not reach completely equal consideration, it is clear that the using and killing of animals, as long as it is unnecessary for human survival, is unjustified.

To conclude, the argument from commonalities gives us good reason to embrace animal liberation. It does not presuppose any particular anarchist convictions but should be accepted in principle by any rational moral agent. We can, however, put forward similar basic points in the form of a critique of oppression, which might be more suited to an anarchist perspective.

THE ARGUMENT FROM OPPRESSION

Many anarchist authors use the terms *oppression* and *domination* roughly synonymously. In this chapter, I will distinguish between the two using dictionary definitions. By *domination* I will understand the "exercise of power or influence over someone or something, or the state of being so controlled" (*Oxford English Dictionary*). *Oppression* is defined by the same dictionary as "Prolonged cruel or unjust treatment or exercise of authority." So in general usage, domination is not necessarily a bad thing, whereas oppression has a moral evaluation written into the concept.

Anarchists naturally oppose oppression as well as domination, at least where human beings are concerned. The basis for the anarchist idea that there should be no government or hierarchies of power and domination between people is of course their idea that people are perfectly capable and willing to exercise their capacity of autonomy and make their own decisions, individually and collectively. When it comes to animals, however, this capacity can be challenged, at least in relation to domesticated animals, which are our main focus here. So while it might therefore not be obvious that anarchists need to oppose a domination of animals, it is clear that they oppose any oppression. Therefore, I will distinguish these two claims and deal with the question of oppression first.

Recent authors arguing for animal liberation from an anarchist perspective often claim that right now animals are oppressed by humans (Watkinson and O'Driscoll 2014; Torres 2007; Cudworth 2015, 98; Dominick 1997). If oppression by definition constitutes an unjust abuse of power, it is uncontroversial that oppression is to be abolished. The controversial question then is if the term really applies to the situation of animals, that is, if it is cruel or unjust to use animals for the production of meat, milk, and eggs. It is not necessarily straightforward to determine—it depends on the definition of "cruel"—whether the treatment of animals in "humane" farms or within hunting qualifies as cruel, but the argument from commonalities can be used to show that it is unjust.

This treatment has already been established to be ethically unjustified because it is based on an unjustified discrimination against animals. The term "just" is usually characterized as applying to institutions rather than individual acts, therefore belonging to the realm of political theory rather than ethics. And accordingly, the term "oppression" applies to institutions in the sense of continuous social arrangements and practices. Now, it can be said that the established practice of using and killing animals institutionalizes an action that is judged to be ethically wrong. In society, laws, economic relations, ideology, and other factors serve to maintain a practice of humans harming and exploiting animals that they would not judge to be acceptable if the victims were humans. Since the distinction is unjustified, so is the practice.

With these clarifications at hand, many points made by anarchists using the terms *oppression* or *domination* do not add anything new to the arguments already discussed. The analysis of the treatment of animals as oppression, however, allows us to see the phenomenon in a different context than the purely ethical discussed in the section before, and this social-political context is important for an anarchist perspective. On the one hand, it is important to recognize the institutionalized nature of the problem instead of seeing it simply as a consequence of a misbehavior of individuals. Torres, for example, cites a sociological analysis of oppression by David Nibert and writes:

> Nibert argues that when we individualize the notion of speciesism and understand it as merely an individual prejudice, we lose the notion that certain social, economic, and legal logics are set in place that perpetuate animal exploitation at a deeper level within the social order. (Torres 2007, 71)

Apart from that, the idea that animals are oppressed often comes with two further points. The first claim is that there are a number of similarities and interconnections between the oppression of animals and other oppressive dynamics in society. Nibert's theory of oppression, which Torres relies on, draws from other sociological work on the oppression of human groups and applies these findings to animals—which works, of course, only because there are significant similarities in the motivations, forms, and consequences of these phenomena. Nibert identifies three factors as "necessary for the development and perpetuation of oppression of humans and other animals." The first is economic exploitation or competition: "Humans tend to disperse, eliminate or exploit a group . . . when it is in their economic interest to do so." The second factor is unequal power, largely vested in control of the state: "The oppressing group must have the power to subordinate members of the at-risk group." The last factor is ideological control: "Ideological manipulation fuels prejudiced attitudes and discriminatory acts that help protect and maintain oppressive economic and social arrangements" (Nibert 2002, 13). So the claim is that the oppression of animals is shaped and driven by roughly the same factors that also shape and drive racial oppression, among others.

The parallels go even deeper. Dominick (1997) refers to several scholarly works that demonstrate the "correlations between speciesism and racism—

between the treatment of animals and people of color" (10) and also the connections between patriarchy and animal exploitation. For example, Marjorie Spiegel has described how specific practices like branding, force-feeding, the separation of families or forced breeding as well as the general use of violence to ensure compliance characterize both the treatment of slaves and the treatment of animals (Spiegel 1996). Even more importantly, it is often very similar ideological tools that are used to justify these practices—objectification, de-individualization, denying members of the oppressed group certain capacities like intelligence or autonomy. Carol Adams (2010) has described corresponding parallels between the oppression of women and animals, like the depiction of both as passive objects for (sexual or actual) consumption.

Also, all of these authors point out how different oppressions hang together and reinforce each other—for example, meat-eating or hunting are promoted by widespread conceptions of masculinity. Also, the current animal industry could not function as it does without the brutal oppression of small farmers and Indigenous people, who are driven from their land in order to grow feed crops, or without the exploitation of workers in slaughterhouses.

This understanding leads to the second point endorsed by some writers connecting anarchism and animal liberation. That is the claim that all these oppressions have ultimately the same cause. Whereas Dominick in some places identifies "the establishment" as the driving cause, Watkinson and O'Driscoll speak of the liberal-capitalist system that is inherently characterized by relations of domination and commodification. On the one hand, these analyses are somewhat simplistic not only because they do not examine the complex conditions of the current animal industry in any detail but also because they seem to ignore the fact that animal abuse is prevalent also in non-capitalist societies and is often practiced and endorsed by groups of humans that are themselves oppressed so it does not only benefit a so-called establishment. On the other hand, the way that animals are exploited within the global "animal industrial complex" (Noske 1989) is certainly significantly shaped by capitalist relations and power structures, which are at the same time responsible for environmental destruction and human exploitation (Nibert 2017). Therefore, the profitability of animal abuse and the economic power of the corporations involved is one of the major obstacles to change the situation. That again links the struggle for animal liberation to other emancipatory struggles.

So what do we make of these points, and how do they relate to the question of animal liberation? In my view, all of them are well sustained. For one thing however, we need to make a qualification. Since they all refer to the institutionalized oppression of animals in current society, they cannot easily be applied to all kinds of treatment of animals that might be judged to be ethically problematic. For example, authors like Peter Gelderloos or Derrick

Jensen would claim that when they go hunting, they are not part of a structure of oppression, let alone a structure of oppression that is serving the capitalist system or the establishment. Also, it is not obvious whether an imagined future society which practices a form of animal farming seen as benign by its proponents could be charged with oppressing animals in such a way that all these points hold true.

The points are, however, relevant to the demand for animal liberation in at least two ways. First, they help to undermine the devaluation of animals by showing that it is part of an ideology, similar to other ideologies we have already discarded. So we might actually say that in this way, even Gelderloos or Jensen are within the system because they buy into the traditional idea that animals may legitimately be killed and eaten even though they do not equally argue that humans may be hunted and killed by other humans.

Second, I think the three claims can underpin the importance of the demand for animal liberation. The oppression of animals is not a marginal issue to be addressed at some point in the future when there is time, but at least within industrialized Western societies, it is intimately tied into the oppressive dynamics of capitalism. Therefore, it has to be taken seriously now and included in any comprehensive struggle for a more just world.

EXCURSION: THE PROBLEM OF THE UNAVOIDABILITY OF HARM

Gelderloos puts forward some arguments against veganism and animal liberation that are based on ecological, not ethical, concerns. For one thing, he claims that vegan products can be very destructive because on the one hand, they are often produced by industrial farming with the use of chemical fertilizers and pesticides, on the other, they are produced by big capitalist corporations that thrive on exploitation.

The second claim he makes is that also for the future, a truly sustainable society would be one that makes use of animals and animal products. He writes, "In eco-harmonious societies, lifestyles or economies (including diet) derive from different ways of relating to the natural environment that prove to be sustainable over time. In other words, outside of consumerism, possible lifestyles vary according to local environmental conditions. In most parts of the world, a vegan lifestyle is simply not sustainable: foods, fuels, and materials for clothing and tools would have to be imported. This is to say, in most parts of the world it is more ecologically sustainable for humans to kill animals" (Gelderloos 2008).

In my view, the first of the two arguments is more easily refuted. Gelderloos is of course right that veganism as a lifestyle choice does not challenge the root problems of current society and is not even successful in what is often claimed, namely to be cruelty free or not harming animals. In this chapter, I am not focusing on veganism as a lifestyle choice, but talking about the political struggle for animal liberation. As Watkinson and O'Driscoll note, however, this might be understood as being part of a more comprehensive conception of veganism. At the same time, it is important to note that under current conditions veganism is the least ecologically harmful diet that is available to most people in industrialized societies, and even more so when it is combined with an effort to consume organic and regional produce. This is because animal production consumes such a huge amount of resources and has such negative social and environmental effects (Springmann 2016).

The second claim made by Gelderloos also rightly points out that ecologically sustainable societies need to adapt to their local circumstances. In my view, however, we have to beware of visions of utopia otherwise known as primitivist. There is no reason why a sustainable society should not involve technology and also the transportation of some goods, especially if it has ecological advantages. Vegan-organic farming, permaculture, and plant-based agroecology can be efficient and have positive effects on surrounding ecosystems and their biodiversity. In order to feed the world's population, we cannot rely on hunting and gathering or on some backyard chickens as Gelderloos suggests. To be sure, the point of animal liberation is not to get rid of every backyard chicken as soon as possible. The point is to fundamentally change the way humans relate to animals and accordingly to change the way we produce food. But as Torres (2007, 26) points out, even if keeping chickens in your backyard for eggs "may not be horribly torturous for the animals," by doing this, "you turn another being into a subject whose primary ends are to fulfill your wants; it reifies human dominance, and exploits another for your ends." So we need to further develop techniques and practices that allow us to produce food with the least possible harm to animals and the environment generally.

One might object at this point that the cultivation of land and agriculture in itself is harmful since it destroys the living spaces of countless animals and requires the control of so-called pests. Does this treatment of animals not also amount to oppression? That is the problem of the unavoidability of harm, meaning that in order to live on this planet, we cannot only have positive and cooperative relations with animals (which Kropotkin highlights) but we also necessarily stand in competition and therefore in combat with some other animals. I would argue, however, that especially if we use the best methods to work within an ecosystem and not against it, promoting biodiversity and natural balances, there is far less killing involved than if we keep livestock to eat or hunt animals (Matheny 2003). Also and maybe more importantly, we do not establish a fixed category of beings that can be used and killed whenever it seems beneficial to us. In my view, these categories are what ultimately amplify and deepen oppression.

Gelderloos and others appear to imagine a society that practices some sort of mythological respect toward animals and is thereby able to avoid devaluing them while still using and eating them.[7] That is, in my view, self-deceit since it excludes the perspective of the victim. Also, I don't think that it is realistically available to us in the foreseeable future, and certainly not at current global population levels.

THE QUESTION OF DOMINATION

For most anarchists writing on the topic, liberation of animals from oppression seems to coincide with complete freedom and independence from humans. That is also due to the fact that they use the terms *oppression* and *domination* synonymously. So Dominick describes his political aim as "total freedom for all," and Watkinson and O'Driscoll (2014, 15) write, "Animal Liberation can be defined as the freedom for non-human animals to live outside of human society."

Also, the fact that many animals are under the control of humans is often seen as a problem in and of itself, leading to calls for animal liberation, without any apparent regard to whether any actual harm is being caused. So the idea is that animals living with humans or in the custody of humans (implying that they are having their freedom restricted in at least some ways) is problematic in itself. But this idea does not follow from the critique of oppression alone. So how could it be motivated? The first reason, which seems to be crucial for Watkinson and O'Driscoll, is the worry that as soon as animals are under the control of humans, they necessarily run the danger of being exploited. They write:

> There are few relationships between "man and beast" that can be deemed mutualistic; rather their foundation is exploitative. From the cute kittens purchased for company and entertainment, to the dogs that form a status symbol, there are few, if any, ways in which people interact in conventional western society with domesticated animals that can be deemed equal and respectful. The simplest way to address this issue is through freeing animals from the tyranny of human society and by doing this, essentially just leaving them alone. (Watkinson and O'Driscoll 2014, 15)

The upshot of this is that, in my terminology, domination is bad because it tends to become oppression. So whereas the authors do not deny that there could be relations between humans and animals that are equal and respectful, they think they are not very widespread today and therefore not very likely, at least in "conventional Western society." This, however, does not provide a further reason for animal liberation since it does not show that domination in itself is a problem. I will address this concern in the conclusion.

The second reason is the idea that for animals, living under the custody of humans is harmful because it restricts their freedom. Watkinson and O'Driscoll (2014, 15) write, "Non-human animals don't (for the most part) choose to be a part of society, so it makes no sense from an anarchist perspective to pursue an agenda where they are forced to do so for our own perceived gain."

That, however, might be true for free-living animals that avoid close relationships with humans—even though many of them choose to live near humans. But not all domesticated animals have or are able to make that kind of choice. We might however assume that not having that sort of choice is in itself a restriction of the freedom of the animals, and add to that the many other ways in which animals living with humans are restricted in their freedom.

As mentioned earlier, Cochrane claims that a restriction of the freedom of animals is only a problem insofar as it causes suffering, like the confinement in stalls and sheds certainly does. His idea is that since animals lack the sort of autonomy that is characteristic for healthy adult humans, they don't have an interest in being free in the same sense as we have. So for them, to be in the custody of well-meaning humans would not harm them, except insofar as they suffer under specific aspects of their situation (Cochrane 2012, chapters 2 and 4).

Also, we have to see that in relation to domesticated animals that currently exist, animal liberationists do accept that certain restrictions of freedom are legitimate—either in the interest of the animals themselves, like forced medical treatment, or in the interest of other or future beings, like reproductive control on sanctuaries or keeping some animals from hurting others. If we are honest, even with the most well-intentioned humans, there never is a truly equal relationship in terms of power to take decisions—the humans are in charge. So are these restrictions of freedom problematic in themselves and therefore a reason to strive for an end to all close relationships of humans and animals?

In my view, it is very hard to argue that a truly respectful and informed guardianship would still harm the animals. In fact, in many sanctuaries animals enjoy fulfilling lives, able to exercise their natural capacities, protected from predators and many diseases. I think that Cochrane is right that a full-blown autonomy in the sense of being able to determine one's own life plans is not important for animals. I would, however, disagree with his claim that since animals do not have that kind of autonomy, it is only about suffering. Animals do have the capacity to make decisions for themselves, they can decide what to eat, what to do during the day, which companions to spend time with, and so on. And just as Cochrane infers from the human capacity for autonomy that we have an interest in exercising our autonomy, I think we should infer from the animals' capacity to make decisions that they have an interest in exercising that capacity. Therefore, respect for animals involves, to some degree, respecting their decisions and enhancing their freedom as much as possible.[8]

Concerning our relation to domesticated animals we might draw an analogy with the relation to human children. Whereas a certain inequality in decision power cannot be eliminated, we can and should try to respect and foster the children's interests and their independence as far as it is not detrimental to their well-being. Insofar as we are able to do so, the inequality alone does not necessarily lead to oppression or exploitation.

To summarize this section: Although for many anarchists an objection to domination in the sense of there being relations of power and control seems to motivate the demand for animal liberation, I have argued that this reasoning is not conclusive since there can be benign cases of humans dominating animals.

CONCLUSION AND FUTURE PROSPECTS

I have discussed several grounds for criticism of the current treatment of animals and for the demand for animal liberation. Aesthetic revulsion and emotional responses to the ways animals are commonly treated are important as a starting point for a critical examination of established practices. Furthermore, it can be argued on a rational basis that the discrimination of animals based on the fact that they are not human cannot be justified. The argument from commonalities shows that we need to take the interests of animals seriously. Harming and killing them for food and other benefits can and should be recognized as oppression and injustice. An anarchist's struggle for justice therefore needs to embrace the political aim of animal liberation.

Contrary to what some authors claim, this aim does not obviously entail the demand that animals need to be freed from every involvement in human society. The next question then is, of course, how it could look like to integrate animals into a human society on the basis of fundamental anarchist principles like equality, cooperation or voluntary agreements. In other words, how can we actually realize the idea, embraced by Reclus, that animals might be "neither our servants nor our machines but rather our true companions" (Reclus 2013, 136)? One very difficult task would be to ensure that the interests of animals are taken into account in collective decision procedures where they cannot directly take part themselves. There should be representatives of one sort or the other in order for the interests of animals to be seriously heard and defended. At the same time, this won't work without a general, ethically motivated willingness to show serious consideration to beings who cannot effectively defend themselves against unjust and inconsiderate treatment. So it will not only be a question of procedures, but of attitude and ideology.[9]

Related to that, even before thinking about political participation we might need to consider the need to establish agreements and organizations that are effective in preventing animals from being exploited and harmed for human benefit—after all, they will always be vulnerable, and even if we generally accept the goal of animal liberation it will be in the interest of some humans to confine, kill, and eat animals. Also, we need to consider future scenarios—even if we achieve some kind of utopian society where domesticated animals are considered members of society, will they really be cared for in cases of natural catastrophe or famine? And if we suspect that they would not, is that not a reason to agree with those animal liberationists who think we should take measures to ensure that domesticated animal breeds die out?

While all these questions are theoretically interesting, the answers do not make much difference to the actual task at hand: to build a comprehensive movement against all oppressions and injustices and to include the quest for animal liberation in it, thereby showing solidarity with animals, rather than exploiting them, and supporting the struggle against the animal industrial complex and the ideologies that sustain it.[10]

NOTES

1. See also Schmitz 2016.

2. On the same page he first champions an association of hunters and then writes, "Uncle Toby's Society at Newcastle, which has already induced over 260,000 boys and girls never to destroy birds' nests and to be kind to animals, has certainly done more for the development of human feeling . . . than lots of moralists and most of our schools" (Kropotkin 1902/2006, 230 f.).

3. See, for example, Donovan and Adams 2007, 4.

4. Dominick mentions alienation as an important factor for the continued existence of animal exploitation: "This is precisely why late capitalism has entirely removed the consumer from the process of production. The torture goes on elsewhere, behind (tightly) closed doors. Allowed to empathize with the victims of species oppression, humans would not be able to go about their lives as they presently do" (Dominick 1997, 14). Brian Luke (1995) gives a similar analysis in 'Taming Ourselves or Going Feral'.

5. There are exceptions here, too, namely humans in a persistent vegetative state. But in these cases it is actually doubtful whether fundamental rights still apply as

it may be deemed morally acceptable to end someone's life if it is certain that they won't ever gain consciousness again.

6. See, for example, Francione 2006; Cochrane 2012, chapters 2 and 3.

7. A similar idea is expressed by Murray Bookchin (Bookchin 1982, 99).

8. See also Donaldson and Kymlicka 2011, chapter 4.

9. In recent years, some authors have put forward ideas about animals' political participation that can be very fruitful for this discussion even though these authors do not operate within an anarchist framework but rather, like Sue Donaldson and Will Kymlicka, argue that animals should be accepted as citizens within liberal-democratic nation-states. Their ideas on how to relate to animals in practice are nevertheless instructive for our purposes; however, there is not room in this chapter to elaborate on these. See Donaldson and Kymlicka 2011 and 2015.

10. I would like to thank the Fritz Thyssen Foundation for financially supporting my research.

REFERENCES

Adams, Carol J. 2010. *The Sexual Politics of Meat*. New York, London: Continuum.

Bookchin, Murray. 1982. *The Ecology of Freedom*. Palo Alto, Calif: Cheshire Books.

Cochrane, Alasdair. 2012. *Animal Rights without Liberation*. New York: Columbia University Press.

Cudworth, Erica. 2015. "Intersectionality, Species and Social Domination." In *Anarchism and Animal Liberation*, edited by Anthony J. Nocella II, Richard J. White, and Erika Cudworth. Jefferson: MacFarland.

Dominick, Brian. 1997. "Animal Liberation and Social Revolution." Zine by Critical Mess Media. Text online available at <https://theanarchistlibrary.org/library/brian-a-dominick-animal-liberation-and-social-revolution> (accessed October 27, 2018).

Donaldson, Sue, and Will Kymlicka. 2011. *Zoopolis: A Political Theory of Animal Rights*. New York: Oxford University Press.

Donaldson, Sue, and Will Kymlicka. 2015. "Farmed Animal Sanctuaries: The Heart of the Movement?" *Politics & Animals*, vol. 1, no.1, Fall, pp. 50–74.

Donovan, Josephine, and Carol J. Adams (eds.). 2007. *The Feminist Care Tradition in Animal Ethics*. New York: Columbia University Press.

Francione, Gary. 2006. "Equal Consideration and the Interest of Nonhuman Animals in Continued Existence: A Response to Professor Sunstein." *University of Chicago Legal Forum*, Issue 1.

Gelderloos, Peter. 2008. "Veganism Is a Consumer Activity." *The Anarchist Library*, <https://theanarchistlibrary.org/library/peter-gelderloos-veganism-is-a-consumer-activity> (accessed July 6, 2018).

Gelderloos, Peter. 2011. "Veganism: Why Not. An Anarchist Perspective." *The Anarchist Library*, <https://theanarchistlibrary.org/library/peter-gelderloos-veganism-why-not> (accessed July 6, 2018).

Jensen, Derrick. 2006. *Endgame, Vol. 1, The Problem of Civilization*. New York: Seven Stories Press.

Kheel, Marti. 2007. "The Liberation of Nature: A Circular Affair." In *The Feminist Care Tradition in Animal Ethics*, edited by Josephine Donovan and Carol J. Adams. New York.

Kropotkin, Peter. 1902/2006. *Mutual Aid*. Mineola, NY: Dover Publications.

Luke, Brian. 1995. "Taming Ourselves or Going Feral." In *Animals and Women: Feminist Theoretical Explorations*, edited by Carol J. Adams and Josephine Donovan. Durham: Duke University Press.

Matheny, Gaverick. 2003. "Least Harm: A Defense of Vegetarianism from Steven Davis's Omnivorous Proposal." *Journal of Agricultural and Environmental Ethics* vol. 16, no. 5.

Nibert, David. 2002. *Animal Rights/Human Rights: Enganglements of Oppression and Liberation*. Lanham, Md.: Rowman & Littlefield.

Nibert, David (ed.). 2017. *Animal Oppression and Capitalism, Volume 1: The Oppression of Nonhuman Animals as Sources of Food*. Santa Barbara, California: Praeger.

Nocella II, Anthony J., Richard J. White, and Erica Cudworth (ed.). 2015. *Anarchism and Animal Liberation*. Jefferson: MacFarland.

Noske, Barbara. 1989. *Humans and Other Animals*. London: Pluto Press.

Reclus, Élisée. 2013. *Anarchy, Geography, Modernity, Selected Writing*, edited by John Clark and Camille Martin. Oakland, CA: PM Press.

Regan, Tom. 2005. *Empty Cages, Facing the Challenge of Animal Rights*. Lanham, MD: Rowman and Littlefield.

Schmitz, Friederike. 2016. "Animal Ethics and Human Institutions: Integrating Animals into Political Theory." In *The Political Turn in Animal Ethics*, edited by Robert Garner and Siobhan Sullivan. Rowman & Littlefield.

Spiegel, Marjorie. 1996. *The Dreaded Comparison. Human and Animal Slavery*. New York: Mirror Books.

Springmann, Marco. 2016. "Plant-Based Diets Could Save Millions of Lives and Dramatically Cut Greenhouse Gas Emissions." *PNAS*, vol. 113, no. 15.

Torres, Bob. 2007. *Making a Killing: The Political Ecology of Animal Rights*. Oakland, CA: AK Press.

Watkinson Kevin, and Donal O'Driscoll. 2014. *From Animals to Anarchism*. Dysophia, open letter #3.

Werkheiser, Ian. 2013. "Domination and Consumption: An Examination of Veganism, Anarchism, and Ecofeminism." *PhaenEx* vol. 8, no. 2, Fall/Winter.

Chapter 2

Political Ecology and Animal Liberation: Emancipating Non-Humans from a Leftist Anti-Capitalist Perspective

Patrik Gažo

INTRODUCTION[1]

We often hear about ethical consumption and responsible consumerism, a discourse that extends beyond the environmental movement. Yet few of us actually realize that the alleged ethics of the product itself is not just about the social aspect or the adverse impact on the environment or ecosystems. In order to identify the product as ethical, many vegans and animal liberationists argue that it is also necessary to remove the possibility of nonhuman animals suffering, especially those exploited in agriculture, fashion, health care, and cosmetic industries.

Political ecology is attempting to blur the edges between nature and society and at the same time to raise awareness about the fact that political and economic processes are also inherently ecological (Hornborg 2017, 41). Animal agriculture is currently one of the biggest producers of greenhouse gases and thus a major contributor to climate change (FAO 2006). The "externalities" that are destroying the environment are mostly produced through a capitalistic production logic, ergo the effort to maximize profit and growth. However, economic processes are not a satisfactory explanation to the primarily anthropocentric and carnistic society. Speciesism (Singer 2009) is a hierarchical stance that is ingrained just as much, if not more, in cultural constructs too. Political ecologists realize that environmentally unfriendly social systems are also achieved by cultural processes that help to create a notion of natural social constructs, for instance, that nature is a commodity (Paulson 2015, 47). This research framework emphasizes a strong connection between political, economic, cultural, and ecological processes and offers a suitable space for raising questions about the power relationships between human and nonhuman animals.

Authors who belong to the wide range of political ecology approaches frequently try to give a voice to those who are marginalized or oppressed (Robbins 2012). This work has several goals. One of them is to upset the power imbalance, this time in favor of nonhuman animals, since their voices are often overlooked. In political ecology, nonhuman animals (or hunting areas and fisheries) are often perceived as commonly shared property and available resources (Robbins 2012, 51), rather than as beings with their own interests and needs. Thus, a thorough elaboration of the idea of animal liberation and the declassification of human superiority over nonhuman animals will bring even deeper understanding of the nature–society dichotomy in pushing political ecology forward. I begin by introducing a strong ethical relationship to nonhuman animals from the view of two of the leading predecessors of political ecology, Pyotr Alexeyevich Kropotkin and Élisée Reclus. These two anarchist thinkers expressed a radical stance, not only toward our relationship with nature and nonhuman animals but also toward the political, economic, and social order of their day. They laid a foundation for an anarchist view of hierarchical structure, which I will employ to analyse people and movements that define themselves as standing against the dominance of one group over the other in the context of speciesism, which has similar parallels with economic domination, racism, and sexism. I will examine the dialog about animal liberation and veganism between radical animal liberators and anarchists. Finally, I will look at how this discussion contributes to political ecological knowledge, or rather to the development of an anarchist political ecology.

RECLUS'S AND KROPOTKIN'S LEGACY

Kropotkin (1842–1921) is one of the most significant historical figures of anarchism, advancing the approach of anarcho-communism. He was aware of the connection between society and nature, and he is considered to be the predecessor of contemporary social and political ecology. Part of his studies focused on understanding and explaining ethics, and it is the conjunction of ethics and ecology that indicates the appropriate presumption to formulate positive relationships with nonhuman animals. What then exactly was Kropotkin's approach?

He analysed ethics in his work *Anarchist Morality* (1897), though he concentrated mostly on relationships between humans. Despite his specific focus, it is possible to find references there, which he might not have realized himself, which point us onto a better attitude toward nonhuman animals. I will try to identify them.

Kropotkin argued that moral sensitivity should not be accorded only to humans (Kropotkin 1897, 4). His life's work is interwoven with examples drawn from nature and the lives of nonhuman animals, where he tries to apply them to human morality. He realized that all organisms seek joy instead of pain and distress, and he regarded that as the very foundation of life, since without it, life would be impossible (Kropotkin 1897, 7). He uses examples of various nonhuman animals to show that human and animal morality concur in the notion of what is good and bad (he uses it as an argument against the necessity of religion as a representative of values in society): "The ant, the bird, the marmot, the savage have read neither Kant nor the fathers of the Church nor even Moses. And yet all have the same idea of good and evil" (Kropotkin 1897, 9). Concurrently, we can regard this idea as an argument that connects us to nonhuman animals. He explains later why we stand up for victims of violence, such as children. It is precisely because we can empathize with their situation. Nevertheless, he adds that this empathy is not a human prerogative, but that other animals are capable of it too (Kropotkin 1897, 11). He concludes that solidarity is a natural law, more important than struggle and competition in terms of how evolution theory has typically been presented. We can safely use this logic also in interspecies relationships and empathy, even though Kropotkin did not mention it within his own thesis. An animal in a slaughterhouse or in a research laboratory is an anonymized object, making it hard to empathize and build a sense of solidarity with because of the depersonalization of individuals within the system of certain industries or structures of the laboratory. In the conclusion of his work on morality, he talks about human beings representing a higher ideal: "The life of a beast cannot satisfy him" (Kropotkin 1897, 19). We can look at this sentence from two perspectives. As an insulting view of nonhuman animals that positions them as subservient to humans and do not measure up to their qualities, or as a higher moral principle that should obligate us to disembark from harsh natural laws and create greater consideration toward nature and its nonhuman inhabitants. Based on this discussion, we can assume that it is the latter.

Kropotkin was never a vegetarian, unlike his long-time colleague and friend Élisée Reclus, and generally he was more focused on the power relations of humans (Purchase 1996a). That does not negate the fact that many of his ideas and opinions reflect a relationship to nonhuman animals based on an advanced human morality. Anarchism as an ideology in Kropotkin's understanding can define this relationship as positive since it disables the view of all "others" as subservient. He once said: "Equality in all things, the synonym of equity, this is anarchism in very deed" (Bruce 2014, 6). If we could take his words seriously and aim for the essence of his statement, anarchist followers should think about his ideas of equity and justice as applicable on the nonhuman world of nature and animals too.

Élisée Reclus (1830–1905) and Kropotkin were connected through a strong friendship (Ferretti 2011). While they were both convinced that society should be organized along anarcho-communist lines, Reclus was much more radical in the issue of animal liberation. According to Reclus, an anarchist society should aim to end cruelty toward nonhuman animals too. Yet Reclus was far from a pacifist in his thinking, as he considered violence in the human domain as inevitable in certain cases and even necessary in the defense of weaker humans and animals. While Kropotkin rationalized in his anarchist morality the principle "Do to others what you would have them do to you in the same circumstances" (Marshall 2010, 343), Reclus's attitude of the inevitability of violence came from a completely different set of beliefs, which I will now analyse. He summarized his position toward vegetarianism and animal rights in two essays, specifically *On Vegetarianism* (1901) and *The Great Kinship of Humans and Fauna* (1933).

In the first mentioned text, he mostly expresses his own impressions and experience with vegetarianism. Reclus argued that contact with animals should make us feel like we are meeting our friends, not food. He rejected vivisection and various kinds of dangerous experiments. He realized, of course, that it is not necessary to go into absurdities and to dogmatically avoid water with bacteria and make a new religion of it. He considered eggs, grains, and fruits as appropriate food, arguing that they are the fruits of nature with concentrated vitality available without unnecessary killing (Reclus 1901).

The Great Kinship of Humans and Fauna (1933) shows, unlike his first, more personal work, his geographic and anthropologic erudition, where the text is focused mostly on proving a much-needed symbiosis of the human and animal realm. His whole text is built upon a comparison of the different views of nonhuman animal domestication from the position of both civilization and "primitive" native peoples. Reclus points out that while our society perceives domestication only in the terms of slavery, Indigenous peoples regard these beings as companions. He describes many examples of mutual aid and harmony between native peoples and nonhuman animals. In contrast, he criticizes domestication as a practice of so-called developed humans. Animals are deformed and degraded to "a walking meat" that barely walks to the slaughterhouse and is completely unable to integrate in nature. However, this is not happening only to the so-called farm animals, since the lives of many other animals are affected and destroyed by humans and their activities (Reclus 1933, 3). His thoughts are concluded with the idea that civilized humans should perceive animals as faithful companions and not as servants or machines and thus re-establish friendships that would be beneficial for us too. Just as anthropological studies of "primitive" people significantly contributed to a better understanding of "modern" people, understanding of animal habits would help us to pervade deeper into the very patterns of life (Reclus 1933, 4). In this last notion, Reclus would agree with his colleague Kropotkin who built his anarchist morality on this presumption.

Reclus's view on "primitive" tribes and their harmonic coexistence with nonhuman animals may seem unduly uncritical and naive. Many of his examples do not question the ownership of nonhuman animals, and he rationalized their exploitation by the provision of "natural" environment, friendship, and so on. With respect to his vindication of eggs as an appropriate food and the idea of domestication (which he considered as a symbiosis rather than a form of slavery) we could probably classify him as a welfare advocate who rejected the idea of slaughtering animals for meat. Élisée Reclus was very radical for his time not only with respect to the issue of socio-economical order of society but as we saw earlier, also in regard to the question of our relationship with nature and its other inhabitants. Many of his ideas, opinions, and remarks are progressive from the point of animal liberation and are also applicable to our age. Thus, we can include him in the group of other great historical figures of the anti-authoritarian movement who demonstrated their interest in animal liberation to the same extent as they did to the question of human emancipation.

ANIMAL LIBERATION AS HUMAN LIBERATION

After the preceding short historical prologue, which pointed out the connection to nonhuman animal interests in anarchist thinking, I now want to shift the focus to contemporary authors and texts that reflect the interconnection of social and environmental themes with activism. In this section, I look at the ideas of anti-authoritarian and radical animal liberators who consider veganism as a necessity for the achievement of animal liberation and a just society.

The first author I consider, for whom veganism is as important as the political-economic change of society, is Steven Best. Best's principal text is *Rethinking Revolution: Animal Liberation, Human Liberation, and the Future of the Left* (Best 2006). He pursues a constructive criticism of leftist approaches toward the concept of rights and toward animal liberation. At the same time, he points out the insufficient reflection on economic, social, and political structures in the thinking and practices of movements advocating animal rights. Unlike Best, who analyzes leftist tendencies as a whole, I am focused only on anti-authoritarian practices. Despite that, I think it is important to present his overall arguments to the left in analysing anarchists who reject veganism.

I will start with his definition and typology of animal protection approaches, which is important for emphasizing the context of this text. He called this social movement an Animal Advocacy Movement (AAM), which he split it into three main branches that often have very different goals and methods. The first branch is striving for welfare; the main theme of the second one is the issue of animal rights; and the third one is the least popular, the Animal Liberation Movement. Many other authors and activists from the anti-authoritarian left use similar divisions in their analyses and thoughts, (see, e.g., Forkasiewicz 2012; Watkinson and O'Driscoll 2014).

According to Best, the ultimate goal of welfare organizations was never about the elimination of the institutions that exploit nonhuman animals. He says that their goal is to reduce or to mitigate the suffering in these repressive and violent structures. Followers of this thinking believe that animals can be used if it is done painlessly and "humanely" (Best 2006). On the other hand, people with the label of Animal Rights Advocates (ARA) refuse this utilitarian view, and their thinking mostly reflects the concepts of American philosopher Tom Regan and his book *The Case for Animal Rights*, originally published in 1983 (2004). For ARA, animals have their own intrinsic value; they argue that animal rights cannot be oppressed for any greater good. Best classifies this branch as a part of the new abolitionism (Best n.d.), which demands to end the enslavement of nonhumans, not to mitigate it to "tolerable" conditions. He says that while ARA stands in contradiction to welfare organizations in their egalitarianism, conception of animal rights, and the idea of abolitionism, both branches agree that changes can be achieved strictly by legal means through education and change of laws. They do not challenge private property, power institutions, and state-market union (Best 2006).

The third and last part of the AAM he talks about is the Animal Liberation Movement (ALM), which differs from welfare organizations and ARA because it does not believe in change through state-approved means. In the eyes of this group, the state is corrupted and serves private corporate interests. Their tactics consist of direct actions aimed at institutions that profit from animal exploitation. ALM refuses capitalism, imperialism, and any other hierarchical structures, thus it is possible to label it as anarchist movement based on its ideology, tactics, and organizational form. Its main tactics are direct action of the sort employed by the Animal Liberation Front (ALF) when it rescues animals or inflicts economic damage on the property of exploitative companies. Best mentions a small ALM offshoot that rationalizes violence toward people who partake in nonhuman animal exploitation, but ALF members embrace the principle of nonviolence toward all living beings and so they attack only property (Best 2006).

Best pays attention to the criticism of legal procedures within animal advocacy, where he does not blatantly dismiss it, since he considers every improvement as something extra for the animals. His defense of ALM is more important right now though. He sees it as a progressive anti-capitalist movement that he likens to other radical leftist movements. The appearance and tactics of ALM show that ALM perceives the state as a defense and extension of the capitalist economy and thus it challenges the representative democracy with its laws as a whole. It pursues change through direct pressure on the animal exploiters. At the same time though, he makes it clear that the ALM is an anti-capitalist movement and that it has a holistic analysis of hierarchy and oppression. Such a position means that they refuse "single-issue" efforts. The last ALM characteristic rests in its anarchist organization and tactics: small individual cells that hinder repressive forces while creating solidarity and common consciousness. He thinks it is important that while leftist radicals are often locked in theorizing, ALM followers take a practical approach to liberating nonhuman animals by directly attacking the institutions they consider exploitative, and thus create an economic loss to them. However, like Best, they realize that their actions cannot change the system unless the whole movement adopts the same holistic attitude (Best 2006).

In terms of the specifics of his arguments, Best considers animals in laboratories, fur farms, intensive farming facilities, circuses, and many other institutions as economic slaves who are exploited to become significant moving forces in the service of capitalism. He sees capitalism as a system based on growth and profit as having enslaved animals through commodification where they become a mere material for humans within the logic of a market system. Owing to this exploitation he thinks that leftists should take animal liberation as another step in the defense of rights and equality, just as they did in the case of environmental issues, which helped them to deepen critical theory. However, under the speciesistic spell they oftentimes cannot unite the efforts for human, animal, and nature liberation, which Best views as a single resistance against domination, exploitation, and hierarchy (Best 2006). In his ideas we can see a strong tendency to interconnect the movement with causes of oppression, or in other words, a move toward intersectionalism.

Best also focuses on the concept of rights. This concept is criticized from the anarchists' point of view since they consider rights to be secured by the state and valid only in the relationship to it—whereas in an autonomous decentralized democracy rights become insignificant. Best writes that he realizes this connection to the state and agrees that the idea of rights is a bourgeois construct, which is suitable for the capitalist logic of the free market and is related mostly to private property and its state-protected accumulation. Nevertheless, he considers the refusal of the rights discourse in the contemporary setting as a huge strategic mistake because it is one of the main tools for sharing animal and human liberation thoughts and it supports a political imagination that can result in criticisms of capitalism. Above that, he sees rights as the primary difference dividing welfare position and utilitarianism from abolitionism. He writes that rights can disappear in the stateless society, but in the present time they are very important. Similar to Peter Singer (2009), he argues that nonhuman animals do not need a right to vote but they do need the most basic rights—the right to live and the right to be free (Best 2006).

In the attitude of radical leftists, he deals with frequent trivial human preferences over animal interests. Within some circles arguments have emerged that suggest that forbidding the consumption of animal products is an authoritative imposition that is incompatible with personal freedom since it is telling people how to live. Best argues that such a view is problematic since it is underpinned by a logic that would also assume it would be authoritative to ban racism, child molestation, and other forms of violence and slavery too. It would lead to a double morality, and he warns that if anyone could choose to eat meat, it could lead to the re-establishment of intensive farming conditions. There, he writes, animals do not come in voluntarily and happily with the perspective of satisfying human demand for meat and other animal products. He considers this as a highly biased argument and refers to Herbert Marcus who condemned this "repressive tolerance" as a relativistic attitude that refuses to condemn exploitation and violence. He reacts also to an interesting objection in regards to direct democracy—nonhuman animals cannot be represented because it would contradict the very concept of direct democracy. Best answers that whatever form of political establishment will come, it will always "represent" nonhuman interests to some extent. Since animals cannot speak for themselves, they need delegates who will represent their interests based on their expression of emotions, needs, and demands. He adds that the application of unique human conditions of social life to nonhuman beings would be absolutist and imperialist (Best 2006).

He concludes his thoughts with the fact that the recognition of interconnection between animal and human liberation is a huge challenge for the leftist movement. As he says, "Having recognized the illogical and unjustifiable rationales used to oppress blacks, women, and other disadvantaged groups, society is beginning to grasp that speciesism is another unsubstantiated form of oppression and discrimination. The gross inconsistency of Leftists who champion democracy and rights while supporting a system that enslaves billions of other sentient and intelligent life forms is on par with the hypocrisy of American colonists protesting British tyranny while enslaving millions of blacks" (Best 2006). Movements advocating the liberation of humans and animals have a lot to learn from each other, and he deems necessary that their ideas and actions interconnect to achieve more solidarity and compassion within society, wherein cruelty and environmental and social degradation will be diminished.

Now I will focus on the criticism of radical animal liberationists from their own ranks, that is, criticism of the animal advocacy movement. Veganarchists or vegan anarchists are people who want to separate themselves from the liberal and reformist approaches in the animal advocacy movement and also from social anarchists and other radical leftists who have not embraced a vegan lifestyle and the idea of animal liberation. Veganarchism is primarily about the interconnection of green anarchism and anti-speciesist thinking or as the subtitle of the work of Brian A. Dominick, the author of the pamphlet formulating this attitude says, it is about the explanation of his understanding of "*A vegan perspective on anarchism or an anarchist perspective on veganism*" (Dominick 1997, emphasis added).

Dominick agrees with Best in the delineation of his arguments, resources, and opinions. He realizes that the leftist movement often ignores animal liberation, but that also many anarchists, largely from the younger age group, have an interest in ecology and animal issues. Radical animal liberators have begun to perceive other forms of oppression and thus "anarchists and animal liberationists share strategic methodology" (Dominick 1997, 4). He also realizes that they cannot achieve their goal by means of direct action and inflicting economical damage. However, veganarchists define themselves as distinct from liberal means of reform that do not challenge the system.

Dominick views the revolution as an internal process in which the individual changes his personal attitude and thinking in everyday situations. Nevertheless, he explains that the attitudes and opinions of the majority of people were created institutionally rather than by individual free will. The system, which he calls the *establishment*, is using a combination of many types of oppression, from the best known, such as classism, sexism, and racism, to speciesism and ageism. That's why he considers the revolution as a process of gradual confrontation of these system values that will result in a real change (Dominick 1997, 5). He refers to the awareness of various obstacles on the way to the liberation of human and nonhuman animals.

To avoid misunderstanding he focuses on an important explanation of the very concept of veganism. He does not perceive veganism as a diet that should be associated with vegetarianism. He sees it as an informed lifestyle and attitude of living that unlike liberal vegetarianism has the potential to recognize the interconnection of exploitation within a capitalist society (Dominick 1997, 7). He is troubled by the fact that many people who call themselves vegans can accept ethical and environmental values toward nonhuman animals but cannot grasp the close interconnection of the laws of society with nature.

In an effort to illustrate the reasons for holistic revolutionary thought, Dominick states that the main reason for the exploitation of animals is profit. He warns though that the boycott of exploitative industries does not change much, since profit is only one of many factors and social relationships that sustain the use of animals. He also comments on vivisection where he warns political radicals: "We need to observe animals in their natural environment, and mimic their environmental relationships, where applicable, in our own"

(Dominick 1997, 8). In this statement we can find similarity with the thoughts of Kropotkin who was, as we saw in the historical section, thinking in the same way, even though he was not referring to vivisection. Another factor is speciesism, which he puts in context with racism and points to the connection between feminism and veganism.

He also analyses the essential concern for many anarchists, namely the state. Dominick (1997, 9) perceives the state with its laws to be on the side that stands against animals and their interests, whether through subsidies for animal agriculture, vivisection for military reasons, its repressive character against animal liberators, or the fact that it defends industries that exploit animals.

Dominick works with an important concept of *alienation*. Based on that, he explains that the exploitation of nonhuman animals does not come from some bad human essence, but from the fact that people, especially consumers, are alienated from the consequences of such behavior because they are removed from the manufacturing process. That is why we should realize that just as humans are submitted to the presumed human—animal dichotomy, which they can defy from an anti-speciesist perspective, they should also defy other oppressive dichotomies and be interested in the origin of products from the view of human rights (Dominick 1997, 11–12).

Thus, we get to Dominick's solutions. He refers to his understanding of revolution as a change that is primarily a change in our thinking and a confrontation of every thought and every practical step in our lives. Every action in our life represents a potential place for the spreading of the idea of liberation and he considers it important that everyone creates their own alternative world right here and now. That means that challenging all forms of oppression and hierarchy should become a lifestyle for every vegan and anarchist as they should become vegananarchists. Those who do not make this connection are not considered anarchists in his view, since they continue to accept a particular form of oppression (Dominick 1997, 13).

Anarchist tendencies toward an individualistic lifestyle remains a big issue in the radical anti-authoritarian environment (Bookchin 1995). It may seem that this whole concept is very individually focused on a personal change, where in striving for "the right" lifestyle, the rest will somehow come by itself. The revolutionary radicals have reproached Dominick for this reason, and that is why he explains his stance in the epilogue of the pamphlet's later edition. He realizes that even if a great number of people would change, it would not impact the structures of society. However, he does not regard it as a reason to desist from the lifestyle that they want to achieve after the revolutionary change, and he does not see a chance for creating a meat-free and oppression-free society unless they give it up in the present (Dominick 1997, 15). Therefore, he warns against the trend of the traditional leftist economic reductionism.

Anti-authoritarian animal liberators, whether we will classify them under Best's typology as ALM or under the Dominick's concept of vegananar-chism, can be defined as people who are striving for a holistic analysis of the causes of oppression and for that reason they object to the weak reflec-tions from radical leftists and animal advocates. At the same time, they feel a strong conviction that veganism, as a lifestyle, is a necessary condition for consistency between theory and practice.

Among the main points of their criticism toward other radical leftists are: (1) Insufficient confrontation of anthropocentrism and its inseparable mani-festation as speciesism in thoughts, acts, and lifestyle; (2) frequent reduction-ist view on the causes and expressions of oppression and domination only toward economic structures; (3) inconsistency of attitude—their welfare attitude toward animal rights in contrast to an abolitionist attitude toward human rights; (4) weak analysis of the social relations that arise from animal and nature oppression.

Best and Dominick's criticism toward animal advocates is comprised mostly of the following: (1) Insufficient awareness of the interconnection of human and nonhuman oppression, which according to them, is predominantly based on a capitalist economy; (2) this first point is the basis of their criticism of the "single-issue" tendency of advocates, that is, of focusing only on non-human animals without broader context; (3) incomprehension of the state and laws as means of legitimizing exploitation; (4) in the long term, ineffective and counterproductive tendencies toward reformism, legislation, and purely legal means of change, which legitimize the system based on the commodifi-cation of animals; (5) contrary to the leftists, the effects of the hierarchy that arise from social processes and relations (economic and political) toward the oppression and abuse of nonhuman animals are misunderstood.

At the same time, we can find certain contradictions in the definition of what vegan anti-authoritarians should do to achieve their goal. While Best emphasizes intersectionalism in the terms of ALM, building a strong radical social movement in concert with leftist movements and direct actions, Domi-nick points to inconsistency. His understanding of the revolution as an inter-nal process, which culminates in the structure change in the society, contrasts with the change of values in people while they are under the influence of gov-erning society institutions. Even though he literally pronounced that he does realize it, he still does not explain how such a change in people should come about, and he offers a solution associated only with an individual lifestyle and the effort to change their surrounding area. Though it is interesting that in his most recent essay titled *Anarcho-Veganism Revisited*, Dominick (2015) does partially leave this attitude and considers changing the institutions as more important than eating habits.

VEGANISM—IMPULSE OR BRAKE OF LIBERATION?

For some anarchists, the idea of animal liberation is not necessarily associated with veganism. Owing to this relationship, I will compare such anarchists' views with Best's description of ALM and the concept of vegananarchism from Dominick. The following anarchists are striving to look critically at the idea of animal rights and veganism from their perspective, though their texts are not (by the very essence of anarchism that hierarchies should be destroyed) in explicit contradiction with the previous discussion, it is rather a different point of view toward nonhuman animals.

Anarchism always stood side by side with movements fighting against human oppression. However, anarchists warned other movements not to become focused only on their own emancipation struggle, but to connect with other movements since staying in one's own interest group often ended up only in reforms to the system. Nonhuman liberation implies a similar situation. Inasmuch as anarchism can be assembled with ecology into eco-anarchism (Purchase 1996b; Bookchin 2005; Bruce 2014), the work of many anarchists reflects upon speciesism as another unacceptable form of hierarchy. Yet this situation does not mean though that they uncritically accept the opinions, lifestyles, and methods presented by animal advocates, whether moderates, liberals or radicals. I will analyse and compare texts of radicals from both groups while I will try to pick out the most important arguments.

As mentioned before, the greatest problem for many anarchists is the lifestyle connected with their efforts toward animal liberation, namely veganism. They often label it as a *consumerist activity and a kind of a religion* (Gelderloos 2008), as *fake opposition* (Anonymous 2010), as *devastatingly liberal* (Anonymous 2009), or as something that cannot stop the violence caused to animals in the capitalist society, and because of that the effort for consumer purity and diet puritanism is often (for many reasons) counterproductive (Subversive Energy 2012). These different individuals and collectives write that because of their anarchist position they acknowledge a desire to undo the human—animal dichotomy, but they are uncertain why it should encompass veganism too when they argue that even many vegans know that the boycott of animal products does not lead to the rescue of animals and that the desire of absolute ethical purity is unattainable. These anarchists feel that vegans are forced into a specific role that accepts the consumer status and encourages them to practice "ethical" consumption instead of confronting capitalism. Thus they point out that all responsibility for what people buy and consume falls onto themselves and that is the reason why it is presented as a choice, not as a role, into which they are violently forced (Gelderloos 2011, 8). Well-known sociologist Ulrich Beck works with a similar thesis. He points out that most of the social and ecological risks in the individualized society are deputed onto individuals and their individual (consumer) behavior, and it pushes them to resolve it by changing their habits (Beck 1992).

While Best, Dominick, and other radicals from the ALM ranks regard veganism as an important part of the resistance against speciesism, and they consider it necessary to make it part of their lifestyle, these other anarchists often remark that "a person can be against speciesism without being vegan in the same way that one can be against industrial civilization while driving a car" (Subversive Energy 2012, 5). At the same time they realize that "unlike veganism, animal liberation is . . . an important part of a full anarchist movement" (Gelderloos 2008, 11). However, they understand consumerism coupled with veganism as something that supports social violence (Subversive Energy 2012, 5), or as something that sustains capitalism and destroys the planet and its boycott does not work in the final consequence (Gelderloos 2011, 8). For this reason they sometimes mention stealing, which they consider as morally justifiable (Gelderloos 2011, 12), and freeganism as alternatives. As the well-known anarchist collective CrimethInc states on its website, "In the meantime, rather than practicing veganism, I practice "freeganism." I know that as long as I participate in the mainstream economy, whether I am buying vegan or non-vegan products, I am supporting the corporations which represent world capitalism" (CrimethInc Ex-Workers Collective 2000).

The collective known as Subversive Energy views Dominick's thesis about revolution being a personal change as naive, and instead they agree with Best's definition of ALM because they emphasize direct action and attack on hierarchical structures. On the contrary, they do not agree with Best in seeing veganism and vegans as a potential revolutionary power, since they consider veganism as a mere lifestyle that diverts attention from creating a real revolutionary anti-capitalist project. They see the problem as being the "apolitical" essence of a vegan lifestyle and its ability to fit into every sphere. That's why they consider it possible to join their struggle with ALM radicals in terms of direct action, but they do not agree in their moralizing and the focus on nonhuman animals. They hold moralizing as something that forces individuals into living by certain moral constructs, which they reject since they emphasize desire and passion (Subversive Energy 2012, 11–12), or needs and wishes (Gelderloos 2008, 5). Authorities create morality and they oppose it and let people themselves decide their actions in terms of how to respond to the contemporary system. Unlike the morality that bids them what is good and what is bad, free decisions come with a feeling of personal liberation (Anonymous 2010, 14–16). These arguments point to a strong emphasis on individual freedom within their anarchist thinking.

In their texts we can find implications that Best unduly idealizes the ALM as primarily anti-capitalist and that their "single-issue" focus is still visible— that is, in the frequent overlapping and participation of members of the ALM in the legal parts of the ARA or because in their ALF communiques they often note that they fight for animal liberation without mentioning humans or capitalism. They also highlight the misanthropic behavior of some ALF radicals with which the anarchists cannot identify. Misanthropy should not emerge in the anarchist conviction, and it proves inconsistency in tendency toward holistic thinking in the ALM, which is why they do not regard it as anarchist, but just as militant offshoot of animal advocates (Anonymous 2009, 19–22; Subversive Energy 2012, 10; Anonymous 2010, 24–26).

The other discrepancies are not based on the understandings of law, but rather on the theoretical and practical attitude toward them. While Best, as we saw before, presents ALM as transcending the limits of law if the particular law is bad for the animals, these anarchists do not divide it into good and evil, but they want to defy everything that the state defines. Again, they point to the inconsistency of the ALM's attitudes, which celebrates legal bans on certain types of animal exploitation (Anonymous 2010, 30), and at the same time argue that they want to defy the state. They mention that the state will permit only such laws that do not threaten it or that indirectly suppress rebellion. Their understanding of the concept of rights does not represent the stimuli for political imagination, as Best states, but rather it forces people into a reformist attitude instead of destroying the system that they regard as exploitative. Thus it strengthens state power (Subversive Energy 2012, 12), since "humans and all other animals are much more free and full outside of legal frameworks, without rights" (Gelderloos 2008, 5).

The last issue I will focus on is the common referring to the naturalness of human—animal relations in so-called primitive and Indigenous societies, which they consider as a harmonic part of the Earth. We can find these examples also in Reclus's historical thinking, and some of the contemporary anarchists refer to them too. At the same time, we can find common reference to the arguments against veganism. Graham Purchase, an Australian author following anarchism, demonstrates a similar mindset in his book *Anarchism and Ecology* (1996b). He writes that while the ethical arguments for veganism are not unfamiliar to anarchists, ecological arguments are much less convincing (Purchase 1996b). While these anarchists rightly point to the fact that a vegan diet in today's system does not have to be environmentally positive (Gelderloos 2008, 7), and that there can be a sustainable society that consumes meat (Subversive Energy 2012, 6), it does not automatically mean that Indigenous and native communities always lived in a pure harmony with nature and nonhuman animals. Their arguments often resemble "the myth of noble savage." Thus the welfare approach (which does not have to be just a part of the state society) emerges among the anarchists too when they refer to the animal exploitation in terms of ecologically sustainable agriculture, such as fertilization and raking of the soil by hens which can also be used for eggs or meat (Gelderloos 2008, 4), or for cattle grazing and cultivating the landscape (Gelderloos 2008, 5). Others prefer the so-called micro-farms which are less environmentally demanding (Purchase 1996b). Therefore, these anarchists highlight the fact that the trouble is not in the nonhuman animal products and their consumption, but rather it is the very organization of contemporary industrial agriculture system.

They see nothing wrong in the act of killing. Again, they refer to nature and its laws. They argue that in nature, there is no violence during the killing of another animal since they regard violence as an act of domination attained by social control. Therefore, they consistently reflect that every conflict in which killing may occur requires contextual analysis: "There is no systematic violence in the wild, but, instead, momentary expressions of specific passions" (Subversive Energy 2012, 14). They contend that "there is no coherent morality or ethics rooted in nature that can view the killing and eating of animals as wrong. In nature, killing and eating something is a respectful, intimate activity, and a necessary part of natural cycles" (Gelderloos 2008, 5). They consider killing in general as justifiable. Their inconsistency with respect to nonhuman animals manifests itself when it comes to reciprocity among humans, who they argue should not be subject to social control, such as imprisonment and exploitation for human benefit. As Ambrosch warns, such perception of reciprocal relationships is very problematic: "No victim voluntarily enters into a deadly 'relationship'" (Ambrosch 2017, 17).

Both radical sides slip into inconsistencies. These discrepancies do not imply that one is good or bad, it just implies that they have different preferences and approaches toward the perception of anarchism and anti-authoritarian thoughts, its practical implementation, and its overlapping with the nonhuman world. They conclusively agree in their criticism of capitalism and toward moderate and purely legal means of animal liberation. They share the idea that direct action is an important method of direct confrontation with powerful institutions. They also share an emphasis on defying speciesism, which they all regard as one of the hierarchical structures bearing out oppression.

Nevertheless, they cannot agree on the lifestyle that should accompany the idea of animal liberation. Best, Dominick, and other radicals from ALM emphasize practical veganism, in the current system and in the potential stateless non-capitalist order. Even though they point out, like the anarchists, that ethical consumption in capitalism is an oxymoron, they consider it important and theory-appropriate to refuse the consumption of nonhuman animals and their products now. On the contrary, many anarchists currently prefer freeganism or stealing because they assume that the necessity to moralize, which they regard as authoritative, will cease in a decentralized society and it will also end the possibility of slipping into reformism for achieving partial wins toward veganism. This leads to their criticism of the ALM radicals, pointing out their inconsistency in holistic thinking about rights, at the danger of misanthropy and the ever-present "single-issue" view and idealization of their anti-capitalist overlap.

Conversely, in the texts of anarchists that I analyzed we can identify their reflection of anthropocentrism and speciesism (even if not absolutely consistent) and intersectionalist approaches, the emphasis on the confrontation of causes and manifestations of oppression and dominance even beyond economic factors. But despite the fact that they separate themselves from the left (Subversive Energy 2012: 8–9), these anarchists meet two out of four points we defined as Best's criticism of radical leftists. First, they exhibit elements of thinking in the direction of an animal welfare attitude, which they defend with environmental arguments and its benefits for the ecological renewal of ecosystems. Second, Best's reproach, applicable to these anarchists, is the weak analysis of social relations, which arise from the oppression of nonhuman animals and nature. This is obvious in their referring to the naturalness of killing in nature while they do not consider the act of killing as violent because of the nonexistence of social control and hierarchical authority in the potential nonhierarchical stateless society. However, this control is reestablished in the domestication of nonhuman animals and their exploitation. They establish the possibility of the reinstatement of master–subservient relations between humans on the one hand, and nonhuman animals and nature on the other.

CONCLUSION

Robbins (2012, 87) argues that "political ecology stories are stories of justice and injustice." That undoubtedly applies when the subjects of the stories are humans, communities, and entire ecosystems. Do the stories of political ecology seek justice and injustice even in our behavior toward nonhuman animals which do not have a privileged position in our society and whom many people regard as food? Should we seek and create such stories?

I hope that the foregoing text and discussion of the radical antiauthoritarian environment can supply a clear answer. If we want to foster anarchist political ecology, we cannot avoid the issues of interspecies hierarchy and its practical consequences. Of course, it is always problematic to apply our own notions and our own morality on the parts of the world where the alternative to consumption of nonhuman animals is hunger and subsequent death. However, this cultural relativism does not apply to a significant part of the industrial world.

What does anarchist theory and the results of the described dialog bring to political ecology? First, Robbins considers Kropotkin's criticism of the state as problematic and inadequate because of stateless corporate and market power (Robbins 2012, 28). The arguments of anarchists criticizing the strong connection between a market system and the state and its laws could create a space for more complex analysis of power imbalances. If the state is a condition for the current capitalist economic system, it is time to think about its real role in ecological devastation and environmental injustice.

Second, unlike an "apolitical" ecology, political ecology is trying to look at things from the broader perspective and separate itself from the mainstream environmentalism. That can be a point of contact with those radicals who criticize the moderate parts of the animal advocacy movement. Environmentalists often emphasize the right, ethically and environmentally conscious consumerism, whether under the label of fair trade or organic. Even though we can take these products as a positive change and that we can adjust our lifestyle to more environmental requests that we would like to achieve globally, a political ecology analysis (just as an anarchist one) considers it important to reflect on socio-economic and political relations in society to advance solutions to the causes of environmental devastation. That is, they seek to challenge the "single-issue" focus. Such an approach does not reserve a space for misanthropy and other human-centered hateful displays that could incite tendencies toward eco-fascism and other ideologies that suppress human freedom under the pretext of protection of nonhuman animals.

Apart from the perception of consequences about political and economic relations, this chapter has argued that reflection on the consequences of inter-species relations is of great benefit for political ecology. Consistent criticism of anthropocentrism and commodification of nonhuman nature requires a critique of speciesism and the commodification of nonhuman animals too. Such criticism points to the significance of cultural (i.e., economically inexplicable) constructs for the creation of society. Adopting such a view will help us not to fall into typical Marxist economic reductionism while qualitatively and quantitatively expanding the space for the analysis of oppression among humans, nonhumans, and nature. Including nonhuman animals and nature into our idea of a non-hierarchical and environmentally, democratically, and economically sustainable society is probably the most difficult role humankind has ever faced. However, it is very likely (as Reclus, Best, and many other authors and scientists remind us) that if we omit the needs and rights to live for sentient and not-so-distant-to-us beings in such a society, it would lead once more to the domination of human over human. Mutual aid and cooperation bring stability, integrity, and development into human society. It is time to expand these values outside of our species and to defy speciesism.

NOTE

1. This chapter is an overwritten and updated version of a bachelor thesis submitted to Masaryk University in Brno, Czech republic, see Gažo 2015. Supported by the Specific Research Project of Masaryk University, No. MUNI/A/1158/2018.

REFERENCES

Ambrosch, Gerfried. 2017. *Defending Veganism, Defending Animal Rights.* S.l.: Active Distribution

Anonymous. 2009. "Animal Liberation: Devastate to Liberate, or Devastatingly Liberal?" 2009. http://theanarchistlibrary.org/library/anonymous-animal-liberation-devastate-to-liberate-or-devastatingly-liberal.html.

——. 2010. "The Harvest of Dead Elephants: The False Opposition of Animal Liberation." *Translationcollective* (blog). February 25, 2010. https://translationcollective.wordpress.com/2010/02/25/the-harvest-of-dead-elephants-the-false-opposition-of-animal-liberation/.

Beck, Ulrich. 1992. *Risk Society: Towards a New Modernity.* Theory, Culture & Society. London; Newbury Park, CA: Sage Publications.

Best, Steven. 2006. "Rethinking Revolution: Animal Liberation, Human Liberation, and the Future of the Left." *The International Journal of Inclusive Democracy*, no. 2. http://www.inclusivedemocracy.org/journal/vol2/vol2_no3_Best_rethinking_revolution.htm.

——. n.d. "The New Abolitionism: Capitalism, Slavery and Animal Liberation." Accessed March 27, 2015. http://www.drstevebest.org/TheNewAbolitionism.htm.

Bookchin, Murray. 1995. *Social Anarchism or Lifestyle Anarchism: The Unbridgeable Chasm.* Edinburgh, Scotland; San Francisco, CA: AK Press.

——. 2005. *The Ecology of Freedom: The Emergence and Dissolution of Hierarchy.* Oakland, CA: AK Press.

Bruce, Corin. 2014. "Green Anarchism: Towards the Abolition of Hierarchy." 2014. http://theanarchistlibrary.org/library/corin-bruce-green-anarchism-towards-the-abolition-of-hierarchy.

CrimethInc Ex-Workers Collective. 2000. "CrimethInc.: Veganism." CrimethInc. 2000. https://crimethinc.com/2000/09/11/veganism.

Dominick, Brian A. 1997. "Animal Liberation and Social Revolution." Syracuse, NY: Crit—ical Mess Media. The Anarchist Library. http://theanarchistlibrary.org/library/brian-a-dominick-animal-liberation-and-social-revolution.

——. 2015. "Anarcho-Veganism Revisited." In *Anarchism and Animal Liberation: Essays on Complementary Elements of Total Liberation*, edited by Anthony J. Nocella, Richard J. White, and Erika Cudworth. Jefferson, NC: McFarland & Company, Inc., Publishers.

FAO. 2006. *Livestock's Long Shadow.* Rome: Food and Agriculture Organization of the United Nations. http://www.fao.org/docrep/010/a0701e/a0701e00.HTM.

Ferretti, Federico. 2011. "The Correspondence between Élisée Reclus and Pëtr Kropotkin as a Source for the History of Geography." *Journal of Historical Geography*, vol. 37, no. 2, pp. 216–222. http://dx.doi.org/doi:10.1016/j.jhg.2010.10.001.

Forkasiewicz, Kris. 2012. "Fragments of an Animalist Politics: Veganism and Liberation." Scribd. 2012. https://www.scribd.com/doc/117372198/Fragments-of-an-Animalist-Politics-Veganism-and-Liberation.

Gažo, Patrik. 2015. "Animal Liberation from the Leftist Anti-Capitalist Perspective." Bachelor's thesis, Faculty of Social Studies, Masaryk University. https://is.muni.cz/th/417027/fss_b?info=1;zpet=%2Fvyhledavani%2F%3Fsearch%3Dga%C5%BEo%26start%3D1.

Gelderloos, Peter. 2008. "Veganism Is a Consumer Activity." 2008. http://theanarchist library.org/library/peter-gelderloos-veganism-is-a-consumer-activity.html.

———. 2011. "Veganism: Why Not." 2011. http://theanarchistlibrary.org/library/peter-gelderloos-veganism-why-not.html.

Hornborg, Alf. 2017. "Political Ecology and Unequal Exchange." In *Routledge Handbook of Ecological Economics: Nature and Society*, edited by Clive L. Spash, 39–47. Routledge International Handbooks. London: Routledge.

Kropotkin, Petr Alekseevich. 1897. *Anarchist Morality*. Mother Earth Pub. Association. https://theanarchistlibrary.org/library/petr-kropotkin-anarchist-morality.pdf.

Marshall, Peter. 2010. *Demanding the Impossible: A History of Anarchism*. Oakland, CA: PM Press.

Paulson, Susan. 2015. "Political Ecology." In *Degrowth: A Vocabulary for a New Era*, edited by Giacomo D'Alisa, Federico Demaria, and Giorgos Kallis, 45–48. New York ; London: Routledge, Taylor & Francis Group.

Purchase, Graham. 1996a. *Evolution and Revolution: An Introduction to the Life and Ideas of Peter Kropotkin*. Petersham, N.S.W: Jura Books.

———. 1996b. *Anarchism and Ecology*. Montréal; New York: Black Rose Books.

Reclus, Élisée. 1901. "On Vegetarianism." *Humane Review*. http://dwardmac.pitzer.edu/Anarchist_Archives/bright/reclus/onvegetarianism.html.

———. 1933. "The Great Kinship of Humans and Fauna." http://theanarchistlibrary.org/library/elisee-reclus-the-great-kinship-of-humans-and-fauna.html.

Regan, Tom. 2004. The Case for Animal Rights. Updated with a new preface, [2004 ed.]. Berkeley: University of California Press.

Robbins, Paul. 2012. *Political Ecology: A Critical Introduction*. 2nd ed. Critical Introductions to Geography. Chichester, West Sussex; Malden, MA: J. Wiley & Sons.

Singer, Peter. 2009. *Animal Liberation: The Definitive Classic of the Animal Movement*. Updated edition, 1st Ecco pbk. ed., 1st Harper Perennial ed. New York: Ecco Book/Harper Perennial.

Subversive Energy. 2012. "Beyond Animal Liberation | The Anarchist Library." 2012. http://theanarchistlibrary.org/library/subversive-energy-beyond-animal-liberation.

Watkinson, Kevin, and Dónal O'Driscoll. 2014. *From Animals to Anarchism*. Dysophia.

Chapter 3

Anarchism, Feminism, and Veganism: A Convergence of Struggles

Ophélie Véron and Richard J. White

We can no longer accept the decaying, hideous, and archaic geographies of hierarchy that chain us to statism, capitalism, gender domination, heteronormativity, radical oppression, speciesism, and imperialism.

—Simon Springer (2016, 3)

INTRODUCTION

Compared alongside other dissident and radical movements, anarchism, not least by virtue of its unconditional commitment to identifying, resisting, challenging and transgressing multiple sites of oppression and their associated "multivariate apparatuses of domination" (Springer 2016, 46) stands alone. In this way, by refusing to rarefy and privilege any *one* source of dominatory power anarchist praxis has been "highly open to intersectionality, if not already characterized by it" (Cudworth 2015, 93). Importantly, this commitment has encouraged anarchists to critically reflect on how questions of emancipation, freedom, and autonomy readily transgress the boundaries of human society, and are intimately bound to concerns that extend toward nonhuman and more-than-human worlds (Hall 2011). In the context of political ecology generally, and the body of theoretically and empirically driven research that informs this chapter more specifically, there are many rich veins to be tapped into within the existing body of anarchist praxis. A strong emphasis on questions of interspecies social justice and liberation, for example, animated some of the most brilliant contributions by key anarchist geographers including Élisée Reclus (1877, 1901) and Peter Kropotkin (1902). More recently, Bookchin (2015, 39) considered that "perhaps the most fundamental message that social ecology advances is that the very idea of dominating nature stems from the domination of human by human," and Pepper (2002), through his work on Eco-Socialism (1993) suggested how anarchism and deep ecology can be synthesized as part of a radical green politics. Here, and other contributions notwithstanding there is still much more to that needs to be said, and urgently so, that speaks to the crises that all life faces in the midst of the anthropocene (White et al. 2016).

In this context of advancing an anarchist political ecology in important directions, the chapter argues that there are two powerful manifestations of oppression, namely *patriarchy* (the institutionalized domination of men over women) and *anthroparchy* (the human exploitation of other species, in particular, nonhuman animals) where an intersectional anarchist praxis has been largely conspicuous only by its absence. In these intersections, anarchists have only recently, particularly through *anarcha-feminist, veganarchist,* and critical academic-activism, more generally forged within both critical animal studies (e.g., Nocella et al. 2014; Nocella et al. 2015; Matsuoka and Sorenson, 2018) and critical animal geographies (see Gillespie and Collard, 2015; White, 2015; White and Springer, 2018), begun to address this considerable oversight.

The timeliness of realizing this potential cannot be underestimated, not least as the horrifying abuse and exploitation of other animals continue to escalate. Focusing on farmed animals alone, Nibert (2017, xi) notes,

> more than 65 billion land-based beings are killed to be consumed as food every year, while the water-based other animals killed for food number in the hundreds of billions. The physical and emotional suffering from such horrific treatment experienced by each individual being, multiplied by the billions of individual animals who undergo it, results in a degree of severe distress and pain—every second—that defies comprehension.

In the face of such appalling injustice one would assume that anarchists, and feminists, would be at the forefront of merging trans-species narratives of social and spatial justice. Yet, troubling, and depressing in equal measure, this has yet to take place, and arguments which have advocated for a radical anarcha-feminist and/or vegan-anarchist praxis (e.g., White and Cudworth, 2014) have been met with overt hostility from within anarchist movement (e.g., Gelderloos, 2011). We find it remarkable, how otherwise critically reflexive anarchists are unwilling to acknowledge their own speciesist privileges, and continue to invest great energies to close down constructive dialog, either through engaging in a politics of denial and avoidance, and/or being overtly hostile toward the very notion of inter-species expression of justice and solidarity. To acknowledge and constructively address this in a chapter which, hopefully, will attract a broader spectrum of anarchist readers, we feel is incredibly desirable and important. In this context, the chapter provocatively calls into question the nature of the emancipatory grounds upon which anarchists and anarchism stand upon. Where *choice* exists (and therefore questions of ethics and ethical praxis come into consideration) is it possible in any meaningful sense:

- To be an anarchist who maintains a deep commitment to fighting against both patriarchal and paternalistic forms of social domination *while* actively supporting forms of anthroparchy (e.g., the consumption of non-human animal corpses (meat) and dairy and eggs ("feminized protein" (Adams, 2015)?
- To be feminist or anti-speciesist that is committed to fighting against sexist and speciesist forms of social domination while acting in ways that upholds statist and capitalist forms of exploitation and domination?

If it is *not* possible then, where it continues to be upheld, how is the radical promise of anarchism (or feminism) blunted and diminished as a consequence? For those who maintain this internal inconsistency, how might recognizing these intersectional blind spots inspire new radical lines of flight into being: and empower anarchists to engage more purposefully and urgently at this time of unprecedented crises. A critical visibility around interrogating the critical intersections between anarchism, veganism, and feminism necessarily evokes strong synergies with political ecologies. Perhaps one of the strongest examples of this is an ongoing desire to envisage and enact a deep care-based ethics that extends toward all life. Thus for anarchism to succeed in encouraging a radical spirit of care and justice into the world, as Reclus so beautifully articulated, it must recognize that this vision rests on ecological premises. Moreover, as John Clark (201, 21) argued, "Far from being anthropocentric, Reclus's view of humanity's place in nature is dialectical, critical holistic and developmental."

Similarly, feminists have contributed greatly to agitate and propel political ecology toward new domains. Feminist scholarship and activism (not least through advocating for veganism) over the past forty or so years have repeatedly foreground an ethics of care into the question of animal rights and liberation. As Seager (2003, 172) argues:

> Insistence on contextualizing the caring for animals within a political analysis brings animal rights into synergy with political ecology, the point of entry for most feminist geographical work in this field.

In making the connection between the exploitation of humans and non-human animals, vegan ecofeminists such as Carol A. Adams and Marti Kheel have extended the scope of feminist political ecology. By examining the historical relations between the domestication of animals and the emergence of patriarchy and slavery, they have argued that the killing of any animal—whether human or not—is part of a larger system of oppression that should be ended:

> In countless ways, the exploitation of animals rebounds to create crises within the human world itself. The vicious circle of violence and destruction can end only if and when the human species learns to form harmonious relations "non-hierarchical and nonexploitative" with other animal species and the natural world. Human, animal, and earth liberation are interrelated projects that must be fought for as one. (Best, 2006: 2)

Before continuing, it is timely to offer a fuller outline of what is understood by vegan(ism) and feminism in the context of this chapter.

DEFINITIONS

Just as there were thousands of years of social forms of organization which would be consistent with anarchism and anarchist praxis before Proudhon declared himself to be "an anarchist," so too were there many individuals who would be considered "vegan" before the term itself was coined in 1944 with the birth of the Vegan Society in England. One of these individuals, almost certainly, would have been the brilliant French anarchist geographer, Élisée Reclus, who spoke of vegetarianism (1901), but who lived according to what we would consider a vegan anarchist praxis (White and Cudworth, 2014). The coining of the word "vegan" by Donald Watson and others in 1944, and the definition veganism used by The Vegan Society from 1979 is still, arguably, the most accessible, and influential today:

> A philosophy and way of living which seeks to exclude—as far as is possible and practicable—all forms of exploitation of, and cruelty to, animals for food, clothing or any other purpose; and by extension, promotes the development and use of animal-free alternatives for the benefit of humans, animals and the environment. In dietary terms it denotes the practice of dispensing with all products derived wholly or partly from animals.[1]

This notwithstanding, we would like to acknowledge a lesser-referenced definition of veganism, one proposed by Eva Batt in 1964, which would appear highly attuned to an anarchist sensibility around prefigurative praxis (and resisting religious overtures!):

> Veganism has no connection with any political party or system, national or international. Similarly, individual vegans may be deeply religious, perhaps devout Christians or disciples of one of many other faiths and creeds in this world, but this is not a requisite of veganism, which is an everyday, fundamental

way of life concerned with living without hurting others. The hereafter may, or
may not, solve all our problems; but what we do now certainly affects all those
around us. (no date)

It is important to note that both definitions explicitly extend the concept of
veganism beyond being merely a "food" or "lifestyle" choice (Watkinson and
O'Driscoll, 2014). Rather, *according to its original use*, veganism—*to be
vegan as envisaged by Watson*—demanded an explicit ethical commitment
to end animal exploitation *and* an intersectional praxis that benefited humans,
other animals, and the environment.

While it is relatively unproblematic to cite a broadly consensual definition of veganism, the same cannot be said of feminism. Each definition of
feminism is informed by specific political perspectives and values, and there
are probably as many definitions of feminism as there are different feminist
movements. We will refer, in the first instance, to the definition proposed by
Wikipedia, which characterizes feminism as:

> A range of political movements, ideologies, and social movements that share a
> common goal: to define, establish, and achieve political, economic, personal,
> and social equality of sexes.[2]
>
> Feminist movements have campaigned and continue to campaign for wom-
> en's rights, including the right to vote, to hold public office, to work, to earn fair
> wages or equal pay, to own property, to receive education, to enter contracts, to
> have equal rights within marriage, and to have maternity leave.

Many reflections can be held against this definition, and examples given, but
we shall restrict our opening analysis to three main points. First, it is an egalitarian definition. The idea here is to ensure that women and men are equal,
without further consideration for the wider structures in which they evolve—
which may still be hierarchized and divided in classes, races, and nations.
Second, it is a liberal definition, which seeks to apply the principles of political liberalism to women on the same terms as men. Third, it is a reformist
definition. Feminism is reduced to achieving equality through legal reforms.

While probably the most common definition of feminism, as reflected by
the popularity of Wikipedia, it is nonetheless contested by many feminist
movements for providing a limited understanding of feminism. Following
this definition uncritically, for example, feminism would appear to be simply
about agitating for, protecting and enforcing women rights *within* the current
social, political, and economic system, without ever questioning the institutions in which these rights are negotiated. Yet, one of the main contributions
of radical feminism, at the end of the 1960s, was precisely in the questioning
of the inequalities induced by—and intrinsic to—these institutions. The status
and emancipation of women will not be improved by merely changing the
existing/orthodox legislation—what *must* be addressed and dismantled is the

patriarchal system that animates these institutions and therefore perpetuates the subordination of women.

INTERSECTIONALITY

For the highly influential activist and author bell hooks (2015), feminism is the struggle to end sexist oppression. According to her, this struggle "takes place anytime anywhere any female or male resists sexism, sexist exploitation, and oppression. Feminist movement happens when groups of people come together with an organized strategy to take action to eliminate patriarchy" (hooks, 2015: xii). When hooks (2015: 33) goes on to argue that feminism "directs our attention to systems of domination and the interrelatedness of sex, race, and class oppression," she is clearly indicating that feminism cannot be reduced to a single-issue lens, and a feminist perspective should include an intersectional framework approach. Coined by critical race theorist Kimberlé Williams Crenshaw (see Crenshaw 1991), the origins of intersectionality "are feminist, specifically, black feminist scholarship's attempt to theorize the overlapping qualities, as well as the tensions between formations of 'race' and gender" (Cudworth 2015, 93). Intersectional scholarship has shown how different systems of power and injustice, not only racism and sexism but also classism or ableism do not act independently of each other and, to be understood more properly, should be examined as interrelated forms of discrimination. In other words, it is *impossible* to adequately tackle patriarchy without simultaneously addressing other forms of oppression, such as capitalism or white supremacy, which take part in individual experiences of sexist oppression. Liberal understandings of feminism are therefore restrictive. Feminism should be seen as a struggle for total liberation, one that includes resistance to male domination, and a human domination over species, too.

In terms of the structure of this chapter, first the chapter will offer a deeper insight into what anarchism is, and the emancipatory grounds upon which it stands. Second, a case for vegan anarchism will be made, which will be followed by an equivalent case for anarcha-feminism being articulated. Before concluding the chapter will focus on critical attention toward the ways in which inter-species struggles converge, with a critical reading of capitalism, and the commodification of women and non-human animals.

The Emancipatory Grounds upon Which Anarchism Stands

Anarchy is commonly perceived as being synonymous with disorder, chaos, and violence. However, anarchy does not mean the absence of law and order—

it is *an-arkhê*, "without authority," "leadership," or "hierarchy" (see White and Williams, 2012). More generally, anarchy means rejecting any form of domination or exploitation, any system of *archy*, such as hierarchy, monarchy, oligarchy or patriarchy. While anarchism embraces and upholds a diverse and radical diversity of approaches; it is only a half-joke to say that there are as many anarchisms as there are anarchists, since at its heart there are significant common grounds upon which they stand. Anarchism is a political theory and practice that aims to abolish traditional forms of institutions. More precisely, it seeks to abolish dominant institutions, whether capitalist, patriarchal, racist, colonialist, or heterosexist. Anarchism is a principle or a theory of life and behavior based on horizontality, self-management, and consensus-based decision-making rather than hierarchical and centralized structures (see Goodwin 1989, Kropotkin 2002; Ward, 1982). Therefore, anarchism advocates self-governed societies based on voluntary institutions. It holds the state to be unnecessary and harmful since it is governed by a dominant class that monopolizes decision-making and through its police represses any practice that endangers its monopoly on power.

Anarchism is therefore opposed to any form of domination through which a majority would establish its privileges on a minority under the guise of social order. As Simon Springer (2017: 3) writes, it entails "the rejection of all the interlocking systems of domination, including capitalism, imperialism, colonialism, neoliberalism, militarism, classism, racism, nationalism, ethnocentrism, sexism, Orientalism, ableism, genderism, ageism, speciesism, homophobia, transphobia, organized religion, and, of course, the state." The idea is not to prioritize some of our commitments, or to fight particular oppressions one after the other, but to completely and simultaneously oppose them. An anarchist perspective therefore will not hierarchize one struggle over another, nor assume that one must precede the other—which is precisely what distinguishes anarchism from orthodox Marxism, which emphasizes the importance of anti-capitalist struggle. Unlike Marxism, anarchism rejects the idea of the revolution as a final goal that may be reached after many transitive steps, including a dictatorship of the proletariat. This difference also helps separate anarchism from other anti-capitalist struggles, which assume systems of oppressions will automatically disappear with the abolition of capitalism.

Most of all, anarchism seeks to establish anarchy, that is to say a society in which individuals are brought to cooperate as equals, not before a law imposed from above, but based on non-hierarchical free associations. Anarchism is therefore not only a process of abolishing institutions but also a process of establishing autonomy before these institutions. It seeks to dismantle any unequal power relation through voluntary cooperation, altruism, self-management, and mutual aid.

Discussion I: Should Anarchists Be Vegan?
A Case for Vegan-Anarchism

Given that anarchism is opposed to social domination and oppressive violence, it seems reasonable to suppose that such an opposition would be naturally (empathetically) extended toward other sentient beings, in ways that fundamentally reject speciesism and *anthroparchy*. To offer a deeper reading of what we understand to be anthroparchy, we draw attention toward Erika Cudworth's original reflection:

> I have developed the term "anthroparchy" to capture the social ordering of human relations to the "environment." Anthroparchy literally means "human domination," and I see anthroparchy as a social system, a complex and relatively stable set of relationships in which the "environment" is dominated through formations of social organization which privilege the human. . . . I consider that anthroparchy has certain advantages over other possible terms such as "anthropocentrism" and "speciesism." (Calvo 2008: 34)

As to what the advantages are over speciesism, Cudworth considers that this term

> suggests a practice, a kind of behaviour and is a parallel term to those describing other undesirable practices, such as racism, sexism, and class discrimination. [But] we do not (just) live in societies which discriminate against non-human species. Rather, we live in societies which are organized around a species hierarchy, a hierarchy in which the needs, desires, interests and even whims of human beings shape the kinds of relationships we are likely to have with non-human species. (ibid)

And yet, the 21st-century anarchist movement, despite enjoying a popular resurgence of interest among a whole spectrum of social movements and within critical academic communities across the social sciences, has yet to deal adequately with its speciesist privileges. As underlined by Ian Werkheiser (2013), there is debate and disagreement among anarchists as to how nonhuman animals ought to be regarded. For some branches of anarchism, human beings are classified at the apex of a hierarchically structured "animal kingdom"; indeed the human status is reified to the extent that they are seen as not a part of nature, but *apart from* nature (an entity that includes nonhuman animals). This hierarchy reflects the supposed superiority of "the human," and human exceptionalism is therefore used to justify the ongoing dominion over nonhuman animals, who can be exploited in whatever ways deemed appropriate for the benefit of humans (Hall, 2011: 378).

Challenging this deeply rooted, yet both ontologically and ethically problematic demarcation between "human" and "animal" is often met with aggression and hostility. This is particularly evident when calling out the rights-violations inherent in the instrumental (ab)use of nonhuman animals for human ends. For example, though the chapter draws favourable attention to social ecology as advanced by Murray Bookchin, it is important to acknowledge that Bookchin was one of the most outspoken critics of the idea of "animal rights." Indeed Bookchin (1982: 362) argued that drawing attention toward our ethical duties in the relationship between nonhuman animals might "cheapen the meaning of real [human] suffering and cruelty" (Bookchin (1982: 362). This is a particularly extreme position to take: even those, like Kant, who argued that we have no direct duties toward other animals, acknowledged a causal link between animal abuse and human abuse.

> If a man shoots his dog because the animal is no longer capable of service . . .
> his act is inhuman and damages in himself that humanity which it is his duty to
> show towards mankind. If he is not to stifle his human feelings, he must practice
> kindness towards animals, for he who is cruel to animals becomes hard also in
> his dealings with men. (Kant, 1997: 212)

Elsewhere, key anarchist figures have disagreed with Élisée Reclus's premise that killing is a form of domination and rather consider that there is nothing wrong with harming or killing sentient creatures. In this view, death and predation are inevitable parts of nature and killing for food cannot be seen as a form of domination as long as it is necessary. Anarcho-primitivists, for instance, support hunting. One of the main advocates of this sub-current, Derrick Jensen, justifies the eating of nonhuman animals out of necessity: "When you take the life of someone to eat or otherwise use so you can survive, you become responsible for the survival—and dignity—of that other's community" (2006: 138). As Peter Gelderloos (2011: 5) points out, "The predator does not dominate the prey, nor does it negate them. It enters into a relationship with them, and this relationship is mutual—or in other words, of a sort that anarchists should find interesting and potentially inspiring." According to these authors, as Ian Werkheiser (2013: 175) writes, vegans are "so alienated from nature that they are able to imagine that suffering and death are not necessary parts of a natural and whole life, and to imagine that it is possible to consume without causing suffering to non-human animals." This sentiment shows that for some, far from necessarily implying each other, anarchism and veganism can be thought as separate if not opposite perspectives.

While there are still many anarchists who are unreconstructed speciesists and, certainly not vegan, a significant (and increasing) current of the anarchist movement condemns wholeheartedly the consumption and exploitation of nonhuman animals by human beings. As mentioned earlier, this is the case where a choice exists, and the decision to use (kill) another sentient being is not essential, that is, a matter of survival. This current of thought has been, in particular, developed by Brian Dominick (1995) who coined the concept of "veganarchism" in his famous essay, *Animal Liberation and Social Revolution: A Vegan Perspective on Anarchism or an Anarchist Perspective on Veganism.* Yet, it was not the first time that the connection between anarchism and the fight against animal exploitation was made. As early as 1901, Élisée Reclus (1901: 2) wrote an essay *On Vegetarianism* in which he questioned the fickleness of morality when applied to nonhuman animals— these "brothers" whom we eat and who nonetheless "love as we do, feel as we do, and, under our influence, progress or retrogress as we do." In making the connection between our treatment of nonhuman animals, the human history of wars and colonization and, more generally, our aspiration to dominate nature, Reclus draws vital attention toward several neglected relationships. Of these, arguably the most relevant to consider here is, first, the importance of an antispeciesist perspective taking root within the anarchist movement. Second, some of the key ecological questions of his era—and equally our own—are politicized. To him, the violent mistreatment of nonhuman animals is symptomatic of how humans destroy the environment to meet their own ends and acts as a basis for violence against fellow humans. Despite the term "speciesism" being coined only 70 years later, it would have been no surprise to find it in the writings of Reclus. Indeed, to Reclus, overcoming intrahuman oppressions, such as nationalism or racism, and human-animal oppression is part of the same process—both imply viewing one another as part of a global extended family composed of all living things. He writes:

> For the great majority of vegetarians, the question is not whether their biceps and triceps are more solid than those of the flesh-eaters . . . for them the important point is the recognition of the bond of affection and goodwill that links man (sic) to the so-called lower animals, and the extension to these our brothers of the sentiment which has already put a stop to cannibalism among men. The reasons which might be pleaded by anthropophagists against the disuse of human flesh in their customary diet would be as well-founded as those urged by ordinary flesh-eaters today. The arguments that were opposed to that monstrous habit are precisely those we vegetarians employ now. The horse and the cow, the rabbit and the cat, the deer and the hare, the pheasant and the lark, please us better as friends than as meat. We wish to preserve them either as respected fellow-workers, or simply as companions in the joy of life and friendship. (Reclus, 1901: 4)

While uncommon at the time, Élisée Reclus's opposition to meat-eating and the oppression of nonhuman animals was not completely isolated within the anarchist movement. The Russian anarchist Piotr Kropotkin (1993, 136) also claimed that "civilized man (sic) . . . will extend his principles of solidarity to the whole human race, and even to the animals." This shared perspective comes as no surprise given that anarchism advocates rejecting any form of domination or exploitation without any gradation between the different social struggles. As Dominick argues:

> I am vegan because I have compassion for animals; I see them as beings possessed of value not unlike humans. I am an anarchist because I have that same compassion for humans, and because I refuse to settle for compromised perspectives, half-assed strategies and sold-out objectives. As a radical, my approach to animal and human liberation is without compromise: total freedom for all, or else. (1995: 4–5)

Since human and nonhuman oppressions are linked, veganism is an essential part of anarchism. Veganarchism here shows its proximity with feminist approaches (such as that of Carol J. Adams), ecofeminist perspectives (according to Dominick, the destruction of the environment is due to anthropocentrism) and critical race studies. To Dominick (1995: 8), "to decide one oppression is valid and the other not is to consciously limit one's understanding of the world; it is to engage oneself in voluntary ignorance, more often than not for personal convenience." According to veganarchists, the source of these oppressions is the establishment—the dominant institutions, which are presided by the statist and capitalist system. As Torres argues, "As a needless and unnecessary form of hierarchy, anarchists should reject the consumption, enslavement, and subjugation of non-human animals for human ends, and identify it as yet another oppressive aspect of the relations of capital and a needless form of domination" (2007: 209). Therefore, veganism cannot remain only a consumer choice within the capitalist system. Consumption alone will not change a system based on the exploitation of human and nonhuman animals—the entire system must be changed.

Brian Dominick's wholehearted rejection of appeals to consumerism as the means to enact a new peaceable future underpins his criticism of "liberal" veganism. Put succinctly, "liberal" veganism is a form of veganism underpinned by individuals concerned about the exploitation of nonhuman animals, but one which fails to connect such exploitation with capitalism. For veganarchists such a thought that simply consuming products from the capitalist industry will help fundamentally change things is, shall we say at best, naive. Veganism should be conceived as the natural consequence of the resistance to social exploitation. Many anarchists are therefore quite critical of the current trend of existing institutions and social movements, which pushes us toward defining our civic actions in terms of consumption, as if our action could be reduced to consumption—even if sustainable and ethical.

Similarly, veganarchism is essentially abolitionist and opposed to reformism. Animal welfare regulations will not free nonhuman animals. According to

Brian Dominick (1995: 9), the law is "anti-animal," as is shown by state subsidization of the meat and dairy industry and vivisection and by its opposition to animal rights activists. According to a classic anarchist perspective (e.g., that of Mikhail Bakunin or Emma Goldman), state laws are fundamentally unjust since they are based on coercion. Because they are used to serve the interests of those who are already in power, they reproduce unjust power relationships. Even if the state might authorize certain reforms regarding nonhuman animal exploitation, this will not change the fundamental power relationships between human and nonhuman animals. The state's lack of concern for animals is the reason why veganism should be anarchist.

Moreover, there is sometimes a temptation to think that anarchism is guided by the ideal of a revolution that would dismantle any existing institutions. Yet, the anarchist revolution is not so much external than internal. Driven by "the confluence of action, being, and rebellion, wherein there is no separation of theory and practice," it is a philosophy of everyday life, encouraging people to "tak[e] control of one's own individual life and creat[e] alternatives on the ground" (Springer 2015, 213). The revolutionary ideal that inspires anarchism may therefore be understood as an inward process of freeing ourselves from our own alienation. Alienation here designates the inability of people to see their exploitation and the resulting belief that domination is justified (Zerzan, 2002). Therefore, to dis-alienate oneself means challenging the beliefs and cultural norms that guide our representations and practices since birth. As argued by Dominick (1995, 6), "It is we who are the enemy; overthrowing the oppressors in our heads will be the revolution." It is precisely this alienation that vegans seek to overthrow when they address the speciesist beliefs rooted in society.

According to veganarchists, alienation includes the ignorance—or rather a more or less conscious refusal—of the reality of nonhuman animal exploitation. Yet, this ignorance is not natural, but results from our oppressive capitalist society. Human beings have a natural compassion toward each other, which vegananarchists extend to all sentient beings. Causing pain to another living being requires both a cultural construction and a moral effort. In order to silence our feeling of compassion and the cognitive dissonance resulting from meat consumption, one must either conceal the reality of animal exploitation (e.g., by placing slaughterhouses outside cities) or make people believe that it is natural, normal, and necessary to eat nonhuman animals—a powerful combination that Melanie Joy (2011) refers to as "carnism." Because veganism places this dis-alienation as a major step of its fight against animal exploitation, it can be considered an anarchist process.

Another common mistake about anarchism is to conflate the revolutionary *project* and *process*. The anarchist revolution should not be seen as an event, but a process. Anarchism rejects the idea of the revolution as a final goal that may be reached after many transitive steps. Unlike Marxism, it does not seek to pursue a revolutionary project, but a process that should be realized *here and now* (Springer, 2012). As a result, what is at stake is an "infinitely demanding" struggle (Critchley, 2007) led by individuals in their daily practices. Anarchism is therefore not a project, but a praxis. As argued by Dominick,

> Action is not so limited. It can be found in our daily lives, our routine and not-so-routine activities. When we assert our beliefs by speaking out in conversation, on the job, at the dinner table, we are *acting*. (Dominick, 1995: 12–13)

As for anarchists, it is in their ordinary, everyday practices, at breakfast, lunch, and dinner, at home, in the street or at work, that vegan activists attempt to fight these dominant ideologies and devise alternative ways of living (see Véron, 2016; White, 2017). Because our most ordinary actions testify to our alienation, it is also through these actions that we can free ourselves and change things. Acknowledging that the revolution must become part of our lifestyle is a major step toward freeing everyday life from alienation and making it a truly revolutionary process. Activism is thus no longer extraordinary, temporarily cutting us from our everyday life, but it is ordinary—present in our smallest and seemingly most insignificant actions as a practice that seeks to transform everyday life via everyday life (see Véron, 2016; White, 2017).

Such an understanding of activism echoes the anarchist notion of "propaganda of the deed," understood not as a form of violent action, but as a form of prefigurative politics (Graeber, 2002). The concept implies that activists must not only advocate something, not only fight to achieve it, but they must also show in their own lives that such things are possible and they must attempt to realize them (Werkheiser 2013). This idea is in line with the definition of the activist by Dominick:

> The role of the revolutionist is simple: make your life into a miniature model of the alternative, revolutionary society you envision. You are a microcosm of the world around you, and even the most basic among your actions affect the social context of which you are a part. Make those effects positive and radical in their nature. (Dominick, 1995: 13)

Therefore, veganism can be perceived as anarchist. It opposes an unjustified form of domination and should logically oppose the other oppressions to which it is linked. It is an everyday life movement, that is to say a movement that changes everyday life via everyday life. Both veganism and anarchism are rooted in our actions and routines. The reunion of both movements within veganarchism is not only theoretical—it is also methodological and practical since both assume the same mode of action. Unlike liberal veganism, veganarchism indicates the need for "total liberation" (see Springer's chapter, this volume). It also suggests how this everyday revolution could be carried out and what non-hierarchized and non-exploitative relationships could mean.

Discussion II: Should Anarchists Be Feminists?
A Case for Anarcha-Feminism

According to L. Susan Brown (2003), "Anarchism is a political philosophy that opposes *all* relationships of power, it is inherently feminist. An anarchist who supports male domination contradicts the implicit critique of power which is the fundamental principle upon which all of anarchism is built." While this might theoretically be true, anarchism does not always entail gender oppression within its struggle against all forms of domination.

Historically, anarchism has often ignored feminism and the question of women in society. When the concept of anarchism emerged, in the second half of 19th century, anarchist philosophy was almost entirely devoted to men, as were communism and socialism. What mattered most was to organize male workers and ensure them good wages and working conditions in order for them to protect their families. Pierre-Joseph Proudhon, one of the most influential theorists of anarchism, was fiercely opposed to the emancipation of women. Arguing that certain hierarchies of power are legitimate, among which was a father's patriarchal authority over his wife and children, he maintained that the woman's place was at home, as a wife and mother (Proudhon, 1860). Convinced of the natural inferiority of women, he even wrote a deeply anti-feminist pamphlet, *La Pornocratieou Les Femmes dans les temps modernes* (1875). While Proudhon's defense of patriarchy was subject to debates and controversies in his lifetime, it has nonetheless influenced anarchists and was later concealed by many analysts.

Moreover, anarchist circles are far from being free from sexism. Many anarchist men behave in sexist ways and activist groups are marked by patriarchal and paternalistic power relationships, illustrated by misogynistic views and sometimes even sexual aggressions. Feminist perspectives or critical discussions of gender have often been subjected to backlash within these groups. Anarcha-feminism, which we will present in the next section, has therefore often been a way for anarchist women to oppose and overcome sexism within anarchist circles.

Besides, the history of anarchism—and many other social struggles—has been marked by the idea that men's struggles are general and universal, whereas women's are specific and particular. This view has been constantly reproduced in anarchist narratives, which have often considered male experience as the default. By forgetting how gender deeply impacts any form of social experience, condition, or struggle, anarchist scenes have helped maintain this default sexist notion of politics. Another key example of how activist circles have helped reproduce power relations is the fact that the oppression of women is often eclipsed by the primacy of the fight against capitalism as the fundamental root of all oppression. Feminist struggles have therefore been perceived of as having lesser importance than the struggle of male wageworkers, which illustrates a hierarchization of struggles in conflict with the anarchist ideal.

Finally, for a large number of anarchists, only virile and aggressive direct action is regarded as useful activism. Any other form of participation in anarchist struggle is deemed marginal and accessory, which demonstrates another form of hierarchization—that of the means of struggle. However, there are many other ways of working toward anarchy that are not based on violence, including but not limited to DIY projects and mutual aid. This perspective demonstrates a particularly gendered view of activism, since anarchist women are often the ones who are involved in such practices. Glorifying only virile action is sexist since it leads to underestimating the role of women in anarchist struggle.

Promoting only confrontational direct action and marginalizing the issue of women's emancipation and oppression are part of the internal contradictions that affect the anarchist movement. Anarcha-feminism can be an assertion that it is essential for anarchism to overcome this contradiction and, more generally, to fight against gender dynamics within social movements.

Anarcha-feminism

While the term "anarchism" emerged in the 1840–1850s and that of "feminism" in the 1870–1880s, the term "anarcha-feminism" was not coined until the 1970s. At the end of the 19th century and the beginning of the 20th century, most anarchists did not use the term "feminism" to discuss gender issues, but rather "the woman question" or "women's emancipation." While the term was already in use during the lifetime of Emma Goldman and although she is today regarded as a feminist icon, she never used it in her writings to identify herself. We have previously evoked how the topic of feminism has been dealt with in anarchist circles, bearing in mind that these circles were predominantly composed of a male audience. Rather than underlining how anarchist men have dealt with gender, we suggest to now look at how anarchist women have laid the foundations for anarcha-feminism as we know it.

One of the first feminist critiques of traditional anarchism stemmed from anarchist women, such as Mary Wollstonecraft, Louise Michel, Lucy Parsons, Emma Goldman, Voltairine de Cleyre, and Virginia Bolten. According to them, women's emancipation is not an "added challenge" in the struggle against alienation. It is impossible to understand capitalist oppression without understanding that the oppression of women is an integral part of this system. Similarly, no anti-capitalist revolution can be carried out without the full and equal participation of women. It is precisely the convergence between "The Woman Question" and the anti-capitalist struggle that explains the divergences between anarcha-feminism and other currents of feminism.

Historically, anarchists have advanced equality, but not as equal integration of living beings into oppressive systems. The anarchist understanding of equality means opposing any forms of hierarchies and oppressions, including capitalism, racism, nationalism, sexism, and patriarchy. This understanding of equality goes beyond the liberal feminist idea of equal rights for women. Here lies one of the main differences between anarcha-feminism and traditional feminism—the view that the exploitation of women cannot be dissociated from the wider context of economic and political exploitation. According to anarchist feminists, there is no point in fighting for equal integration of women in an oppressive, unequal, and exploitation system. When feminists campaigned for women's right to vote in the late 19th century and early 20th century, most anarchist women did not support the suffragette movement. As argued by Emma Goldman,

> Her [a woman's] development, her freedom, her independence, must come from and through herself. First, by asserting herself as a personality, and not as a sex commodity. Second, by refusing the right to anyone over her body; by refusing to bear children, unless she wants them; by refusing to be a servant to God, the State, society, the husband, the family, etc. . . . Only that, and not the ballot, will set woman free, will make her a force hitherto unknown in the world, a force for real love, for peace, for harmony; a force of divine fire, of life-giving; a creator of free men and women. (1913: np)

Anarchist women argue that only by themselves can women become emancipated and empowered. Neither men, neither the laws nor the state can bring about their liberation—women need to become the only agents of their own freedom. As pointed out by Carol Ehrlich (1977: np) in her essay *Socialism, Anarchism, and Feminism*:

> Because they are anarchists, they work to end all power relationships, all situations in which people can oppress each other. Unlike some radical feminists who are not anarchists, they do not believe that power in the hands of women could possibly lead to a non-coercive society. And unlike most socialist feminists, they do not believe that anything good can come out of a mass movement with a leadership elite. In short, neither a workers' state nor a matriarchy will end the oppression of everyone. The goal, then, is not to "seize" power, as the socialists are fond of urging, but to abolish power.

Despite this early awareness for feminist issues by anarchist women, only the second-wave feminist generation in the 1970s will more systematically theorize the relationship between feminism and anarchism by connecting the oppression of women to capitalist and statist oppression. Yet, the anarchist legacy is more than relevant for the feminist movement. By opposing all forms of oppression and promoting instead self-government and non-hierarchical associations, it does not pretend that feminist struggles are secondary, unlike other anti-capitalist movements. In that sense, anarchism should always be feminist: anarcha-feminism simply emphasizes the fact that feminism is inherent to anarchism.

Discussion III: Recognizing the Convergence of Inter-species Struggles: Capitalism, and the Commodification of Women and Non-human Animals

In order to understand the intersection of oppression and the need for interconnected social struggles, attention is now turned toward the process of capitalist appropriation of human and nonhuman animals. While it is important to note that speciesist relations were evident long before capitalism, as Sanbonmatsu (2017, 1–2) argues, "By the end of the twentieth century, speciesism under advanced capitalist conditions had at last reached its zenith as a totalitarian, global system of surveillance, technological control, and mass murder without moral, spatial, temporal, biological, or ontological limits."

We will here distinguish two components of this appropriation: the commodification of individuals (women/nonhuman animals) and the commodification of social struggles (feminism/veganism).

(1) The Capitalist Commodification of Women and Nonhuman Animals

Commodification is a process by which goods, services, ideas, and people are turned into commodities, that is to say, objects of economic value. When applied to women, this process is marked by an objectification of the female body (see Wrenn, 2017). Women are reduced to their bodies and constantly commodified by the capitalist society. Advertising and media messages judge, mould, and mutilate their bodies through weight loss diets, plastic surgery or cosmetic products in order to create a unified, racialized, and eroticized model of the female body, which informs the collective psyche. This commodification of the female body goes hand in hand with its hypersexualization. Regarded as a mere sexual object, the female body is fragmented and reduced to certain body parts that can be sold or bought—often the breasts and buttocks. Women are thus reduced to consumer goods.

Similarly, capitalism reduces nonhuman animals to resources and to commodified and deindividualized objects, designated by collective or generic terms, such as "livestock" or "meat." While recognizing that nonhuman animals were already exploited and killed before capitalism, the latter has brought nonhuman animal commodification to another degree. According to David Nibert (2002:237),

> "Capitalism continued the ten-thousand-year-old tradition of exploiting humans and other animals for the production of wealth and privilege, an exploitation that continued to bind the fate of devalued humans and other animals."

In other words, they are biologically engineered for profitable exploitation and valued accordingly. That is to say in ways that "serve to maximize the owner's profit, even if these fundamentally override and violate all ethical norms" (White, 2017, 275).

Commodification affects women as it does nonhuman animals, and it remains as one of the main processes through which capitalist exploitation establishes and consolidates its power. The work of eco-feminists has been particularly important in making explicit the connections here, particularly focused on the fragmentation, objectification, and ultimate consumption of female bodies (through the male gaze) and animal bodies (through the human gaze). Therefore, addressing the continuing oppression of women and nonhuman animals implies understanding the interconnectedness of such a process. As Kathryn Gillespie (2013: 2) points out, "Understanding this commodification is important both for the sake of the individual animals laboring and dying within the industry and for the more extensive project of uncovering the consequences of gendered commodification of all bodies—nonhuman and human—and the violent power structures to which they are subjected." These connections are essential to understand how capitalist modes of domination and violence operate and to address human and nonhuman exploitation as part of the same process. By highlighting the connection between the domination of nature and the domination of women and non-human animals, vegan ecofeminism has extended traditional approaches of political ecology. One of the most radical and influential individuals around intersectionality and vegan-feminism is Carol Adams. The expression of feminism she advances is one that is entirely on point with the radical possibilities of feminism we draw on here:

> We believe that feminism is a transformative philosophy that embraces the amelioration of life on earth for all life-forms, for all natural entities. We believe that all oppressions are interconnected: no one creative will be free until all are

free—from abuse, degradation, exploitation, pollution, and commercialization. (Adams and Donovan, 1995, 3)

Other feminists such as Gena Corea (1984), Marti Kheel (1987), Val Plumwood (1993; 2002), and Lisa Kemmerer (2011) have similarly exposed the interconnections between the oppression of nature, women, animals, and people of color, thereby clarifying why intersecting forms of oppression must be challenged in order to end the oppression of all beings.

(2) The Capitalist Commodification of Feminism and Veganism

One of the main strengths of capitalism lies in its capacity to absorb, reduce, and commodify political values, including radical movements for social justice. This power explains why capitalism succeeds not only in commodifying women and nonhuman animals but also their struggles—feminism and veganism.

The capitalist commodification of feminism is blatant when considering women's magazines. One of the most emblematic examples of this "commodified feminism" is probably *Elle* magazine, whose French edition dreams of a "pop, light and uninhibited" feminism,[3] that is to say "a grown-up and generous feminism, which would not be a mask put on indescribable and ancestral drives—neither the hatred of men and their sexual desire nor the hatred of women."[4] According to its colleague *Glamour*, feminism should be "relaxed" and "non-aggressive" and it should express the voice of women who are "too much in love with men to want to dominate them."[5] Feminist killjoys please abstain. This form of "feminism" perfectly complements the numerous advertisements for beauty products, clothes, and pressures to be thin that can be found in these magazines. Feminism is here reduced to a pink and sparkly "girl power" theme, which can be bought long before puberty. Most clothing or cosmetics brands have understood this very well and turned feminism into a marketing strategy. Here, capitalism not only re-appropriates feminist themes, but it invents a new form of feminism consistent with consumerist values. In this perspective, being a feminist means daring to buy three new Vuitton handbags, "Because I'm Worth It." The emancipation of women is stripped of its meaning and assimilated to a form of "personal development," without any further questioning of gendered values and practices, which in turn helps maintain patriarchal domination.

A similar trend can be identified with veganism. Whereas veganism is a political strategy to end animal exploitation, capitalism manages to strip it of its radical impetus via a new packaging—that of a "healthy" and "alternative" lifestyle. Veganism becomes a highly profitable business opportunity, characterized by a huge amount of "green juices," "detox meals," and "veggie burgers," which Hollywood celebrities are quick to adopt. Many enterprises involved in animal exploitation find in veganism a new way of greenwashing their activities in the form of "ethical washing." They start invading supermarket shelves with non-dairy milks and seitan sausages along with their traditional animal-based products. This form of "neoliberal veganism"—that is, veganism reduced to a lucrative venture—is encouraged by capitalism since it does not question or threaten the wider social and political system and fits in perfectly with its consumerist perspective.

Both the feminist and vegan struggle are continuously neutralized and reduced to capital assets by the logic of profit and financial gains. However, capitalism is not the only system of power that contributes to neutralizing social struggles. As underlined by Brian Dominick (1995), the state is on the side of those who exploit animals and the law is decidedly anti-animal, as shown with the numerous government subsidies to the meat and dairy industries. The connection between the state, the legal system, and the meat and dairy industries has been demonstrated in many countries with the proliferation of ag-gag laws, which criminalize whistleblowers and those who oppose animal exploitation. The dairy industry has recently bended the European Union to its will by preventing dairy nouns to be applied to non-dairy products, such as milk or yogurt. In France, it is now compulsory for public institutions to serve meat, eggs, or dairy products in their canteens since the introduction of a legislative decree in 2011.

These elements explain why a deeper understanding of the statist and capitalist system of power and domination is essential to understand the roots of women and nonhuman animal exploitation, which is precisely what an anarchist reflection offers. By questioning the role played by the state, the economic system, and other forms of social hierarchies, anarchism offers a political perspective on human interactions and on human/more-than-human interactions. This perspective enables us to espouse an ethic of justice inclusive of humans, nonhuman animals, and ecosystems, and to follow a holistic revolutionary strategy with the potential to combat all forms of inequality and oppression.

CONCLUSION

Many critical animal studies and ecofeminist scholars, such as Carol J. Adams or Marta Kheel, have connected the exploitation of non-human animals with the oppression of nature and of marginalized groups of humans. However, these works sometimes underestimate or minimize how these oppressions are closely interwoven in our social, cultural, economic, and political systems. In addition, few have attempted to offer a revolutionary program that would allow human and nonhuman society to advance toward non-hierarchical relationships. An important component of anarchism is its profound critique of power and exploitation, along with its strategies for social change and environmental advocacy. Adopting an anarchist perspective would enable feminist and vegan movements to reassess these power relationships as well as their own strategies and modes of action.

In the final analysis, we contend that feminist and vegan praxis are not only close to anarchism—to realize their full potential they actually *should* be anarchist. Anarchism offers a systematic understanding of the roots of the exploitation of women, nonhuman animals, marginalized groups and ecosystems, by highlighting the role played by the state, capitalism, and other hierarchical organizations in this exploitation. It also suggests how to resist these relations of power and domination. Therefore, anarchism should be given better recognition among the vegan and feminist movements. On the other hand, anarchism cannot pretend to dismantle existing oppressions without fighting against sexist and speciesist oppression both theoretically and practically within activist circles. This explains why a convergence between the (eco)feminist, vegan, and anarchist struggles is not only desirable but essential to the success of their fight for social justice, freedom, and liberation. Such a perspective seems integral to advancing a contemporary anarchist political ecology, conceived as a holistic strategy aimed at identifying the interdependency between the exploitation of humans and more-than-humans, and with the potential to fight all forms of injustice and oppression.

NOTES

1. Source: https://www.vegansociety.com/go-vegan/definition-veganism [accessed December 17, 2017].
2. Source: https://en.wikipedia.org/wiki/Feminism [accessed January 10, 2018].
3. http://www.elle.fr/Societe/News/Cette-semaine-dans-ELLE-la-parole-a-une-nouvelle-generation-de-feministes-3443510.
4. *Elle*, « trop de féminismes? », March 1, 2013, http://www.elle.fr/Societe/Edito/Trop-de-feminismes-2362260 [accessed December 10, 2017].
5. *Glamour*, « On peut être blonde et féministe », n°154, mars 2017.

REFERENCES

Adams, C. J. (2015). "Why Vegan-Feminist?" http://caroljadams.com/why-vegan-feminist/. Retrieved on March 7, 2018.

Adams, C. J., and Donovan, J. (1995). *Animals and Women: Feminist Theoretical Explorations*. Durham, NC: Duke University Press.

Batt, E. (no date). "Why Veganism?" http://www.abolitionistapproach.com/media/pdf/why-veganism.pdf/. Retrieved on March 27, 2018.

Best, S. (2006). "Rethinking Revolution: Animal Liberation, Human Liberation, and the Future of the Left." *Journal of Inclusive Democracy*, 2 (3): 1–28.

Bookchin, M. (1982). *The Ecology of Freedom: The Emergence and Dissolution of Society*. Palo Alto, CA: Cheshire Books.

Bookchin, M. (2015). *The Next Revolution: Popular Assemblies and the Promise of Direct Democracy*. London: Verso Books.

Brown, S. (2003). *The Politics of Individualism: Liberalism, Liberal Feminism and Anarchism*. Montreal: Black Rose Books.

Calvo, E. (2008). "'Most Farmers Prefer Blondes': The Dynamics of Anthroparchy in Animals' Becoming Meat." *Journal for Critical Animal Studies*, VI, (1): 32–45.

Clark, J. (2004). "The Dialectic of Nature and Culture." In J. Clark and C. Martin (eds.), *Anarchy, Geography, Modernity: Selected Writings of Elisée Reclus*. Oakland: PM Press. pp. 16–34.

Corea, G. (1984) "Dominance and Control: How Our Culture Sees Women, Nature and Animals." *The Animals' Agenda* 4 (May/June): 20–21, 37.

Critchley, S. (2007). *Infinitely Demanding: Ethics of Commitment, Politics of Resistance*. London: Verso.

Cudworth, E. (2015). "Intersectionality, Species and Social Domination." In A. Nocella, R. J. White, and E. Cudworth (eds.), *Anarchism and Animal Liberation: Critical Animal Studies, Intersectionality and Total Liberation*, Jefferson, NC: McFarland Press.

Dominick, B. (1995). *Animal Liberation and Social Revolution: A Vegan Perspective on Anarchism or an Anarchist Perspective on Veganism*. Syracuse, NY: Critical Mass Media.

Ehrlich C. (1977). *Socialism, Anarchism, and Feminism*. Baltimore, MD: Research Group One. https://theanarchistlibrary.org/library/carol-ehrlich-socialism-anarchism-and-feminism/. Retrieved on January 17, 2018.

Gelderloos, P. (2011). "Veganism: Why Not—An Anarchist Perspective." *Infoshop News*, news.infoshop.org.

Gillespie, K. (2013). "Sexualized Violence and the Gendered Commodification of the Animal Body in Pacific Northwest, U.S. Dairy Production." *Gender, Place, and Culture*, 21 (10): 1321–1337.

Gillespie, K., and Collard, R. C. (eds.) (2015). *Critical Animal Geographies: Politics, Intersections and Hierarchies in a Multispecies World*. London: Routledge.

Goldman, E. (1910). *Anarchism and Other Essays*. New York: Mother Earth Publishing Association. http://theanarchistlibrary.org/library/emma-goldman-anarchism-and-other-essays. Retrieved on January 17, 2018.

Goodwin, D. (ed.) (1989). *For Anarchism, History, Theory, and Practice*. London: Routledge.

Graeber, D. (2002). "The New Anarchists." *New Left Review*, 13: 61–73.

Hall, M. (2011). "Beyond the Human: Extending Ecological Anarchism." *Environmental Politics*, 20 (3): 374–390.

hooks, b. (2015). *Feminist Theory: From Margin to Centre*, 3rd ed. New York: Routledge.

Jensen, D. (2006). *Endgame, Vol. 1: The Problem of Civilization*. New York: Seven Stories Press.

Joy, M. (2011). *Why We Love Dogs, Eat Pigs, and Wear Cows: An Introduction to Carnism*. San Francisco: Conari Press.

Kant, I. (1997). *Lectures on Ethics* (Vol. 2). Cambridge University Press.

Kemmerer, L. (2011). *Sister Species: Women, Animals, and Social Justice*. Champaign, IL: University of Illinois Press.

Kheel, M. (1988). "Animal Liberation Is a Feminist Issue." *The New Catalyst Quarterly*, 10 (Winter): 8–9.

Kropotkin, P. (1993). *Fugitive Writings*. Montréal; New York: Black Rose Books.

Kropotkin, P. ([1902] 1993). *Mutual Aid: A Factor of Evolution*. London: Freedom Press.

Kropotkin, P. (2002). *Anarchism: A Collection of Revolutionary Writings*. New York: Dover Publications.

Nibert, D. (2002). *Animal Rights/Human Rights: Entanglements of Oppression and Liberation*. Lanham, MD: Rowman & Littlefield.

Nibert, D. (2017). "Introduction." In D. Nibert (ed.), *Animal Oppression and Capitalism, Volume 1: The Oppression of Nonhuman Animals as Sources of Food*. Santa Barbara, CA: Praeger Press.

Nocella, A., Sorenson, J., Socha, K., and Matsuika, A. (eds.) (2014). *Critical Animal Studies Reader: An Introduction to an Intersectional Social Justice Approach to Animal Liberation*. New York: Peter Lang Publishing Group.

Pepper, D. (2002). *Eco-socialism: From Deep Ecology to Social Justice*. London: Routledge.

Plumwood, V. (1993). *"Feminism and the Mastery of Nature*. London: Routledge.

Plumwood, V. (2002). *Environmental Culture: The Ecological Crisis of Reason*. Abingdon, Oxon: Routledge.

Proudhon, P.-J. (1860). *De la justice dans la révolutionetdansl'Église*. Paris: Fayard.

Proudhon, P.-J. (2009). *La Pornocratieou Les Femmes dans les temps modernes*. Paris: L'Herne.

Reclus, E. (1877). *Nouvelle géographie universelle*. Paris: Hachette.

Reclus, E. (1901). "A propos du végétarisme." *La réforme alimentaire*, 5 (3): 37–45.

Sanbonmatsu (2017). "Capitalism and Speciesism." In D. Nibert (ed.), *Animal Oppression and Capitalism*. Westport, CT: Praeger.

Seager, J. (2003). "Pepperoni or Broccoli? On the Cutting Wedge of Feminist Environmentalism." *Gender, Place and Culture: A Journal of Feminist Geography*, 10 (2): 167–174.

Sorenson, J., and Matsuoka, A. (2018). *Critical Animal Studies: Towards Transspecies Social Justice*. London and New York: Rowman & Littlefield International.

Springer, S. (2017). "Anarchist Geography." In Douglas Richardson, Noel Castree, Michael F. Goodchild, Audrey Kobayashi, Weidong Liu, and Richard A. Marston (eds.), *The International Encyclopedia of Geography*. New Jersey: John Wiley & Sons.

Springer, S. (2015). "Radical Political Geographies." In: J. Sharp, J. Agnew, V. Mamadouh, and A. Secor (eds.), *Wiley-Blackwell Companion to Political Geography*, 2nd ed., 206–219.

Springer, S. (2016). *The Anarchist Roots of Geography: Towards Spatial Emancipation*. Minneapolis and London, MN: Minnesota Press.

Torres, B. (2007). *Making a Killing: The Political Economy of Animal Rights*. Oakland, CA: AK Press.

Véron, O. (2016). "(Extra)Ordinary Activism: Veganism and the Shaping of Hemeratopias." *International Journal of Sociology and Social Policy*, 36 (11/12): pp. 756–773.

Ward, C. 1982, "Anarchy in Action. London: Freedom Press.

Watkinson, K., and O'Driscoll, D. (2014). *From Animals to Anarchism*. Dysophia. Open Letters. Leeds, UK: Footprint Workers Co-operative Ltd.

Werkheiser, I. (2013). "Domination and Consumption: An Examination of Veganism, Anarchism, and Ecofeminism." *PhaenEx*, 8 (2).

White, R. J. (2015a). "Critical Animal Geographies and Anarchist Praxis: Shifting Perspectives from the Animal 'Question' to the Animal 'Condition.'" In K. Gillespie and R.-C. Collard (eds.), *Critical Animal Geographies: Power, Space and Violence in a Multispecies World*. London: Routledge.

White, R. J. (2015b). "Following in the Footsteps of Élisée Reclus: Disturbing Places of Inter-species Violence that Are Hidden in Plain Sight." In A. Nocella, R. J. White, and E. Cudworth (eds.), *Anarchism and Animal Liberation: Critical Animal Studies, Intersectionality and Total Liberation*. Jefferson, NC: McFarland Press.

White, R. J. (2017). "Rising to the Challenge of Capitalism and the Commodification of Animals: Post-capitalism, Anarchist Economies and Vegan Praxis." In D. Nibert (ed.), *Animal Oppression and Capitalism*. Westport, CT: Praeger.

White, R. J., and Springer, S. (2018). "Making Space for Anarchist Geographies in Critical Animal Studies." In J. Sorenson and A. Matuoka (eds.), *Critical Animal Studies: Towards Trans-species Social Justice*. London: Rowman & Littlefield International.

White, R. J., Springer, S., and de Souza, M. L. (2016). *The Practice of Freedom: Anarchism, Geography, and the Spirit of Revolt*-V. 3. New York and London: Rowman & Littlefield.

Wrenn, C. (2017). "Toward a Vegan Feminist Theory of the State." In: Nibert, David, ed. *Animal Oppression and Capitalism*. Santa Barbara, CA: Praeger Press, pp. 201–230.

Zerzan, J. (2002). *Running on Emptiness*. Port Townsend, WA: Feral House Publishing.

Chapter 4

Vegan-Washing Genocide: Animal Advocacy on Stolen Land and Re-imagining Animal Liberation as Anti-colonial Praxis

R.D.

INTRODUCTION

This chapter examines the animal liberation movements in settler colonial contexts, specifically movements primarily composed of and largely led by white settlers, and their potential to both reify and challenge the structure of Settler State. I problematize the understandings of animal advocacy that rely on legal rights frameworks that appeal to state sovereignty, and erase Indigenous cosmologies of nonhuman relations and obligations, rendering such movements ineffective in settler colonial contexts wherein animal bodies are simultaneously produced as subjects of colonization and deployed as weapons of colonization and dispossession. My hope is to provoke settler animal advocates to critically engage anti-colonial solidarity.

"Intersectional" animal advocacy is *en vogue* (has gained traction in recent years), but attempts to bridge gaps in theory and practice have been little more than hollow moves to innocence (Tuck and Yang 2012). Adopting slogans such as "One struggle, one fight, human freedom, animal rights!," this cursory analysis of "intersectionality" erases the differences and experiences that should inform radical animal liberation struggle, solidarity, and strategy. This is especially true on stolen land. Rather than recognizing the strategic centrality (Olson 2009) of settler colonization to challenging mass animal enterprise, this use of homology flattens incommensurate experiences of dispossession, oppression, and marginalization. Assimilating decolonization struggle into an "intersectional" animal advocacy framework reproduces the logics of colonization and white supremacy. This process renders settler animal advocacy movements ineffective in terms of the material lives of animals, while also positioning animal advocacy, and more particularly, vegan advocacy, as an instrument of dispossession and colonization.

Indigenous resurgence is intrinsically committed to returning non-hierarchical interspecies relations (Coulthard 2014). Borrowing from Andrea Smith (2009), Billy-Ray Belcourt (2014) reveals the operation of anthropocentrism as a pillar of white supremacy, showing how animal advocacy movements that fail to name and challenge settler colonialism uphold colonial relations and the politics of recognition. Similarly, Anderson (2004) traces dispossession and colonization to the invasion of European animal agriculture, epistemologies, and cosmologies onto Indigenous land.

This chapter fosters a praxis that figures animals as both colonial subjects and weapons of colonization, while prefiguring an animal liberation movement on stolen land that centers Indigenous decolonization, repatriation of land and relations, and anti-colonial solidarity. Before turning to the critical content of this chapter, I want to attend to my experience and background, both as a settler and as an active participant and organizer in the animal liberation movement.

I arrived at this writing through a decade of experience in the animal advocacy movement in North America. My organizing background was primarily developed through localized, grassroots animal liberation collectives, which worked to develop coalitions with other communities in struggle, particularly through solidarity with anarchist and abolitionist struggles, "radical" eco-defense, environmental and climate justice work, Indigenous land defense, and Palestinian liberation.

My observations of and participation in settler animal advocacy movements in North America have left me cynical that meaningful change can be affected for nonhuman animals without situating both animal enterprise and the animal liberation movement in the context of the settler colonial-capitalist state. There has been a provocative emergence of literature on the relationship of animality and animal enterprise to settler colonization and white supremacy over the past decade (e.g., Deckha 2006; Tallbear 2011; Robinson 2013, 2014; Powell 2014; Belcourt 2014; Watts-Powless 2014; Todd 2014, 2015, 2016; Zahara 2015; Kanji 2017; Gossett 2015; Alloun 2017). However, there is still a need for a substantive analysis of the animal advocacy movement(s) that operate on stolen land. They hold the potential to either uniquely challenge anthropocentrism as a formation of whiteness and capital, or to reproduce the very structures that render animal enterprise visible, material, and profitable. That powerful potential requires a great degree of responsibility on the part of settler animal liberation advocates, particularly white settlers.

I am interested in the array of settler animal advocacy movements, whether stylized as "animal welfare," "animal rights," "animal liberation," "intersectional," or "total liberation." As Belcourt (2014) notes, "total liberation" and "intersectionality" as radical frameworks for animal advocacy movements both fail to attend to the specificity and singularity of settler colonization as a structure on stolen land that is "irreducible" and incommensurable to the aims and analysis of even the most radical social justice-oriented animal advocates (Belcourt 2014). Robinson (2013, 2014), Belcourt (2014), and Gossett (2015) argue that Indigeneity, Indigenous cosmology, decolonization, land defense, anti-colonial, and Black struggle are not only compatible with animal liberation, but they also always already resist violent constructions of animality and capitalist animal enterprise. This chapter is intended to address the range and contrast of settler and Indigenous animal advocacy as they exist in settler colonial contexts. It is the animal liberation work at these radical margins and intersections that holds the most promise for transformative and accountable struggle for decolonization, Indigenous solidarity, and anti-colonial resistance. White settlers engaged on this level of the movement subsequently must be accountable to reimagine animal liberation on stolen land.

If settler colonization engenders the "biopolitical and geopolitical management of people, land, flora and fauna within the 'domestic' borders of the imperial nation" (Tuck and Yang 2012, 4), then how do animal advocates and organizers attend to settler colonialism, white supremacy, anti-Blackness and the building and maintenance of capitalism and empire on this land? How will that change the trajectory of movement work and the allocation of resources? What will base-building look like? What sorts of grassroots campaigns will be generated? What is sustained and measurable resistance to animal enterprise as an extension of the larger colonial project? What do solidarity and sovereignty look like as an interspecies affair if we recognize reciprocity and agency among nonhuman actors (e.g., Hribal 2011, Coulter 2016)? How do we measure efficacy and what metrics are appropriate?

THE SETTLER COLONIAL STUCTURE OF ANIMALITY

> The question of genocide is never far from discussions of settler colonialism. Land is life—or, at least, land is necessary for life. Thus, contests for land can be—indeed, often are—contests for life. (Wolfe 2006, 387)

Settler colonialism is materially distinct from other colonial formations through the regular operation of structural violence on appropriated land and the deployment of the "logic of elimination" (Wolfe 2006). As Tuck and Yang (2012) argue, while colonial relationships are often understood to be either *external* or *internal*, vis-à-vis the metropole, settler colonialism is both. Situated in this context, the sovereignty of the nation-state is necessarily derived from the daily violent occupation of Indigenous land, the perpetual elimination of the Indigenous population, and the production and projection of settler life and imagination:

> The most important concern is the land/water/air/subterranean earth. . . . Land is what is most valuable, contested, required. This is both because settlers make Indigenous land their new home and source of capital, and also because the disruption of Indigenous relationships to land represents a profound epistemic, ontological, cosmological violence. (Tuck and Yang 2012, 5)

Settler colonization is more than an antecedent to the modern nation-state and prerequisite for capital accumulation—"invasion is a structure, not an event" (Wolfe 2006, 388). Dispossession, colonization, and settlement are recurring relational themes that must be produced and reproduced in order to materially register whiteness and capital across Indigenous land. In this way, settler colonialism is both dispossessing and generative (Wolfe 2006). It works simultaneously to empty the Indigenous land of the original inhabitants while deploying and weaponizing settlers onto these lands, configuring and imagining them as native. Settler colonialism as a structure requires settlers to secure native identity and connection to the land through culture, economy, agriculture, food, and mythology. Meanwhile, Indigenous populations are evacuated of these identities and relationships to place and eliminated through war, murder, and assimilation into the body of the occupying settler state. In the words of Patrick Wolfe, "Settler colonialism destroys to replace" (Wolfe 2006, 388). As Andrea Smith argues,

> This logic holds that Indigenous peoples must disappear. In fact, they must *always* be disappearing in order to allow non-Indigenous peoples rightful claim over this land. Through this logic of genocide, non-Native peoples then become the rightful inheritors of all that was Indigenous—land, resources, Indigenous spirituality, or culture. (Smith 2006, 68)

As a field of geo-economic arrangements, settler colonialism is critical to nation-state formation and capitalist political economy on a global scale. Morgensen elaborates that the biopolitics and necropolitics of settler state power are organized through the logic and governance of global capital— "The colonial era never ended because settler colonialism remains the naturalised activity projecting Western law and its exception along global scales today. Theories of the biopolitical state, regimes of global governance, and the war on terror will be insufficient unless they critically theorise settler colonialism as a historical and *present* condition and method of all such power" (Morgensen 2011, 54).

Settler colonialism is a spatial modality of global capital and state power. The generation of wealth and capital needed for state building and governance is not possible without the processes of colonial dispossession and the disciplining of colonized bodies, including not only Indigenous peoples but African slaves, migrants, women, queer, and trans people and, as I will argue later, nonhumans. In his critique of Marx's concept of primitive accumulation, Glen Coulthard notes that dispossession "never ceases to structure capitalist and colonial social relations in the present" and that colonial-capitalist production is "territorially acquisitive in perpetuity" (Coulthard 2014, 151). Sylvia Federici similarly expands upon the traditional reading of primitive accumulation to center the disciplining of the animalized and feminized body in the process of capital accumulation and state formation (Federici 2014). Thus, especially in the context of settler colonialism, capital and the state generate proletarianization *alongside* dispossession, racialization, feminization, and animalization.

It is for the reasons outlined earlier that anarchist activist and scholar Adam Lewis has argued that white supremacy and settler colonialism are "strategically central" to anarchist, anti-authoritarian, and anti-state organizing, and that anti-colonial solidarity forms the foundation for radical social movements on stolen land (Lewis 2015 and 2017). However, as I will argue, despite the empirical centrality of white supremacy anti-Blackness and settler colonialism to global animal enterprise, settler animal advocacy and animal liberation movements have largely failed to attend to Indigenous resurgence and anti-colonialism as advancing the struggle for animal liberation, or to strategize meaningful engagements in anti-colonial solidarity. The work of animal advocates of color is often marginalized, while the work of Indigenous solidarity is often ostracized.

Settler colonialism is a field of material relations through which whiteness and capital deploy their mutually constituted logics. Animality is the background logic against which settlers project both their humanity and their whiteness:

The settler, if known by his actions and how he justifies them, sees himself as holding dominion over the earth and its flora and fauna, as the anthropocentric normal, and as more developed, more human, more deserving than other groups or species. (Tuck and Yang 2012, 6)

For Tuck and Yang, the normalization of anthropocentrism anchors whiteness and settler identity. This process of animalization is related to Mbembe's concept of necropolitics. For Mbembe, the power to inscribe death on the bodies of the subaltern is the ultimate source of political sovereignty in modernity.

The power to confront and control death is the ontology of humanity and whiteness: "In other words, the human being truly *becomes a subject*—that is, separated from the animal—in the struggle and the work through which he or she confronts death" (Mbembe 2003, 14). Inversely, to be marked for death is the ontology of race and animality. Mbembe elaborates that "the function of racism is to regulate the distribution of death and to make possible the murderous functions of the state" (2003, 17). Interrogating the normalization of genocidal death in settler colonial contexts, Mbembe asserts that "*savage life* is just another form of *animal life*, a horrifying experience, something alien beyond imagination or comprehension" (2003, 24) and is thus rendered dead, disappeared, and dispossessed. In the logic of necropolitical power, "the figure of the animal is always already wrapped up in colonial and racial discourse" (Gossett 2015). Put more bluntly, "Our particular co-constitutions of human and nonhuman matter *for who lives and dies* in this world, and *how*" (Tallbear 2011). It is through this necropolitical logic of racialized and animalized cleansing and regulation of the social body that the state manages populations surplus to the requirements of capital (Marx 1993). These operations are "primarily a way of introducing a break into the domain of life that is under power's control: the break between what must live and what must die" (Foucault 1975–1976, 254). The sovereignty of the modern state is derived from the perpetual production and elimination of aberrations—savageness, animality, blackness, indigeneity, queerness—the "others" from which the society of capital must be defended and made secure (Foucault 1975–1976; Agamben 1998).

In *Dangerous Crossings*, her pivotal analysis of modernity, race, and species, Claire Jean Kim argues that animality is produced through the anxieties of whiteness, at the same time that race, as the correlative of animality, is produced through the anxieties of humanity: "Race is forged in the crucible of ideas about animality and nature" (Kim 2015, 25). Through the construction of what Kim calls "taxonomies of power"—biopolitical ontologies and epistemologies—it is *animality* that becomes an organizing principle of white supremacist society:

> As a taxonomy of power, race has been elaborated in the United States in intimate connection with species and nature. From the 1600s to the 1800s, [racialized groups] were imaginatively located in a human-animal borderlands where they were at once lumped together and painstakingly differentiated, depending on the exigencies of the situation. Remarkably, the racial stories crafted during these centuries . . . continue to structure the American cultural imaginary today. (Kim 2015, 60)

The processes of racialization that order the colonial-capitalist state are not only metaphorically and discursively linked to the production of animality and operations of animal enterprise. According to Anderson (2000, 4),

"Animality has informed rhetorics of race, class, and gender, and other identity constructs" critical to the functioning of state sovereignty and governmentality. Animality played a crucial role in the persecution of female sexuality, providing pretext for the witch trials, the subjugation and disciplining of the body, and the accumulation of capital through the system of wage labor and perpetual dispossession (Federici 2014).

Animality is critical to the material operations of whiteness and is a central logic of settler state sovereignty. As Belcourt (2014) posits, anthropocentrism is a "racialized and speciesist site of settler coloniality." Expanding upon Andrea Smith's "Three Pillars of White Supremacy" model, he suggests that "anthropocentrism is the fourth logic of white supremacy" and that "decolonization is only possible through an animal ethic that disrupts anthropocentrism as a settler-colonial logic" (2014, 4). Belcourt echoes Kim in his analysis of animality as the organizing principle of white supremacy:

> The logic of anthropocentrism is also militarized through racial hierarchies that further distance the white settler from blackness and indigeneity as animalized sites of tragedy, marginality, poverty, and primitivism. That is, black and Indigenous bodies are dehumanized and inscribed (and continually re-inscribed) with animal status—which is always a speciesist rendering of animality as injuring—to refuse humanness to people of color and colonized subjects. This not only commits a violence that re-locates racialized bodies to the margins of settler society as non-humans, but also performs an epistemic violence that denies animality its own subjectivity and re-makes it into a mode of being that can be re-made as blackness and indigeneity. (Belcourt 2014, 5)

The necropolitical nature of the settler capitalist state is produced against a cast of capital's residue that includes the other-than-human, nonhuman animals, Indigenous nations, Black and other racialized peoples, women, migrants, and queer and trans people. Animality is a metric by which other groups are rendered into various states of death and dying, or to borrow Dean Spade's terminology, are exposed to vectors of harm and an uneven distribution of life chances (Spade 2013).

ANIMAL ENTERPRISE ON STOLEN LAND: INDIGENOUS DISPOSSESSION AND THE ACCUMULATION OF CAPITAL

> May your lordship realize that if cattle are allowed, the Indians will be destroyed.
>
> —Antonio de Mendoza, first viceroy of New Spain, in a letter to King Charles I of Spain (Nibert 2013, 52)

Settler colonial states and populations consume animals at the highest rates in the world (OECD/FAO 2017). Settler colonization is constituted through capital's drive for nonhuman animal production, accumulation, use, and consumption. Extending Euro-settler agriculture onto Indigenous lands is central to mobilizing expansion and settler invasion and to disrupt Indigenous land-based relations and cosmologies (Anderson 2004, Lavallie 2016). In the context of Turtle Island, Yellowknives Dene scholar-activist Glen Coulthard describes the land as "a relationship based on the obligations we have to other people and the other-than-human relations that constitute the land itself" (Coulthard 2015). European livestock animals were rendered visible and perceptible across native land as evidence of terra nullius and the ostensible failure of Indigenous populations to properly cultivate the crops and domesticate animals to the full impulse of settler capital, absent "an economy predicated on the perpetual exploitation of the human and non-human world" (Coulthard 2013). Decolonization scholars have identified "the biopolitical and geopolitical management of people, land, flora and fauna within the 'domestic' borders of the imperial nation" as essential to the maintenance and advancement of the settler state (Tuck and Yang 2012, 4). Extending this analysis further, Belcourt argues that in settler capitalist formations, nonhuman animal bodies are reproduced simultaneously as subjects and weapons of colonization (Belcourt 2014). Colonization is always already anthropocentric. In these contexts, any concern for animal advocacy must attend to the centrality of settler formations and violence, and support Indigenous self-determination, resurgence and decolonization, rather than erase it.

While settler capital has rendered animal life in the Manichean terms of animality and racialization, prior to colonization nonhumans likely enjoyed more dynamic conceptions in Indigenous cosmologies and epistemologies. Historian Virginia Anderson has noted that in native languages such as Powhatan, Narragansett, and Massachusett, there exists no direct translation for the word *animal*. Early settlers collected words for distinct animal types or species, but no word for animal itself (Anderson 2004). This is suggestive of an ontology that recognized the nonhuman world in diverse relational terms beyond the reductive speciations of capital, humanity, and whiteness. Indeed, Anderson suggests that animals played far more significant social and cosmological roles in Indigenous life. Like Kim, Anderson sees the binary of animality deployed through settler conquest as a specific construction of Western ontology and political economy (Anderson 2004).

Many Indigenous ways of knowing nonhumans explicitly required the recognition of their agency. While Mi'kmaq scholar Margaret Robinson asserts that there is "no view on animals that is shared by all Aboriginal people," she suggests that in Mi'kmaq tradition, the "view of the world is rooted in our relationship with the other-than-human animals that share our territories"

(Robinson 2014, 672–673). She further extends the concept of personhood to nonhuman animals and argues that Mi'kmaq cosmology presents human and nonhuman life existing on a continuum, rather than in dichotomous relation in the logics of white supremacy and anthropocentrism. Reciprocity is articulated as an operational factor determining the relations between human and nonhumans, Robinson argues, and underpins traditional hunting practices in Mi'kmaq society. Notably, she elaborates this same principle in specific contexts in settler states to articulate a defense of Indigenous veganism and opposition to commercial fishing, sport hunting, the fur industry, and farmed animal industries (Robinson 2013, 2014). Thus, for Robinson, there is a clear continuity between the work of animal liberation and Indigenous sovereignty.

Using the optic of colonial subjectivity to understand animal relations in settler colonial contexts, as advanced by Belcourt, nonhuman agency becomes perceptible across colonial histories. Zoe Todd uses the human–fish relationships of northern Indigenous peoples to explore the dynamics of reciprocity and accountability in human and other-than-human relations in Indigenous life (Todd 2014, 2015, 2016). Drawing from the legal orders of northern Indigenous societies, she illustrates how, through relationships of mutual duty that extend throughout the human and other-than-human world, "resistance to colonial dispossession is articulated and mobilized not only through human means, but also through the bones, bodies, and movement of fish" and other nonhumans (Todd 2016). Zahara and Hird, directly drawing from Belcourt's analysis of animals as colonial subjects, show how both the Inuit peoples and the so-called trash animals (ravens and sled dogs) of Nunavut are assimilated and biopolitically managed populations (Zahara & Hird 2015).

The common thread in these understandings is that, however differentiated and complex, Indigenous cosmologies of the nonhuman, other-than-human, or inhuman are not structured through patterns of dominance or subjugation, or hierarchies of ontological value. Rather, they constitute a field of human and nonhuman relations that collectively constitute the land. Reciprocity is a recurring theme in what Vanessa Watts refers to "Place-Thought," which is "based upon the premise that land is alive and thinking and that humans and non-humans derive agency through the extensions of these thoughts" (Watts 2013, 21). Consequently, she identifies colonization as an attack on these Indigenous cosmologies, relations, and societies in which "non-human beings are active members," adding that "colonialism is operationalized through dismantling the essential categories of other societies" (Watts 2013, 23 and 31). Thus, settler colonial capital operates to disrupt Indigenous land-based relations, including non-hierarchical relationships with other-than-human life and respect for nonhuman agency.

In many ways, the story of settler colonization on Turtle Island is the story of animal agriculture and accumulation by dispossession. Karl Marx, in *Capital*, presents primitive accumulation as a historical impetus for the capital relation: "nothing other than the process which divorces the worker from the ownership of the conditions of his own labour" (Marx 1990, 874–875). For Marx, this event was the dispossession of peasants from their land and the enclosures of the commons that occurred in England, beginning in the late 15th century, which simultaneously served to generate a proletarian class and privatized land base for production. Since the publication of *Capital*, Marxist theorists have refined and updated the concept of primitive accumulation to account for the unfolding economic and material realities of the times. Lenin, Luxemburg, and Harvey have argued that the accumulative impulse of capital is the driver of imperialism, colonialism, and neo-colonial extractivism over the past half-century (Lenin 2011; Luxemburg 2003; Harvey 2004). Thus, it does not suffice to relegate the dispossessing register of accumulation to a particular, historical, and static antecedent. The process of dispossession is as ongoing and central to capitalism as accumulation itself. Indeed, to draw any logical distinction between capitalist exploitation and dispossession remains a dubious endeavor. Importantly, Harvey notes that the state acts as an interlocutor and arbiter in the development of capitalist accumulation and dispossession, having been pressed by capital into biopolitical and disciplinary functions. Capitalism is as critical to the reproduction of state power as the state is to the generation and accumulation of capital.

In his book *Red Skin, White Masks*, Glen Coulthard reconfigures Marx's original formulation of primitive accumulation to center the *ongoing dispossession of land and the destruction of land-based relations* as the principal feature of capitalism (Coulthard 2014). This contrasts with Marx and his interlocutors, who understand proletarianization—the violent divorce of the laborer from the means of production—as the primary feature of capital accumulation. Explaining the breadth and impact of this reformulation, Coulthard elaborates that "it's the theft not only of the material of land itself, but also a destruction of the social relationships that existed prior to capitalism violently sedimenting itself on Indigenous territories. And those social relations are often not only based on principles of egalitarianism but also deep reciprocity between people and with the other-than-human world" (Epstein 2015).

This understanding is in sync with the material reality of colonization on Turtle Island. As suggested by Marx, the pretext for primitive accumulation or accumulation by dispossession was need for more land for the growing industry of animal agriculture: "The rapid expansion of wool manufacturing in Flanders and the corresponding rise in the price of wool in England provided the direct impulse for these evictions" (Marx 1990, 878–879). It is no surprise then that animal agriculture immediately tracked English settlers onto Indigenous lands.

In her essential work, *Creatures of Empire*, Virginia Anderson provides an accounting of early English settlers' use of animals and English animal agriculture to dispossess Indigenous inhabitants of their land and to further colonial encroachment. Invoking the concept of *terra nullius*, settlers argued that Indigenous peoples had not adequately conquered or "improved" the land through their own practices and *animal* agricultural systems, so the land itself remained a commons, a wilderness unclaimed but vulnerable to enclosure and settlement through dispossession. In order to elaborate *terra nullius* in English legal and political economic terms, nonhuman animals, particularly cattle and pigs, were deployed throughout New England and the Chesapeake regions, effectively enclosing whatever land onto which the animals roamed. Nonhuman animals, then, were enlisted as the initial colonizers to establish an economic relationship between the English and the land. They also acted as ambassadors in the civilizing project of early English settler colonialism—the domesticated animals representing civilization, capitalism, and human labor. Dispossession and white settlement would follow. When these domesticated animals came into inevitable conflict with Indigenous inhabitants on their ancestral lands, the English would invoke the animals' legal status as chattel. Animals as capital served as material extensions of settler sovereignty. Any harm done to these animals by native populations would constitute property destruction and could be a pretext for more violence and further conquest (2004).

In *Animal Oppression & Human Violence*, David Nibert similarly suggests that "the oppression of pigs and other animals was deeply entangled with the oppression of Native Americans" (Nibert 2013, 53). In addition to the virtually perpetual theft of land that accompanied European animal agriculture, Spanish and English nonhuman animals were vectors of new diseases and were utilized in warfare in mass numbers against the restive Indigenous populations. The fecundity of European domesticated animal populations allowed for rapid proliferation following initial colonization and dispossession, and subsequently, the eradication of Indigenous crop supplies and subsistence base, leading to massive starvation. Through dispossession, starvation, disease, and military incursion, the invasion of European nonhuman animals furnished Indigenous lands and peoples as more vulnerable to colonization, extraction, and capital accumulation, from the tip of what is now Patagonia to the Canadian Arctic (Nibert 2013).

Thus, in settler colonial formations, animals as capital are both subjects and weapons, colonizers and colonized. As of 2015, over half of all land (1.3 billion acres) in what is now the contiguous United States was used for livestock or feed production (Glaser et al. 2015). For perspective, all Indigenous reservation land in the United States totals only 56.2 million acres

(BIA 2018). Animal enterprise on stolen land is operationalized toward dispossession and is a propellant of territorial expansion (Anderson 2004).

A SETTLER COLONIAL GAZE: ANIMAL ENTERPRISE ON A GLOBAL SCALE

As noted earlier, Morgensen argues that settler colonialism structures society on a global scale, beyond the physical borders of the settler state: "We must theorise settler colonialism as historical grounds for the globalisation of bio-power" (Morgensen 2011, 73). If the production of animality as an ontological figure is central to the cast of settler colonization and white supremacy and the political economy of animal enterprise is central to the material dispossession and liquidation of land and accumulation of capital, then it should follow that settler colonialism as a structure would reproduce animal enterprise on a mass global scale. This is precisely the case.

The *Agricultural Outlook*, published by the Organisation for Economic Co-operation and Development (OECD) and the Food and Agriculture Organization of the United Nations (FAO), assesses agricultural practices on a global scale. It uses commodity production and consumption patterns as metrics for agricultural production. One of those metrics is meat consumption per capita. The *Agricultural Outlook* notes that over the next ten years, both meat production and meat consumption rate are expected to increase on the global scale (OECD 2017). At the nation-specific scale, this effect is amplified in Western capitalist, white supremacist and settler colonial nation-states. Included in the top ten consumers of meat in the world are the United States, Australia, Argentina, Uruguay, Israel, Brazil, Chile, Canada, European Union, and New Zealand (OECD 2017). The consumptive patterns of the top ten constitute over 44% of all global meat consumption per capita. Notably, the only offender that is not a settler colonial state is the European Union, the member states of which clearly have violent legacies of colonization.

Similarly, the Lush Prize published *A Global View of Animal Experiments 2014* to assess the global status of animals in biomedical and scientific research. Much like the *Agricultural Outlook*, this paper indicates that the eight countries with the largest populations of animals used in research are all either European colonial powers or settler states like the United States, Australia, and Canada (Lush Prize 2014).

Thus, there seems a correlative link between the ongoing legacies of global capitalism, European imperialism and colonization, settler colonial formations, and expansion of animal enterprise and animal consumption.

BETWEEN VEGAN CAPITALISM
AND FARM SANCTUARIES: ANIMAL
ADVOCACY ON STOLEN LAND

Animal Rights, Recognition, Citizenship, and Assimilation

Animal advocates take for granted a rights-based approach that seeks to assimilate nonhuman animals into the moral and political spheres of human relationships and social systems. Donaldson and Kymlicka's *Zoopolis* (2011) perhaps represents the most sophisticated argument for the political recognition of animals within state and legal structures. They draw from multicultural liberal citizenship theory to elaborate animals as full subjects of settler state sovereignty and present this possibility as the logical extension of animal activism (Donaldson and Kymlicka 2011 and 2012). In Belcourt's words, "*Zoopolis* militarizes recognition as the hegemonic mode of animal activism" (2015, 6). Deploying Coulthard's critique of the colonial politics of recognition, Belcourt rejects this trend in animal advocacy "because it operates within—and consequently upholds—colonial infrastructures of settler citizenship and neoliberal subjecthood that re-orient animal bodies as the mundane surfaces on which settler colonialism is discursively reified" (2015, 6). In *Society Must be Defended*, Foucault argues that state power is contingent upon a dynamic of continuously producing and exterminating alterity—the racialized and animalized "other"—in an "ongoing and always incomplete cleansing of the social body . . . [that] structures social fields of action, guides political practices, and is realized through state apparatuses" (Lemke 2011, 43–44). The state manages external and internal threats as sites of heteropatriarchal, colonial, racialized, and anthropocentric violence at the impulse of capital and its shifting valorization requirements. Those expelled and excluded by capital from the sphere of (re)production are abandoned as wards of the state. Zahara and Hird argue that the state mobilizes this "colonial rhetoric of safety and security" against nonhumans using the same governance and population management *techniques* exercised against Indigenous peoples (2015, 183). Yet, for mainstream animal advocacy and scholarship, the state is understood to be a neutral actor and arbiter, so that in the case of animals, "the main source of injustice is exclusion from the political structure, not the coloniality of the structure itself; and so, recognition, not decolonization, is seen as being the remedy" (Kanji 2017, 73). Like Belcourt, Kanji argues that the assimilation of the animal into political and legal discourse will only reify the settler capitalist relations that render the animal the subject of (re)production, consumption, death, and erasure (2017). Jewish Arab scholar Esther Alloun cautions that in these contexts, "animal advocacy thereby follows the patterns set up by the settler colonial regime, with the type of advocacy on behalf of animals being shaped by the sides taken within the settler state (2017, 4). The work of critical trans scholar Dean Spade suggests that these multicultural and liberal politics of inclusion maintain power relations and population management through the operation of what he calls "administrative violence" (Spade 2015). Similarly, Kim has illustrated the limitations of neoliberalism and multiculturalism in the United States for addressing the intersections of structural racism and violence against animals. She argues that adherence to liberalism positions white settler animal advocates to profess color blindness when engaging with race and Indigeneity (2015).

Animal advocacy—vegan advocacy, specifically—is increasingly presented as a mainstreaming social phenomenon. More and more food processing and agricultural conglomerates are acquiring vegan and plant-based food products and manufacturers. Plant-based protein has significantly increased its market share over the past several years and is projected to account for as much as 30% of the meat market by 2050 (LuxResearch 2014; Cision 2017). Vegan food businesses are increasingly blurring with Silicon Valley technology firms and leveraging investment, finance, and venture capital from across the globe. Even those with highest influence in the system of global capital (e.g., Bill Gates) have generated economic support for growing vegan capitalism (Giammona 2017). In markets like Israel, Europe, and the United States, household names such as Domino's, Pizza Hut, and McDonald's are deploying vegan options on their menus (Zipkin 2017).

Superficially, these are cause for celebration among many animal advocates. They are interpreted as metrics for the efficacy of decades of fighting for animal rights and vegan education. Growth in vegan capitalism is not a metric for the lived experience and material reality of nonhuman animals, regardless of how heavily the movement leans on the trend to generate funds and deflect critical analysis. This is additionally challenging as animal advocacy organizations increasingly adopt the route of incorporation and assimilation into the nonprofit industrial complex (INCITE 2003; Glasser 2015). Glasser notes the recent proliferation of the "corporate incorporation" model of animal advocacy in the United States—strategies of social change that rely on assimilation into corporate formations (professionalization) while working with capitalist animal enterprises and the state. Rather than challenging the material underpinnings of animal exploitation, "moderate animal rights organization are neglecting, and even supporting the economic basis of nonhuman animal exploitation" (Glasser 2015, 369). Despite the cases made by large animal advocacy organizations that this type of animal and vegan advocacy has impacted meat consumption, Glasser establishes that prior fluctuations have more to do with market and environmental factors than any substantive impact from animal advocacy campaigns (2015). She concludes that the route of assimilation and professionalization is likely to support the structures of animal exploitation, rather than challenge them (2015).

In the North American context, Gelderloos argues that veganism has largely become a commodity fetish and is by nature ineffective at challenging the material conditions that generate animal enterprise (Gelderloos 2009). Given that a recent Faunalytics study concluded that there are five times as many former vegetarians and vegans as current ones (2014), Gelderloos's critique seems quite prescient. Stated simply: for Marx, the fetish character of the commodity is its capacity to conceal the real material relations between people (and the land) and project them as social relations between things (1993). In this epistemic field, vegan advocacy is actually immanent to capital. The social relations of dispossession and exploitation (both of humans and nonhumans), relations which constitute the substance of the value-form of the commodity, are reified via struggles over the commodity's natural form (e.g. a product of nonhuman animal bodies). In such a context, veganism as a consumer politics appears to directly challenge animal use, but in reality it cannot attend to the material relations of production concealed by the particulars of animal-based commodities. It mistakes the totality of capitalist relations in which human and nonhuman animals are embedded for the arbitrariness of particular use-values merely because those use-values take their shape from an animal. It cannot see the forest for the trees. It is apparent that vegan advocacy in this siloed formation can be mobilized to drive the accumulation of capital through destructive consumption patterns rather than challenging the material and the economic dimensions of animal enterprise.

Such vegan advocacy work has been severed from the liberation of animals by the mechanisms of capital and colonization. Despite the professionalization of animal organizations and expanding market capitalization of plant-based foods, existing empirical data suggests that the lot of nonhuman animals and other-than-human relations is likely to worsen as capital accumulation lumbers on. In practice, the settler animal "rights" movement either implicitly or explicitly supports the sovereignty of the settler state, the hegemony of whiteness and the colonial-capital relation replicating the very social formations that give rise to the domination of nonhuman animals (Robinson 2013, 2014; Belcourt 2014; Wadiwel 2015).

Settler Animal Advocacy and the Maintenance of Empire

> It was the fervent hope of the friends of humanity that whenever the flag of the United States was planted, the dumb animals might share in the benefits of an advancing civilization.

—Alfred Wagstaff, president of the ASPCA, 1907 (Davis 2013, 565)

By primarily operating through an "optic of cruelty" (Kim 2015) or a liberal politics of state recognition, settler animal advocates run the risk of re-inscribing the state sovereignty on the body of nonhuman animals and Indigenous peoples. A deeper interrogation into the history of animal advocacy shows that beyond shoring up support for vegan capitalism, animal activists have long been engaged in other harmful organizing and campaigns that reproduce colonial power. Erasing Indigenous cosmologies, relations, and obligations concerning nonhuman beings, settler animal advocates have cast Indigenous hunters "backwards" or "savage" and have reproduced the logic of settler colonialism twofold. First, by erasing Indigenous ontology, epistemology, and cosmology, they are participating in the logic of elimination. Second, by characterizing the behavior of Indigenous people as uncivilized, they are utilizing the logics of animalization and racialization that harm both racialized humans and nonhuman animals. Despite these concerns, these patterns of advocacy persist. My goal here is to reveal that pattern and its historical roots in empire-building and the settler colonial project.

Western animal advocacy can be traced to the legislation of the first anti-cruelty laws in the United Kingdom and the United States and their respective colonial territories in the nineteenth and early twentieth centuries (Deckha 2013; David 2013). Maneesha Deckha's historical and legal analysis of anti-cruelty legislation reveals the imperial underpinnings of the legal framework in the context of the larger civilizational discourse. She argues that anti-cruelty statutes and common law interpretations have never been effective at preventing violence toward animals, yet they are effective at criminalizing marginalized and racialized populations within the scheme of empire-building (Deckha 2013). Davis likewise implicates the American Society for the Prevention of Cruelty to Animals (ASPCA) and other anti-cruelty societies for their role in the colonial expansion and nation-building. Animal advocacy organizations were eager to legislate against cockfighting in Cuba, Puerto Rico, and the Philippines, a practice long understood to be an expression of popular identity in contrast to Spanish bullfighting. This endeavor was swiftly taken up by occupying military forces, who believed cockfighting to be an aberrant and idle activity, the abolition of which would increase the productive labor of the colonized populations (Davis 2013). This may be one the earliest examples of the animal advocacy movement operating in the service of colonial subjugation and capital accumulation.

As both Deckha and Davis illustrate, the hegemony of the state and capital are excluded from questions of violence toward animals. The actual impact of legislation and its enforcement against colonized populations "indicate that the focus on animal cruelty was primarily about legitimating colonialism rather than addressing animal suffering in its multitude of forms" (Deckha 2013, 524). The legalizing framework of early animal advocacy provided the pretext for a violent civilizational discourse, imperial ambitions, dispossession, and eliminating logic of state racism. Contrasted with the occupying settler state's massive structural and institutional violence against animals *and* its ability to enact, interpret, and transgress animal cruelty laws, this dynamic constitutes a *state of exception* that structures the sovereign power of the settler state. In this scheme of ostensible civilizing progress, nonhuman animals, racialized populations, and Indigenous populations are rendered as *bare life* (Agamben 1998) and the relationships of the land as *bare habitance* (Rifkin 2009), setting the stage for ongoing dispossession. Given their (non)relation to the engine of capitalist production via wage labor, it might be useful to consider these populations and relations (human and nonhuman) as forms of state-managed 'wageless life' (Denning 2010). This punitive juridical framework is repeated throughout the history of settler animal advocacy.

In the late 1980s and early 1990s, Exxon manufactured a conflict between animal advocates and the Chippewa of northern Wisconsin. The Chippewa had been organizing their community to defend against Exxon's mining interest since the 1970s, asserting that their treaty rights to hunt and fish preserved the land from industrial encroachment. However, Exxon diverted attention toward the Chippewa's traditional practice of spearfishing and was successful in getting animal rights activists to target the Chippewa while they desperately tried to defend their land. Unfortunately, attempts by the Chippewa to redirect animal and environmental activists' concern back toward industrial mining failed (Smith 1999).

Only a few years later, a similar struggle occurred off the shores of Neah Bay. Several well-known animal advocacy organizations, including Sea Shepherd Conservation Society (SSCS), mobilized to protest the resurgence of Makah whaling in the late 1990s. Critical here is the evidence that the Makah Nation was not united around the tribal government's position on whaling, or its political motivations, with many Makah elders opposing the whale hunt (Kim 2015). Instead of organizing a coalition politics to support these elders and center Indigenous perspectives and self-determination, activists allied with right-wing political figures (2015). Asserting that the issue had nothing to do with race, SSCS openly organized with Jack Metcalf, a conservative politician opposed to Makah whaling, on specifically the grounds of dissolving treaty rights (2015). Other organizations simply leaned on color blindness to ignore the legacies of colonialism and questions of food access and sovereignty for Indigenous populations.

More recent conflicts have emerged in Canada. The Harper administration attempted to leverage sympathy for Inuit communities in the north, conflating their sovereignty with the commercial seal hunt to shore support to lift the 2010 EU Commercial Seal Hunt Ban, despite this ban already making an exemption for Inuit hunters, which comprises only three percent of the market.

Nevertheless, as argued by Powell (2014), animal advocates took the bait and engaged in organizing against the Inuit community while the Conservative administrative used them both to further its agenda. When some Inuit activists responded with the "Sealfie" hashtag, posting images of seal fur use, seal hunts, and dead seals in attempt to show the possibility of respect and reciprocity in traditional hunts, they received death threats from animal rights activists (Zahara and Hird 2015). Inuk activist Tanya Tagaq identified this settler demand for dietary assimilation in the context of poverty as a "mini version of colonialism" that effectively divorces Indigenous people from specific means of subsistence adapted to a particular place (Tagaq 2014). As a consequence of this colonial incursion and threat to sovereignty, she suggests that high suicide rates in the Arctic and violence against Indigenous women are connected to the history of settler attempts to stop traditional seal hunting (Tagaq 2014).

In 2012, the Haudenosaunee asserted their treaty right to a traditional deer hunt in Short Hills Provincial Park in southern Ontario. The Haudenosaunee deer hunt was legally granted by the Albany Deed of 1701 but made materially necessary through land theft and the loss of traditional agriculture. Hunting was one exercise of food sovereignty left (Powell 2013). Yet settler animal rights activists quickly took issue and organized a campaign to stop the hunt, which is ongoing as of this writing. Animal advocacy's maintenance of settler colonial-capitalist relations operates through more than animal rights activist opposition to Indigenous hunting. It also discursively erases native populations through settler moves to innocence.

A salient example is the "vegan-washing" of the Israeli colonization of Palestine (Alloun 2017). Vegan-washing is one of the more recent manifestations of the larger Brand Israel propaganda campaign. Brand Israel mobilizes the West's latent colonial, racist, xenophobic, orientalist, and jingoist mentality to rebrand Israel as a politically progressive nation (White 2010). Specifically, it alleges that Israel is making strides in the arenas of feminism and LGBTQI advocacy (pink-washing) or environmental protection and climate policy (green-washing), in an effort to undermine and stifle the momentum of the international Boycott, Divestment, and Sanctions campaign (White 2010). Brand Israel is a correlative expression of what Tuck and Yang identify as "settler moves to innocence," which are

> those strategies or positionings that attempt to relieve the settler of feelings of guilt or responsibility without giving up land or power or privilege, without having to change much at all. . . . Yet settler moves to innocence are hollow, they only serve the settler. (Tuck and Yang 2012, 10)

According to Alloun (2017, 11), the trappings of innocence are self-evident in the Zionist context: "Jewish activists foreground animal rights as a politics-free utopia where activists can think and act as if racism, (hetero)sexism and settler colonialism do not exist. The 'beauty' of animal rights is being used to obscure the violence of politics and of the Israeli settler state." Brand Israel recasts settlers as deserving and capable and Palestinians as undeserving and unable. By associating Israel with pillars of the Western liberal gaze (i.e., LGBTQ advocacy, ecological sustainability, gender equality), the aim is to divorce settlers from notions of colonization and violence, replacing them with notions of progress, development, and virtue—*civilization*. In the process, settlers become married to their own destiny and righteousness while furthering the structural and material violence of settlement, occupation, and eradication. So, rather than securing meaningful justice for marginalized and oppressed populations, including nonhuman animals, rebranding through vegan-washing secures only the future of the settler state.

The Brand Israel campaign is securing that future by leveraging animal advocacy. Co-opting Israel's radical past of anti-colonial animal liberation activism and assimilating it into the body of the nation-state, Israeli institutions and political figures, including the Israeli Defense Forces and Prime Minister Benjamin Netanyahu, are working to soften their image as brutal occupiers by pointing to purported advances being made for animals in Israel (Shalif 2009; Ravid 2013; and Alloun 2017). These dubious claims include an allegedly high vegan population, vegan accessories in the Israel Defense Forces, vegan options in corporate chains like Domino's Pizza and Pizza Hut and cities like Tel Aviv becoming global tourist capitals for vegan cuisine (Strauss 2016; Abunimah 2012c; Cohen 2015; The Vegan Woman 2015; and Kashmin 2015). Nowhere is it mentioned that Israel's occupation is responsible for mass animal death through militarization, massive livestock production, pollution and industrial waste, and destruction of the land and life as a strategy of war and settler colonization (Ali 2015; World Bank 2017a; Sabawi 2011; Lorber 2012). Israel's annual carbon dioxide emissions are 14.7 times higher than Gaza and the West Bank combined (World Bank 2017b). Israel has by far the highest meat consumption per capita of any country in the region (Powell 2015). Israel has some of the highest meat consumption per capita in the world (OECD/FAO 2017). Some haven for animals indeed.

The last example I will explore is a form of animal advocacy that functions both discursively as a settler move to innocence and materially as dispossession through the logic of *terra nullius*. Donaldson and Kymlicka suggest that farmed animal sanctuaries (FASes) are central to the animal advocacy movement in North America: "The animal sanctuary movement is rapidly expanding and represents an important dimension of activist response to human violence against non-human animals" (Donaldson and Kymlicka 2015, 50). FASes, they assert, shape the profile of the animal advocacy movement as a whole and *prefigure* alternative modes of human–animal relations.

While still small, FASes have proliferated since the 1980s, when Farm Sanctuary opened in New York (2015). Now there are over 50 similar models operating in North America. While the work they do is important for the rescued animals, Donaldson and Kymlicka believe that the model is limited by its refugee-advocacy framing and is reduced to paternalizing the animals under care (2015). While not overtly drawing the connection, they suggest that FASes operate as disciplinary institutions, such as psychiatric hospitals or residential care facilities for the elderly (2015).

For these reasons, they argue that the FAS model does not sufficiently respect the animal inhabitants' agency and range of wants and needs. They propose an alternative model that rests on their conception of animal agency, community, and citizenship. The pillars of this model are *belonging, absence of fixed hierarchical relationships, self-determination, citizenship, dependent agency, scaffolded choices* and *reconfigured spaces* (2015). It is this last point that I wish to focus on. Donaldson and Kymlicka argue that unfettered space—land—is essential for animals to realize their agency. They suggest that by blurring the boundaries between the domestic animals' space and the land relations surrounding sanctuaries, the animals can more fully enact their agency and sense of place (2015).

Substantively, this framework is eerily similar to the rationale of early English settlers who deployed their domestic animals onto Indigenous lands to tease out the relationship between animality, wilderness, domestication, Indigeneity, and civilization. Domestic animals on the land served a role in the civilizing project and as evidence of *terra nullius*. Donaldson and Kymlicka suggest that FASes and intentional communities prefigure their *Zoopolis*, and the notions of citizenship in these communities still rely on liberal frameworks. Land is also central to the continued proliferation of FASes, but enclosure and privatization seem to have already been assumed. Domestic animals continue to transform and re-empty the land through advocacy for their denizenship and citizenship. For these reasons, it seems that the current FAS movement and the alternative suggested by Donaldson and Kymlicka foreclose the possibility of a decolonized future for human–animal relations and take for granted settler/animal futurity on Indigenous lands. We can acknowledge alternative models of refuge for nonhumans that better prefigure the decolonization of land and animality, while at the same time rejecting the framework upon which the current trend of FASes rests. It is rendered tangible and operationalized only through the ongoing functions of settler colonial-capitalist relations.

ANIMAL LIBERATION AND THE "STRATEGIC CENTRALITY" OF SETTLER COLONIALISM

I turn finally to the question of organizing alternative models for animal liberation that situate the movement in a settler colonial context. Often the most visible and powerful manifestations of the animal advocacy movement in North America lack attention to the deeply transformative possibilities of seating animal liberation organizing in the framework of anti-colonial and anti-capitalist praxis. The critical work of environmental and food justice advocates and BIPOC vegans and animal liberationists is overlooked, erased, or appropriated by the settler animal advocacy movement at large (Harper 2013; Robinson & Corman 2016; and Ko & Ko 2017). Organizations such as Black Vegans Rock, Food Empowerment Project, and Coalition of Vegan Activists of Color have long been engaging the relationship between white supremacy, anti-Blackness colonization, veganism, and animal advocacy. Yet material resources are accumulated and consolidated into vastly larger organizations unwilling to address critical questions of race, gender, and power (Animal Charity Evaluators 2017). Radical or anarchist animal liberation groups may purportedly reject capitalism and profess "intersectionality" as their modality of animal advocacy, but they struggled to make progress in appropriately identifying and challenging capitalism, colonialism, and white supremacy as an intrinsic praxis of the movement (Harper & Ornelas 2013; jones 2013, Harper 2015).

First, it is necessary to distinguish decolonization from intersectionality. Patricia Hill Collins suggests that the term *intersectionality* is confronted with existential anxiety. It is simultaneously operating in discourse and praxis "as a field of study that is situated within the power relations that it studies; (b) . . . an analytical strategy that provides new angles of vision on social phenomena; and (c) . . . as critical praxis that informs social justice projects" (Collins 2015, 3). So, although intersectionality emerged as an analytical tool for thinking about the matrix of juridical and political economic power and relationships, it is also recognized as a strategy for social movement organization. While there are challenges in defining the scope of intersectional analysis, broadly "intersectionality references the critical insight that race, class, gender, sexuality, ethnicity, nation, ability, and age operate not as unitary, mutually exclusive entities, but as reciprocally constructing phenomena that in turn shape complex social inequalities" (Collins 2015, 2).

Harper (2013) and jones (2013) suggest that the white settler animal advocacy movement as a whole tends to *perform* intersectionality, if acknowledging its existence at all. Harper further argues that as white-led animal activism assimilates intersectional discourse in a reductive manner to further its animal-centric optic, this performance is tantamount to tokenization (Harper and Ornelas 2013). Belcourt points out that this ethic of "total liberation" renders distinct experiences of oppression as commensurable (2015). This dynamic tends to draw analogies across lived experiences, focusing on sameness rather than difference and eliding the social positionality of the players, to express the specific oppression of nonhuman animals in distinctly human, racial, and gendered terms. As Kim argues, the analogy model relies on the passive omission of ongoing specificity, singularity, and lived realities of racialization, colonization, or gendered and sexual violence (2015). It also forecloses the subjective experience of animality on its own terms, erasing the singular role of animality and animal enterprise in white supremacy and the setter colonial project.

Considering these current "definitional dilemmas" of intersectionality (Collins 2015), it important to assess decolonization on its own terms. In the article "Decolonization Is Not a Metaphor," Tuck and Yang assert that when they "write about decolonization, we are not offering it as a metaphor; it is not an approximation of other experiences of oppression" (Tuck and Yang 2012, 3). Decolonization is unsettling and challenges the *differences* between settlers and the native population. In practice, in white animal advocacy communities, intersectionality then risks becoming a "move to innocence" and "colonial equivocation" that does not attend to the singularity of settler colonial relations or the Indigenous repatriation of land and life that is the teleological raison d'être of decolonization (2012). Belcourt argues that intersectionality "stabilizes the settler identity," while decolonization "*cannot* exist within these fleshy and architectural spaces of whiteness through which Indigenous politico-economic structures are anachronized and the totality of decolonization is rendered unimaginable" (2015, 2–3). Thus, an intersectional framework for animal liberation organizing is not only insufficient to address settler colonial power, it has the potential to concretize that power and reproduce the violence of animality that constitutes it.

Instead, I adopt the use of "strategic centrality," as suggested by Olson (2009) and expanded upon by Lewis (2015, 2017), as a framework for animal liberation organizing that centers anti-colonial solidarity. Olson argues that anarchist and anti-capitalist movements need to develop focus on anti-racist organizing and solidarity. Anarchism in the United States "must overcome an analysis of white supremacy that understands racism as but one 'hierarchy' among others. Racial oppression is not simply one of many forms of domination; it has played a central role in the development of capitalism in the United States" (Olson 2009). Consequently, for anarchists, struggle against racial domination is characterized by a "strategic centrality" to the power of the state and capital (2009). Lewis extends

Olson's concept further and argues that all settler movements, especially anarchist movements, in settler colonial contexts need to attend to settler colonialism, Indigenous dispossession, white supremacy, and the regime of capital in order to sufficiently challenge the structures of domination in those contexts: "There can be no resistance on stolen land without resistance to settler colonialism" (Lewis 2017, 479). Lewis moves the strategic center for anarchist resistance from white supremacy broadly to settler colonialism specifically. Lewis further argues that the anarchist concept of *prefiguration*, or "infrastructures of resistance," needs to be reconfigured on Indigenous terms. Solidarity for anarchist settlers should then defer to Indigenous political systems and laws, as Indigenous resurgence is inherently prefigurative and a potentially fertile site of meaningful engagement for other social movements (2017).

As argued before, the structure of animality and political economy of animal enterprise are co-constitutive of settler colonization, whiteness and capital accumulation. Whiteness, and racialization were critical to the formation of animality and nonhuman abjection. Dispossession, accumulation, land theft, and colonization utilized animal bodies as both subjects and objects of settler colonial power. Settler colonialism has propelled animal enterprise into unprecedented levels of accumulation. While intersectional animal advocacy is justifiable and necessarily attends to the complex taxonomies of power, knowledge, structural violence, oppression, and domination, it is insufficient to challenge the material relations of settler colonial capitalism. In these contexts, animal liberation organizing must strategically center resistance to settler colonialism and the settler state, Indigenous decolonization and repatriation, and solidarity with Indigenous resurgence and land defense. There can be no animal liberation on stolen land without resistance to the settler colonial formation. Settler colonialism must be the context for all further engagement and organizing.

CONCLUSION

In this chapter, I have argued why radical animal liberation advocates should attend to the specific structure of settler colonial-capitalism and its generative context on stolen land. Capital, whiteness, and settler colonization render the nonhuman animal visible and perceptible, and thus exploitable, to settlers and industry through the co-constituting logics of elimination, racialization, and animalization. Instrumentalized in the processes of accumulation and dispossession, nonhuman animals are critically engaged as vectors of settler colonization and sites of colonial subjectivity. Animal enterprise is made material on stolen land through conquest and profitable through the rapid capital accumulation of the settler state. As established by Anderson, Belcourt, Kanji, Alloun, Gossett, Powell, and others, settler colonialism and white supremacy are always already anthropocentric; animal use industries are vital to the operation of dispossession and colonization; and settler colonialism is a central social form in the maintenance of animal enterprise on stolen land.

I then argued that although animal enterprise figures necessarily into the narratives of colonization, resistance to animal enterprise is not itself anti-colonial or supportive of Indigenous sovereignty. Most forms of animal advocacy potentially reproduce the process of colonization by operating from a single-optic analysis of animal cruelty and rights, while failing to define the settler colonial-capitalist roots of animal exploitation in the context of stolen lands. Furthermore, I set out to challenge "intersectional" animal advocacy as laudable but insufficient for addressing the irreducible and incommensurate profile of white supremacy, settler colonialism and global capitalism.

Settler animal liberation advocates, activists, and organizers need to identify the settler colonial roots of animal enterprise on stolen land, and the centrality of Indigenous dispossession and white supremacy to the operations of animality and animal exploitation and harm. But naming the power is not enough. Alloun (2017, 3, emphasis added) asserts that, "human-animal relationships constitute one more dimension in which settler colonialism is expressed, engaged with, but also *resisted*." Settler animal activists need to meaningfully engage with Indigenous solidarity while deferring the nature and scope to Indigenous title, sovereignty, and political process. Settler animal activists need to reconfigure their understandings of nonhuman life, ontology and cosmology, the political economy of animal enterprise, and the movement dynamics of animal advocacy to *prefigure Indigenous resurgence as a site of critical animal liberation praxis*.

REFERENCES

Abunimah, Ali. 2012. "Israel's Killer Vegetarians (and Vegans). A Brief History." *The Electronic Intifada*. https://electronicintifada.net/blogs/ali-abunimah/israels-killer-vegetarians-and-vegans-brief-history.

Agamben, Giorgio. 1998. *Homo Sacer: Sovereign Power and Bare Life*. Stanford: Stanford University Press.

Ali, Muna. 2015. "The Animal Victims of the Gaza Bombings." https://pal.ps/en/2015/02/18/the-animal-victims-of-the-gaza-bombings-2/.

Alloun, Esther. 2017. "'That's the Beauty of It, It's Very Simple!' Animal Rights and Settler Colonialism in Palestine—Israel." *Settler Colonial Studies*, 1–16. doi:10.1080/2201473X.2017.1414138.

Alvarez, Linda. n.d. "Colonization, Food, and the Practice of Eating." http://www.foodispower.org/colonization-food-and-the-practice-of-eating/.

Anderson, Kay. 2000. "'The Beast Within': Race, Humanity, and Animality." *Environment and Planning D: Society and Space, 18*(3): 301–320.

Anderson, Virginia D. 2004. *Creatures of Empire: How Domestic Animals Transformed Early America*. New York: Oxford University Press.

Animal Charity Evaluators. 2017. "Recommended Charities." https://animalcharityevaluators.org/donation-advice/recommended-charities/.

Belcourt, Billy-Ray. 2014. "Animal Bodies, Colonial Subjects: (Re)Locating Animality in Decolonial Thought." *Societies, 5*(1): 1–11.

Bureau of Indian Affairs. n.d. "Frequently Asked Questions." https://www.bia.gov/frequently-asked-questions.

Cision. 2017. "Plant Based Foods Sales Experience 8.1 Percent Growth over Past Year." http://www.prweb.com/releases/2017/09/prweb14683840.htm.

Cohen, Tova. 2015. "Why Domino's Only Sells Vegan Pizza in Israel." *The Christian Science Monitor*. https://www.csmonitor.com/World/Middle-East/2015/0721/Why-Domino-s-only-sells-vegan-pizza-in-Israel.

Collins, Patricia H. 2015. "Intersectionality's Definitional Dilemmas." *Annual Review of Sociology*, 41: 1–20.

Coulter, Kendra. 2016. *Animals, Work, and the Promise of Interspecies Solidarity*. New York: Palgrave Macmillan.

Coulthard, Glen. 2013. "For Our Nations to Live, Capitalism Must Die." *Nations Rising*. http://nationsrising.org/for-our-nations-to-live-capitalism-must-die/.

Coulthard, Glen. 2014. *Red Skin, White Masks: Rejecting the Colonial Politics of Recognition*. Minneapolis: University of Minnesota Press.

Coulthard, Glen. 2015. "Land Is a Relationship: In Conversation with Glen Coulthard on Indigenous Nationhood." Interview by Harsha Walia. *Rabble*. http://rabble.ca/columnists/2015/01/land-relationship-conversation-glen-coulthard-on-indigenous-nationhood.

Davis, Janet M. 2013. "Cockfight Nationalism: Blood Sport and the Moral Politics of American Empire and Nation Building." *American Quarterly, 65*(3): 549–574.

Deckha, Maneesha. 2006. "The Salience of Species Difference for Feminist Theory." *Hasting's Women's Law Journal, 17*(1): 1–38.

Deckha, Maneesha. 2013. "Welfarist and Imperial: The Contributions of Anticruelty Laws to Civilizational Discourse." *American Quarterly, 65*(3): 515–548.

Denning, Michael. 2010. "Wageless Life." *New Left Review 66*: 79–97.

Donaldson, Sue, and Will Kymlicka. 2015. "Farmed Animal Sanctuaries: The Heart of the Movement." *Politics and Animals, 1*(1): 50–75.

Epstein, Andrew Bard. 2015. "The Colonialism of the Present: An Interview with Glen Coulthard." *Jacobin Magazine*. https://www.jacobinmag.com/2015/01/indigenous-left-glen-coulthard-interview/.

Faunalytics. 2014. "Study of Current and Former Vegetarians and Vegans." https://faunalytics.org/wp-content/uploads/2015/06/Faunalytics_Current-Former-Vegetarians_Full-Report.pdf.

Federici, Silvia. 2014. *Caliban and the Witch: Women, the Body and Primitive Accumulation*. New York: Autonomedia.

Foucault, Michel. 2013. *Society Must Be Defended: Lectures at the College De France, 1975–1976*. English Series Editor: Arnold Davidson. New York: Picador.

Gelderloos, Peter. 2008. "Veganism Is a Consumer Activity." *The Anarchist Library*. https://theanarchistlibrary.org/library/peter-gelderloos-veganism-is-a-consumer-activity.

Giammona, Craig. 2017. "Bill Gates-Backed Vegan Burgers Hit Mainstream with Safeway Deal." *Bloomberg*. https://www.bloomberg.com/news/articles/2017-05-25/bill-gates-backed-vegan-burgers-hit-mainstream-with-safeway-deal.

Glaser, Christine, Chuck Romaniello, and Karyn Moskowitz. 2015. "Costs and Consequences: The Real Price of Livestock Grazing on America's Public Lands." *Center for Biological Diversity* 44. http://www.biologicaldiversity.org/programs/public_lands/grazing/pdfs/CostsAndConsequences_01-2015.pdf.

Glasser, Carol L. 2014. "Opportunity Fields and Animal Rights: Is Corporate Incorporation a Route to Change?" In *Animal Subjects 2.0*, edited by Jodey Castricano and Lauren Corman, 369–404. Waterloo, Canada: Wilfrid Laurier University Press.

Gossett, Che. 2015. "Blackness, Animality, and the Unsovereign." *Verso*. https://www.versobooks.com/blogs/2228-che-gossett-blackness-animality-and-the-unsovereign.

Harper, Amie Louise. 2013. *Vegan Consciousness and the Commodity Chain: On the Neoliberal, Afrocentric, and Decolonial Politics of "Cruelty-Free."* PhD diss. University of California, Davis.

Harper, Amie Louise. 2015. "The Vegan Praxis of Black Lives Matter." Presented at the 2015 Resistance Ecology Conference, Portland, OR.

Harper, Amie Louise, and Lauren Ornelas. 2013. "Animal Liberation, Tokenizing 'Intersectionality,' and Resistance Ecology." Presented at the 2013 Resistance Ecology Conference, Portland, OR.

Harvey, David. 2004. "The 'New' Imperialism: Accumulation by Dispossession." *Socialist Register*, 40: 63–87.

Hribal, Jason. 2011. *Fear of the Animal Planet: The Hidden History of Animal Resistance*. Oakland: AK Press.

jones, pattrice. 2013. "Intersectionality in Theory and Practice." Presented at the International Animal Rights Conference, Luxembourg, September 2013.

Kanji, Azeezah. 2017. "Colonial Animality: Canadian Colonialism and the Human-Animal Relationship." *Critical Epistemologies of Global Politics*, 63–78.

Kim, Claire Jean. 2015. *Dangerous Crossings*. New York: Cambridge University Press.

Ko, Aph, and Syl Ko. 2017. *APHRO-ISM: Essays on Pop Culture, Feminism, and Black Veganism from Two Sisters*. Brooklyn, NY: Lantern Books.

Kymlicka, Will, and Sue Donaldson. 2011. *Zoopolis: A Political Theory of Animal Rights*. New York: Oxford University Press.

Kymlicka, Will, and Sue Donaldson. 2014. "Animal Rights, Multiculturalism, and the Left." *Journal of Social Philosophy*, 45(1): 116–135.

Lavallie, Jaydene. 2016. "The Colonial Flight of the Honeybee." *Fake Vegan*. https://fakevegan.com/2016/04/05/the-colonial-flight-of-the-honeybee/.

Legge, Melissa Marie, and Rasha Taha. 2017. "'Fake Vegans': Indigenous Solidarity and Animal Liberation Activism." *Journal of Indigenous Social Development.* 6(1): 63–81.

Lemke, Thomas, Monica J. Casper, and Lisa Jean Moore. 2011. *Biopolitics: An Advanced Introduction.* New York: NYU Press.

Lenin, Vladimir Il'ich. 2011. *Imperialism: The Highest Stage of Capitalism.* Martino Publishing.

Lewis, Adam Gary. 2015. "Anti-State Resistance on Stolen Land: Settler Colonialism, Settler Identity and the Imperative of Anarchist Decolonization." *New Developments in Anarchist Studies*, 145–186.

Lewis, Adam Gary. 2017. "Imagining Autonomy on Stolen Land: Settler Colonialism, Anarchism and the Possibilities of Decolonization." *Settler Colonial Studies*, 7(4): 1–22.

Lorber, Ben. 2012. "Israel's Environmental Colonialism and Eco-apartheid." *Links: International Journal of Socialist Renewal.* http://links.org.au/node/2956.

Lush Prize. 2014. "Global View of Animal Experiments." http://www.lushprize.org/wp-content/uploads/Global_View_of-Animal_Experiments_2014.pdf.

Luxemburg, Rosa. 2003. *The Accumulation of Capital.* New York: Routledge.

LuxResearch. 2014. "WhoPea: Plant Sources Are Changing the Protein Landscape." https://members.luxresearchinc.com/research/report/16091.

Kashmin, Roni. 2015. "Two New Reasons Why Tel Aviv Is a Vegan Culinary Capital." *Haaretz.* https://www.haaretz.com/jewish/food/1.681800.

Marx, Karl. 1993. *Capital, Volume I.* London: Penguin Classics.

Mbembe, Joseph-Achille. 2003. Necropolitics. *Public Culture*, 15(1): 11–40.

Morgensen, Scott Lauria. 2011. "The Biopolitics of Settler Colonialism: Right Here, Right Now." *Settler Colonial Studies*, 1(1): 52–76.

Nibert, David A. 2013. *Animal Oppression & Human Violence: Domesecration, Capitalism, and Global Conflict.* New York: Columbia University Press.

OECD. 2017. "Meat Consumption (Indicator)." https://data.oecd.org/agroutput/meat-consumption.htm.

OECD/FAO. 2017. "OECD-FAO Agricultural Outlook 2017–2026." Paris: OECD Publishing. http://dx.doi.org/10.1787/agr_outlook-2017-en.

Olson, Joel. 2009. "The Problem with Infoshops and Insurrection: US Anarchism, Movement Building, and the Racial Order." In *Contemporary Anarchist Studies*, 51–61. New York: Routledge.

Powell, Dylan. 2013. "Don't Want a Traditional Deer Hunt? Then Start Returning Stolen Land." https://dylanxpowell.wordpress.com/2013/11/19/dont-want-a-traditional-deer-hunt-then-start-returning-land/.

Powell, Dylan. 2014a. "An Animal Liberationist Perspective on #Sealfie and the Inuit Seal Hunt." https://dylanxpowell.wordpress.com/2014/04/02/an-animal-liberationist-perspective-on-sealfie-and-the-inuit-seal-hunt/.

Powell, Dylan. 2014b. "Veganism in the Occupied Territories: Anti-Colonialism and Animal Liberation." https://dylanxpowell.wordpress.com/2014/03/01/veganism-in-the-occupied-territories-anti-colonialism-and-animal-liberation/.

Powell, Dylan. 2015. "The Myth of Vegan Progress in Israel." https://dylanxpowell.wordpress.com/2015/02/15/the-myth-of-vegan-progress-in-israel/.

Ravid, Barak. 2013. "Could Netanyahu Be Turning Vegan?" *Haaretz*. https://www.haaretz.com/blogs/diplomania/.premium-1.552142.

Rifkin, Mark. 2009. "Indigenizing Agamben: Rethinking Sovereignty in Light of the 'Peculiar' Status of Native Peoples." *Cultural Critique*, 73(1): 88–124.

Robinson, Margaret. 2013. "Veganism and Mi'kmaq Legends: Feminist Natives Do Eat Tofu." *The Canadian Journal of Native Studies*, 33(1): 189–196.

Robinson, Margaret. 2014. "Animal Personhood in Mi'kmaq Perspective." *Societies*, 4: 672–688.

Robinson, Margaret, and Corman, Lauren. 2016. "All My Relations: Interview with Margaret Robinson." In Jodey Castricano and Lauren Corman (eds.), *Animal Subjects 2.0.*, 229–247.

Sabawi, Samah. 2011. "Palestine: The Environmental Impact of Israel's Military Occupation." *Links: International Journal of Socialist Renewal*. Retrieved from http://links.org.au/node/2574.

Shalif, Ilan. 2009. Interview by Zabalaza Anarchist Communist Front. http://www.anarkismo.net/article/12618.

Smith, Andrea. 2006. "Heteropatriarchy and the Three Pillars of White Supremacy: Rethinking Women of Color Organizing." In *Color of Violence: The INCITE! Anthology*, 66–73. Cambridge, MA: South End Press.

Smith, Justine. 1999. "Native Sovereignty and Social Justice: Moving towards an Inclusive Social Justice Framework." In Jael Silliman and Ynestra King (eds.), *Dangerous Intersections: Feminist Perspective on Population, Environment and Development*, 202–213, Boston, MA: South End Press.

Spade, Dean. 2015. *Normal Life: Administrative Violence, Critical Trans Politics, and the Limits of Law*. Duke University Press.

Strauss, Jennifer. 2016. "Israel's Booming Vegan Culture." *The Culture Trip*. https://theculturetrip.com/middle-east/israel/articles/israel-s-booming-vegan-culture/.

Tagaq, Tayna. 2014. "Eating Seal Meat Is a Vital Part of Life in My Community." *Vice Munchies*. https://munchies.vice.com/en_us/article/z4gdjy/eating-seal-meat-is-a-vital-part-of-life-in-my-community.

Tallbear, Kim. 2011a. "Opening Comments." Presented at *Symposium: Why the Animal? Queer Animalities, Indigenous Naturecultures, and Critical Race Approaches to Animal Studies, UC Berkeley*. http://www.kimtallbear.com/1/post/2011/05/conference-why-the-animal-queer-animalities-indigenous-naturecultures-and-critical-race-approaches-to-animal-studies-april-12th-uc-berkeley.html.

Tallbear, Kim. 2011b. "Why Interspecies Thinking Needs Indigenous Standpoints." *Theorizing the Contemporary, Cultural Anthropology*. https://culanth.org/fieldsights/260-why-interspecies-thinking-needs-indigenous-standpoints.

Todd, Zoe. 2014. "Fish Pluralities: Human–Animal Relations and Sites of Engagement in Paulatuuq, Arctic Canada." *Études/Inuit/Studies*, 38(1–2): 217–238.

Todd, Zoe. 2015. "Relationships." *Cultural Anthropology*. https://culanth.org/fieldsights/799-relationships.

Todd, Zoe. 2016a. "From Fish Lives to Fish Law: Learning to See Indigenous Legal Orders in Canada." *Somatosphere*. http://somatosphere.net/2016/02/from-fish-lives-to-fish-law-learning-to-see-indigenous-legal-orders-in-canada.html.

Todd, Zoe. 2016b. "From a Fishy Place: Examining Canadian State Law Applied in the Daniels Decision from the Perspective of Métis Legal Orders." *TOPIA: Canadian Journal of Cultural Studies*, *36*: 43–57.

Tuck, Eve, and K. Wayne Yang. 2012. "Decolonization Is Not a Metaphor." *Decolonization: Indigeneity, Education, & Society*, *1*(1): 1–40.

The Vegan Woman. 2015. "Is Pizza Hut Going Vegan-Friendly?" http://www.thevegan woman.com/pizza-hut-going-vegan-friendly/.

Von Alt, Sarah. 2014. "Israel Goes Vegan." *Mercy for Animals*. http://www.mercy foranimals.org/israel-goes-vegan.

Wadiwel, Dinesh. 2015. *The War against Animals*. Boston, MA: Brill.

Watts, Vanessa. 2013. "Indigenous Place-Thought & Agency amongst Humans and Non-humans (First Woman and Sky Woman Go on a European World Tour!)." *Decolonization: Indigeneity, Education & Society*, *2*(1): 20–34.

White, Ben. 2010. "Behind Brand Israel: Israel's Recent Propaganda Efforts." *The Electronic Intifada*. https://electronicintifada.net/content/behind-brand-israel-israels-recent-propaganda-efforts/8694.

Wolfe, Patrick. 2006. "Settler Colonialism and the Elimination of the Native." *Journal of Genocide Research*, *8*(4): 387–409.

World Bank. 2017a. "Livestock Production Index." https://data.worldbank.org/indi cator/AG.PRD.LVSK.XD?end=2014&locations=IL-PS&start=2014&view=bar.

World Bank. 2017b. "World Development Indicators: CO2 Emissions (Metric Tons per Capita)." http://databank.worldbank.org/data/reports.aspx?source=2&series=EN. ATM.CO2E.PC&country=.

Zahara, Alexander R. D., and Myra J. Hird. 2015. "Raven, Dog, Human: Inhuman Colonialism and Unsettling Cosmologies." *Environmental Humanities*, *7*: 169–190.

Zenk, Henry, Yvonne Hajda, and Robert Boyd. 2016. "Chinookan Villages of the Lower Columbia." *Oregon Historical Quarterly*, *117*(1): 6–37.

Zipkin, Nina. 2017. "Pizza Hut Now Has a Vegan Pizza." *Entrepreneur*. https://www. entrepreneur.com/article/305388.

Chapter 5

Whose Environment? Epistemic-Political Disputes over a Concept and Its Uses

Marcelo Lopes de Souza

INTRODUCTION: WHAT'S IN A NAME?

For "environmental scientists"—a label that covers the professional identity of many geographers and biologists, among others—*environment* is a key concept, or even *the* key concept; but it has also been a key concept for political activists around the world since the 1960s. However, the contents behind the term are far from being undisputed. The trouble with this concept lies in the fact that in spite of variations due to linguistic differences, a common ground at the international level seems to be the existence of two trends: on the one side, a naturalizing bias (which has been hegemonic both in academia and in the realm of common sense) on the basis of which "environment" is primarily understood as synonymous with "natural environment"; on the other side, a non-naturalizing approach that emphasizes a broader meaning according to which "environment" should *not* be primarily understood as non-anthropogenic processes, landforms, and so on.

Such a disagreement is not restricted to academic debate, and its relevance is by no means only a theoretical one. Different approaches to environment have different implications for "environmental protection" and more generally for the questions and discussions regarding rights—from human rights to animal rights. In light of this, the concept of environment and its uses are at the core of crucial epistemic-political disputes. "Preservationists" versus "conservationists"; radically "ecocentric"/"biocentric"-oriented thinkers and activists ("nature is everything, humans are nothing") versus radically "anthropocentric"-oriented thinkers and activists ("humans are everything, nature is nothing")—there seems to be an abyss, an incommensurability between these rival "paradigms."

The theoretical edifice (and subjacent worldview) that has predominantly animated the interdisciplinary and ideally *trans*disciplinary field of political ecology since the 1970s is Marxism; albeit never absolute, Marxism's hegemony has been clear in some contexts (such as Anglo-American geography), even if it has also been increasingly contested. However, some problems cannot be adequately addressed from this perspective. To begin with, attempts at making Marxism fully compatible with a non-productivist/non-economist approach to the transformation of nature by social relations (i.e., one that is free from a "domination of nature" bias) are intrinsically vulnerable to charges of inconsistency; moreover, Marxist political ecologists deal with the anti-anthropocentric claims made by ecocentrically minded environmental activists typically in a problematic way, as they just reassert a conventional anthropocentric worldview and underestimate or dismiss as irrelevant concerns about the sentience and rights of non-human animals, for instance. Within such a framework, it is difficult to reconcile human needs and rights with bioethical concerns, and humanism with an ecological viewpoint.

In comparison with Marxist thought, left-libertarian contributions—such as those made by anarchist Élisée Reclus (1830–1905), neo-anarchist Murray Bookchin (1921–2006), and libertarian autonomist Cornelius Castoriadis (1922–1997)—are much more suitable to help us finding a coherent, reasonable, and fertile balance of different aspects and arguments, within the framework of a simultaneously flexible and critical conceptualization of the environment. My aim in this chapter is to contribute to this (re)conceptualization, and in doing so also to contribute to the building of a left-libertarian approach to political ecology.

In Shaekespeare's *Romeo and Juliet* (Act II, Scene II), a desperate Juliet offers a clever analogy to show Romeo the foolishness of being too proud about family names such as her Capulet and his Montague:

Juliet

O Romeo, Romeo! wherefore art thou Romeo?
Deny thy father and refuse thy name;
Or, if thou wilt not, be but sworn my love,
And I'll no longer be a Capulet.

Romeo

[Aside] Shall I hear more, or shall I speak at this?

Juliet

'Tis but thy name that is my enemy;
Thou art thyself, though not a Montague.

What's Montague? It is nor hand, nor foot,
Nor arm, nor face, nor any other part
Belonging to a man. O, be some other name!
What's in a name? That which we call a rose
By any other name would smell as sweet;
So Romeo would, were he not Romeo call'd,
Retain that dear perfection which he owes
Without that title. Romeo, doff thy name,
And for that name which is no part of thee
Take all myself.

She has a point, and to a large extent, she is undoubtedly right. But in contrast to what Juliet's wisdom suggests, words are not "just words": discourse and the concepts that are expressed through words both reflect the cultural-historical-geographical situatedness of all knowledge (obviously including common sense) and condition the way we think—and the way we politically mobilize and fight. Discourse is shaped by culture, mentality, and ideology, but it also shapes them in return. "Environment" is in this sense one of the least innocent terms we could imagine, and I hope to demonstrate it in the remaining of this chapter.

FROM NATURALIZATION TO SECURITIZATION: SOCIALLY CONSERVATIVE USES OF "THE ENVIRONMENT"

Robert Kaplan's statement according to which "the environment [is] *the* national-security issue of the early twenty-first century" (Kaplan 1994, 58) has been often cited since it was published two and a half decades ago. Incidentally, since the end of the 1980s and the beginning of the 1990s conservative geopolitics has nurtured a concept of (and an agenda for) so-called environmental security. It seems that from scientists to activists to government officials to geopolitics and "defense" experts, "the environment" lies now at the core of the interest and concerns of a very heterogeneous set of people. However, what is "the environment"? The idea is far from univocal, but the shadow of a reductionist reading is always present: environment as "natural environment."

For preservationists walking in the footsteps of John Muir, "the environment" is basically (or even exclusively) the non-human nature that "surrounds" us. Not only misanthropic-minded people such as Muir but virtually all preservationists seem to believe (and often explicitly say) that "the humans" are the problem, because "the humans," in an indistinct way that does not identify social classes or modes of production, "disturb" nature's beauty and "harmony." For them, a statement such as the one made by Élisée Reclus—a French geographer and anarchist that embodied what I have termed a "critical and dialectical conservationism" (Souza 2015, 428)—according to which society can *both* degrade *and* improve and embellish nature (Reclus1864, 763), probably does not make any sense. For them, not only Western(ized) societies and their project of "domination of nature" is a factor of "disturbance" but society in general. From such a viewpoint, there is nothing wrong with creating national parks and other protected areas for the sake of (a mythical) "wilderness" while evicting traditional inhabitants who have lived in those areas for many generations, both influencing and being influenced by non-human nature. The ignorance of facts related to European colonialism and U.S. American white supremacy and their relationship with a certain kind of environmental protection is inexcusable.

Sure, pre-capitalist and "non-Western" (or not highly Westernized) societies and cultures should not be romanticized. However, the fact (illuminated by many historians) that large-scale environmental degradation and self-induced environmental tragedies were not invented by capitalism or the West does not mean that all cultures and modes of production have been equivalent to each other in terms of eco-stress (or "entropy" in Nicholas Georgescu-Roegen's thermodynamic parlance). "Harmony" between society and non-human nature is certainly an imprecise, romantic, and even a little naive ideal, especially when we take into account the findings and theoretical assumptions made by recent *non-equilibrium ecology* studies, according to which nature is always changing (emphasis on *flux* and not on *fixity*) so that ideas such as "nature's stability," or "balance" and "ecological climax" appear as too simplistic (e.g., Zimmerer 2000). None of these points, however, imply that we can neglect or underestimate that differences between cultures/modes of production as well as asymmetries inside specific societies can determine very different responsibilities and impacts, as far as "environmental degradation" is concerned. A concept of environment built on Malthusian oversimplifications and abstract assumptions about society—which is usually reduced to an "anthropic factor"—cannot but be a threat to environmental justice and human dignity in general.

"Environment" means originally a set of objects and circumstances that "surround" a specific being; if taken literally, it is implicit, hence, that one does not belong to its/his/her environment—actually, the environment is external to it/his/her. However, it should be evident that we must adopt a relational approach to the concept. Even if we consider the environment of a certain being as consisting of *all* other beings (living and non-living), the total environment consists of all beings—*including oneself.* Seen in this light, "environment" is in fact a more comprehensive concept than "geographical space," as the latter in its strict sense does not always and necessarily comprise elements such as movable goods or even animals and people; though it is not possible to draw a clear dividing line between geographical space and those earthly entities that are not fixed as well as flows of power and information (as concepts such as "territory" and "place" and even "landscape" show space and social relations are inextricably linked with each other and partially even overlap), "environment" is intuitively all-encompassing from the very beginning.

Whenever naturalistic-minded observers act as if they would interpret the "natural environment" as the complex of physical, chemical, and biological factors that act upon human organisms and societies, but not human and societies themselves, they are inducing us to commit a fallacy. After all, the kingdoms *plantae* and *animalia* (as well as *fungi, protista* [*protozoa* and *chromista*], and *monera* [*eubacteria, archeabacteria,* and *archezoa*]) do belong to the "(natural) environment"; why should only humans be excluded from it? Are humans not living organisms as well?

As soon as we agree with Reclus that "humankind is nature becoming self-conscious" (*l'Homme est la nature prenant conscience d'elle-même* [Reclus 1905–1908, vol. 1, 4]), things begin to look differently. "First nature" and "second nature" (Reclus's *première nature* and *seconde nature* [Reclus 1868–1869, vol. 1, 541], certainly inspired by Schelling's and Hegel's *erste Natur* and *zweite Natur*) may refer to two different aspects or levels of reality (respectively called *physis* and *nomos* by ancient Greeks), but the noun "nature" already indicates they share something essential. Such a point of   AuQ1 view, which refuses to draw a sharp dividing line between human and non-human nature (and which overlooks, for a moment, the ontological differences between human society/culture and non-human nature, along with the epistemological and methodological consequences it maintains for scientific research and philosophical reasoning), the environment is not restricted to the landforms, soils, and climate that "surround" humans; it also includes all "biotic factors" and their agency, as well as humans beings. The environment is ultimately *cosmos*, in the sense of an orderly totality (sure, an "order" that is both objective and [inter]subjective or culturally and historically conditioned). In both conventional ecocentric and anthropocentric views, humans are more or less excluded from the idea of "environment" for cultural reasons, as the Western mentality tends to treat humans or human society and nature as two "ontological sets," clearly, "Cartesianly" distinct from each other. (Although, on the other hand, the positivist science generated by this same society has always insisted on the opposite extreme, wanting to subject the study of both non-human nature and society to the same scientific method— something that seems to configure one of the contradictions in which our neurotic culture inherited from the Enlightenment is immersed.)

Back to Kaplan and the like. One of the indirect products of naturalism (actually an offspring of naturalism and political "realism") is the debate around "securitization" of the environment as the best example of the "new security agenda" (Buzan et al. 1998; Frédérick 1999; Dalby 1999; Deudney 1999). Always reduced to "natural environment," this environment that is supposed to be treated from the viewpoint of "security" is regarded in two basic, different ways: *security of the environment* ("It considers the security of states in only a minor way; its main concern is the security of the planet taken in its totality" [Frédérick 1999, 97]) and *the environment as a component of state security* ("Environmental security . . . takes on the meaning of 'the environmental component of national security'" [Frédérick 1999, 98]). These differences do not seem relevant to the point of breaking with naturalism, however; and even conservatism is somehow latently present even in the first conceptualization, though Frédérick apparently sees in it a "progressive" alternative to the second one. Simon Dalby (e.g., Dalby 1999) has tried to raise reservations and objections from the inside of this debating arena: for him, "environmental security" is an ambiguous concept, and "much of the policy literature linking environmental issues and security (broadly defined) is in danger of overlooking important political issues unless analysts are alert to the persistent dangers of the traditional ethnocentric and geopolitical assumptions in Anglo-American security thinking" (Dalby 1999, 157). Dalby's warning is undoubtedly important (and two decades later his words are still valid, unfortunately)—but this is not enough. The "securitization of the environment" is only the most reactionary face of a "governmentalization" of nature that is politically very dangerous and regressive, since it expresses a tendency to control social processes and individual behaviours—or, in Foucault's words, to "conduct conducts"—using ecological arguments that, in the end, can even help introject and disseminate an "eco-fascist" mentality.

ECOCENTRISM VERSUS ANTHROPOCENTRISM AND THE LIMITS OF MARXIST POLITICAL ECOLOGY

Taken in their strong senses, anthropocentrism and ecocentrism (or biocentrism)[1] means respectively a viewpoint that ascribes the *homo sapiens sapiens* at least some privileges or priority in comparison with non-human nature and a viewpoint that vehemently deny any such privileges or priority (or at least strongly relativize them). The first trouble with these perspectives lies in the tendency of dogmatism and oversimplification that characterizes their extreme versions, what generates an intellectual and political climate that gives us the impression that bridges between these positions are impossible or illusory (or irrelevant). Sure, extreme anthropocentrism—a position that refuses to take themes such as animal rights seriously—and extreme ecocentrism—a position that refuses to acknowledge any anthropocentric concern as ethically legitimate—are clearly antipodal to each other and therefore irreconcilable. However, what if they could at least listen to each other without (too much) prejudice, so that concerns and reservations raised by one perspective could be at least partly incorporated by the other? In this case, we could have some (implicit or explicit) dialog and intermediate or mitigated forms of anthropocentrism and ecocentrism would gain terrain against the most extreme versions.

Would these mitigated forms correspond to "weak" variants, or could they be actually *stronger* (intellectually richer and more sophisticated) than the extreme variants? I firmly believe in this latter possibility. But that is still not all, as this talk about extreme and mitigated variants remains culturally and politically too abstract. In fact, there have been *many* anthropocentrisms (and the differences are so huge that the common ground looks like a thin layer) as well as many ecocentrisms (idem). Furthermore, there are some relevant facts related to ecocentrism and anthropocentrism that must be stressed, as they show the distance or the frictions between these abstract concepts and the cultural and political reality:

- The cosmology that permeates a specific society can be ecocentric and nonetheless remarkably ethnocentric at the same time—in fact, traditional cultures have usually presented both characteristics.
- Extreme ecocentrism seems to be rather a discourse produced by (Western) thinkers, activists and academics than a massive social phenomenon that could be found throughout human history. To my best knowledge, "ecocentric" cultures have always been only moderately ecocentric, in the sense that reverence for and sacralization of (aspects of) "first nature" and the universe, as well as the acknowledgment of non-humans as souled subjects, have not prevented their members from making the well-being of the tribe or reference group their highest priority. Misanthropy was surely not invented by Western intellectuals, but John Muir's famous quip, "and if a war of races should occur between the wild beasts and Lord Man, I would be tempted to sympathize with the bears," seems unlikely to be shared by members of so-called traditional cultures—who did not see human beings simplistically as "destroyers of nature" either, although in many cases (e.g., Easter Island, to mention only one among a plethora of examples), humans literally depleted the resources of their environment fatally.
- Anthropocentrism does not correlate as directly and strongly with true altruism, ethical universalism, or interpersonal solidarity as one could naively think. Christian and capitalist "anthropocentrisms" have been historically compatible with the oppression and exploitation (or even serfdom and slavery) of specific social classes or groups or even entire populations, and massacres (to the point of genocide sometimes) have been committed in the name

of "civilization" and "progress." In the context of some "anthropocentrisms," the motto "humans first" obviously does not mean "*all* humans first."

Different cultural, philosophical, and ideological backgrounds condition and imply very different interpretations about "privileges," "priorities," and "rights" (and "responsibilities"). A Western, vegan, biocentric activist, for instance, stands in a clear contrast to an *indígena* of the Andean region whose duties toward *Pachamama* (= "Mother Earth") lies at the core of an ecocentric perspective, which nevertheless accepts as normal ancient traditions and customs related to animals (including even animal sacrifice for religious reasons) that would probably appear as shocking to a vegan person in a Western (or highly Westernized) country. But also inside a single cultural group or society we can find enormous differences and tensions due, for instance, to political and ideological questions. For example, an eco-anarchist vegan and supporter of "animal liberation" does not share the same worldview of a politically conservative "deep ecologist" who fights for the preservation of "wilderness" but for whom human rights are of secondary importance. (Nonetheless, of course, contradictions and some similarities can occur in concrete individual cases: if individualism is strong and cultural and social sensibility is weaker than ecological sensibility, even an eco-anarchist can nurture ethnocentric and anti-popular positions sometimes—a problem against which Murray Bookchin tried to offer immunization by means of his "social ecology" [e.g., Bookchin 1995, 2005, 2007].)

We should avoid romanticizing non-human nature and the processes that shape naturogenic forms and the structures and dynamics of the environment. The expression "Mother Earth," for instance, sounds nice, but such an anthropomorphism also carries with it its own problems. "Mother Earth" suggests benevolence, the nurturing, compassionate and caring presence of a mother, the love associated with motherhood; but what about . . . the "Father"? As *mestiza*-Aymara sociologist and "border thinker" Silvia Rivera Cusicanqui stressed (during a lecture delivered on April 25 in La Paz and attended by me), there is both *Pachamama* and *Pachatata* ("Father Earth") in Aymara cosmology. Within the framework of this cosmology, while "Mother Earth," as the personification of the feminine in the universe, takes care of her children and nurtures them, "Father Earth," the personification of the masculine, is severe and punishes (it may sound mean to men, but the analogy is historically justifiable). So we also have earthquakes, volcanic eruptions, tsunamis, floods, and so on—always *Pachatata* doing his job. Aymara cosmology interestingly also unites both principles in a single word, as the term *pacha* is formed by two words: *pa* (= two) and *cha* (= "force" or "energy"). *Pacha* is then actually the totality: *mama* and *papa*, love and strength; in a nutshell, the whole vital force of the universe.

Geographers have drawn attention to the Western explicit or implicit classification of certain aspects of nature as bad ("bad nature," as Kaika [2004] says). However, in the face of rates, "bad bugs" or cold, the Western tradition is driven by an attempt to *submit* or *domesticate* or even (whenever possible) to *eliminate* the "bad" side. Although Descartes's famous formula *maîtres et possesseurs de la nature* ("masters and possessors of nature") (Descartes 1894, 102) smells after patriarchy with its tacit comparison of nature to a woman who needs to be "tamed" and "conquered" (a thought not unusual among 17th-century philosophers), considered against the background of Aymara cosmology the Western mentality of a "bad nature" to be eliminated curiously resembles Freud's psychoanalytic thesis of the symbolic murder of the father.

In light of this complexity, Marxist political ecology appears as an intent to pay tribute to the ecological dimension of human welfare while at the same time haunted by the ghost of a humanistic philosophy committed from the very beginning with a very problematic form of anthropocentrism. On the one side, Karl Marx was able to produce wise remarks such as the following one, a passage from volume 3 of *Das Kapital* often quoted by "eco-Marxists" in support of their thesis about Marx's conservationist ethics:

> From the standpoint of a higher socio-economic formation, the private property of particular individuals in the earth will appear just as tasteless [*abgeschmackt*] as the private property of one man in other men. Even a whole society, a nation, or all simultaneously existing societies taken together are not owners of the earth. They are only its occupants, its beneficiaries, and have to bequeath it in an improved state to succeeding generations, as *boni patres familias*. (Marx 1983, 784)

On the other side, however, Marxist philosophy reveals (very much in the spirit of capitalism itself) a remarkably economistic/productivistic and rationalist side, which ranges from a certain technological fetishism to an ontological devaluation of "first nature." On this basis, it is clear that an internal tension between ecological sensibility and humanistic sensibility is inevitable. The problems of typical Marxism, or of a Marxism that is attached to what can be considered as the typical elements of and predominant readings in the work of Marx himself, are several: from hierarchy and verticality (political parties and vanguards) to the "socialist state" and the "dictatorship of the proletariat"; from the weak (or non-existent) criticism of the contradictions of the Enlightenment to, as already said, an economistic and rationalistic productivism and a quasi-technolatry whose dependence on the capitalist imaginary can be no longer successfully dissimulated.[2] Especially, since the middle of the 20th century, neo-Marxists linked with the tradition of "Western Marxism," which originated with György Lukács in the 1920s (Frankfurt School, Henri Lefebvre, etc.), feeling increasingly uncomfortable with both the theoretical orthodoxies (such as Friedrich Engels's interpretations about "dialectical materialism") and political ones (Leninism, Stalinism, *et caterva*), have relativized some of these principles and assumptions. But have they not, in the wake of this process, been forced to free themselves also from substantial portions of the very thought of Marx himself, although (understandably) they are seldom willing to admit it? Even worse than this is the tendency, already visible in Henri Lefebvre in the 1960s, and brought to paroxysm by all the Holloways and Negris of the past decades, of wanting to renew Marxism by *mimicking* left-libertarian thought—without giving due credit to it—traditionally so despised and vilified by Marxists (Souza 2016). Self-deception and opportunism may combine in variable doses according to each specific author, but both problems are part of the process of mutation in the context of which neo-Marxist political ecology and "eco-Marxism" emerged on the improbable ground of "Western Marxism," so averse to giving real importance and validity to the category of nature (Vogel 1996 offers both a brilliant synthesis and a paradigm case itself and the same time).

Figure 5.1 tries to graphically depict the four understandings of the relationships between society and (non-human) nature. Two of them (Figure 5.1A and 5.1B) are clearly antipodal to each other, but they share as a common ground an idea of environment as something basically understandable as "naturalness," in the sense of "without the humans." Figure 5.1A corresponds to *anti-humanistic ecocentrism*, from the perspective of which "wilderness" is to be protected from the "disharmony" and "degradation" imposed upon it by human beings; nature should be accordingly preserved and altered as little as possible, being also object of contemplation and even worship. And not just that: respect for human rights and concerns about human dignity are more often than not almost virtually absent.[3] On the other hand, from the viewpoint of Figure 5.1B, nature is regarded as a mere instrument for the satisfaction of human beings' needs; interestingly, this *provincial anthropocentrism*, so typical of what Marxists traditionally call "bourgeois thinking" (e.g., Gifford Pinchot's classical capitalist version of conservationism and all its contemporary variants) is at the same time basically what constitutes Marxism's approach to nature. In contrast to these two extreme positions, Figure 5.1C and 5.1D represent views where there is no sharp distinction (not to speak opposition) between advocacy for humans and non-humans, or between concerns about human needs satisfaction and about limiting and reducing eco-stress. Figure 5.1C could be termed *humanistic ecocentrism*, and Figure 5.1D could be called *cosmophilic anthropocentrism*. The difference between them is one of degree, not substance; both regard the environment as comprising humans and non-humans alike, and the relationship between humans and non-humans is never reduced to simplistic assumptions (usually ideological projections of specific values and desires).

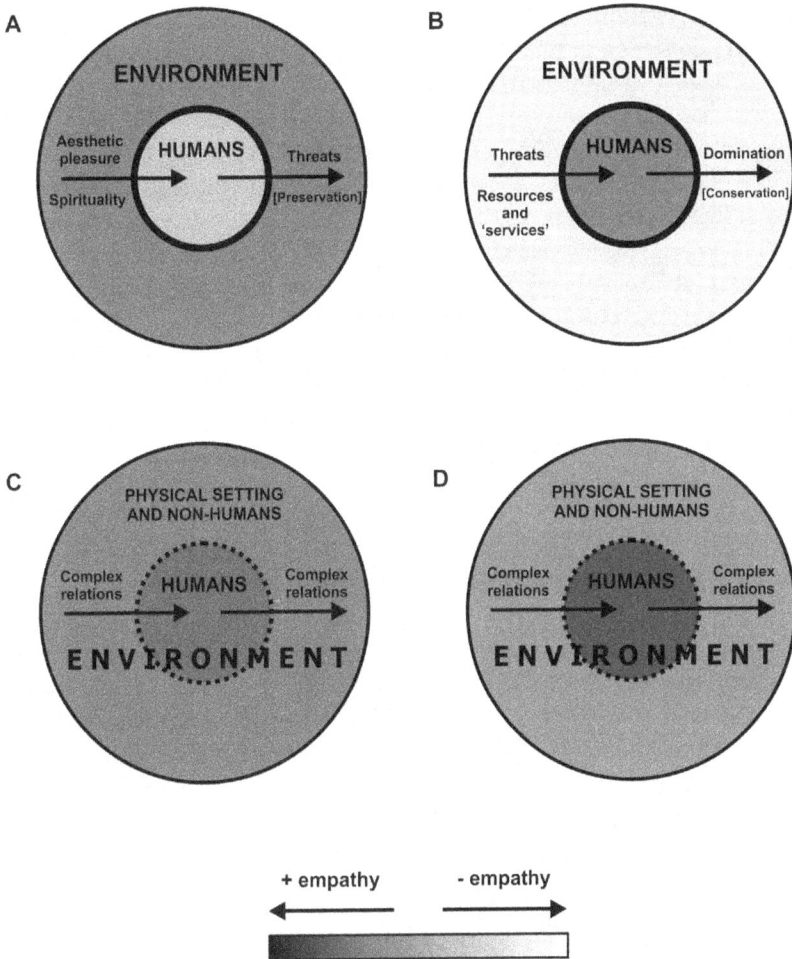

Figure 5.1. The Notion of "Environment" and its Range: relationships between humans and non-human nature, emphasizing the degree of empathy of the first toward the latter. A: anti-humanistic ecocentrism; B: provincial anthropocentrism; C: humanistic ecocentrism; D: cosmophilic anthropocentrism.

While humanistic ecocentrism decidedly rejects misanthropy and socially conservative values, cosmophilic anthropocentrism for its part embraces a not narrow-minded concern about human rights and needs that, despite professing an explicit and pragmatic "preferential option for the humans," takes very seriously bioethical and ecological concerns and approaches such as animal rights, agroecology, and the need of an ecological or "liberatory" technology.[4] From the perspective of this kind of mitigated anthropocentrism,

a particularly strong empathy toward humans and the ethical priority pragmatically conceded to intra-species solidarity do not prevent us from seeing
human beings as ultimately nothing than "cosmic dust," a tiny part of the
cosmos that should never try to evade its moral responsibility toward other
living forms and the totality of the environment. As for humanistic ecocentrism, although those who espouse this view chose to place in the foreground
their ethical commitment to all sentient beings, they nonetheless never compromise or neglect intra-species solidarity and socially emancipatory values
in favor of any socially regressive preservationist principles. Both humanistic
ecocentrism and cosmophilic anthropocentrism are essentially compatible
with a left-libertarian viewpoint, no matter their different emphases; both attitudes are compatible with left-libertarian key values such as radical territorial
decentralization and economic-spatial deconcentration, self-management,
horizontality, and dignity for all living and sentient beings.

ENVIRONMENTAL JUSTICE FROM
A LEFT-LIBERTARIAN PERSPECTIVE

The movement for environmental justice emerged in the United States on
the eve of the 1980s. According to several authors, it could be understood to
some extent as an unfolding of the civil rights struggle of the black population
of the previous two decades; in fact, the problem of environmental injustice
has been, in the U.S. American case, inextricably linked to the problem
known as "environmental racism" (e.g., Schlosberg 2009, 45 ff.). In terms of
politico-philosophical values and worldview, liberalism has had a great deal
of weight, given the hegemonic role it plays in the context of U.S. American
political culture (other than continental European or Latin American political
culture, the U.S. American one has historically been much more averse to a
radical Marxist or left-libertarian thinking). That is to say that, despite serious
denunciations and sometimes blunt criticisms of political and economic institutions, in the United States, the conceptual horizon and political mobilization
around environmental justice have often been confined within the ideological
limits of representative "democracy." Within this framework, the maximum
possible "radicality" is related to reforms; "revolution" is a word that simply
does not belong to the usual vocabulary. This means that the central problem of environmental injustice—above all, the socially unequal distribution
of environmental risks and economic benefits related to the production of
goods that inevitably generate problems such as environmental pollution and
contamination, waste, and so on—was already clearly put by environmental
justice activists in the United States four decades ago, but the solution has
been often tied to politically overly unambitious benchmarks. Beyond the

levels of local and national politics, the problem of exporting toxic waste and dirty technologies (banned by domestic laws) to other, "southern" countries has also been a major concern of liberal environmental justice activists and theorists—and again the repertoire of strategies and tactics is a narrow and shallow one, as too much optimism regarding the power of formal laws, agreements, and conventions (or institutional reform more generally) is not uncommon.

As a critical approach to environmental problems, political ecology has incorporated the environmental (in)justice discourse as part of its agenda. Having Marxism as its ideological mainstream in some contexts, radical political ecology has therefore tried to translate Marxism's traditional concerns about social (in)justice into the language of environmental (in)justice narratives. Sure, there are different Marxisms; considering that Marx's body of work was itself everything but free of contradictions or serious internal tensions (as Marxists themselves admit sometimes), there is no wonder that we have found Marxists of all kinds. Does it prevent us to speak about Marxism in singular form? Surely Marxism has been proved able to adapt itself to new circumstances (recently by means of the mimicry of left-libertarian concepts, strategies, and organization forms such as self-management), but if Marxism is everything, it is nothing at the same time. Honest Marxists should acknowledge that Marxism (beginning with Marx himself) has been fundamentally characterized by a *fondness or at least ambiguity toward hierarchical, vertical types of organization* (state apparatus, "vanguard" political parties, etc.) and *economism, that is the more or less sophisticated reduction of social facts to its economic dimension.* Marxists who deeply and sincerely disagree with both aspects should stop calling themselves Marxists.

In a nutshell: if a politically moderate (be it "left-liberal" or social democrat) environmental justice approach is doomed to halt in the middle of the road without being able to suggest anything but reforms within the capitalist state, could an approach inspired by neo-Marxist political ecology do it better? It is certainly capable of a much more radical and profound analysis of the anti-ecological and inequality implications of capitalism and the limitations of the capitalist state to cope with them, but it will surely be entrapped in a dilemma at the very moment when it will try to propose alternatives to the status quo: *either* it will resort to well-known, typical authoritarian formulas, such as the emphasis on leftist political parties as the main agents of change (the social movements organizations being generally seen as mere "transmission belts" on behalf of a vanguard party) and the goal of building a "socialist state" (including of course "nationalization" of companies and other forms of centralization in this context), *or* it will be forced to adopt left-libertarian principles and strategies, as it has already been the case.

In comparison with Marxism-inspired political ecology, what do left-libertarians have to offer? In contrast to the rare, isolated episodes used by neo-Marxists to try to sustain their "horizontal/self-management turn" with the help of Marxist writings (such as Marx's "quasi-anarchist" text on the Paris Commune of 1871 and the passages in which Engels advocates a radically deconcentrated spatial organization), left-libertarians have to offer a continuous tradition of two centuries of discussions on *and practices of* territorial decentralization, economic-spatial deconcentration, horizontality, and self-management—from some of Proudhon's writings to Kropotkin's seminal works to the land collectivizations led by the anarchists during the Spanish Civil War to Murray Bookchin's and Cornelius Castoriadis's views and proposals. Furthermore, left-libertarians also have a long tradition, at least since Élisée Reclus, of consistently discussing environmental problems and issues regarding conservation and animal welfare from an emancipatory perspective, as well as (since the mid-twentieth century) alternative technology and several types of bioethical problems, such as animal research. Let us briefly consider specifically three left-libertarian direct or indirect contributions to the contemporary debates around environmental justice: Reclus's environmental ethics, Bookchin's "social ecology" and Castoriadis's "project of autonomy." All three thinkers and activists established benchmarks for a distinctively left-libertarian approach to the subject.

Although Reclus was in many respects a son of the Enlightenment, his belief in "progress" was so critical and dialectical, and his respect for all forms of life was so central to his thinking that his position could be regarded as a kind of humanistic ecocentrism. In his essay, "La grande famille" ("The Great Kinship"), he synthesizes his thought in an impressive and unmistakable way:

> Some day our fiercely individualist civilization, dividing the world into as many small enemy states as there are private properties and family households, will have suffered its last collapse, and it will be necessary to resort to mutual aid for the sake of common survival; the search for friendship will then replace that for material well-being, which sooner or later will be sufficiently assured. Some day enthusiastic naturalists will have revealed to us all that is charming, amiable, human, and often more than human in the nature of beasts; we will then think of all these species left behind in the march of progress, and we shall endeavor to make them neither servants nor machines, but true companions. (Reclus 1897, 12)

Calling animals our "brothers" (*frères animaux*), Reclus, a vegetarian, nevertheless was miles away from regarding humankind merely as a threat for (first) nature. As young Élisée once wrote in an interesting essay called "De l'action humaine sur la géographie physique" ["Human Action on Physical Geography"], the human action instead gives the greatest diversity of aspect to the Earth's surface. On one side it destroys, on the other it improves; according to the social condition and progress of each people, sometimes it contributes to degrade nature, sometimes to embellish it. (Reclus 1864, 763)

He did not see (first) nature as something "sacred," from which a "corrupting" human influence should be as completely as possible removed. He understood humanity as a part of nature (taken as a whole), and *as such* human beings would not play the role of *homo devastans* in an absolute manner: The way how (and the degree to which) society would destroy/degrade or improve/embellish the environment would depend on historical and social factors. His concern was ultimately one about how human beings' needs could be satisfied without domination as well as without causing unnecessary harm to other forms of life. Reclus was definitely no forebear of today's "deep ecologists" (he even avoided the term "ecology" due to the fact that it was originally coined by German biologist E. Haeckel, a notorious reactionary, eugenicist, and racist) and for that matter any anti-humanistic ecocentrist. His vehement refusal of capitalist exploitation, state domination, and actually all forms of heteronomy clearly means that for him environmental protection should never be achieved at the cost of compromising human rights and dignity.

In contrast to Reclus, Bookchin and Castoriadis share with us the same historical age: an age in which optimism about "progress" (since the mid-twentieth century rephrased as "economic development"), "modern" science, and (capitalist) technology was largely replaced by various degrees of pessimism and skepticism, and an age in which concerns about "the environment" reached very often the point of paranoia, giving rise to a dangerous entanglement of environmental, "(national) security" and even nationalist/racist preoccupations, sometimes expressed in some form of "eco-fascism." In the context of what he (actually echoing E. Gutkind) called "social ecology," Bookchin claimed for an "ecology of freedom," stressing that the ecological problem was at its core a social problem, in a sense shared by neo-Marxists such as Horkheimer, Adorno, and Marcuse, that the "domination of nature" was a product of social inequality and heteronomy: "The notion that man [sic] must dominate nature emerges directly from the domination of man by man" (Bookchin 2004, 24 [essay "Ecology and Revolutionary Thought"]). From his perspective, social ecology

is based on the conviction that nearly all of our present ecological problems originate in deep-seated social problems. It follows, from this view, that these ecological problems cannot be understood, let alone solved, without a careful understanding of our existing society and the irrationalities that dominate it. To make this point more concrete: economic, ethnic, cultural, and gender conflicts, among many others, lie at the core of the most serious ecological dislocations

we face today—apart, to be sure, from those that are produced by natural catas-
trophes. (Bookchin 2007, 19)

"Unless we realize that the present market society," Bookchin warned,
"structured around the brutally competitive imperative of 'grow or die,' is
a thoroughly impersonal, self-operating mechanism, we will falsely tend to
blame technology as such or population growth as such for environmental
problems" (Bookchin 2007, 20). This also means that the root causes of those
environmental problems, "such as trade for profit, industrial expansion, and
the identification of 'progress' with corporate self-interest" (Bookchin 2007,
20). Therefore, "in short, we will tend to focus on the symptoms of a grim
social pathology rather than on the pathology itself, and our efforts will be
directed toward limited goals whose attainment is more cosmetic than cura-
tive" (Bookchin 2007, 20).

> Unconsciously following in Reclus's footsteps, Bookchin stated that [w]e are
> part of nature, a product of a long evolutionary journey. To some degree, we
> carry the ancient oceans in our blood. . . . Our brains and nervous systems did
> not suddenly spring into existence without long antecedents in natural history.
> That which we most prize as integral to our humanity—our extraordinary capac-
> ity to think on complex conceptual levels—can be traced back to the nerve
> network of primitive invertebrates, the ganglia of a mollusk, the spinal cord of a
> fish, the brain of an amphibian, and the cerebral cortex of a primate. (Bookchin
> et al. 1991, 32–33)

However radical in some senses Marxist-inspired environmental injustice
analysts may be, Marxists have been traditionally fond of statecraft and other
forms of verticality, so that the spirit contained in a book such as Bookchin's
The Ecology of Freedom (Bookchin 2005) with its deep refusal of hierarchical thinking implicitly indicates a potentially deep difference in terms of
openness to a radically non-heteronomous future between a left-libertarian
approach to environmental (in)justice and a Marxist one.

Obviously, Marxists can accept that superficial reforms designed to merely
mitigate residential segregation and alleviate poverty are insufficient anti-
dotes against environmental injustice; what they have trouble grasping is that
it does not suffice to overcome capitalism and the capitalist state: it is necessary to overcome statecraft *as such* as well as all other forms of heteronomy
if we want to build true freedom. For Reclus and Bookchin, true freedom
means *anarchy* ("without rulers"); for Castoriadis, it is expressed by something different but whose *ethos* is basically the same: *autonomy* ("one who
gives oneself one's own law"). Within the framework of his approach to individual and collective autonomy,[5] Castoriadis developed a high appreciation

of ecology's revolutionary and liberatory potential (largely convergent with Bookchin's views), as ecological concerns can—once correctly understood and radically formulated, far beyond the environmental approaches and policies advocated by political parties, states, and international organizations like the United Nations—lead us to question the very foundations of our society in terms of mode of production, political structure, and values.[6] From such a perspective, only in the context of an autonomous society one can achieve social justice—environmental justice included—not because it is a "perfect" society, but only because the absence of structural heteronomy (class stratification, exploitation of labor, and other kinds of asymmetry and oppression such as racism and patriarchy) allows for the possibility of arriving at fundamentally just arrangements, which should be nonetheless constantly open to debate and improvement.

While Reclus's perspective could be regarded as an instance of humanistic ecocentrism, Bookchin's and Castoriadis's positions are better described as examples of cosmophilic anthropocentrism. But in all three cases the approach to the relationships between society and nature as well as to those between human beings themselves is very different from what both liberals and typical Marxists have offered.

CONCLUSION: TOWARD A "COSMIC" PERSPECTIVE

The fact that we can accept as understandable and legitimate that our empathy toward fellow *homo sapiens sapiens* is more intense than that toward other "living creatures"—including primates and other mammals—and the possibility of admitting some "priority" on the basis of intra-species solidarity (a universal phenomenon that only humans seem to relativize sometimes) *do not necessarily mean or imply*, however, any neglect or underestimation of other living beings' sentience (and therefore rights, with or without quotation marks). As Peter Parker ("Spider-Man") famously (at least to comics fans) said, "With great power comes great responsibility." Seen from both the humanist and ecological point of view implied by such a wisdom, *homo sapiens sapiens*'s ability to reshape geographical space and create a "second nature"—often in ways that are dangerous not only to ecosystems, other species, or biodiversity in general, but also to many human beings, and particularly to those who are most vulnerable by virtue of their class or ethnicity—is both a privilege and a burden. We *can* do many things, but we *should not* do all things we can. Human "privileges" or alleged "superiority" (in terms of our complex abilities) must be hence understood in a strictly dialectical way, and our "priority" must be relativized—but clearly not denied in absolute terms.

In reality, in spite of the contradictions of extreme (anti-humanistic) eco-centrism and in spite of the politically conservative and socially regressive forms that this ecocentrism usually takes, mainstream anthropocentrism is ultimately a "provincial" perspective. If we take the information and theories provided by astrobiologists and astronomers like Carl Sagan seriously, there is a high probability that humans are far from being the sole "intelligent" or "rational" life form in the universe or even in our galaxy. Let us then consider the possibility of a technologically and scientifically much more advanced civilization visiting Earth and contacting us. How would we feel if the aliens denied our right to self-determination or even to existence, or at least kill and torture some of us for the purpose of scientific research? As for now, that is a matter of pure speculation and a nightmare restricted to science fiction, but the thought experiment can be of pedagogical importance for us here and now.

The argument that we could "talk" to them to express our feelings and pre-sumed "rights" while dogs and even primates cannot "talk" to us to express their feelings is flawed for two reasons: first, our communication efforts could appear to a materially much superior civilization as not much more sophisticated than the barking of a dog from a human perspective; second and more relevant, we are more than clever enough to perceive the sentience (feelings of pleasure, suffering, fear, etc.) of dogs and other animals or even of plants, we have just chosen to ignore them, partly for material, cultural, and historical reasons.

It could also be argued that while humans evolved from the very begin-ning within an existential (question of survival) framework of hunting and domesticating other animals, extraterrestrial beings have not regularly eaten or domesticated humans for serving their own purpose—in other words, kill-ing and enslaving humans have not been a part of their culture or material necessities. This second argument is ethically (and obviously historically) much less fragile, but it does not correspond to an absolute alibi, either.

In the end, sacrificing other living beings for the sake of satisficing human beings' needs has been widely historically and culturally accepted, and per-haps we can at least admit that there are huge differences between hunting for sport (can culture and tradition sanction *everything*, as if it were an absolute taboo for all of us?) and hunting for survival, as it was the case during the most part of *homo sapiens sapiens*'s existence. But this question will prob-ably remain open, and answers regarding what could be seen as acceptable or not will vary according to the cultural context, the worldview, and the epoch. Many or most of us, for instance, may condemn the way how animals are bred, fed, confined, and killed in the context of capitalist food industry, though some of us might find it exaggerated to characterize the killing of animals under these circumstances as "murder." Nonetheless, what about ani-mal sacrifice and blood rituals as part of animist religions? Although we may find these practices regrettable, most of us intuitively see that a simplistic condemnation would be probably a sign of Eurocentrism and intolerance.[7] In these two cases, are there a difference of degree, not substance? The situation becomes even more complicated when we introduce the theme of cannibalism and human blood rituals. Anthropophagy and human sacrifice have not been uncommon phenomena in the history of humankind until at least the nineteenth century. The obvious point here is: if culture cannot sanction everything in absolute terms (i.e., for everybody, forever, and regardless of the circumstances), how should one react? Trying to impose one's ecocentric, vegan, and so forth values on others while ignoring or underestimating all the ethnocentric, imperialistic-geopolitical, and class-based implications can be as authoritarian and ethically problematic as simply silencing in the face of "unnecessary" (in terms of human survival) animal slaughter and various forms of cruelty to animals (e.g., bullfighting and cruelty to animals in laboratories). As we see, there is no easy answer. But left-libertarian streams—from Reclus's critical conservationism and animal welfare concerns to Bookchin's "social ecology" to Castoriadis's "project of autonomy"—seem to provide a more balanced, reasonable, and fair approach to these matters than Marxism or liberalism can do.

A "cosmic" perspective, in a nutshell, underlies the special empathy that human beings should foster toward each other, impying a radical refusal of heteronomy as a basis and precondition for justice and fairness, and stresses the fact that humankind is ultimately nothing more than "cosmic dust" when considered in terms of geological (not to mention cosmological) time, as well as our lack of centrality in the universe. We are an evolving species (technologically evolving much faster than biologically or even ethically), and if we do not destroy ourselves in a probably not very remote future (capitalism is trying its best in this direction), perhaps we will have time to learn that "environment" is an idea that designates our home as much as it designates the home of other, equally evolving species, everything in a highly complex (and only partly understood) whole of interrelated factors and elements, so that heteronomy (all forms of oppression) but also capitalism-driven "amoral" instrumentalization and consumption of soils, fauna, flora, etc. ("biotic and abiotic factors") are not compatible with an appropriate and just balance of needs and rights—of humans and non-humans alike.

NOTES

1. Many people suggest that there is a difference between ecocentrism and biocentrism; however, there is no consensus on this question, and not few people use these terms interchangeably. Those who emphasize a difference between them see an

ecocentric ethic as one that stresses the importance of whole ecosystems rather than just of Earth's living beings, while a biocentric ethic would be specifically concerned with the well-being of organisms. Although both positions are largely similar and convergent, many scientists and activists (self-)described as ecocentric can under some circumstances accept the killing of animals if it is necessary to reduce the population of a certain animal species whose unbalanced proliferation threats endangered species—a position biocentric and animal liberation activists have difficulties in accepting. Considering such an example, there is indeed some disagreement in terms of perspective and behavior, regardless of the labels we use.

2. On economism/productivism, rationalism, and technological fetishism in Marx's work, see Castoriadis 1975 and 1978; on the heteronomous/authoritarian dimension of Marxian thought and Marxist ideology and practices, see, among many other works, Castoriadis 2013a and b. Recent treatments of these subjects from the point of view of socio-spatial research can be found, for instance, in Springer 2014 and Souza 2016.

3. See, e.g., the famous debate between Murray Bookchin's "social ecology" and Dave Foreman's reactionary positions [Bookchin et al. 1991].

4. See on this latter point the essay "Towards a Liberatory Technology" in Bookchin 2004.

5. "Project of autonomy": see, e.g., Castoriadis 1975 and 1990.

6. See Castoriadis 2005a, b; Castoriadis and Cohn-Bendit 2014.

7. Interestingly, tribal and Indigenous cultures and cosmologies in Latin America and Africa acknowledge the existence of "non-human subjects" (to use contemporary Western parlance), but surely in a different way in comparison with Western approaches based on bioethics, animal rights, and vegetarianism/veganism: after all, recognizing non-human animals (or even mountains, rivers, etc.) as "subjects" or souled entities did/does not mean that many of these "non-human subjects" could not/cannot be hunted and killed, and that their feathers, fur, and leather could not/cannot be used.

REFERENCES

Bookchin, M. (1995). *From Urbanization to Cities: Toward a New Politics of Citizenship*. London: Cassel.

Bookchin, M. (2004 [several years; first edition of the book: 1971]). *Post-Scarcity Anarchism*. Edinburgh and Oakland: AK Press, 3rd edition.

Bookchin, M. (2005 [1982]). *The Ecology of Freedom: The Emergence and Dissolution of Hierarchy*. Edinburgh and Oakland: AK Press.

Bookchin, M. (2007 [several years]). *Social Ecology and Communalism*. Edinburgh and Oakland: AK Press.

Bookchin, M. et al. (1991 [1989–1990]). *Defending the Earth: A Debate between Murray Bookchin and Dave Foreman*. Montreal and New York: Black Rose Books.

Buzan, B., et al. (1998). *Security: A New Framework for Analysis*. Boulder and London: Lynne Rienner.

Castoriadis, C. (1975). *L'institution imaginaire de la société*. Paris: Seuil.

Castoriadis, C. (1978). "Technique," in *Les carrefours du labyrinthe*. Paris: Seuil, 221–248.

Castoriadis, C. (1990 [1988]). "Pouvoir, politique, autonomie," in Castoriadis, C. *Le monde morcelé—Les carrefours du labyrinthe III*. Paris: Seuil, 113–139.

Castoriadis, C. (2005a [1992]). "L'écologie contre les marchands," in Castoriadis, C. *Une société à la dérive: Entretiens et débats 1974–1997*. Paris: Seuil, 237–239.

Castoriadis, C. (2005b [1992]). "La force révolutionnaire de l'écologie," in Castoriadis, C. *Une société à la dérive: Entretiens et débats 1974–1997*. Paris: Seuil, 241–250.

Castoriadis, C. (2013a [1974]) "La question de l'histoire du mouvement ouvrier," in Castoriadis, C. *Quelle démocratie? (Tome 1)*. Paris: Éditions du Sandre, 383–458.

Castoriadis, C. (2013b [1964]) "Le rôle de l'idéologie bolchevique dans la naissance de la bureaucratie," in Castoriadis, C. *Quelle démocratie? (Tome 1)*. Paris: Éditions du Sandre, 191–212.

Castoriadis, C., and Cohn-Bendit, D. (2014 [1981]). *De l'écologie à l'autonomie*. Paris: Éditions Le Bord de l'eau.

Dalby, S. (1999). "Threats from the South? Geopolitics, equity, and environmental security," in Deudney, D. H., and Matthew, R. A. (eds.), *Contested Grounds: Security and Conflict in the New Environmental Politics*. Albany: New York University Press, 155–185.

Descartes, R. (1894 [1637]). *Discours de la méthode, Pour bien conduire sa raison, et chercher la vérité dans les sciences*. Paris: Bibliotèque Nationale.

Deudney, D. (1999). "Environmental security: A critique," in Deudney, D. H., and Matthew, R. A. (eds.), *Contested Grounds: Security and Conflict in the New Environmental Politics*. Albany: New York University Press, 187–219.

Frédérick, M. (1999). "A realist's conceptual definition of environmental security," in Deudney, D. H., and Matthew, R. A. (eds.), *Contested Grounds: Security and Conflict in the New Environmental Politics*. Albany: New York University Press, 91–108.

Georgescu-Roegen, N. (1971). *The Entropy Law and the Economic Process*. Cambridge, MA: Harvard University Press.

Kaplan, R. (1994). "The coming anarchy." *The Atlantic Monthly*, February, 44–76.

Marx, K. (1983). *Das Kapital* [Bd. III, Sechster Abschnitt] in Marx, K. and Engels, F., *Werke*, Band 25. Berlin: Dietz Verlag.

Reclus, E. (1864). "L'Homme et la Nature: De l'action humaine sur la géographie physique." *Revue des Deux Mondes*, 54, 762–771.

Reclus, E. (1868–1869). *La Terre: Description des phénomènes de la vie du globe*. Paris: Hachette, 2 vols. Online (facsimile reproduction): Librairie Nationale Française (http://gallica.bnf.fr [the specific address varies according to the volume]).

Reclus, E. (1897). "La grande famille." *Le Magazine International*, January, 8–12. Online (facsimile reproduction): Librairie Nationale Française (http://gallica.bnf.fr/ark:/12148/bpt6k660250.r=reclus.langPT).

Reclus, E. (1905–1908). *L'Homme et la Terre*, 6 vols. Paris: Librairie Universelle. Online (facsimile reproduction): Librairie Nationale Française (http://gallica.bnf.fr [the specific address varies according to the volume]).

Schlosberg, D. (2009). *Defining Environmental Justice: Theories, Movements, and Nature*. Oxford: Oxford University Press.

Souza, M. L. de (2015). "From the 'right to the city' to the right to the *planet*: Reinterpreting our contemporary challenges for socio-spatial development." *City*, 19(4), 408–443.

Souza, M. L. de (2016). "'Feuding brothers'? Left-libertarians, Marxists and socio-spatial research at the beginning of the twenty-first century," in Souza, M. L. de et al. (eds.), *Theories of Resistance: Anarchism, Geography, and the Spirit of Revolt*, vol. 2. London: Rowman & Littlefield, 123–153.

Springer, S. (2014). "Why a radical geography must be anarchist." *Dialogues in Human Geography*, 4(3), 249–270.

Vogel, S. (1996). *Against Nature: The Concept of Nature in Critical Theory*. Albany: State University of New York.

Zimmerer, K. S. (2000). "The reworking of conservation geographies: Nonequilibrium landscapes and nature-society hybrids." *Antipode*, 90(2), 356–369.

Chapter 6

A Future Eco-Anarchic Society and the Means to Achieving It

Shane Mc Donnell

If we do not do the impossible, we shall be faced with the unthinkable.

—Murray Bookchin

INTRODUCTION

This chapter is an attempt to, on the one hand, highlight some of the necessary global changes that must occur for better ecological and human health, and, on the other hand, to promote a pragmatic approach to and use of the state and its apparatuses as a tactic for *our* end. This essay will be split in two. Part I will encourage the adoption of a vegan lifestyle not only for personal well-being but the well-being of the environment too. Animal products will be shown to have negative impacts on human health, while animal agriculture will be shown to have negative impacts on the environment. Separately, hemp will be promoted as a crop to replace the vast amounts of trees used in paper production. The use of hemp will be shown to halt deforestation and be beneficial as a replacement crop needing less herbicide, pesticide, and water. Finally, in part I, the concepts of the commons and permaculture will be examined and a synthesis proposed in order to maximize food production (for areas of poor soil health) and distribution. My presumption in part I is that significant mass change must happen immediately. The ecological disasters of recent years alone are evidence to this. Though class is not discussed, recent research[1] has shown that the upper classes consume more, thus necessitating greater sacrifices on their part.

Part II should be treated as a thought experiment that will discuss interim changes that could occur now initiating the creation of a better world. Part II is admittedly reliant on state apparatuses. The recurring message of part II is

141

Percentage of CO₂ emissions by world population

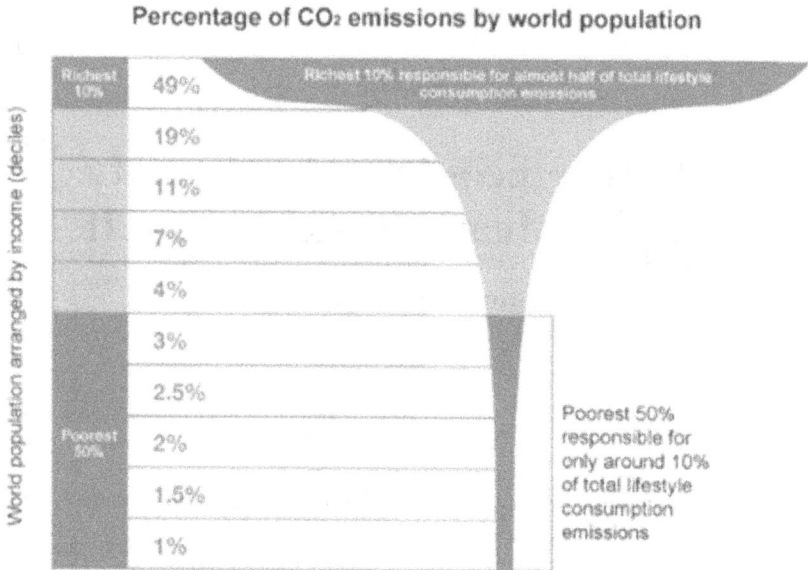

Figure 6.1. Global Income Deciles and Associated Lifestyle Consumption Emissions. *Source*: Oxfam.

tactics not goals. As such, working within the system, with laws and policies already in place, from a strictly ecological point of view will be argued for. It is not my goal to support the state or capitalism, however, as a tactic I can choose to work within it to subvert and disrupt it. Examples from France, Rojava (in northern Syria), and Freetown Christiania (in Denmark) will be examined for methods of managing and disposing of waste. Finally, as per the premise of Part II, that is, interim changes and relying on state apparatuses, it is my presumption that there is a likelihood amid all these changes of making contact with non-governmental bodies. Existing alongside and amongst these typically non-radical organizations will be examined. A pragmatic response will be offered while acknowledging that NGOs support the status quo. Nonetheless, it is unlikely that without coordination, communication, and cooperation across the planet by a variety of groups, the idealized mass change of Part I, and arguably in the rest of these volumes, will not occur.

Part I—The Environment and Us

The political right, and those attempting to maintain the status quo, have bastardized people's natural orientation toward the community and the land. The Nazi slogan *blut und boden* ('blood and soil') is not particularly gratifying to utter, yet the historicity of such bastardization is clear. It is unfortunate and discouraging that such care for one's community and surrounding environment is synonymous with the consequential nationalisms of *blut und boden*. Though this chapter is not explicitly focused on that issue, by discussing both anarchism and ecology, it is hoped that the bad taste left by the right on issues like the land and the community is thoroughly washed away for good. My goal is that, by the end of this chapter, readers will associate community, nature, and the environment with anarchism and leftist principles.

A Plant-Based Approach

COWSPIRACY: The Sustainability Secret is a scathing documentary film focusing on the global beef industry. In addition to the documentary, an online fact sheet exists, created by the documentary's creators Anderson and Kuhn.[2] Shocking details are shared for all to read, not only about animal agriculture's impact on climate change, but other resource extractive methods like hydraulic fracturing or fracking.

On top of this, in recent years, several U.S. doctors have come out with many documented cases in medical science literature showing how a vegan or plant-based diet[3] is healthier for one's body. Drs. Neal Barnard, Michael Greger, Caldwell Esselstyn and Kim A. Williams (at the time of writing, Dr. Williams is president of the American College of Cardiologists), among others, are leading examples of medical personnel who are recommending a vegan diet for better health in conjunction with regular amounts of daily exercise.[4] Further, Chris Hedges's article "Eating Our Way to Disease" outlines the darker side of the animal agriculture industry vis-à-vis lobbying, funding-biased research and, as a consequence, a corrupt medical practice. The issues raised in Hedges's article are explored further in Anderson and Kuhn's second documentary *What the Health?*. In *What the Health?* both Anderson and Kuhn critique the pharmaceutical and medical establishment for needlessly medicating and operating on people with preventable diseases. While Anderson and Kuhn never state that lifesaving medication or surgeries ought not be used, they promote lifestyle changes before undergoing extremely invasive and costly procedures and medications.

Hedges illustrates the incredible amounts of money involved in preventable diseases by showing two cardiovascular examples, that is, a $5 billion stent industry and a $35 billion statin (cholesterol-lowering drug) industry. Hedges muses that those benefiting from these profits do not want to see the stent or statin industries lose money. More than just recommending good nutrition, this is also a deeper tactic of disrupting big business, specifically the pharmaceutical industry. The regular long-term consumption of meat, dairy, and eggs in some cases directly results in and in other cases increases the risk of developing dietary-related cholesterol[5] (a leading cause in contracting atherosclerosis and may also be related to an increased risk of abdominal aortic aneurism), Alzheimer's disease,[6] breast cancer,[7] declining kidney function,[8] DNA damage,[9] inflammation,[10] sexual dysfunction,[11] and type 2 diabetes.[12] The list could go on, however prevention is certainly better than cure.[13] Though none of these doctors are rash enough to suggest that animal products cause cancer outright, they do suggest, with medical science very much supporting them, that animal products greatly contribute by raising IGF-1 levels, a contributing factor in many illnesses/diseases.

The fault for contracting these illnesses and diseases lies in a society and culture that values and promotes consumerism and consumption. Poor nutritional choices are made readily available to communities marginalized by poverty and/or crises.[14] A 2017 documentary, *Ireland's Health Divide*,[15] highlighting the health divide in the Republic of Ireland noted that people from poorer communities prioritize cheap and easy-to-access food, albeit unhealthy choices. In an interview about the documentary, Dr. Eva Orsmond (who presented *Ireland's Health Divide*) stated, "Mothers trying to cope with chronic illness or domestic violence or substandard housing have enough going on without thinking about healthy eating" (Pownall, 2017). Further discoveries showed that poorer children are likely to die several years younger; three times as likely to die of cancer; twice as likely to become obese; and twice as likely to have mental health problems (Pownall, 2017). Further, access to health care and education was shown to be highly restricted with one percent of children from poorer communities likely to receive a college education; have access to one community doctor (GP or general practitioner) per 2,500 where the national average is one GP per 1,250 (Pownall, 2017). Dr. Orsmond notes, contrasting the environments of affluent and impoverished communities, vis-à-vis the impact on health, that "for most of these people their environment is grey and depressing, there are no trees, no parks, no playgrounds. If they do have a shop nearby it's just a corner shop offering limited choices such as fizzy drinks, cakes and frozen food. There are a huge concentration of takeaways" (Pownall, 2017). This type of data, while coming from a small Western country on the periphery of Europe, is just as applicable to other Western states. Poor communities have poor opportunities, poor infrastructure, and poor investment. This leads to poor lifestyle choices.

In the introduction to Greger's book,[16] *How Not to Die*, Greger informs the reader that physicians (in the United States) get very few hours of nutritional training. Keeping Greger's claim in mind, Hedges and the documentary *What the Health?* point out that certain health institutions like the American Diabetics Association (ADA), recommend patients eat a varied diet of red meat and poultry despite medical evidence suggesting that these meats are particularly harmful for diabetics. Further, the World Health Organization classified red meat as a type 2 carcinogen, that is, a probable cause of cancer, whereas processed meats are classified as a type 1 carcinogen, that is, known cause of cancer.[17] Hedges shows us that huge investments are made by the meat, dairy, egg, and pharmaceutical industries in health institutions like the ADA, the American Heart Association, and the Academy of Nutritional Dietetics. On top of this, Hedges alludes to a worse and often unspoken problem, that is, the meat, dairy, and egg industries fund and publish ninety percent of the nutritional and dietary research. Some might correctly suspect an agenda or bias, especially given the profits involved. This leaves a very small percentage of authentic independent[18] research which invariably results in forming positive conclusions about a vegan diet and condemning animal-based diets. Indeed, Barnard, Willett, and Ding (2017) discuss the misuse of meta-analyses in nutritional research in a recent online publication. Unfortunately, however, Hedges's article begins by showing just how far such authentic and independent nutritional research can go—even on a government committee they are shut down, thrown out, and replaced with animal agriculture representatives.

Though some may toot the horn of moderation in everything, a recent catastrophe has put a dampener on that. Reports in late July 2017 of an area the size of New Jersey off the Mexican coast had become a dead zone. To put that into perspective, that's roughly an area of 22,608 km² (8728.9 mile²) off the coast of Mexico where no life exists.[19] Marine life either fled or died due to hypoxia. A larger expanse in the Indian ocean was deemed a dead zone in 2016 covering an area of roughly 59,569.7 km² (23,000 mile²).[20] The surprising culprit was the meat industry. Though the prophets of moderation may cry a combination of consumerism, capitalism, and poor environmental infrastructure and policies; it is not often that the unregulated broccoli industry creates a dead zone! On top of that, the first waves of climate refugees are already migrating,[21] and the effectiveness of animal agriculture on global food supply and the environment has proven to be a failure alongside poor and inefficient distribution methods under capitalism.

This is more than an ethical and nutritional discussion. Though both overlap, we can clearly see political and environmental issues in the obfuscation of the truth regarding the impact on our health and the environment by animal agriculture and the pharmaceutical industry. This is not an isolated issue. Climate change is a planetary problem. Sickness and disease are universal issues too.

Hallelujah Hemp

That wonderful and misunderstood plant—hemp! Its versatility is astounding: paper, bricks, cement, medicine, clothing, milk, and so on. Accordingly, hemp produces four times the amount of paper trees produce per acre. Hemp, for the purpose of paper, therefore takes up less land. In essence, paper production (from writing to toilet paper) could use seventy-five percent less of the land it currently is using if current production levels are sufficient. Alternatively, by using the same amount of land hemp would produce four times the amount of paper that trees are currently producing. "When grown for fibre, industrial hemp is planted in narrow rows to reduce branching and increase stalk height" (Fortenberry and Bennett 2004, 99). The fact that hemp can produce more paper than trees combined with the added bonus of this cultivation technique, hemp is a win-win regarding land use at least. On top of that, hemp can also be fashioned into bricks—a more environmentally friendly means of building with much less carbon emissions than cement. Though carbon neutral items may be used for domestic construction, for example, timber, hempcrete may replace concrete and be used on more publicly used structures such as pavement, buildings, and other structures.

I will momentarily return to the issue of toilet paper due to the number of trees used in its manufacturing[22] and the thoughtless waste that can accompany such everyday products. Some have put forth the idea of replacing toilet paper with a bidet. Others have also encouraged the use of dry toilets and, regarding women's products, using reusable sanitary pads and/or a cup (specifically designed to sit comfortably and collect menstrual blood). Though "green" in terms of paper use, in some groups, women's sanitary products are typically pushed as an option by men, not recognizing that not all women are comfortable or want to use them. Never mind that a group not affected by the issue is making such decisions. This thinking typically puts the burden of tackling climate change solely on women and risks impacting hygiene standards. It's not a worthy society if poor hygiene standards are widespread for the sake of "greenness." Though anecdotal, I recall several men in what would be termed a *leftist leaning "green" discussion* stating that women don't really need sanitary products if it is a question of reducing tree/paper consumption. Furthermore, in such scenarios, misogynistic elements slip into environmental topics. It's a worrisome trend that may have combined toxic masculinity with already scientific and ecological ignorance. However, the ideas mentioned earlier are laudable if accompanied by consent.

Some of the claims attributed to hemp's added greenness is the fact that less herbicides and pesticides are required, thus reducing the amount that can leak into groundwater or as run off. Fortenberry and Bennett point out that hemp is very competitive with weeds, though this may depend on the purpose for the hemp as some agro-uses reduce hemp canopy and thereby allow for weeds (Fortenberry and Bennett 2004, 100). Having said that, less herbicide is more, and both Fortenberry and Bennett acknowledge this by recommending hemp as a rotational crop. Further, hemp paper is rumored to need less ink and bleach additives than tree paper. As these are only rumors and research around hemp is hard to find, more studies need to be conducted to substantiate these claims and made available for other researchers. However, supposing these to be true, though there would be less cost involved for the producers, for example, regarding herbicide, pesticides, and so on, the major cost saved would be for the stakeholders or those who would feel the effects of the change. Some may scoff at this bonus, but the mass leakage of chemicals into groundwater and the food chain is a concern. Given the scale of pollution and the crisis we face, the stakeholders are certainly many!

Fortenberry and Bennett briefly assess the political climate around hemp in the United States, namely the DEA's tight control over the plant, even for industrial purposes (Fortenberry and Bennett 2004, 115). Having said that, a number of states have legalized medicinal marijuana essentially behind the federal government's back. There surely could be no reason not to similarly legalize a regulated industrial hemp industry. This legal path combined with workers seeking to set up such companies/industries may be particularly feasible. Imagine worker-owned hemp industries or hemp cooperatives that are eco-friendly. In this conversation about politics and ecology, one area of overlap is industry. Though dated, Long informs us of the success of the Mondragon Co-operative Federation of País-Basque, Spain:

> Studies have shown that the co-ops have consistently outperformed surrounding capitalist industry on all the usual measures, and while unemployment in Spain has hovered around 20% for many years, full employment has been maintained within the Federation. All this has been achieved with a level of internal democracy and concern for social justice undreamt of by most workers struggling under exploitative state systems, whether capitalist or authoritarian socialist. (Long 1996)

Of course, funding may be difficult to acquire especially if one's cooperative/anarchist collective sounds nonsensical to the capitalists likely to approve of funds. Pragmatically "playing the game" may be necessary. If acquiring funding becomes difficult, other paths may be very well open, for example, online start-up campaigns, asking for a loan from friends, family, and other co-ops. The Mondragon Co-operative Federation was able to begin when sympathetic community members loaned what money they had. However, Fortenberry and Bennett note that small-scale hemp industries could satisfy current demand (excluding the demand for medicinal marijuana). But, one may predict a rise in demands/popularity for the use of hemp in clothing, paper, construction, foods, and so on. A form of expansion may happen. As noted earlier vis-à-vis the medical, farming, and pharmaceutical institutions promoting each other, a similar support network against the use of hemp ought to be expected. It is nonetheless a very versatile plant and very green regarding the use of land, herbicides, and pesticides.

A Permacultured Commons

A commons can be defined as a shared resource managed by a community who create rules to make the resource long-lasting, wherein the resource cannot be monopolized by one or a group of individuals. A commons is meant to be as open as possible, where the resource is neither private nor public. The idea of the commons as land-based and agricultural appears to be dispersed globally and surviving in small communes of radical groups. Contrary to this, tech-based commons exist, for example, the internet. Agricultural commons can of course come back in a nuanced, widespread, and synthesized form, complimented by modern green technology. The Solar-Punk sub-culture attempts this. The so-called tragedy of the commons, a popular straw man argument, is really the inevitability of capitalism, that is, over-fished, acidified, and ruined seas and oceans; degraded soil; deforestation; desertification; and so on ad nauseam.[23] Permaculture, however, is a response to the disastrous agribusiness idea of single crops dominating swathes of land creating a monoculture, such as wheat for miles, impacting the surrounding eco-system. Permaculture has very egalitarian and leftist ideas about sharing surplus crops, utilizing manageable scales, and naturally integrating plants to work harmoniously together, for example, some plants help the shared soil chemically, others may physically repeal or distract pest, and others again attract pollinators.

Building on the wider vegan movement, with less land given to livestock and their feed,[24] more land can be allocated for human crops and other essential spaces including recreation, housing, medical facilities, schools, and so on. On top of this, slaughterhouses can be repurposed. This process can easily be derailed if lacking a sufficient number of involved and dedicate groups of people. It is not enough to have individuals involved at this point in time. Large groups of people have to already be mobilized and actively involved. Wholescale reorganization of land use and the decision-making processes involved is a mighty feat. For example, if housing is an issue in a particular community, building well-designed and properly sized apartments (instead of housing estates)[25] may be an option; if having a recreational area or other facilities is desired, so be it.

Adding to the issue of maximizing the use of available space, the Venus Project discusses concepts like vertical farms[26] and hydroponics. These concepts are viewed as a necessity in order to both reduce waste and as a response to poor soil health. As a quick note, organic farms reportedly have twenty-six percent more potential to sequester carbon in the soil and thirteen

percent more soil organic matter, that is, humus (Nargi, 2017). Soil maintenance is important ecologically as well as for food production. Vertical farms,
however, as the name might suggest, are planted vertically. The area of space
they occupy is therefore limited though the yield is increased. Hydroponics is a subset of hydroculture, the method of growing plants without soil,
using mineral nutrient solutions in a water solvent. Terrestrial plants may be
grown with only their roots exposed to the mineral solution, or the roots may
be supported by an inert medium, such as perlite or gravel. The nutrients in
hydroponics can come from an array of different sources; these can include
but are not limited to animal manures and/or normal nutrients. The adoption
of vegan lifestyle and animal ethics would, however, complicate the use of
animals for their faeces as a separate but equally exploitative animal industry may emerge. As such, nutrients derived from composts are the preferred
option. Carver and Bradley[27] praise hydroponics for being able to "provide
only what the plant uses in controlled and easily maintained systems—it is
a viable alternative to traditional farming methods. The amount of control in
these systems also ensures that crops are contaminant free, which helps stem
outbreaks of *E. coli* and *Salmonella*" (2012, 44).

This proposed commons is far more difficult to discuss than other commons as it relates to land, food production, and so on. The internet acts like
a commons of sorts via access to vast amount of information and is defended
by many (cf. net neutrality). Net neutrality has come under threat numerous
times and has awoken mass global protests. Though algorithms for searches
and content are manipulated by Google and Facebook, a degree of commons
remains:

> Clearly, when we talk about the commons we are not speaking of some universal
> panacea that will magically resolve everything. It is rather about understanding
> that there are links beginning to be forged between the old, traditional collective
> ways of managing resources, goods and subsistence, and new forms of coopera-
> tion and collective creation of value linked to great technological change and to
> globalisation. And so, faced with problems that purely marketised options and
> purely state-owned options have had, the existence of a cooperative, communal
> nexus expressed in the idea of the common good open up new possiblities for
> research, transmission and experimentation. (Subirats 2012)

Subirats's article, while discussing Ostrom's death and the legacy Ostrom
left on theories and research about common goods and spaces, hearkens back
to Kropotkin's treatise on cooperation in his *Mutual Aid*. Indeed Kropotkin
([1902] 2009, 231) concludes this work by stating that "the periods when
institutions based on the mutual-aid tendency took their greatest development were also the periods of greatest progress in arts, industry, and science."
The underlying point is that cooperation works and can work on a city-wide

scale.[28] Of course, tactics for organizing groups of people to this point pre-date the juncture being discussed.[29] Rather, "the abiding logic of the com-mons is not based, as we have seen, on a balancing act between the roles of the state and the market," instead the logic of the commons is a polycentric and decentralized agreement between those affected by shared and indeed common problems (Subirats 2012). In short, more cooperation and less competition.

Part II—Interim Changes (Tactics Not Goals)

Among leftist circles, there is sometimes a heated discussion as to whether individual changes trump systemic widespread change or vice versa. Are ste-reotypical and caricatured ragtag leftie groups tactically beneficial vis-à-vis public reception or tools for the prevailing system to bash anti-capitalist and anti-state sentiments, however slight or strong? Worse, such a motley crew could be labeled and prosecuted as terrorists.[30] Having said that, we shouldn't compromise convictions simply to gain members, but extreme actions ought not to alienate the very people we wish to support and show solidarity with. Given the world we live in and the number of voices, interest groups, and lobbying powers, a certain amount of realism and pragmatism is necessary, which ought not to quell hope or idealism. A balancing act, no doubt! That said, none of the proposals given in the following ought to be interpreted as a capitulation to the state or other institutions. Working within the system is necessary tactically.

The purpose of this section is to recognize that the global changes we want from Part I may require us to work within the system. For some anarchists, having anything to do with the state is an indefensible compromise. This sec-tion will try to help differentiate between a tactic and a goal. Working within and for the system and participating in the accompanying bureaucracy are not goals. These are tactics. Supporting government policy is a tactic. The main "system" that will be discussed is from an Irish-EU perspective, as these are the jurisdictions I am accustomed to and can speak better about.

Working the System and Working within It (A Tactic Not a Goal)

The European Commission is clear on what environmental crime is: "The most known areas of environmental crime are the illegal emission or discharge of substances into air, water or soil, the illegal trade in wildlife, illegal trade in ozone-depleting substances and the illegal shipment or dumping of waste" (European Commission). However, this appears to be an aesthetic matter, disapproving of impropriety, that is, the *illegal* nature of trading wild animals or ozone-depleting substances, and so on, not the acts or substances themselves. But, the 2008 European Union (EU) directive stipulates more clearly the illegality of "the production, importation, exportation, placing on the market or use of ozone-depleting substances" (3(i)). Though Article 3 and 4 of the EU directive stipulate several offences, I will focus on the offence 3(a): "the discharge, emission or introduction of a quantity of materials or ionizing radiation into air, soil or water, which causes or is likely to cause death or serious injury to any person or substantial damage to the quality of air, the quality of soil or the quality of water, or to animals or plants." On the surface, Article 3(a) of the EU directive appears to be a progressive policy that environmentalists can support. Enforcement however is another matter.

The provision of satisfactory basic amenities, such as appropriate waste disposal and wastewater treatment facilities, is sorely lacking in the Republic of Ireland as Melia (2017) discusses. The case is clearly in violation of the EU directive mentioned before. The point of such superficial legal analysis is that a motley crew of anarchists installing a sewage system, though admirable, is likely to end badly. A certain amount of working the system and working within it is required. Further, the fine Melia outlines as imposed upon Greece was of course a fine the working people had to pay. It is worrying that Ireland can toy with environmental damage, lack of necessary infrastructure, and potentially worsening public debt. The Irish government, at the time of this writing, has spent millions[31] in legal fees contesting the EU's demands that Apple pay back taxes of €13 billion though the original figure owed was roughly €19 billion.[32] Though the corporate tax rate in the Republic of Ireland is 12.5%, it has been revealed that Apple paid significantly less. Apple paid less than 2%, while two of its subsidiaries Apple Operations International (AOI) and Apple Sales International (ASI) paid 0% and 0.05%, respectively.[33] I hope that this tangential example illustrates how much money and resources states will exhaust to halt standard legal/economic procedures, for example, collecting corporate taxes and back taxes owed. One can only speculate the level of cover-ups and deceit that may occur if radical or progressive laws around industries and climate crimes were shirked.

Supplying appropriate bins for waste, recycled materials, glass, and organic waste (food peelings, etc.) is not an across-the-board policy by privatized waste collection companies. Furthermore, the growing method of waste collection, known as "pay and weigh," whereby the heavier one's bin the more one pays, has led to cross-contamination as certain waste goods, specifically nappies/diapers, are put into the wrong bins to cut down on waste collection bills. This puts unnecessary pressure on homes with a baby/babies and increasing bin collection bills, of which some cannot afford. Further, the consequence has been contamination and potential pollution or the use of illegal waste disposal groups.[34] This situation has raised many questions locally. Calls to nationalize waste collection were made alongside the imposition of maximum charges and/or have worker-led waste collection facilities. However, an example of collectivized waste collection can be seen in the organizational structures created in Rojava in Northern Syria.[35] Basic services like waste removal and disposal are now democratically controlled and directly accountable to the people's councils[36] in districts, neighbourhoods, and villages (Knapp et al. 2016, 107).

Nonetheless, the expense for recycling and disposing of separated waste is costly. Once again, the expense is on customers who have no choice but to purchase the food packaged as is. Industries are not discouraged from using plastic packaging, which spoils food quicker in the heat and may not be recyclable. Street markets and small groceries are known for selling mostly unpackaged foods. The customer can bring their own bags. Often a variety of reusable plastic or paper bags are provided. However, food packaging facilities are not encouraged to use recyclable/biodegradable packages just as recycling facilities are not encouraged to upgrade their equipment to recycle all goods. Pope (2017) acknowledges in his article that not all recyclable products are able to be recycled in Ireland. This is a well-known complaint from households seeking to cut down their general waste as a means of cutting down waste collection bills.

A recent French law forbids food waste forcing unsold food to be given to food banks and charities. Though this does not manage the problems of overproduction, poor storage methods, or the expense of living healthily, at least food waste became a public issue, and an agreeable solution was implemented. Unfortunately, no statistics exist comparing how better the situation is in reality; are poorer people able to access better quality food because of this particular law; and how has this affected France environmentally. This law however was a response to findings that stated that in France every year 10 million tons of food was either lost or wasted, costing €16 billion annually (French Agency for the Environment and Energy Management 2016). The negative impact on the environment was shocking as the food waste emitted 15.3 million tonnes of CO_2, representing three percent of the country's total CO_2 emission. Though a small figure, this three percent is clearly manageable. This law interestingly targets supermarkets over a certain square meter and other premises that produce more than a certain tonnage of food waste including the hospitality sector. Though no figure can be found for how costly this was for France's hospitality sector, in Denmark it reportedly costs over €80 billion! Unfortunately, if the language is money, learning to speak it may reap more rewards.

Appropriate and enforceable environmental laws appear to be lacking across Europe. Though implying a reliance on the state, it is true that tactically one must work through state apparatuses to achieve justice at times. A further consideration is how much pollution is done domestically versus industrially. When examined, is it the case that domestic pollution occurs due to affordability, whereas industrial pollution occurs due to greed and profitability? Should laws be created and enforced to lessen and stop industrial pollution and the unnecessary creation of unrecyclable products? Should appropriate provisions be made for people to separate and dispose of waste properly? I think so. While single-use plastic bag bans have seen a decrease in the number of bags ending up in landfills, there has been a corresponding increase in the purchase of plastic bags. The latter is of thicker quality, therefore more plastic is used which typically contains more ink as Thornton (2017) explains. A more widespread ban aimed at companies who package both food and other items could be more successful particularly if aimed at plastics that are not or cannot be recycled, complimented with the introduction of better reusable bags made from canvas or hemp.

On a more local and immediate level, communities can come together to create a change they desire. Community gardens (even in urban settings) are becoming increasingly popular. Initiatives like community gardens form bonds, provide skills, feed people, save money on food, and reduce unnecessary use of plastic. Organic waste, from both food and sewage, can be used as fertilizer. With respect to the latter example, dry toilets may be the preferred option of collection if human waste is to be used as a fertilizer. Though considered a vulgar topic, these are real issues and real solutions. A more long-term benefit of starting such an initiative is that similar groups can be started and organized, such as community child minding or community meals. In the 1980s in Mexico City, poor locals developed what they called the *colonia ecologica productiva* (productive ecological settlement). In Queensland, Australia, in 2009, neighbors similarly started to collectively grow crops.[37] Unfortunately, such communal activities only come out of a need. However, they repeatedly show the possibilities of community organization, cooperation, and mutual aid.

Amorós (2015) discusses how rural lands are no longer the source of food but the endpoint of waste treatment. Further, as capitalism commodifies all, Amorós shows how even waste has become a profitable commodity. As a form of resistance, interrupting this commodification and profitization is necessary to dismantling both state and capitalist power, but also to create more ecological values and culture. Though Amorós encourages ruralization and de-industrialization, the Curious George Brigade (an anarchist collective in Queens, New York) praises the city but proposes communal changes to stop the massive pollution cities cause.[38] Communities must however come together and decide on collective action. Gelderloos (2010, 71–72) briefly outlines how Freetown Christiania in Copenhagen, Denmark, managed their waste via cooperation and a garbage committee answerable to the general meeting. Such committees may not be as necessary in much smaller communities, however, the spirit of cooperation is. Gelderloos points out that it is only when we see the true extent of our consumption that we may choose to do something, such as not ship our e-waste to the Global South. Again, this seems predicated upon visible needs and a community coming together. Some may pre-emptively be willing to discuss with other neighbors developing urban/guerrilla gardens.

In *Anarchy and Action*, Ward argues that "in a society where urban land and its development are in the hands of speculative entrepreneurs and where the powers of urban initiatives are in the hands of local and national governments, it was inevitable that the processes of change and innovation should be controlled by bureaucracies and speculators or by an alliance between the two" (Ward 2008, 76). While Ward's main claim that "Community organisations . . . have resulted from the new consciousness that local as well as central governments exploit the poor" (Ward 2008, 165), we should also consider Smucker's warning that using unnecessary leftist or academic language with such community organizations can be alienating. Smucker cautions against inadvertently alienating allies who may not be totally convinced of leftist values. Rather than the rhetoric of old/in-group jargon, one may tactically frame and phrase typically leftist issues, such as the rise of food prices and the cost of living, as potential reasons in a "non-partisan discussion" for a community garden.

Inevitable Contact—Tactical Response

In terms of working with others on campaigns, coming into contact with NGOs and other groups working on similar issues can happen. Though this chapter focuses on ecology, there are groups already in existence who we may need to help, learn from, or reshape. Working with such groups to force policy implementation or close down an industry infamous for pollution may be a pragmatic necessity. A non-governmental organization (NGO) is usually defined as a non-profit organization that operates independently of any government, whose purpose is typically to address social or political issues. Having said that, in practice, NGOs can operate very differently than the proposed definition would suggest,[39] with considerable support from politicians, governments, and political institutions. Tackling climate change globally won't be successful if scattered pockets of resistance do not cooperate and communicate. Global change will necessarily bring us in contact with different groups and communities. Pragmatically and tactically then, NGOs will be discussed.

Regarding NGOs, Crn Blok argues that "the representatives who promise to fight in our name not only do not care about our problems, but also they profit from our miserable conditions of living. That is why we know that if we want to start struggling for a total liberation from the chains of the state and of our bosses, the last place we will go to is an NGO." However, Crn Blok continues by illustrating a pragmatic approach I am in agreement with: "of course, that doesn't mean that in various specific occasions we shouldn't use the loopholes and the contradictions of the legal system in order to defend ourselves from any legal attacks." However, Crn Blok also cautions us stating that "neither the law, nor any other institutional 'remedy' the state is offering us can be our main means of struggle against the state oppression and against our exploiters at work. We should remember that the law that (we think) is protecting us today, can be withdrawn overnight if the elites find it too menacing to their privileged position" (Crn Blok n.d.).

Crn Blok makes clear the anarchist distaste for NGOs. Though we may be working on similar issues, we shouldn't be lulled into a false sense of solidarity with groups who habitually support both capitalism and the state. A pragmatic tactic to use NGOs and their access to resources (money, food, clothing, medicines, contacts, etc.) may be employed. Though this may nonetheless complicate relationships, it will broaden the outreach of our message and allow us to be better informed about the issues we are working on, whether it be social housing, domestic violence, fracking, industrial pollution, or otherwise. One such activity could be working with a refugee NGO in a government detention center to supply information about the rights and entitlements or help with legal paperwork. Further, working with certain groups gives one access to their collated information, data, and political platform. Working alongside Médecins Sans Frontières or Human Rights Watch in the Middle East, for example, is not necessarily the same as other NGOs who pocket donations and turn a blind eye to corruption. Certainly in crises one cannot pick and choose. Solidarity and mutual aid must occur whether in Yemen or with migrants crossing the Mediterranean. War zones and natural disasters are obviously different in their immediacy than "stable" countries campaigning for social issues. However, NGOs like the Red Cross cannot enter certain areas without a military escort, limiting, therefore, who receives help. Under similar conditions we see anarchists or those un/knowingly adopting anarchist principles ignoring so-called sound advice and escorts. By entering these "no go areas" they splinter the prevailing narrative and help those "beyond help" or "in difficult to reach places."

The case of Hungary under Orbán shows a different side of NGO involvement. Wright and de la Chapelle highlight in one particular case domestic abuse against women who are being ignored by the state:

> Victims complained they were ignored by police and social services while being repeatedly abused by their partners. This included, HRW [Human Rights Watch] says, while being stabbed and chopped at with knives, axes, and swords;

kicked and punched in the abdomen while pregnant; raped; beaten with sticks, prams, iron rods, and thick cables to the point of broken bones and skull fractures; locked in sheds without clothes in winter; thrown off balconies; dumped in remote areas in the middle of the night; and subjected to severe psychological violence.

Orbán and his followers make the case that various NGOs, especially those being funded from abroad, are negatively influencing Hungarian society. The opposite appears to be the case. With the insistence upon traditional societal values, more negative impacts created from within Hungary will be felt by marginalized groups.

Lessons from NGO-ized areas of Africa further the need for a nuanced and pragmatic approach to NGOs, specifically when, as Bah and Anumo point out (2017), NGOs force the involvement of men in community feminist groups. While feminism ought not to be solely "a woman's issue," it ought not to be decided by a third party who is to be involved and to what extent. Certainly, in the context Bah and Amuno outline, forcing women (who may be victims of domestic/other abuse) to accept the presence of men in their group is potentially damaging to their mental health, sense of well-being, and confidence in group discussion/activity. The fear of course is that this NGO could be forcing victims to be around their abuser(s). While elements of restorative justice may use such scenarios, this is not such a case. Neither is it receptive to what these women actually want, feel, and demand nor thoughtful about how this decision may negatively impact women's attendance or participation. The ultimate issue being outlined in this segue of course is the muddy waters surrounding NGOs and the varying contexts they may exist within.

That, albeit important, case aside, the main focus is ecology. One can see though how complicated this can become. With that, it's worth noting that there is a contentious case among some groups, particularly in the vegan community, regarding hunting and fishing practices. Some equate Indigenous tribes hunting, animal agriculture, and super trawlers, seeing no ethical difference between these activities. There is no doubt that super trawlers scraping the sea floor for fish not only ruin marine ecosystems but also obliterate their populations via bycatch. It is extremely unlikely that any of the remaining Indigenous tribes left in the world who hunt could possibly be the reason for the damage done to ecosystems. Generally speaking, such Indigenous groups have a particularly noteworthy view, oftentimes tied to their spirituality, of nature and their place within it. On top of this, according to the International Fund for Animal Welfare (IFAW), commercial seal hunts waste roughly ninety percent of the meat compared to Indigenous hunts.[40] Oceana, an NGO seeking to protect marine ecosystems, suggests that by the EU reducing its trawler fleet (estimated to be 15,000—this is differentiated from the number of vessels, and it is not specified whether these include super trawlers or not) it could reach its own goal of a forty percent reduction in fishing capacity[41] as opposed to enforcing quotas, fleet capacity restrictions, and controls on the amount of time spent at sea.[42] All of which do not prevent sea floor scrapping or bycatch. As a side note, Dr. Michael Greger recommends removing fish from one's diet due to the unhealthiness of it nutritionally and as pollution in the sea works its way up the food chain.[43]

Expanding on that, the double exploitation in the poaching industry (of animals and poor communities where these animals live) is sickening. Hunters, typically wealthy and Western, often pay huge sums of money to be able to kill an animal. Some justify this lifestyle with the motto: eat what you kill. But, the fact that these animals live in poorer parts of the world can have an impact on locals turning a blind eye to these hunters, however illegal it may be, in the hope that some money may flow their way. Niraj et al. briefly show the failures of the lack of policy enforcement regarding wildlife in India (2012, 13). Poor infrastructure and lack of knowledge by the general population counted as two main aspects for failure. Other concerns focused on low conviction rates, lack of coordination between agencies and departments, and poor resources including training and funding for local-level officials (2012, 14). I view this to mean poor enforcement and a community too ill-informed to be aware of the issue. Niraj et al. conclude, however, that communities ought to be involved in policy-making and implementation (2012, 17). This conclusion by Niraj et al. is welcomed. Community involvement in not only the maintenance but prosperity of one's locality. Community involvement is preferable to outside groups' involvement. This situation does not make outside help unwelcome, however, local knowledge, leadership, and activity are more important, especially given Bah and Anumo's exposé of one NGO's negative involvement. Community involvement would have a secondary effect of maintaining traditional skills and knowledge, informing locals regarding best practice and benefiting communities via communication, mutual aid, and solidarity to help with new skills, such as literacy and technology.

Building on community involvement, credible and appropriately messaged information, which debunks myths about certain animal appendages' medicinal properties, is also a necessity. Debunking myths of medicinal properties of animal appendages is not solely an issue in poorer regions of the world. There is a growing trend of bathing in the blood of severed deer antlers in Russia (Pleitgen and Ilyushina 2018). Reasons put forth for this vary from alleviating erectile dysfunction to better athletic performance. This pseudo-science is regressive and borders on totemic-animism, where the strength of a specific animal can supposedly be absorbed via consuming and/or wearing it. More concerning is how this may be symptomatic of toxic masculinity whereby bathing in an animal's blood, for example, reinforces one's manhood and hetero-normativity. The same totally unnecessary toxic masculinity occupies the space of the hunter, who is often seen as the idealized human, fighting against or taming the harsh savage wild. The trade in ivory, for example, though widely considered objectionable, still occurs. However, the largely unknown tagua seed will hopefully replace ivory, just as faux leather and fur will hopefully replace real leather and fur. Tagua seeds are particularly versatile and can be fashioned into various shapes for both jewelry and ornamentation, making ivory an unnecessary product.

However, the earlier discussion about NGOs can be adapted to NGOs specifically designed for the environment, animal welfare, and anti-poaching. Butler (2017) outlines how NGOs which protect minorities and are against state interests are targeted by the state and put through a smear campaign. For the moment NGOs protecting the environment have not come up against such pressure/violence. This may not be the case forever. At a certain point, industries will be targeted by such eco-groups/NGOs whether they be in animal agriculture, fishing vessels, or more generally simply responsible for pollution and contributing to climate change. In the latter half of 2017, in response to a campaign by a group called Go Vegan World, dairy giants in the United Kingdom began spending over £1 million on counter-propaganda (Feltcher 2017). When discussing ecology and steps toward beneficial change, coming up against industrial unions or powerful lobbying industries is a significant concern.

CONCLUSION

This chapter has demonstrated how plants can and will occupy more space in our lives in the future, from tagua seeds and hemp to a vegan lifestyle. The disastrous effects of animal agriculture on the environment are unfortunately ignored or written off as a necessary evil to feed people. Listening to some of the named medical professionals mentioned in this chapter is necessary to counter the erroneous and dangerous view that animal agriculture is good and necessary. Veganism is beneficial for our human and ecological health. Furthermore, it disrupts Big Pharma's pill-pushing monopoly and the capitalist interests in agriculture. Hemp, though requiring a much better analysis, is the plant of the future. Its versatility and lack of need for resources (land, pesticide, and herbicide) are strong reasons for its use and acceptance in society. Its nutritional and medical qualities are additional reasons for using hemp to make our future greener. However, at the time of writing this, there are attempts by Big Pharma to turn hemp into a profit-making machine. The voraciousness of capitalists is to be expected and resisted.

The commons of the future will not be the same as that of the past. It will be different by being complimented with new technology and practices, such as vertical farming and hydroponics. Having commons will benefit communities more than private property and laws protecting it. Creating these permacultured commons is about maximizing food production for places where soil health could be appalling and where population density is unbalanced to meet the societal needs. Futher, by involving communities, better food distribution methods can be achieved than the prevailing distribution methods under capitalism. On top of this, a better view and value toward food, land, and cooperative work can be created, a necessity in a future culture. An empowered populace achieving results is a threat to the prevailing ideology and powers of oppression.

The left has often been criticized for isolating itself, while the right has not been. Working the system is about using the system's own laws and policies against itself. My overarching message in part II of this chapter was tactics not goal. This situation may necessitate working with NGOs and political/ legal groups to prevent industrial pollution or update sewage systems, and so on. Working with other groups (including NGOs) implies intersectionality, which itself necessitates vetting of which groups to be in solidarity with, for example, a racist eco-feminist group is not an ally. We don't and ought not to need to rely on governments or NGOs to work the system. However, we should expect encountering them and responding appropriately. Having such tactics provides a variety of tools to achieve our goal.

Global solidarity and communication are a necessity for the paradigm shift dreamed of. As with all activities, when going into another community, not being insulting, patronizing, or demeaning is paramount. Being invited into a community is not the same as deciding to enter uninvited. Further, if promoting a lifestyle like veganism, which affects farming, industry, and jobs, all of which are very important in rural and poor communities especially when value is placed on such generational traditions, it should not be promoted as a new fashionable trend that the privileged class in the more affluent regions of the world are spreading across the poor global south. My fear is that this would appear to be an aesthetic re-fashioning of neo-colonialism. Though well intentioned as it may be, a variety of poorly constructed and poorly thought-out tactics can be both alienating and insulting as Bah and Anumo describe. Working within the system and with specific groups to tackle specific problems and crises can act as a foundation in solidarity. Choosing which groups to work with, though, is another matter! It can also be an access point from which to spread radical means of organizing.

A concluding warning, though: discussing ecology and certain changes we may make inadvertently welcomes views and opinions in conflict with anarchism. This contradiction can come in the form of so-called anarchoprimitivism or accompanying misogyny as noted previously. Further, outside groups may wish to participate for their own nefarious ends contrary to our principles and goals. Intersectionality, though not discussed, is assumed, by me, to be a foundational block in anarchist political movements. Promoting veganism while turning a blind eye to racism is not acceptable. Dropping our anti-fascist values to spread our message is not acceptable either. There is a limit to working the system and working with others. It cannot be so far that we lose credibility, nor can it be so close that we isolate and alienate others from us.

NOTES

1. The poorest half of the global population are responsible for approximately 10% of total global emissions: https://www.oxfam.org/sites/www.oxfam.org/files/file_attachments/mb-extreme-carbon-inequality-021215-en.pdf.

2. Anderson and Kuhn's Cowspiracy facts page: http://www.cowspiracy.com/facts/.

3. Though I understand the difference between veganism as a lifestyle and the diet aspect of just a plant-based diet, "vegan diet" will be the term used henceforth.

4. For more, see The Physicians Committee for Responsible Medicine: http://www.pcrm.org/.

5. Physicians Committee for Responsible Medicine on heart disease (atherosclerosis) and cholesterol: http://www.pcrm.org/health/health-topics/cholesterol-and-heart-disease.

6. Physicians Committee for Responsible Medicine on Alzheimer's disease: http://www.pcrm.org/health/diets/ffl/employee/eating-to-prevent-alzheimers-disease.

7. See https://nutritionfacts.org/topics/breast-cancer/ and Physicians Committee for Responsible Medicine on meat consumption and cancer risk: http://www.pcrm.org/health/cancer-resources/diet-cancer/facts/meat-consumption-and-cancer-risk.

8. See https://nutritionfacts.org/topics/kidney-disease/.

9. See https://nutritionfacts.org/topics/dna-damage/.

10. See https://nutritionfacts.org/topics/inflammation/.

11. See https://nutritionfacts.org/topics/sexual-dysfunction/ and Physicians Committee for Responsible Medicine on erectile dysfunction: http://www.pcrm.org/nbBlog/index.php/diet-away-erectile-dysfunction.

12. See https://nutritionfacts.org/topics/diabetes/ and Physicians Committee for Responsible Medicine on causes of Type 2 Diabetes: http://www.pcrm.org/nbBlog/does-sugar-cause-diabetes.

13. Physicians Committee for Responsible Medicine argues that prevention is better than relying on pharmaceuticals that only treat symptoms not the underlying issue: http://www.pcrm.org/nbBlog/prevention-over-pharmaceuticals.

14. FEMA provides Skittles and Cheez-Its to Hurricane Harvey survivors: https://www.washingtonpost.com/news/wonk/wp/2017/10/24/why-fema-sent-junk-food-to-puerto-rican-hurricane-survivors/?utm_term=.8babd538d372.

15. https://www.rte.ie/player/ie/show/irelands-health-divide-30004817/10851865/?ap=1.

16. Highly recommended book, see also https://nutritionfacts.org.

17. See https://www.cancer.org/cancer/cancer-causes/general-info/known-and-probable-human-carcinogens.html and http://www.aicr.org/press/press-releases/2017/new-report-whole-grains-link-to-lower-colorectal-cancer-risk-for-first-time.html.

18. By independent, I mean not aligned with any outside company, institution, group, think tank, or other. These researchers stick to the scientific method regardless of conclusions.

19. See https://www.theguardian.com/environment/2017/aug/01/meat-industry-dead-zone-gulf-of-mexico-environment-pollution.

20. See http://www.express.co.uk/news/nature/740946/dead-zone-miles-bat-bengal-scientists.

21. According to the UNHRC (in 2015), since 2008, 22.5 million people have become displaced due to climate/weather-related disasters: http://www.unhcr.org/en-ie/climate-change-and-disasters.html.

22. An estimated 270,000 trees are used as toilet paper daily: http://wwf.panda.org/how_you_can_help/live_green/fsc/tissue_issues/?.

23. See Springer, *The Anarchist Roots of Geography*, pp. 7–12 for a better introduction into the concept of the commons.

24. According to the Food and Agricultural Organisation of the United Nations (2006, p.4): "Directly and indirectly, through grazing and through feedcrop production, the livestock sector occupies about 30% of the ice-free terrestrial surface on the planet."

25. If saving space and maximizing efficient use of available land, especially with climate change concerns, is desired then vertical structures ought to be considered.

26. See Bowery, a contemporary vertical farming industry: http://boweryfarming.com/how-it-works.

27. Note: Carver and Bradley's article is mainly a discussion on a lesson plan for science classes in the United States. They nonetheless conclude hydroponics can be cross-curricular (p. 48). Their lesson plan also has the added benefit of teaching groups, adaptable to all ages, how to construct sustainable means of growing food.

28. The World Bank notes how Porto Alegre in Brazil, a city (in 2003) of 1.3 million inhabitants, makes radical democratic decisions on budgets and resource management. See https://openknowledge.worldbank.org/bitstream/handle/10986/11309/274620PAPER0snd71.pdf?sequence=1.

29. For reading on tactics vis-à-vis organizing, I suggest Smucker's *Hegemony How-To*. For tactics about fighting in work, I suggest Van Meter's *Guerrillas of Desire*.

30. Over 90,000 signatures calling on White House to recognize Antifa as terrorists: https://www.rt.com/usa/400272-petition-us-antifa-terrorist-trump/.

31. Irish government spent €3.6 million in appeal: http://www.thejournal.ie/apple-tax-legal-fees-3594252-Sep2017/.

32. Apple owes Ireland billions in back taxes: https://www.irishtimes.com/business/economy/eu-to-find-apple-owes-ireland-billions-in-back-taxes-1.2772178.

33. Apple and subsidiaries' corporate tax rates: https://www.rte.ie/news/business/2013/0521/451564-apple-tax-arrangements/.

34. Nappies/diapers and hazardous waste illegally dumped: http://www.independent.ie/irish-news/news/hundreds-of-nappies-and-hazardous-waste-discovered-in-beauty-spot-36131747.html.

35. For more on this interesting and complex development and political structure created in Rojava, I highly recommend reading Knapp's book: *Revolution in Rojava* (cf. bibliography).

36. The organizational structure in Rojava has many facets and levels. To properly address it, even briefly, would require additional space in this chapter. Again, I recommend Knapp's book, particularly chapter 6 vis-à-vis Rojava's organizational structure.

37. The street that grows its own food: https://www.sciencealert.com/welcome-to-the-street-that-grows-its-own-food.

38. The Curious George Brigade's zine *Liberate Not Exterminate* (cf. bibliography) was written to collate ideas relating to anarchism, ecology, and cities with the hope of starting a conversation in a similar vein.

39. UN peacekeepers sex abuse cases in Central African Republic and Haiti. See http://www.aljazeera.com/news/2017/07/peacekeepers-hit-allegations-sex-abuse-170701133655238.html and http://www.pbs.org/newshour/bb/un-peace keepers-accused-thousands-cases-abuse-ap-finds/. See also UN peacekeepers cause cholera outbreak in Haiti: https://www.theguardian.com/global-development/2016/dec/01/haiti-cholera-outbreak-stain-on-reputation-un-says.

40. IFAW indigenous seal hunt: http://www.ifaw.org/united-states/our-work/seals/indigenous-seal-hunts; see also Canada's commercial seal hunts: http://www.ifaw.org/sites/default/files/IFAW-2016-Canada's-Commercial-Seal-Hunt-Past-Present-Future-0.pdf.

41. European trawlers are destroying the oceans: http://eu.oceana.org/sites/default/files/reports/european_trawlers_destroying_oceans.pdf.

42. EU managing fisheries: https://ec.europa.eu/fisheries/cfp/fishing_rules/fishing_effort.

43. List of video sources: https://nutritionfacts.org/?fwp_search=sea+food&fwp_content_type=video.

REFERENCES

Amorós, Miguel. 2015. "The Invasion of Waste." Accessed November 11, 2017. https://libcom.org/library/invasion-waste-%E2%80%93-miguel-amor%C3%B3s.

Bah, Valerie, and Anumo, Felogene. 2017. "The Revolution Will Not Be NGO-ised: Four Lessons from African Feminist Organising." Accessed September 28, 2017. https://www.opendemocracy.net/5050/felogene-anumo-and-valerie-bah/four-lessons-african-feminist-organising.

Barnard, Neal, Willett, Walter C., and Ding, Eric L. 2017. "The Misuse of Meta-analysis in Nutrition Research." Accessed November 20, 2017. http://jamanetwork.com/journals/jama/fullarticle/2654401.

Butler, Israel. 2017. "Participatory Democracy Under Threat: Growing Restrictions on the Freedoms of NGOs in the EU." November 9, 2017. https://www.liberties.eu/en/news/participatory-democracy-under-threat-summary.

Carver, Jeffrey, and Wasserman, Bradley. 2012. "Hands-On Hydroponics: A Long-term Inquiry Lesson on Sustainability and Plant Biology." *The Science Teacher* Vol. 79, No. 4, pp. 44–48.

Crn Blok. n.d. "The NGO Sector: The Trojan Horse of Capitalism." Accessed November 9, 2017. https://theanarchistlibrary.org/library/crn-blok-the-ngo-sector-the-trojan-horse-of-capitalism.

Curious George Brigade. n.d. "Liberate Not Exterminate." Accessed November 12, 2017. https://theanarchistlibrary.org/library/curious-george-brigade-liberate-not-exterminate.

European Commission. n.d. "Environmental Crime." Accessed July 18, 2017. http://ec.europa.eu/environment/legal/crime/index.htm.

European Union. 2008. "Directive 2008/99/EC of the European Parliament and of the Council of 19 November 2008 on the Protection of the Environment through Criminal Law." Accessed July 18, 2017. http://eur-lex.europa.eu/legal-content/EN/TXT/PDF/?uri=CELEX:32008L0099&from=EN.

Fletcher, Ian. 2017. "£1.2m Dairy Campaign Hits Back against Vegan Attack." The Metro, September 5, 2017. https://www.metro.news/1-2m-dairy-campaign-hits-back-against-vegan-attack/734818/.

Fortenbery, T. Randall, and Bennett, Michael. 2004. "Opportunities for Commercial Hemp Production." Review of Agricultural Economics, Vol. 26, No. 1 (Spring), pp. 97–117.

French Agency for the Environment and Energy Management. 2016. "Food Losses and Waste: Inventory and Management at Each Stage in the Food Chain." Accessed November 3, 2017. http://www.ademe.fr/en/food-losses-and-waste-inventory-and-management-at-each-stage-in-the-food-chain.

Gelderloos, Peter. 2014. "Anarchy Works: Examples of Anarchist Ideas in Practise." London: Active Distribution.

Hedges, Chris. 2017. "Eating Our Way to Disease." Accessed August 28, 2017. https://www.truthdig.com/articles/eating-our-way-to-disease/.

Henning Steinfeld et al., Food and Agricultural Organisation (FAO). 2006. "Livestock's Long Shadow: Environmental Issues and Options." Accessed August 30, 2017. http://www.fao.org/docrep/010/a0701e/a0701e.pdf.

Knapp, Michael, Flach, Anja, and Ayboga, Ercan. 2016. *Revolution in Rojava*. trans. by Biehl, Janet. London: Pluto Press.

Kropotkin, Peter [1902]. 2009. *Mutual Aid: A Factor of Evolution*. London: Freedom Press.

Long, Mike. 1996. "The Mondragon Co-operative Federation: A Model for Our Times?" Accessed November 9, 2017. https://theanarchistlibrary.org/library/mike-long-the-mondragon-co-operative-federation-a-model-for-our-times.

McMillan, Stephanie. 2016. "Why NGOs and Leftish Nonprofits Suck (4 Reasons)." Accessed July 21, 2017. http://skewednews.net/index.php/2015/10/13/ngos-leftish-nonprofits-suck-4-reasons/.

Melia, Paul. 2017. "European Commission Prosecuting Ireland for 'failing to stop raw sewage entering waters.'" *The Irish Independent*, February 15. http://www.independent.ie/irish-news/european-commission-prosecuting-ireland-for-failing-to-stop-raw-sewage-entering-waters-35453850.html.

Nargi, Lela. 2017. "New Study Shows Organic Farming Traps Carbon in Soil to Combat Climate Change." September 30, 2017. https://popularresistance.org/new-study-shows-organic-farming-traps-carbon-in-soil-to-combat-climate-change/.

Niraj, Shekhar K., P. R. Krausman and Vikram Dayal. 2012. "A Stakeholder Perspective into Wildlife Policy in India." The Journal of Wildlife Management Vol. 76, No. 1, pp. 10–18.

Pleitgen, Frederik, and Mary Ilyushina. 2018. "Russians Soak Up the 'Power' of Siberian Red Deer Blood." Accessed May 29, 2018. https://edition.cnn.com/2018/03/11/europe/russia-deer-antler-blood-intl/index.html.

Pope, Conor. 2017. "Baffled by Recycling Rules? Here's All You Need to Know." *The Irish Times*, August 28, 2017. https://www.irishtimes.com/news/consumer/baffled-by-recycling-rules-here-s-all-you-need-to-know-1.3195917.

Pownall, Sylvia. 2017. "Dr Eva Orsmond Tells How She Was Moved to Tears after Witnessing Deprivation and Poverty while filming for RTE." *The Irish Mirror*, September 3, 2017. https://www.irishmirror.ie/news/irish-news/dr-eva-orsmond-tells-how-11100452

Smucker, Jonathan Mathew. 2017. *Hegemony How-To: A Roadmap for Radicals*. Oakland: AK Press.

Springer, Simon. 2016. *The Anarchist Roots of Geography: Towards Spatial Emancipation*. Minneapolis: University of Minnesota Press.

Subirats, Joan. 2012. "The Commons: Beyond the Market vs. State Dilemma." Accessed August 20, 2017. https://www.opendemocracy.net/joan-subirats/commons-beyond-market-vs-state-dilemma.

Thornton, Trevor. 2017. "In Banning Plastic Bags We Need to Make Sure We're Not Creating New Problems." Accessed August 20, 2017. http://www.theinertia.com/environment/in-banning-plastic-bags-we-need-to-make-sure-were-not-creating-new-problems/.

Ward, Colin. 2008. *Anarchy in Action*. London: Freedom Press.

Wright, Paul, and de la Chapelle, Alice. 2017. "Viktor Orbán and Hungary's Dark Path towards Dictatorship." Accessed September 30, 2017. http://www.ibtimes.co.uk/hold-hungarys-dark-path-towards-dictatorship-1631111?utm_campaign=soficalflowfacebook&utm_source=socialflowfacebook&utm_medium=articles.

Chapter 7

Beyond the Anthropocene, toward the Anarchocene? Notes on the Emergence of the Next Epoch

Randall Amster

INTRODUCTION

What does it mean that we have invented a way to destroy all life on Earth? Nothing much. . . . We are free in TIME—and will be free in SPACE as well.

—Hakim Bey (1991, 35, 47)

In one of his final book-length works, Peter Kropotkin wrote on "modern science and anarchism" in terms that resonate over a century later. "Anarchism originated *among the people*," Kropotkin recalled, "and it preserves its vitality and creative force so long only as it remains a movement of the people" (1923, 1). Reflecting on the egalitarian ethos of the anarchist project, he further observed that "the Anarchists, more than any legislators, aspire to Justice, which . . . is equivalent to Equality, and impossible without it" (1923, 73). And connecting all of this to the core of emerging inquiries, Kropotkin iterated a worldview that subsumes the physical and social sciences: "Anarchism is a conception of the Universe based upon the mechanical [kinetic] interpretation of phenomena, which comprises the whole of Nature, including the life of human societies and their economic, political, and moral problems" (1923, 38). Within this integrative space, Kropotkin himself moved seamlessly among the realms of geography, biology, sociology, and political economy, presenting a nascent vision of decentralized, agrarian, self-sufficient societies built upon a core of values that are both pragmatic and utopian all at once.

I draw upon this text as a starting point for a number of related reasons. First, when we think about concepts like anarchism, politics, and ecology—which encapsulate the scope of Kropotkin's work—we are principally conceptualizing *spaces* in which identities are constructed, power relations are formed, worldviews are manifested, and aspirations are expressed. Yet even beyond its role as a place where events occur, "space" more broadly is a contested and evolving set of conditions that are inscribed with societal meanings and structural conditions, but always admit agentive interventions that alter these inscriptions as we engage them. In other words, as Kropotkin alluded to, it is a dynamic world in which we find ourselves, and despite appearances to the contrary that suggest an immutability or inevitability to dominant systems, conditions are inherently ambiguous and always under construction. It thus becomes imperative to think materially and ideologically in equal parts—to consider both the physical and metaphysical dimensions of existence, to connect the means and ends—to be fully spatial beings.

Historical figures, such as Kropotkin, remind us that space also includes a temporal dimension, beyond its presence as a set of coordinates and a realm of complex power formulations. The collective human story is writ large in the workings of an increasingly globalized system that implicates the political, economic, and environmental domains, and further through the unfolding of history as both a master narrative and benchmark for change. In this sense, we come to grasp the spatio-temporal nature of existence, including the constraints and possibilities therein, and the intrinsic power that we possess as active participants in the unfolding expression of a shared reality. An ambitious framework like "anarchist political ecology" necessarily encapsulates this magnitude, and object lessons will abound. And perhaps none is more critical than the call to reconsider our impacts on the world, and the future. Welcome to the (erstwhile) Anthropocene.

GEOGRAPHIES OF THE ANTHROPOCENE

> Those who would take over the earth
> And shape it to their will
> Never, I notice, succeed.
> The earth is like a vessel so sacred
> That at the mere approach of the profane
> It is marred
> And when they reach out their fingers it is gone.
>
> —Lao Tzu (in Ammons and Roy 2015, 16)

We are living in an era in which the collective human impingements on the natural world (of which we are a part) are undeniable. From climate change and pollution to loss of biodiversity and species extinctions, the biosphere is undergoing an unprecedented transformation. This isn't to say that the global habitat has never changed before—indeed, it is changing all the time—but the rate at which it is presently occurring and our own hand in precipitating these changes render this time unique in the annals of recorded history. As is often the case, the search for a way to neatly name this has led to a remarkable moment in which an ostensible critique of our environmental impacts has yielded a rebranding of both time and space as falling even deeper under human influence. Thus rises the Anthropocene, an epoch in which "we humans have made an indelible mark on our one and only home. We have altered the Earth system qualitatively, in ways that call into question our very survival over the coming few centuries" (Castree 2016).

The designation clearly is not unproblematic, and not only due to its extinction-courting aspects. In order to qualify, the changes wrought must have accrued into the basic workings of the biosphere itself—into the "strata" of rocks, ice, and oceans, in the geological parlance—and not merely have yielded cosmetic changes that can more readily be undone. This indicates that there is an essentially biophysical dimension to the concept that transcends any particular ideological orientation, except insofar as ideologies may be bound up with particular tangible outcomes. It might thus be said that the core of the Anthropocene designation is more about effect than cause, although (as we shall see) the two domains cannot so easily be separated. More to the point at this juncture is that the signification of an epoch defined by human impacts on the life-giving properties of the planet suggests, as Margaret Ronda (2013) has opined, that "we are now in the realm of necessity, not speculation." In other words, how we got here and what we do matters.

Further unpacking the challenges leads us to inquire more deeply into who is meant by "we" in this equation. Surely not all humans (past or present) have contributed to the scaled-up planetary impacts being discerned now, nor are the consequences of this realization evenly distributed: "Critics have found the term itself too anthropocentric and misleadingly general in scope, too keen on evidence of Man and of 'our' collective imprint on the globe, to the exclusion of profound differences of responsibility and vulnerability with regard to contemporary ecological crises" (Howe and Pandian 2016; citations omitted). This is a key point from an *environmental justice* framework that needs to be reiterated, namely that it is often those who contribute the least to a problem who are most severely impacted by it. In this light, "environmental justice activists and scholars have widely criticized the concept [of the Anthropocene] for its limited analysis of the 'human' [as] it generalizes to all humans the effects of particular environmental practices that have only benefited some humans at the expense of others" (Ahuja 2016).

Moreover, even within any cognizable category of "we," who may be more directly implicated through their choices and behaviors, the aggregated conduct driving these processes involves myriad mundane activities that are so ubiquitous (e.g., consuming, transporting, communicating) that they are difficult to pull out for greater scrutiny. Notably, many of those seemingly routine behaviors are being recontextualized today, as some of the leading-edge effects of anthropogenic incursions are realized in real time. Potentially, the hallmark of this era may be an emerging recognition that the same powers that have brought apparent prosperity may spell our collective doom; indeed, "this is the paradox of the human enterprise, namely that too much of the very things that enable us to flourish can sow the seeds of our destruction" (Amster 2015, 194). Still, this self-reflective impetus remains more speculative than pragmatic, as the human capacity to imagine ourselves clever enough to use our tools to solve problems caused by them is marked. Placing human interventions at the center of the discourse can be an invitation to double down:

> Part of the Anthropocene's appeal was . . . its capaciousness—large enough to swallow the whole planet and everything that lives on it. [Paul Crutzen, the atmospheric scientist who coined the term] wished to capture the imagination and frame the world in a word that would create urgency around the issue of climate change and other slow-building dangers accruing to the earth. *But the risk was always that the word would capture the imagination all too well and become more like a summons to further heroic exertions to remake the world in our own image.* . . . Unwinding the damage we've done to the earth now represents a challenge so enormous that it forces us to dream about fantastical powers, to set about creating them and in the process either find our salvation or hasten our demise. (Yang 2017; emphasis added)

In this light, the recommendation by a blue-ribbon working group to designate this epoch as the Anthropocene has raised as many questions as it attempted to answer. On one hand, it offers a sobering assessment of human impact on the planet and its systems—perhaps with a political subtext to foster awareness of climate change and related forms of degradation. However, the Anthropocene potentially reifies the human–environment dichotomy that may be central to the problem in the first place, and further instantiates an anthropocentrism that reflects the hubris underscoring myriad current crises. Equally potent but less discussed are the justice implications, as noted, with the designation implying that *all* humans are responsible—whereas in reality both contributions and impacts are skewed along extant lines of power and privilege. Moreover, it could be argued that the Anthropocene follows a pattern of titling something after that which has been displaced, as with the names of many cities and landmarks in North America, and so on.

Pausing to take all of this in provides a moment to fully apprehend the geographical complexities, which are thoroughly bound up with the magnitude of the stakes in play. This isn't merely a semantic issue or an academic debate; how we define the moment will serve both to condition and constrain the action-space as to the range of responses that may be cognizable. As a discursive exercise, it could lapse into mere branding as "the ultimate act of apex species self-aggrandizement—less a geological -cene, perhaps, than an Anthropo*scene*, a picture of the world as dominated by ourselves" (Howe and Pandian 2016; citations omitted). As a material critique, it can serve to connect the socioeconomic and biophysical patterns that have defined the modern era (as the 2016 Working Group noted), such as changes in "erosion and sediment transport associated with a variety of anthropogenic processes, including colonization, agriculture, urbanization and global warming. . . . It is widely agreed that the Earth is currently in this state."

While there may be a palpable sense of emerging agreement that human-initiated activities are registering at the global scale, the assessment of what specific behaviors are responsible and (even more problematically) what is to be done about it, if anything, is far less unitary. As suggested before, for some, this moment may be coded as a form of anthropocentric validation, an enshrinement of our innate powers, an indicator of progress and evolution, and the steady fulfillment of our human destiny. For others, the conscious demarcation of the Anthropocene is more of a referendum on deeply rooted patterns of exploitation and domination, positing a direr and darker set of possible trajectories and serving to "paint a gloomy picture for the future of contemporary societies" in a worst-case outlook: "Human activities have become so pervasive and profound that they rival the great forces of Nature and are pushing the Earth into planetary terra incognita" (Steffen et al. 2007, 614). Will this nascent "great unknown" yield immolation or innovation?

How we answer this question depends on how we view present social arrangements and how critical we are about the histories that have enabled them. In this sense, an epochal encapsulation of the Anthropocene can serve to reify predominant ideologies and sociopolitical divides. No one really doubts that humankind is powerful enough to impinge upon the planet, but one person's cataclysm may be another's revelation. Nonetheless, the scientific discourse generally paints a picture far more cautionary than celebratory, and we can discern strands of this sensibility in the Working Group's recommendations as well as its relevant precursors: "Global warming and many other human-driven changes to the environment are raising concerns about the future of Earth's environment and its ability to provide the services required to maintain viable human civilizations" (Steffen et al. 2007, 614). More pointedly, subsequent notes have called for prompt action on these issues: "There is an urgent need for a new paradigm that integrates the continued development of human societies and the maintenance of the Earth System (ES) in a resilient and accommodating state. . . . There is increasing evidence that human activities are affecting ES functioning to a degree that threatens the resilience of the ES——its ability to persist in a Holocene-like state in the face of increasing human pressures and shocks" (Steffen et al. 2015).

When notable scientists themselves (some of whom were part of the Working Group) combine grounded analysis with future extrapolations and even calls for action, it becomes apparent that the issues at hand are as much sociopolitical as they are geological and biophysical. When we consider "geographies of the Anthropocene," then, this includes aspects of the stratigraphic and sociocultural records alike, potentially raising profound questions about how to structure present responses, the viable options for action, how the future will be constrained or enabled to manage these issues, and who has the power and opportunity to decide. These spheres of engagement are eminently spatial in nature, implicating physical locations and political relations equally: "The Anthropocene is a worthy point of departure not only for its popularity but, more importantly, because it poses questions that are fundamental to our times: How do humans fit within the web of life? How have various human organizations and processes—states and empires, world markets, urbanization, and much beyond—reshaped planetary life?" (Moore 2016, 2).

In the following section we will look more closely at the implications of naming an epoch and the technical processes for doing so. But at this juncture, bringing a geographical perspective into the mix and mapping the domain of inquiry, we come to understand the Anthropocene as an invitation (perhaps ironically) to more deeply center the locus of human activities in the analysis. The depth to which this interrogation is taken will help determine the salience of the issues and how to respond. Promisingly, belatedly, and somewhat redundantly, it is becoming clear that the challenges of the Anthropocene are as much about how societies distribute political power as they are about how electrical power is generated. But this is merely a surface rendering, leaving more critical dimensions of this unpacking in a contested state. It is one thing to observe that political, economic, and cultural frames matter to the analysis; it is another to assert that the manner in which these frames have been developed and are being perpetuated is in itself part of the problem. Critical insights into these realms will help guide the ensuing analysis of next steps:

> The term shuts down a radical reimagining of the interspecies forces that constitute our planetary webs of life. Finding a geological basis for the anthropocene in preserved rock or ice strata limits the potential of the term, confining it to geological forms in ways that reproduce the divide between human and environment that "anthropocene" could theoretically undermine. This much is evident in the dismissal of the clearest stratigraphic evidence of capitalist transformation of the environment by the top experts in the field and, thus, the exclusion of this evidence from the working group's proposal. . . . Geologists don't need to pick a specific environmental process like climate change or nuclear irradiation to define the so-called anthropocene. *The very ability to conceptualize the planet as a geological system by documenting and reorganizing its strata* may be the

most compelling geologic signal for declaring a new epoch marked by the co-production of planetary systems by humans and other species. (Ahuja 2016; emphasis in original)

Indeed, it may well be that the capacity to manifest, comprehend, and measure our behaviors at a planetary scale *is* the defining aspect of this epoch. This consciousness implies that we find ourselves at a turning point in our collective human trajectory, even as the consequences of the moment are differentially distributed. Navigating a storm, both literally and figuratively, often includes fixing a point and moving toward it. Such a point can be demarcated as a particular geographical location or landmark (e.g., the "Great Divide"), as a discernible sociocultural configuration or demographic (e.g., the "Greatest Generation"), or as a point in time marked by an event (e.g., the "Great Flood")—or as a combination thereof. The problematic of the Anthropocene implicates all of this, turning the present into a proverbial "tipping point" that provides an axis of self-conscious reassessment of the past and prefiguring the future. Marking this axis thus becomes critical, not merely as a discursive exercise but as to how we can proceed.

FROM THE GOLDEN AGE TO THE "GOLDEN SPIKE"

> How often do we hear
> That there is no other choice
> No return—to what?
>
> —Stephen Collis (2016, 120)

To understand how something works (or isn't working), it can be helpful to name it. Yet when we do so, it can reduce a complex set of conditions to an oversimplified slogan or phrase that might promote awareness while at the same time limiting genuine consciousness. This is partly a conundrum of linguistics but also one of the hypermedia age. A meme can play widely, but it is still reductive. And naming an entire epoch isn't like naming a street or a blog post; it attempts to encapsulate the sum of human behaviors across time and space—even as its implications are not so uniformly distributed. The search for a generic name, coupled with the need for an identifiable marker to be discerned, highlights the inevitable tension between attribution and reductionism.

First, a bare reminder that "the Anthropocene deserves to become part of our lexicon—a way we understand who we are, what we're doing and what our responsibilities are as a species—so long as we remember that not all humans are equal contributors to our planetary maladies, with many being

victims" (Castree 2016). This justice-oriented framework needs to be reiterated at every opportunity when we scale up the analysis to a more rarified
global frame (which runs the risk of obscuring differences among localities
on the ground). Nevertheless, a planetary perspective is essential, and is part
of how we arrive at the conclusion that "the case for a new epoch appears
reasonable. . . . Human activity is now global and is the dominant cause of
most contemporary environmental change [and] human actions may well
constitute Earth's most important evolutionary pressure" (Lewis and Maslin
2015, 172). The question is how we typologize this.

The issue of whether humankind has entered the Anthropocene is less
contentious than how and when to mark that milestone. There is broad
agreement that human impacts at the planetary scale are demonstrable and
sufficiently alterative to warrant the designation. (As noted earlier, however,
some may view this with consternation, whereas others may do so as more
of a confirmation—or even a coronation.) But this ostensible consensus is
only the starting point of the debate, leaving open critical questions about (a)
whether the term Anthropocene is the right one to subsume the agreed-upon
human impacts, (b) when the epoch can be said to have properly commenced,
and (c) what artifacts can be discerned in the (geological) record to support
this. In essence, beyond the name itself, the issues turn on locating markers
and memorials of sufficient import to warrant an onset date that focuses the
cumulative impacts into a single, iconic variable.

Beginning with the formalities, the naming and location-fixing of the project (in both time and space), is at root a geological one, and requires substantial accumulation in the planet's core structures: "Defining the beginning of
the Anthropocene as a formal geologic unit of time requires the location of
a global marker of an event in stratigraphic material, such as rock, sediment,
or glacier ice" (Lewis and Maslin 2015, 173). In essence, the search is for
either a signature event (for which the onset date is fixed by its occurrence) or
a particular causal marker (for which a date must be determined). The latter
(pertinent) realm is that of the proverbial "Golden Spike."

The threshold question of impact is fairly settled, as noted: "There is an
overwhelming amount of stratigraphic evidence that the Earth System is
indeed now structurally and functionally outside the Holocene norm" (Steffen
et al. 2016). The matter of causation (and thus of fixing an onset date) has
yielded numerous contenders: "This evidence includes novel materials such
as elemental aluminum, concrete, plastics, and geochemicals; carbonaceous
particles from fossil fuel combustion; widespread human-driven changes to
sediment deposits; artificial radionuclides; marked rises in greenhouse gas
concentrations in ice cores; and trans-global alteration of biological species
assemblages" (Steffen et al. 2016). Taken together, this constitutes sufficient
evidence for a new epoch. But which factor(s) is/are the cornerstone?

A leading contender is the presence of nuclear byproducts, distributed worldwide since the advent of the atomic age (circa 1950): "The era in which we live is now officially described as an atomic Anthropocene . . . and one of its most distinctive features is radiation. The fallout (both literal and figurative) from international nuclear weapons testing, nuclear energy and nuclear disasters are embedded in our environment, but also in our society" (Alexis-Martin et al. 2016). Locating confirmation, however, brings to the fore other contenders, including carbon emissions driving climate change and the impacts of militarism: "Drilled by the US military in Greenland as part of a secret installation intended to mobilize under-ice nuclear weapons, the Camp Century ice core demonstrates the interplay of Cold War nuclear militarization, Arctic colonization, and emerging climate science. The world's first deep ice core is both an expression of high-tech imperialism and a technical basis for linking atmospheric sciences to geological method" (Ahuja 2016). The complex interaction of multiple causal factors thus defies convenient categorization.

This suggests the salience of carbon released through the burning of fossil fuels as a potential spike, which would fix the onset date at the rise of the industrial age (circa 1850). Of note, somewhat ironically, is that "global warming threatens to melt the ice covering the site. Although this is one of the main technical limitations for use of ice as a golden spike, it demonstrates that climate change itself has the potential to undo the progressive temporality of the stratigraphic record" (Ahuja 2016). The implication is that climate change has the capacity to essentially "cover its own tracks" by erasing its records from the ice core databank. This quality of erasure raises a larger concern with the reductive methodologies themselves, since "the ice core scientist literally removes the stratigraphic record from the Earth in order to study it. . . . By focusing on the presence of human-made materials rather than the absence of strata disturbed by extraction technologies, the search for a golden spike is narrowing to more predictable methods" (Ahuja 2016). Looking for an active presence can obscure deeper interrogation into what's been lost.

We might term this conundrum as the "Golden Spike" versus the "Golden Age." Both are temporal constructs, but the latter evokes a distinct sense of romantic longing for a place that transcends a particular location on the map. Whereas the Golden Spike is a function of rational inquiry and testable representation, the Golden Age is a mutable sensibility that places memory and psychology squarely in the mix. The question of what is *present* in the stratigraphic record is indicative of a prevalent mindset of human domination, in itself part of the cultural narrative framing the leading Golden Spike contenders and perhaps the quintessential software of the Anthropocene. But the matter of what is *absent* from the record raises potentially more nuanced and critical concerns, and not merely about extracting (or melting) core samples.

The lacking components in the Earth's record are literally "missing elements" as a result of mass resource extraction—and also include species (animal and biota) lost to human-induced extinctions, deforestation and erosion, depletion of freshwater sources, and more. We have taken a lot from the Earth, perhaps more than we have toxified it, and thus do we long for a more innocent age.

But there is no going back, and the longing for a pristine place to inhabit—either in time as a construct of prehistory, or in space as a retreat from contemporary crises—is fraught with elements of romanticism and resignation. Oddly, despite a deep-seated cultural belief in the virtues of "progress," the dominant (Western) narrative is one of paradise lost, a descent from a simple and bountiful existence into one of scarcity and hubris. The exchange is often coded as inevitable in the sense that expanding mental complexity and the trajectory of evolution were responsible for driving us from a Golden Age into the ravages of conflict and chaos. Simply put, humans could either have remained simple but happy, or become smart yet unsatisfied—with no real commensurability or cross-pollination being possible. We can measure how much we have "fouled the nest" from whence we sprang, but in a sense this further reifies the behavior and conveys a mindset of inevitability in which human impacts are merely a cost of doing business.

This convenient rationalization licenses myriad profligate behaviors in the present, rewrites the lifeways prevalent in the past (and which are still practiced in places today), and threatens to constrain options in the future. We might take the view that such "environmental degradation is a crime against humanity" (Lennard and Parr 2016)—but who is responsible? Culpability for rampant degradation may be attributed to specific corporate or governmental actors in isolated locales, oftentimes with tepid results and an insufficient impetus for change. In reality, however, "environmental crimes" are widespread, with culpable behaviors being globally prevalent yet largely unscrutinized. This becomes clear when *intergenerational justice* is considered, as the greatest impacts of present degradations are visited upon generations yet to come. The search for a Golden Spike can foster an expansive view of environmental incursions to include a wide net of contemporary actors and causal factors, and brings a sense of temporal enclosure to the fore:

> The human species is the agent of a terrible injustice being perpetrated against other species, future generations, ecosystems. . . . Examples include contaminated waterways, mass species extinction, massive fossil fuel consumption and greenhouse gas emissions and unsustainable rates of deforestation, [leading to] extreme and more frequent weather events, expanding deserts, loss of biodiversity, collapsing ecosystems, water depletion and contamination, and the rise of global sea levels. . . . However, humans are not all equally guilty of this crime. Some, such as those advancing the interests of the fossil-fuel industry, or those

whose high-income lifestyles carry a heavy environmental footprint, are implicated more than those living in poverty. . . . Environmental degradation, and in particular climate change, denies future generations their agency through no fault of their own, leaving them with a world that could very well reduce what life remains to that of mere survival. (Lennard and Parr 2016)

What we are talking about here is a complex brew of resources extracted, toxins dispersed, species and habitats lost, and ultimately the potential closure of the future in terms of both space (locational, political, and cultural) and time (the diminution of a window in which to take action). To some degree, the invocation of the Anthropocene may be the right vehicle to raise these issues that converge around what we value, what we deem valuable, and what values we hold. It can serve as a benchmark for what we have inflicted on ourselves and the world, what we have lost in the process, and what needs to be done to alter course while there is still time to do so. The Anthropocene is a retrospective label yet suggests "futures planning" (White 2009) as well. To undertake this in a meaningful way, will it mean that we must return to some mythical Eden?

The question before us thus becomes whether we can be both complex and contented at the same time. The evidence at hand suggests a negative response, as Martin Luther King Jr. intoned in noting the potential for technology to eclipse any sense of morality and humanity: "Modern man suffers from a kind of poverty of the spirit, which stands in glaring contrast to his scientific and technological abundance." As King inferred, the arc of scientific progress may give the impression that equivalent gains had been made in the social, cultural, and political realms. And indeed, in the intervening years, we have witnessed an unprecedented technological explosion that has reformulated every aspect of human life, from transportation and commerce to education and entertainment—and likewise comprising an era typified by perpetual warfare, widening inequality, racialized politicking, and erosion of the public sphere. Core values, and what is valued, are wholly implicated, as King famously observed in *Beyond Vietnam*: "We must rapidly begin the shift from a 'thing-oriented' society to a 'person-oriented' society. When machines and computers, profit motives and property rights are considered more important than people, the giant triplets of racism, materialism, and militarism are incapable of being conquered."

Racism, materialism, and *militarism,* perhaps this is a more illuminating characterization of the Golden Spike, ultimately tracing back to a shared economic framework? "There are two tools corporations use to maximize profits . . . the use of technologies that transfer production from local communities to distant corporations, substitute biodiversity with toxic products, and make everyone into consumers of toxic, nonrenewable products whose cost is high but price is cheap [and] the creation of tools for wealth accumulation. These tools include measuring wealth as capital, thus ignoring both nature's wealth and society's wealth" (Shiva 2011). This has led some to suggest that the epoch be termed the *Capitalocene*, which "does not stand for capitalism as an economic and social system. . . . Rather, [it] signifies capitalism as a way of organizing nature—as a multispecies, situated, capitalist world-ecology" (Moore 2016, 6). The Capitalocene highlights the enclosure of the planet and the commodification of nature, moving it squarely into the discussion of potential epochal labels, and yields space for greater social-ecological synthesis.

It has also opened up room for further creative and highly illustrative linguistic interventions, and indeed "there have been many other wordplays—Anthrobscene, econocene, technocene, misanthropocene, and perhaps most delightfully, manthropocene" (Moore 2016, 6; citations omitted). These are all clever, yet they tend to omit critical aspects of reflexivity (a fundament of spatial analysis), human–nature integration, and a more complex rendering of the interconnected factors that contribute to the anthropocentric dilemma. "I am calling all this the Chthulucene—past, present, and to come," writes Donna Haraway (2015, 160), after considering options like Capitalocene and Plantationocene. (Cthulhu was "a monster of vaguely anthropoid outline," from the writings of H. P. Lovecraft.) This is a more allegorical construct, yet it does tap into an essential attribute of the era, dating at least to Hobbes's resurrection of the *Leviathan* as a stand-in for the inexorable rise of centralized state power and corollary socioeconomic systems.

The depiction of a monstrous creation of our own making encapsulates the fear and self-fulfilling nature of the moment, yet it minimizes the material aspects of our interventions. Is the primary point that it is humankind that has driven the world to the brink, that some humans (but not all) have done so, that our very way of life in many locales is the driver, that the prevailing societal structures are to blame, that it is a set of reinforcing worldviews, or that it is the accumulated footprint of biochemical byproducts from those myriad systems and activities? Or perhaps the point is to lament what we have lost in the process, whether it be biodiversity, squandered resources, maximal freedom, a sense of natural connection and relative innocence, and a capacity to project ourselves into the future? If it is all of these points, then no single name is likely to fit—and thus the case for the Anthropocene may be bolstered in its sheer generic breadth, leaving open the possibility of subsuming many attributes. Yet if the goal is to posit root causes and to spark the prospect of action undoing the same, a more pointed moniker would be warranted.

Herein lies the challenge: the epochal name isn't intended merely to ascribe blame (and certainly not with a broad brush) or yield more disempowerment, but somehow to admit the possibility of constructive intervention. This taps into an essential conundrum of the Anthropocene, serving as both a celebration and lamentation, fixing our gaze on what we have wrought while refusing to yield to its inevitable consequences. The systematization of competitive, acquisitive, dominative behaviors has brought forth so much of "value" that modern societies are increasingly plagued by interpersonal and structural violence, individual and collective dysfunctions, and the results of living on a planet pushed to the brink by the specter of nuclear war and runaway climate change. Under such circumstances, it is little wonder that many resort to forms of virtual escapism and self-medication to bolster their capacity to continue participating in dominant structures. But this sort of double-think—a veritable "geography of dissonance"—can't be sustained indefinitely, as the present deteriorates and future prospects grow dimmer by the day. So if not this, then what?

PREFIGURING THE ANARCHOCENE

We can only choose between worlds
We have already variously altered and harmed
And we do not lack the gas to get away
But lack the imagination of another
Way of inhabiting space
Or fashioning homes without egregious grids
And despite our best efforts there is a
Mutual aid amongst species and materials
And we do not emerge outside nature
To disrupt it but all things live in us
And we live in all things that surround us
And even in the direst circumstances
Even in the moment of our disappearance
Resistance has continued

—Stephen Collis (2016, 120)

However we choose to fix the label in the present, we must return to the underlying patterns of inequity and domination residing at the core of the epoch-naming conversation, as well as the eschatological sensibilities contained within the project in the first place. The Anthropocene (or equivalent) isn't a celebration of our cleverness and ascension; it is a recognition of "paradise lost" and how we may have squandered the bestowal of the robust gifts of time and space. We can couch this in strictly geological terms, yet at root this is a political intervention—not in a party sense, an ideological view, or an economic framework—that recognizes the limited time in which to act if we are to retain even a modicum of stable human societies on this planet. And if we are to dare imagine a future in which humanity has survived, and perhaps even somehow flourished, it is going to be one inscribed with deeply rooted hallmarks beyond mere cosmetic amendments. This won't be about repackaging or rebranding the same structures that brought us to this point; whatever means may carry us across the breach will have to be truly trans-formative. In this light, "It is futile to try and solve the harms being inflicted upon the environment using the same mechanisms that produced the problem in the first place" (Lennard and Parr 2016).

Unpacking this further requires a consideration of mutually reinforc-ing factors of responsibility and self-infliction. As Fredy Perlman wrote in *Against His-story, Against Leviathan!* (1983, 4–5): "There are many ways to speak of the wrecking of the Biosphere. From the standpoint of a single protagonist, Earth herself, it can be said that She is committing suicide. With two protagonists, Mankind and Mother Earth, it can be said that We are murdering Her. Those of us who accept this standpoint and squirm with shame might wish we were whales. But those of us who take the standpoint of the trapped animal will look for a third protagonist. . . . It is the monster's body that destroys the bodies of human communities and the body of Mother Earth." Beyond analogies, the difference between Cthulhu and Leviathan is akin to that between nightmares and torture; the former is a projection of our fears, whereas the latter is their implementation as social policy. Yet they do converge in one critical respect: both constrain our actions and aspirations in equal parts.

As an antidote to this tendency toward spatio-temporal delimitation, we might consider an approach that seeks prospectively to engage the next epoch, since the proposed one may already be nearing its coda, and with due regard for incipient counter-trends that provide evidence for speculations about what might ensue. Thus it is posited for discussion that the "Anarchocene" may be at hand—replete with possibilities for emergence, spontaneity, horizontal-ism, scalability, and other patterns of socio-ecological reflexivity that could become stratigraphically significant. "Indeed, for many anarchists, the asser-tion of human supremacy over nature and the domination of humans by other humans are thoroughly intertwined processes, and both sets of forces are seen as contributing to widespread environmental degradation that inexorably pushes the world toward the brink of apocalypse. . . . [As such] it is rapidly appearing that the choice before us is anarchism or annihilation—meaning that the effort to achieve an anarchist social order is no longer a mere idyllic vision but is an urgent necessity for human survival" (Amster 2012, 64).

What I am suggesting here is that the proposed construct of the Anarcho-cene must by definition be reflected in the stratigraphic record if we are to survive the Anthropocene with all of its confluent causal factors. Perhaps it will be an epoch defined by what has been forestalled or remediated—a measure of what has *not* been done, or what has been undone—or by the affirmative presence of life-giving properties infused throughout its prevailing social and biophysical systems, or a combination of both. Either way, it will have to be substantial enough to inure at the planetary level, since the crises it will have surmounted are firmly located there. How can an anarchist vision be scaled up to achieve this, with its penchant for decentralization and participatory decisional methods? One way is to stay deeply rooted in ecological principles:

> "Earth rights" are . . . the right to food and water, the right to health and a safe environment, and the right to the commons (the rivers, the seeds, the biodiversity, and the atmosphere). . . . Living democracy enables democratic participation in all matters of life and death—the food we eat or lack; the water we drink or are denied due to privatization or pollution; the air we breathe or are poisoned by. Living democracies are based on the intrinsic worth of all species, all peoples, all cultures; a just and equal sharing of this earth's vital resources; and sharing the decisions about the use of the earth's resources. . . . Violence is the result when our dominant economic structures and economic organization usurp and enclose the ecological space of other species or other people. (Shiva 2011)

> We humans are kin to one another and to all the other beings on the planet . . . and we will share a common fate. . . . The necessity of achieving a concordance between ecological and moral principles, and the new ethic born of this necessity, calls into question . . . our current capitalist economic systems, our educational systems, our food production systems, our systems of land use and ownership. It calls us to re-examine what it means to be happy, and what it means to be smart. [This] will release the power and beauty of the human imagination to create more collaborative economies, more mindful ways of living, more deeply felt arts, and more inclusive processes that acknowledge the ways of life of all beings. (Blue River Quorum 2011)

> [The Earth] was made to be a common Store-house of Livelihood to all Mankind . . . without exception. . . . For buying and selling is the great cheat, that robs and steals the Earth one from another; It is that which makes some Lords, others Beggars, some Rulers, others to be ruled; and makes great Murderers and Thieves to be imprisoners. . . . What Law then can you make, to take hold upon us, but Laws of Oppression and Tyranny, that shall enslave or spill the blood of the innocent? (Diggers and Levellers [1649], in Ammons and Roy, 2015, 20)

The annals of anarchism are replete with consonant perspectives and extrapolations: elevating the commons, participation, interdependence, inclusivity, property as theft, resistance to tyranny. The Anarchocene would be an epoch in which sociopolitical structures reflect and integrate with environmental processes, rather than the current model that flouts ecological principles at every turn and produces grotesque outcomes as the inevitable product.

Whereas the Anthropocene disconnects us one from another and all of us from nature, the Anarchocene will serve to reconnect. Where the Anthropocene controls, extracts, and toxifies, the Anarchocene liberates, creates, and remediates. The Anthropocene is built on a foundation of carbon and uranium, and the concomitant political economies that accompany them; the Anarchocene will be fueled in a manner consistent with attributes of sustainability and self-sufficiency. The Anthropocene courts cataclysm at every turn and narrows the future, while the Anarchocene is inherently open-ended.

Anarchism provides perhaps the most trenchant critique of contemporary value structures and their historical precursors: "Without a Golden Age to emulate or a utopia to create, we find ourselves seemingly trapped in a rather uninspiring if overawing present. Banality is raised to the level of the sublime. We retain bits and pieces of the fragmented myths of the past and increasingly find ourselves left with disconnected bits and pieces of self. At worst, we merely accumulate and discard; at best, we recycle" (Clark and Martin 2004, 4). The roots of this run deep in history: "Domination within a society is not unrelated to domination of nature. . . . We have taken a monstrously wrong turn . . . from a place of enchantment, understanding, and wholeness to the absence we find at the heart of the doctrine of progress. Empty and emptying, the logic of domestication, with its demand to control everything, now shows us the ruin of the civilization that ruins the rest. Assuming the inferiority of nature enables the domination of cultural systems that soon will make the very earth uninhabitable" (Zerzan 1994, 35, 46).

Anarchists have been promulgating these insights for a long time, before such thinking was even remotely popularized. When Kropotkin's *Fields, Factories and Workshops* was re-released after World War I, it included an added preliminary note: "It pleads for a new economy in the energies used in supplying the needs of human life, since these needs are increasing and the energies are not inexhaustible" (in Ward 2004, 90). As Colin Ward (2004, 90) has observed: "In those days this was a rare recognition of the limits of growth. Today we have a vast literature on the problems of resource depletion and environmental destruction." The intersecting crises of the Anthropocene are parallel to the problems that anarchism has confronted from the beginning, and a full recognition of the magnitude of the choices before us has been central to its core project:

> It is obvious that we have but one planet that holds the essential life preserving mechanisms with which we must learn to live in harmony. If we do not do so we face extinction, or at the very least, condemn future generations of our species to live upon a planet pitifully degraded and totally devoid of the vast majority of the life forms which it now supports. Our species must make enormous changes

in society in order to begin to make the transition from a world dominated by multinational capitalist imperialism and the artificial boundaries of the Nation-State" (Purchase 1997, 26). "Human survival depends . . . upon the adoption of cooperative and nurturant ways of life. . . . People everywhere are realizing that our survival is dependent upon environmental stability, and that the pathological interests of governments and multinational corporations pose the single biggest threat to the health of the Earth. . . . Today, anarchism is emerging as the only credible philosophy of survival. (Purchase 1994, 3–6)

We thus come to glimpse the set of social, political, economic, and environmental arrangements that anarchism has strived to present; these are rooted in a deeply critical posture, yet balanced by an equivalently constructive sensibility that is non-prescriptive and unflinching all at once:

No philosophy or movement for liberation can ignore the connection between human exploitation of the environment and our exploitation of one another, nor can it ignore the suicidal ramifications of industrial society. . . . Capitalism is the first social arrangement in human history to endanger the survival of our species and life on earth in general. Capitalism provides incentives to exploit and destroy nature, and creates an atomized society that is incapable of protecting the environment. . . . An ecologically sustainable world would have to be anti-authoritarian, so no society could encroach on its neighbors to expand its resource base; and cooperative, so societies could band together in self-defense against a group developing imperialist tendencies. Most importantly, it would demand a common ecological ethos, so people would respect the environment rather than regarding it simply as raw material to exploit. (Gelderloos 2010, 134–150)

It is important to see some of these grounded visions unfiltered, to convey the earnestness and urgency in which they have been formulated. Anarchists are used to being told how impractical, idealistic, and impossible their ideas are (which is interestingly juxtaposed with being treated in a manner that views them as dangerous). The architects of the Anthropocene will be dismissive of ideologies or practices that threaten to expose the core of the operation, either by demonizing or incapacitating them. Consider that the main causal factors undergirding the Anthropocene—from petroleum economies to nuclearized militaries—are also underscored by the application of force in order to maintain their primacy; in this light, perhaps the defining feature of the Anthropocene is its institutionalization and normalization of *violence*, which is directed at people, societies, and ultimately toward the planetary systems themselves. The Anthropocene, in its full expression, is an interlocking system of "geographies of violence" that reverberates through time and across space. It can be supplanted by something like the Anarchocene, but only if action is taken now.

CONCLUSION

The "children of mother earth" claiming their right to live—what else could
it be about?

—P.M. (1995, 19)

The naming of an epoch is no minor task, and no small matter. No single word
or concept can possibly encapsulate all of the many factors and variabilities
involved in producing a long-term set of impacts at the global scale. For all
of its ostensible flaws in terms of equity, precision, and more, the invocation
of the Anthropocene does have at least one core (and perhaps ultimately saving) virtue: it subsumes all of the effects yielded in the modern/mechanical
age under a single rubric of "human causation," thus identifying the locus of
responsibility and potential alteration. The label transcends particular dimensions of human "progress"—from our economic structures and militarized
incursions, to our consumerist practices and worldviews—in favor of a more
unitary appellation that defines the trajectory of time and space as integrative.
In so doing, it provides a model for how we might change course today and
establish a vision for tomorrow.

The next epoch—if it is to exist at all—will be known for its stratigraphi-
cal impacts on the biosphere in a positive sense, as a record of accumulated
patterns of remediation and reinvigoration. Its hallmarks will be found in
what is not there, or more accurately, in what was there previously but slowly
diminished over time. Ultimately, the record of the next epoch will be one of
restoration, juxtaposed with the multifarious existence of complex societies
and myriads of people. How will they live cooperatively and sustainably,
undoing the damage done by their forebears yet still reaching for the stars
and deepening their connections to the Earth and one another? How will
they—we—cultivate forms of progress that are actually progressive in the
sense of continually opening more options for the future rather than steadily
foreclosing them? At a minimum, it will require self-critical engagement:
"Anarchism doesn't merely ask us to live in harmony with nature. [It] hopes
rather, that through the proper balancing of economic, cultural and ecological factors upon a regional basis, we can actively enhance and improve upon
the beauty, generosity and creative potentiality of organic life and nature"
(Purchase 1997, 108).

Unfortunately, however, "the current debates are doubling down on the
conceptual split between humans and the planet, society and nature, in ways
that foreclose a broad rethinking of the planetary processes through which
energies, life forms, and processes are formed and reproduced" (Ahuja 2016).
In some ways, the debate over the invocation of the Anthropocene devolves

upon many of the factors that have brought us to this point: linear causation, human separation from nature, reductive methodologies, valorizing impacts over losses, obscuring differential contributions and consequences, failure to effectively interrogate political economies, backgrounding issues of power, and the reification of human domination. Still, one thing remains clear—a sense of urgency: "Which trajectory the Anthropocene follows depends on the decisions and actions of global society today, and over the next few decades" (Steffen et al. 2016). Mere longing won't turn the tide, as P.M. (1995, 56) said: "There is no hope. We have to choose *now*."

The aim here has been to address the immediacy of these issues while projecting toward a better future—one that is informed by the present but not delimited by it. A mechanism for this effort comes in the attempt to prospectively explore (and even hesitatingly name) what the next epoch might entail, an exercise rarely undertaken in the quest to finalize a caption for the current one. This sort of project has some inherent pitfalls, including that it might literally be a projection of both our hopes and dreams, as well as our limited imaginations as a product of this time. It may be that it is anthropocentric thinking, after all, that set this in motion in the first place—and we, as children of the Anthropocene, barely have the linguistic or conceptual tools to map out the contours of our own paradigm, let alone the next one. In either case, may we somehow find our way there.

REFERENCES

Ahuja, Neel. 2016. "The Anthropocene Debate: On the Limits of Colonial Geology," *University of California, Santa Cruz* (September 9). Accessed December 15, 2017. https://ahuja.sites.ucsc.edu/2016/09/09/the-anthropocene-debate-on-the-limits-of-colonial-geology/.

Alexis-Martin, Becky, Stephanie Malin, and Thom Davies. 2016. "The Anthropocene Is a Nuclear Epoch—So How Can We Survive It?" *The Conversation*, December 8, 2017. https://theconversation.com/the-anthropocene-is-a-nuclear-epoch-so-how-can-we-survive-it-69393.

Ammons, Elizabeth, and Modhumita Roy, eds. 2015. *Sharing the Earth: An International Environmental Justice Reader*. Athens, GA: University of Georgia Press.

Amster, Randall. 2012. *Anarchism Today*. Santa Barbara, CA: Praeger/ABC-CLIO.

Amster, Randall. 2015. *Peace Ecology*. New York: Routledge.

Bey, Hakim. 1991. *T.A.Z.: The Temporary Autonomous Zone, Ontological Anarchy, Poetic Terrorism*. Brooklyn, NY: Autonomedia.

Blue River Quorum. 2011. "The Blue River Declaration: An Ethic of the Earth." *New Clear Vision*, November 4, 2011. http://www.newclearvision.com/2011/11/04/the-blue-river-declaration/.

Castree, Noel. 2016. "An Official Welcome to the Anthropocene Epoch—But Who Gets to Decide It's Here?" *The Conversation*, August 30, 2016. https://thecon versation.com/an-official-welcome-to-the-anthropocene-epoch-but-who-gets-to-decide-its-here-57113.

Clark, John P., and Camille Martin, eds. 2004. *Anarchy, Geography, Modernity: The Radical Social Thought of Elisée Reclus*. Lanham, MD: Lexington Books.

Collis, Stephen. 2016. *Once in Blockadia*. Vancouver, BC, Canada: Talonbooks.

Gelderloos, Peter. 2010. *Anarchy Works*. San Francisco Bay Area, CA: Ardent Press.

Haraway, Donna. 2015. "Anthropocene, Capitalocene, Plantationocene, Chthulucene: Making Kin." *Environmental Humanities* 6: 159–165.

Howe, Cymene, and Anand Pandian. 2016. "Introduction: Lexicon for an Anthropocene Yet Unseen." *Cultural Anthropology* (January 21). https://culanth.org/fieldsights/788-introduction-lexicon-for-an-anthropocene-yet-unseen.

Kropotkin, Peter. 1923. *Modern Science and Anarchism* (2nd edition). London: Freedom Press.

Lennard, Natasha, and Adrian Parr. 2016. "Our Crime against the Planet, and Ourselves." *New York Times*, May 18, 2016. https://www.nytimes.com/2016/05/18/opinion/our-crime-against-the-planet-and-ourselves.html.

Lewis, Simon L., and Mark A. Maslin. 2015. "Defining the Anthropocene." *Nature* 519 (March 12): 171–180. doi: 10.1038/nature14258.

Moore, Jason W., ed. 2016. *Anthropocene or Capitalocene? Nature, History, and the Crisis of Capitalism*. Oakland, CA: PM Press.

Perlman, Fredy. 1983. *Against His-story, Against Leviathan!* Detroit, MI: Black & Red.

P. M. 1995. *bolo'bolo*. Brooklyn, NY: Semiotext(e).

Purchase, Graham. 1994. *Anarchism and Environmental Survival*. Tucson, AZ: See Sharp Press.

Purchase, Graham. 1997. *Anarchism and Ecology*. New York: Black Rose Books.

Ronda, Margaret. 2013. "Mourning and Melancholia in the Anthropocene." *Post45*, June 10, 2013. Accessed December 15, 2017. http://post45.research.yale.edu/2013/06/mourning-and-melancholia-in-the-anthropocene/.

Shiva, Vandana. 2011. "Earth Democracy and the Rights of Mother Earth." *Tikkun*, December 12, 2011. http://www.tikkun.org/nextgen/earth-democracy-and-the-rights-of-mother-earth.

Steffen, Will, Paul J. Crutzen, and John R. McNeill. 2007. "The Anthropocene: Are Humans Now Overwhelming the Great Forces of Nature?" *Ambio* 36 (8): 614–21.

Steffen, Will, et al. 2015. "Planetary Boundaries: Guiding Human Development on a Changing Planet." *Science* 347 (6223). doi: 10.1126/science.1259855.

Steffen, Will, et al. 2016. "Stratigraphic and Earth System Approaches to Defining the Anthropocene." *Earth's Future* (August 12). doi: 10.1002/2016EF000379.

Ward, Colin. 2004. *Anarchism: A Very Short Introduction*. New York: Oxford University Press.

WGA (Working Group on the Anthropocene). 2016. "What Is the Anthropocene? Current Definition and Status." *Stratigraphy.org*. Accessed December 15, 2017. http://quaternary.stratigraphy.org/workinggroups/anthropocene/.

White, Rob. Ed. 2009. *Environmental Crime: A Reader*. Portland, OR: Willan.
Yang, Wesley. 2017. "Is the 'Anthropocene' Epoch a Condemnation of Human Inter-ference—or a Call for More?" *New York Times Magazine*, February 14. https://www.nytimes.com/2017/02/14/magazine/is-the-anthropocene-era-a-condemnation-of-human-interference-or-a-call-for-more.html.
Zerzan, John. 1994. *Future Primitive and Other Essays*. Brooklyn, NY: Autonomedia.

Chapter 8

Chthulucene Compacts: An Anarchist Guide to Multispecies Troublemaking

Benjamin O'Heran

Reckless societies allow themselves to meddle with that which creates the beauty of their domain, they always end up regretting it.

—Élisée Reclus

Anarchists have a reputation for being known as troublemakers. And this is a very well-founded reputation. Our slogans of "No Gods, No Masters" and "Anarchy Is Order" put us at odds with most of society's normal beliefs and institutions. Our practices of creating new stories, worlds, and possibilities, based on abolishing all forms of oppression and domination through a prefigurative practice built upon the desire to meet the needs of those most disadvantaged though a do-it-yourself (DIY) ethic, are not accepted as being "legitimate" or serious strategies for creating social and systemic change in the eyes of liberal elites or state-centered Marxists. Combining our desire to abolish all forms of oppression and domination with anarchism's strong stance against using the state as the primary nexus of economic, social, and political change means that we are often lonely troublemakers in trying to create the worlds that we wish to embody.

Although lonely, we are seldom alone. Anarchists have a habit of finding solace and making relations with other unwanted troublemakers. While you may think that these troublemakers are our fellow non-statist, anti-capitalist, and anti-oppressive socialists and communists, these are not who I am talking about. Instead, these troublemakers are our non-human accomplices and kin who appear on our book fair posters, our screen-printed patches, and those who sit underneath (and sometimes at) our kitchen tables. Seldom thought of, although vitally important, these critters and plants are troublemaking accomplices in our attempts to create anarchist worlds.

It is hard to attend any sort of anarchist gathering without seeing some sort of anarchist identification with non-human troublemakers. From noticing the similar behaviors of dumpster diving freegans and raccoons who rummage through trash receptacles, to prison abolitionists using dandelions and other "pest" plants to signify a future without prisons, it is hard to discern if anarchists build their practices before or after identifying with non-human troublemakers. Even the posters for anarchist gatherings, book fairs, and picnics are often emblazed with society's unwanted and misunderstood plants and critters.

For example, the posters and announcements for the annual Victoria Anarchist Book Fair (held on the unceded, traditional, and ancestral lands and waters of the W̱SÁNEĆ and Esquimalt peoples) has featured the pesky, too smart for its own good, troublesome raven taking part in anarchist activities (Figure 8.1). In this year's rendition, the raven is seen standing above a maple leaf emblazed with the number "150" in front of the provincial legislature with what appears to be claw and peck marks all over the leaf. Here the anarchist raven reminds attendants that as part of our anarchist practice of abolishing all forms of oppression, we have an obligation and responsibility to work with local Indigenous nations to dismantle the capitalist, heteropatriarchal, white supremacist settler colonial state that is responsible for one-hundred and fifty years of continued Indigenous genocide and dispossession.

Perhaps the most infamous anarchist iconography and cross-species relation belongs to humanity's "neighbor species"—cats. Cats are probably the most beloved and adorned anarchist critter, with the most famous one being "The Black Cat" or Sabo-Tabby. With its arched back, bushy tail, and bared claws, the angry cat is featured prominently in the early literature of the Industrial Workers of the World (IWW). Created by IWW member Ralph Chaplin (perhaps better known for "Solidarity Forever"), "The Black Cat" served as a silent code for Wobbly members to use direct action in the workplace. Specifically, to take part in workplace sabotage. Hence, the name Sabo-Tabby as a play on the word *sabotage*. When IWW members drew the black cat, it was code for their fellow Wobblies to partake in slow-downs, strikes, and other forms of workplace sabotage ("The Black Cat [Sabo-Tabby]" 2011). Sabo-tabby and other feline co-conspirators still serve as a powerful symbol and ideal for anarchist practices of liberation, autonomy, and telling the police to go away.

Yet, while we anarchists often identify with our troublemaking animal and vegetable companions, I want to challenge ourselves to question what it would mean if we were to take these stories and inspirations of non-human anarchism and multispecies troublemaking seriously? Instead of seeing our identification with anarchist-like critters and plants as a powerful metaphor, aesthetic, or ideal to live up to, what if we accepted an anarchist practice of

Figure 8.1. Poster for the 12th Annual Victoria Anarchist Book Fair Hosted on the Lands and Waters of the Songhees, Esquimalt, and W̱SÁNEĆ Nations in What Is Currently Known as Victoria, British Columbia. *Source*: Courtesy of the Victoria Anarchist Book Fair.

multispecies troublemaking? A way of creating worlds with these species and individuals that sees them as political actors and allies in the struggle for the creation of anarchist societies. What would it mean for anarchists to seriously speculate and attempt to create practices of multispecies response-ability, solidarity, and mutual aid? These are questions that I am interested in attempting to think through, work with, and (re)create.

In our troubled times of prolonged capitalist crisis, anthropocentric climate change, and the increasing precarity of life itself we need new stories to tell ourselves and others. We need new stories that serve as an inspiration for creating more egalitarian dreams, worlds, and everyday practices of care among humans and non-humans. Stories inspire new ways of living and relating, and so my storytelling in the rest of this chapter attempts to do just that. I seek to outline my belief of an anarcho-symbiogenesis—a form of anarcho-communism with its political actualization in the form of Chthulucene compacts between particular humans and non-humans.

To tell such a speculative tale, I trace the tentacular threads and hidden seeds of posthumanism in anarchist thought beginning with Peter Kropotkin. Starting with his seminal text *Mutual Aid*, I argue that a theory of and practices of multispecies solidarity and mutual aid are an important part of the anarchist intellectual tradition. While mutual aid between animals foregrounds Kropotkin's work on mutual aid, this is overshadowed by the importance of mutual aid amongst humans leading Kropotkin to neglect forms of mutual aid between individuals and communities of different species. To think through this relational gap requires bringing anarchist geographer Élisée Reclus into our tale. Reclus's "The Great Kinship of Humans and Fauna" and "On Vegetarianism" are two key anarchist texts that address Humanity's relationships to Nature over half a century before environmentalism would become a central part of anarchist thought. Both essays seek to elaborate a way of anarchist relating between humans and non-humans. They are stories that we should return to, complicate, and compost.

The second step in this story is to bring these anarchist works and ideas into conversation with present-day thinkers who are dealing with the complicated task of human/non-human troublemaking. French philosopher Isabelle Stengers offers a glimpse into a posthuman cosmopolitics by forgoing the traditional Kantian politics of a universal world. Here she turns this concept on its head by proposing that the world is a constructed process built through mutual relations between entities. Especially, seeing the world as being co-created between the intentional actions of humans and non-humans. Feminist scientist Donna Haraway, the dog mother of contemporary multispecies thought, will teach us with her canine companion Ms. Cayenne Pepper about an ethic of co-flourishing. Her work advances a practice of responding, presencing, and respecting those whom we are in relation with. Their work hints at the ends and means needed to practice forms of multispecies anarchism necessary for surviving on our damaged Terra.

Finally, this story concludes where others begin. I investigate where anarcho-symbiogenesis is taking place in the form of Chthulucene compacts. In these stories humans and non-humans are speculating and acting together to create new, contingent, and precarious multispecies politics. To see how anarchists can and are (re)creating intimate and tenuous multispecies acts of solidarity and mutual aid we will travel to the battered landscapes of neoliberal Greece and Chile to examine how Loukanikos the Riot Dog, Negro Matapacos, and their human co-conspirators are creating new forms of multispecies mutual aid and solidarity in the ruins of capitalism. From these fleshy doggo/human worldings, we sojourn to the northwest coast of Turtle Island to see how art, DIY tree planting, and multispecies response-ability collide in cellulose practices of multispecies care.

AN ANARCHIST ORIGIN OF MULTISPECIES MUTUAL AID AND SOLIDARITY

In the biological sciences, it is increasingly popular to say that bacteria "have done it all," meaning that if someone is looking for some sort of biological phenomena or property to observe, then it is a good bet that you should start by looking at what bacteria are doing. More often than not, when scientists observe bacteria long enough, they do find what they were looking for. This includes coming to realize that bacteria have solved problems relating to biological complexity and interdependence, surviving in unfriendly or quickly changing environments, and established forms of multispecies and intraorganism solidarity long before multi-cellular organisms learned to do so (McFall-Ngai 2017, 61–65).

Perhaps the same can be said for anarchist ideas and strategies for multispecies relating? If we look back long enough within our own intellectual history, can we see whether prior anarchist thinkers and practitioners thought of how to imagine and practice forms of multispecies politics? Indeed, it does look like we can. Intellectual heavy-weight Murray Bookchin immediately comes to mind in discussions of green anarchism and environmental stability. Or perhaps the early writings of literary anarchist and deep ecologist Gary Snyder could serve as a starting point for rethinking multispecies relations (Cornell 2017, 183). However, they both do not quite fit the needs of solving the problems associated with our troubled times of the Capitalocene and the Anthropocene. While Bookchin's proposals signaled the arrival of a rational way out of our ecologically damaging capitalist society, it flies too close to the sun of transhumanism and the eco-modernist techno fixes that are so popular amongst today's neoliberal elites. Synder's influence on the development of early green anarchism could lead us back to an earthier co-existence with non-humans. However, its development into misanthropic primitivism seems more like a dead end then a beginning of new tales yet to be told. Instead, we must dig deeper.

If bacteria have already done it all, then why not just go back to the beginning? By attempting to figure out an anarchist conception of multispecies mutual aid and solidarity we are sent back to the beginning of contemporary anarchism. To times of revolutionary fervor, transnationalism, and anarchist cross-pollination. Here, our tale begins with those spun by Peter Kropotkin and Élisée Reclus. While not specifically laying out the foundations for multispecies mutual aid and solidarity, Kropotkin's work in *Mutual Aid* shows that anarchism and mutual aid are not solely traits belonging to humans.

Written in 1902, *Mutual Aid: A Factor of Evolution* serves as a powerful reminder as to why Kropotkin is regarded as one of anarchism's most important intellectuals and propagandists. On one hand, like other pieces written by Kropotkin, the book seeks to establish anarchism as genuine science and way of knowing. Often with the belief that anarchism was the logical end-point of science or using science to explain why the ultimate evolution of humanity would be that of anarchism (Mac Laughlin 2016, 93–99). On the other hand, the book acts as a powerful form of anarchist propaganda by speaking back to bourgeoisies, scientists, and politicians who weaponized the ideas of Charles Darwin to argue that the evolution of life on Earth was only brought about due to the law of competition, where only the fittest would and should survive. This hierarchical and anthropocentric sentiment act as the foundational logic for the commodification of non-humans, the destruction of ecosystems, and the origins of the Capitalpocene.

As such, *Mutual Aid* sets out to tell a tale of science. A science of how mutual aid and solidarity (sociability), two of anarchism's most cherished ideals and practices, arose through the evolutionary development. According to Kropotkin, mutual aid and sociability were an innate part of life on Terra and developed over the course of evolutionary millennia as a necessary trait for survival. Critiquing Darwin for their preoccupation with the "law of competition," he traced the origins of mutual aid from observable cases in animal and various human societies with his hypothesis being that sociability was an evolved trait that manifested itself in all forms of life. Stating that, "As soon as we study animals—not in laboratories and museums only, but in the forest and the prairie, in the steppe and the mountains—we at once perceive that though there is an immense amount of warfare and extermination going on amidst various species, and especially amidst various classes of animals, there is, at the same time, as much or perhaps even more, of *mutual support, mutual aid, and mutual defense amidst animals belonging to the same species, or at least to the same society*" (Kropotkin 2006, 5; emphasis added).

Encountering species-specific forms of sociability ranging from insects and crabs, to cranes and parrots, and even among "competitive" animals like lions and wolves, Kropotkin spins numerous yarns as to how individuals of the same species partake in acts of mutual aid. While praising ants, bees, and mites as having "risen to the conception of a higher solidarity embodying the whole of the species," he documents how the social instincts of ants extends beyond the limits of the hive and the nest (Kropotkin 2006, 15). They demonstrate the sociability of two different species of ant, *Formica exsecta* and *F. pressilabri*, because even though they were two different species, they were able to co-create immense colony systems made up of multiple nests.

Similarly, in their study of ant colonies in the Panama Canal Zone, Eben Kirksey documents similar behavior in the species *Ectatomma ruidom* (Kirksey 2015, 15). While most species of ants strongly guard their colonies, *Ectatomm* often had no problems letting ants from other colonies into theirs. They also had a strong habit of carrying larvae, workers, winged queens, and even food that Kirksey put out in their experiments to nests that were not their own. Rather than rejecting all non-kin, these ants often exhibited "sociable" behavior among ants of different colonies and species. Instances of these ants biting, dragging, or fatally stinking non-kin were only occasionally observed.

Instances of mutual aid and sociability were not only found in "lower order" species, but also in "higher order" ones too. According to Kropotkin, only a few species were truly unsociable and this trait posed the risk of being a potential evolutionary dead end. These forays into the sociable worlds of non-humans served as a powerful scientific examples and propaganda tools for placing mutual aid and solidarity as an inherent part of the evolutionary process. Although Kropotkin's evolutionary understanding of mutual aid presupposes that it is found in critters, plants, and even ecosystems, their work places a special emphasis on its full realization in humans.

Mutual aid only becomes "conscious" as animal's progress through evolution. "Association (sociability) is found in the animal world at all degrees of evolution. . . . But, in proportion as we ascend the scale of evolution, we see association growing more and more conscious. It loses its purely physical character, it ceases to be simply instinctive, *it becomes reasoned*" (Kropotkin 2006, 43; emphasis added). Acts of association and mutual aid manifests itself amongst animals due to the physical and material nature of survival needed by individuals and species. Humanity, as Earth's rational and political animal, was capable of association and mutual aid because we are able to reason why it is beneficial to us. If this was the case, then only humans are truly capable of practicing forms of multispecies mutual aid because we can rationalize that our survival is dependent on the survival of other non-humans.

Later in our story I seek to prove that this is not true. Non-humans are capable of partaking in acts of association, sociability, and mutual aid across species differences if we cared to leave behind our anthropocentric hubris.

To fill in this gap left by Kropotkin requires a horizontal transference of ideas. As bacteria do to swap genetic material horizontally, so must we for Kropotkin and anarchist geographer Élisée Reclus's "On Vegetarianism" and "The Great Kinship of Humans and Fauna." While Kropotkin's scientific anarchism leads us to believe that mutual aid and solidarity are the result of evolution, Reclus articulated an early theory of "emergence" whereas humanity emerged out of nature it created a dialectic relationship where humanity owed nature its due care and respect (Clark and Martin 2013, 21).

Because humanity emerged out of nature both partners helped to co-shape the other. Due to their dialectic relationship, humanity developed a moral recognition of nature as a place of meaning, value, and creativity (Clark and Martin 2013, 25). Although Reclus saw nature as a place where humanity found its meaning, he also noted how important the material relationship between the two was. Believing that, "the brutal violence with which most nations have treated the nourishing earth" leads "foremost among the causes that have vanquished so many successive civilizations" (Reclus 1866, 352–381). Prophetic advice from someone watching the beginning of the Capitalopocene unfolds.

Much like Kropotkin, Reclus was a theorist of mutual aid- though their interpretation was largely an anthropocentric affair. Reclus's mutual aid was also a story of revolution. Where revolution was a struggle by the oppressed to overthrow their dominators. Those who joined in the revolutionary endeavor to create a society based on cooperation and mutuality would ultimately demonstrate that they outnumbered those who did not. Combining their larger numbers with solidarity, the dominated would overturn the prevailing systems of oppression. When human intelligence was combined with mutual aid, it showed itself to be the force for social revolution (Clark and Martin 2013, 66).

While not directly addressing matters of multispecies mutual aid, we can see aspects of his views on mutual aid and humanity's relationship with nature in their progressive stance on environmental ethics, animal liberation, and human/non-human relations. "On Vegetarianism" makes the case for an anarchist practice of vegetarianism. Echoing today's calls for animal liberation and vegetarian practices, Reclus saw the killing and consumption of animals as morally and ethically wrong. More in line with the acts of cannibalism than an act that modern humans should partake in. He also based this view on seeing the relationship between humans and animals as being part of the larger kinship of life itself. Stating:

For the great majority of vegetarians, the question is not whether their biceps and triceps are more solid than those of flesh-eaters, nor whether the organism is better able to resist the risks of life and the chances of death, which is even more important; for them the important point is the recognition of the bond of affection and goodwill that links man to the so-called lower animals, and the extension to these our brothers of the sentiment which has already put a stop to cannibalism among men. . . . The arguments that were opposed to that monstrous habit are precisely those we vegetarians employ now. The horse and the cow, the rabbit and the cat, the deer and the hare, the pheasant and the lark, please us better as friends than as meat. We wish to preserve them either as respected fellow-workers, or simply as companions in the joy of life and friendship. (Reclus 2010, 4)

Vegetarianism for Reclus was an endeavor to recognize the beauty of Nature in non-humans that helped to shape our existences. Viewing them as friends, companions, and fellow workers brings humans a profound sense of happiness and meaning. Referring to them as fellow workers also obliges us to think of the formal and informal labor that non-humans do to make our lives possible.

In "The Great Kinship of Humans and Fauna," Reclus images how non-humans could be viewed once again as companions and kin by humanity. In line with Kropotkin's beliefs about the evolution of sociability, Reclus believed that humanity learned how to practice mutual aid from our early multispecies relationships. Explaining that "the world of animals, from which we derive our genesis and which was our tutor in the art of existence, which taught us fishing and the chase, and the rudiments of healing and of house construction, the habits of work in common, and the storing of food—this world has become a stranger to us" (Reclus 2010, 7). Mutual aid and solidarity were skills not practiced consciously by just humans. Nor were they practiced just between individuals of the same species or of kind. Instead, they were created and learned through the relationships between entities of differing species trying to understand how to live together. Mutual aid was, in short, a gathering of multispecies troublemakers trying to figure out how to create livable worlds with each other. These skills are much in need today, just as they were in Reclus's time.

Reclus closes the text by telling readers when the great kinship of humans and fauna will be recreated.

When our civilization, ferociously individualist as it is, and dividing the world into as many little hostile States as there are separate properties and different family households- when its last bankruptcy shall have been declared, and recourse to mutual help shall have become necessary for the common salvation, when the search for friendship shall have taken the place of the search for wealth—that wealth which, sooner or later, will be sufficiently assured for all; and when the enthusiasm of naturalists shall have revealed to us all that there is of charming, of lovable, of human, and often more than human, in the nature of animals, then we shall remember all these species that have been left behind on the forward route, and shall endeavor to make them, not servants or machines, but veritable companions. (Reclus 2010, 11)

Multispecies kinship relations will be recreated when it becomes necessary for the common survival of humans and fauna. In a time of anthropocentric climate change, the sixth-mass extinction, and the increasing sense of precariousness of all life on Terra it does seem as though it has become necessary to renew the great kinship of humans and fauna. To (re)create the multispecies practices of mutual aid necessary to aid in the building of livable worlds on our increasingly damaged home.

COMPOST COSMOPOLITICS

Stories yet to be told and worlds to be created are projects of compost. And composting is a troublesome process. It combines dead, dying matter and detritus with micro and macro sized multispecies assemblages to work together across species boundaries to create, renew, and restore life. Troublesome because the breaking down of older organic and inorganic materials requires one to get dirty. It also requires a composter to know what materials work best to create the types of matter needed. It is a wonderful and often tiring process by which the composter and the compostables learn to work together—often through trial and error, after which, most of the materials are used as fertilizer for the generation of life. A common practice found in nature that allows for the growth and maintenance of ecosystems, multispecies assemblages, and communal livelihoods. Composting is precisely the method and practice necessary for creating new forms of anarchism(s). Forms capable of meeting the needs of multispecies troublemakers and troublemaking.

As composting starts with the gathering and recycling of older materials, we can view the previous section as the necessary first step in the creation of fertile multispecies troublemaking compost where Kropotkin and Reclus serve as the initial nutrients and ideas for our multispecies compost bin. If we take Kropotkin seriously, mutual aid between individuals is an evolutionary characteristic needed for survival, growth, and development. One that seems to be evident in both Kropotkin's own time and increasingly in our own as neoliberalism and environmental devastation seem to be pushing humans and non-humans into tighter, more precarious relations. Reclus's insights into the multispecies relationships of non-humans and their hominid companions, co-workers, and kin hint that mutual aid is not just enacted between individuals, individuals of the same species, or of the same kind, but it was a learnt activity of multispecies living, learning, and flourishing.

As any batch of compost requires more materials, it is time to add some more. The cosmopolitical project of French philosopher Isabelle Stengers is mixed with the insights of feminist scientist Donna Haraway. Stengers's cosmopolitical project seeks to recognize the constructed nature of world-making, including those between humans and non-humans. Haraway brings to this compost an ethic of "staying with the trouble," where humans learn to live, dine, and die with their multispecies companions. By bringing them into conversation with Kropotkin and Reclus, I seek to compost the ideas and practices necessary for multispecies survivance and troublemaking in the ruins of our Capitalocene present. Examples of which will be explored in the concluding section.

As anarchists, we are quite familiar with being cosmopolitans of a different sort. Today, cosmopolitics and cosmopolitanism is generally tied to the concept of liberal citizenship, the state, and capitalist globalization (Plackek 2012). All of which stand in opposition to any anarchist theory and practice of cosmopolitics. Ironically, they are also the reasons behind many anarchist cosmopolitical projects. While this traditional view of citizenship and world-making can be traced back to Immanuel Kant and his "Perpetual Peace," anarchist cosmopolitics have always sought to problematize the notion of fixed citizenship, state borders, and an adherence to capitalist ways of relating. Because of anarchism's relationships to other systems of world-making and relating, we have often been transnational cosmopolitians. Transgressing the perceived boundedness of state and capitalist-centered communities to organize for anarchist futures, reunite with kin who have been separated because of capitalist induced diasporas, and to escape various forms of persecution.

Instead of liberal citizenship and Kantian cosmopolitics, anarchists have focused on building "cultures of affinity" (Struthers 2017, 63) and "affective communities" (Gandhi 2006, 8–9). Creating spokes, linkages, and networks where the common principles and practices of anarchism serve as the central point of relating, organizing, and hospitality. Spaces, bubbles, and nodes where transnational anarchists could find support from the violence of the State or the Boss, share ideas and practices to further the realization of the social revolution, and to practice an ethic of mutual aid and solidarity among one another. Contrary to the fixed nature of traditional cosmopolitics, anarchist cosmopolitics are often tenuous and precarious. They are mutually dependent on others for their maintenance, renewal, and progress. Just like compost.

Much like transnational anarchists with their fluidity, vibrancy, and precarity, Isabelle Stengers wishes to create a form of cosmopolitics not determined by a Kantian universal. One with little to do with the world as the citizens of antiquity saw it too. Nor of an Earth finally united, where everyone is a citizen of a world society like the globalized statist and capitalist society we now live in. While politicians, the bourgeois, and others with economic, political, and social power urge us to create a society built around the notion of a "good common world," Stengers wants to slow down the creation of any common world so that there is a space for hesitation. Hesitation allows for a moment of investigation into what it means to say or to create the "good" in a "good common world" (Stengers 2004, 2).

Anarchist projects, spaces, and instances of multispecies relations should also intend to follow Stengers's advice and create moments of hesitation. To ask how we humans (and anarchists) can challenge what it means to conduct politics amongst ourselves and with non-humans. Creating the reciprocal thought of what must be done to transform these relations.

"Cosmos" in anarchist cosmopolitics often refers to an unknown. A form of prefigurative politics where we come to know by doing a coherence of means and ends. In Stengers's cosmopolitics, "cosmos" also refers to the unknown—an unknown that is constituted by multiple, divergent worlds, and articulates that they could eventually be linked to create new "common" world(s) (Stengers 2004, 8). Both seem to be opposed to the temptation of creating a peace or a world that is intended to be final and ecumenical. They also do not demand a transcendent peace where the power of asking anything that diverges from the universal, recognizes itself as a purely individual expression that constitutes the point of convergence for all (Stengers 2004, 3). A cosmopolitical proposal and practice demands that a "common world" must be free to emerge from the multiplicity of disparate links that exist because of the role each has in the creation of the other's world. Thus, cosmopolitical worlds can only emerge through the co-creation of the common world through the building of small worlds where actors help to create linkages between them. The very practice of mutual aid and solidarity.

Such cosmopolitical worlds are produced through contingent political articulations against an unknown cosmos. Forming such worlds means making high-stakes, sometimes politically groundless, distinctions between "enemies" and "allies." It means building new worlds by working together in concert with others (Kirksey 2015, 18). Entailing a necessary sense of vulnerability from both the collective individuals (humans and non-humans involved in micro level relationships and interactions) and communities (possibly human and non-human populations and species) involved in the interconnected world-building process. Yet, this vulnerability is not a form of weakness. Instead, it is a form of strength demonstrating the courage to envision and actualize new modes of being, relating, and world-building. This cosmopolitan process of co-creating a common world requires having the necessary tools to think, act, and be in relation with our non-human troublemaking kin.

Donna Haraway is a dog lover. A dog lover who is also focused on examining how their entanglements in capitalism, the inherited process of settler colonialism, and scientific technological assemblages effect and shape our relations with dogs, which is seen especially in the sport of dog/human agility racing. Centering her own relationship with her agility dog co-competitor, Ms. Cayenne Pepper, Haraway demonstrates that humans and non-humans share a much more tenuous relationship than what we might expect. To succeed in the sport of agility racing (and in multispecies relating more generally), both humans and dogs must have the ability to ethically relate to one other. To do so, from within or between species, ethics is practiced and maintained through ongoing alertness to what Haraway calls "otherness-in-relation" (Haraway 2016a, 142). When objects, individuals, and species are in relation, they are never alone in the world. Never without relations or relationships to others. Never the autonomous liberal individual so commonly propagated in our society.

In the sport of agility racing, both Haraway and Cayenne Pepper are working co-operatively to navigate an obstacle course that includes see-saws, high jumps, and interpersonal emotions. They are not a single entity though. They are still Cayenne Pepper, the energetic and attentive young dog, and Donna Haraway, the middle-aged human just trying to keep up. Yet, their ability to succeed in navigating the physical, mental, and emotional obstacles created in the act of relating to one another and running the course depends on their ability to get along together. When Donna and Cayenne Pepper are tackling the obstacle course, they are obliged to ask, "who is present?" and "who is emergent" in these interactions. In this interpersonal encounter, as well as, when species meet, the situated emergence of more livable worlds depends on a differentiated responsibility. In these relationships humans and non-humans create responsibilities to each other. To enact these responsibilities demands that actors pay attention to each other, respect the other actor(s), and respond appropriately.

Through giving attention, respect, and responsiveness to each other, a relationship of reciprocal possession is created between human and non-human troublemakers. We are both caught up in the ongoing and unfolding relationships with each other where each partner is owed attention, respect, and a continued response. Like Stengers's theory of cosmopolitics, participants in Haraway's ethic of flourishing are remodeled by the reciprocal possession created by human/non-human relationships (Haraway 2016a, 144). Neither is the same as what they were before the relationship started (if a beginning can ever be found in a cosmopolitical project). While each continues to develop, grow, and change from being a part in it.

Cosmopolitical relationships based on building contingent worlds through relations of reciprocal possession are not just a human/non-human phenomenon. It has been demonstrated that many species of plants secrete substances that attract certain species of ants, including *Ectatomma ruidom*. These ants have built vibrant and contingent relations and worlds with these plants. Which includes attacking insect species that attempt to eat the plant, spreading the plant to new ranges that it would not be able to do on its own, and are known to "farm" their plant relations for their own benefit (Kirksey 2015, 33). Arctic foxes are also known to create multispecies worlds using the power of compost and cosmpolitics. In the vibrant and precarious ecosystem of the high Arctic, Arctic foxes act as "ecosystem engineers," where they leave the remains of their prey on top of their dens to rot. The decomposition of these bodies allows extra nutrients to soak into the soil, increasing the amount of dune grasses, willows, and wildflowers that grow on top of the den. Making them stand out as islands of flowers and greenery on the tundra landscape. Greenery and flowers then attract herbivores such as caribou, hares, and lemmings who manage the grasses, as well as other scavengers who are interested in the left-over remains (Kives 2016). All of this makes for high-stakes relations between entities commonly thought of as predator and prey. A cosmopolitical world of contingent relations created and maintained through the multiple actions of Arctic foxes, decomposing bodies, vegetative life, and other critters.

Anarchist practices of multispecies cosmopolitics that I aim to develop are predicated on this ethic of flourishing and multispecies response-ability (Haraway 2016a, 256–260). Where the reciprocal possession of individuals and species entails an ability to continually respond and an ability to act on that response. As climate change brings about new emerging ecologies and political actors, anarchists must realize that non-humans are entangled in relationships of reciprocal possession with us and vice versa. As the climate continues to change we will be brought into closer and more dependent relationships of reciprocal possession with various non-humans. Intertwined in the lives, deaths, and ongoing becomings of each other.

ANARCHO-SYMBOGENESIS AND CHTHULUCENE COMPACTS

From bacterial beginnings to compost cosmopolitics, this story ends where others are just beginning. As this is a project of compost, our starting materials—the multispecies mutual aid of Kropotkin and Reculus's interspecies ethics—and our new materials—Stengers's contingent cosmopolitics and Haraway's co-flourishing through otherness-in-relation—needs to be turned. The process of turning compost helps to mix new materials with the old, aerate it so that it can breathe and continue to re/decompose, and gives the composter a moment of hesitation to get their hands (or paws) dirty to see what still needs to be done. I see this batch as the fertile materials needed for the sympoiesis of certain aspects of anarchism and multispecies troublemaking.

Sympoiesis simply means "making with." As I have tried to demonstrate, world-making is never done alone, either by humans or non-humans. We are all in this complicated dance of living on Terra together. Our world's continuous (re)making is done unevenly by humans, animals, plants, and abiotic forces. Yet, if we wish to create more livable worlds, anarchists need to recognize the importance of working with non-humans to create such worlds.

In reevaluating the evolution of life on Earth, scientists have begun to question the common-place notion of the linear advancement of life from "simple" to more "complex" based on individual competition and survival of the fittest (McFall-Ngai 2017, 52). Lynn Margulis leads this debate by advocating that evolution is predicated on sympoiesis (making with) between cells, individuals, and species. Arguing that we are all holobionts—assemblages of different species that form complex ecological units—and symbionts—organisms in symbiotic relationships with each other trying to navigate heterogeneous relationships of mutuality and competition. Haraway states, "Margulis's view of life was that new kinds of cells, tissues, organs, and species evolve primarily through the long-lasting intimacy of strangers. The fusion of genomes in symbioses, followed by natural selection—with a very modest role for mutation as a motor of system-level change—leads to increasingly complex levels of good enough quasi-individuality to get through the day, or the eon. Margulis called this basic and mortal life-making process *symbiogenesis* (emphasis in the original)" (Haraway 2017, 26–27).

Through the process of composting, we can see the development of a form of *anarcho-symbiogenesis*. Where complex relationships between humans and non-humans creates micro and macro level world building processes where humans and non-humans are both holobionts and symbionts with one another. Recognizing this complex relationship exists on many different levels of relationality means that the worlds we inhabit are precarious and mutually constructed like Stenger's cosmopolitics. Recognizing that these relations, linkages, and systems that connect Stenger's cosmopolitical projects resemble transnational anarchist cosmopolitics, we need to combine the anarchist ethics of solidarity and mutual aid with Haraway's ethics of response-ability and co-flourishing to allow us to relate to non-humans who exist in relations of reciprocal possession with us.

I term the speculative and embodied relationships of anarcho-symbiogenesis "Chthulucene compacts." A form of multispecies anarchist politics and practices made between certain humans and non-humans that are grounded in the cosmopolitics of contingent world-building. Here, certain groups of humans and non-humans are caught in relationships of reciprocal possession; where the health, survivance, and flourishing of both communities is dependent on an ongoing response-ability that demands that actors pay attention to each other, respect the other actor(s) involved, and respond appropriately. Recognizing the fragility and contingency of these interdependent worlds necessitates that humans partake in political practices aimed at creating forms of multispecies mutual aid and solidarity. Occurring when humans reorient their political struggles to focus on the (re)creation of an ecological commons beyond the realm the of the State and capitalism, where multispecies politics is an embodied and everyday practice, and where the human subject is decentered as the main actor of history-making (Papadopoulos 2010, 135–136).

I borrow the word "Chthulucene" from Haraway who uses it to demonstrate that solving the ongoing crises of the Anthropocene and Capitalocene requires multispecies string figure games and speculative fabulations. Tentacular thinking through ways of knowing, living, and relating that embodies practices like interconnected spider webs and fleshy octopi tentacles. The Chthulucene, as Haraway terms it, serves a new way thinking and relating that moves our politics beyond the anthropocentric hubris of the Anthropocene and the fetishization of capitalist modes of production and potential state capitalist solutions found in Capitalocene logic (Haraway 2016b, 47–57). Compact refers to an agreement, treaty, or contract between nations, communities, or individuals of matters in which there is a common concern. World-making is a common concern, as is suriviance during the sixth-mass extinction is a common concern, and producing life in the ruins of capitalism is a common concern between humans and non-humans. Chthulucene compacts are an "agreement" between humans and non-humans that posits that humans and non-humans attempt to speculate and act together in the creation of multispecies politics.

Now let us turn to places and spaces where the stories of anarcho-symbiogenesis and Chthulucene compacts are being spawned.

In 2011, an unlikely hero emerged amongst the blasted landscape of neoliberal Greece. Materializing from behind a tear gas smokescreen and amongst blacked clothed anti-austerity and anarchist protesters, Loukanikos surprised and wooed the local and international media with tenacity and solidarity. From attacking tear gas containers to confronting and being assaulted by heavily armed police officers, Loukanikos showed no fear in the face of steep physical assaults and threats to themself and their kin. Their courage against the economic, social, and political violence of the state and international capital would enable him to be one of TIME Magazine's nominees for Person of the Year: The Year of the Protestor in 2011 (Meet Loukanikos 2011).

What made the story of Loukanikos all the more tantalizing was that he was not just any protester. What set him apart was that Loukanikos was a dog. Stray dogs are a common sight in Athens where they are considered "citizens" of the municipality and are tagged and vaccinated by the city (Zournazi 2015). As members of the body politic, dogs freely roam the city. Giving themselves enough relational and physical space to navigate numerous micro and macro level relationships of reciprocal possession with city officials responsible for the individual and overall health of Athens's dog population, tourists who serve as an easy source of food, and whomever else they please. For Loukanikos (or Sausage), this meant making particular relationships and entering into world-building projects with those suffering from chronic housing insecurity, students, and local anarchists (also a common sight in Athens). When he saw that his human companions were out protesting in 2008 he quickly trotted up to offer whatever kind of support a good doggo could.

Loukanikos is not the only dog known to build contingent multispecies worlds with anarchists. In Chile, stray dogs were commonly seen accompanying student protesters in 2010 in their own confrontations against the police, the state, and the neoliberal economic order (En Marcha 2013). Negro Matapaco is the most well-known of these dogs, in part because of the award-winning documentary, *Documental Matapaco* and his human cultivated Facebook and Twitter accounts.

Not much is known about Matapaco before he was seen joining the Santiago student protests. Preferring the area between the Metropolitan Technological University and the Central University of Chile, Matapaco was recorded fighting the police and navigating water cannons and tear gas canisters one minute and then going and making friends with the student protesters the next (RT En Español 2013). Students often reciprocated Matapaco's kindness, solidarity, and mutual aid by giving him colorful bandanas to wear, providing food, and offering shelter from the police. His Facebook page notes that Matapaco is "an innate revolutionary, father of 32 children (recognized) and husband of six ladies, a friend of the people and the worst nightmare of the police" (RT En Español 2013). Facts only known because of the intimate lives of Matapaco and his human companions.

From barking at the police, to moving tear gas canisters; in addition to offering mental and emotional support for humans engaging with the oppressive forces of the state and capitalism, Loukanikos and Negro Matapaco represent and exemplify a multispecies practice of solidarity and mutual aid. Here, the multispecies mutual aid enacted in the Chthulucene compacts between Loukanikos, Matapaco and their human co-conspirators is recognizable and different from how we would normally expect solidarity and mutual aid to be enacted. Their physical participation in the protests resembles the anarchist practice of direct action. Directly confronting the police, moving tear gas containers, and putting themselves in front of protestors allows us to see the easily recognizable forms of solidarity that they enacted. Yet, they both practiced intangible forms solidarity and mutual aid. Primarily, by being able to offer mental and emotional support due to their physical presence at the protest and in their intra-personal relations they cultivated before, during, and after the protests were finished.

Anarcho-symbiogenesis and Chthulucene compacts require us to rethink what solidarity and mutual aid may be. They should also not be viewed as just occurring between humans and animals either. We should be conscientious to include the power of vegetative, microbial, and abiotic life in our attempts to make more livable worlds in the ruins of capitalism. Vegetative life—from microscopic plant life to the great forests of the Amazon Rainforest and Boreal Arctic—is what makes life as we know it possible. The earliest plants did so by pulling carbon dioxide out of the atmosphere and producing the oxygen that we breathe (Darroch 2015, 1), consequently creating the first mass extinction—an example of how life and symbiogenesis is never just a process of mutuality.

In the pacific northwest of Turtle Island, artist Deanna Pindell uses DIY art and direct action to simultaneously fight capitalist-induced clear-cutting of forests while (re)building contingent multispecies worlds. After driving by one of the numerous clear-cuts near their home, Pindell became inspired to do something about it. Remembering the story of the Lorax, where greedy capitalists cut down forests to make sweaters, Pindell sent a call-out for people's' unwanted wool sweaters. After felting them, she combined them with chicken wire to create small felted balls. Calling them Thneeds Reseeds, in honor of the Lorax, Pindell seeds these balls in recently clear-cut forests. By soaking them in buttermilk and adding bits of *Bryum argenteum*, silvery bryum moss, the Thneeds Reseeds act as source for tree seeds to germinate and sprout from. They also act as homes for mice, salamanders, and other small critters displaced from the forest due to the holes Pindell puts in them (Kirksey 2014, 148).

Pindell also includes a tongue-and-cheek recipe for those who want to make their own Thneeds Reseeds:

Thneeds Reseeds

To restore your clear-cut forest:

1. Break the mosses into fragments.
2. Mix the moss with buttermilk.

3. Place Thneeds in clear-cut.
4. Keep the Thneeds moist with buttermilk until tree seedlings can take hold.

Note: Enough Thneeds for one square meter of forest (Kirksey 2014, 150).

Pindell's Thneeds Reseeds project epitomizes the type of thinking and reciprocal projects needed for creating life in our troubled times. She did not wait for the benevolent hand of the market, the state, or local governments to reclaim and heal these lost forests. Instead, she embraced an anarchist-like DIY ethic to start it herself, one meter of forest at a time. Recognizing the response-ability that they had to the forests, Pindell created an easy way to reseed them while also cutting down on community's waste through using recycled materials. The Chthulucene compact(s) enacted between Pindell, the forest, and the numerous small animals that live in the Thneeds Reseeds show that not all multispecies relations will be as reciprocal as those we saw with Loukanikos and Matapacos. Humans will, at times, have an asymmetrical responsibility and capacity to be the primary world-builders in anarcho-symbiogenesis.

I will admit that creating new forms of life and (re)building multispecies worlds is no easy task. It requires completely reexamining our relationships to other humans, the particular non-humans that we interact with, and the political projects that we are creating. It will also take a lot of speculation, trial and error, and most importantly, patience. We cannot expect to (re)create new worlds in one fell swoop. After centuries of capitalist exploitation of human and non-human bodies and relationships created by anthropocentric hubris, there is a lot of work to be done. Yet, as anarchists, we are up to such a task. We have always been troublemakers accused of being utopian dreamers and that is our strength. We know the worlds that we want to create and we have the tools to do so. What we now have are more troublemakers to make trouble with. More companions, co-workers, and kin to make lives with. As Loukaniko and Matapaco tell us:

Rise up pupper!!! You have a world to bork at!

REFERENCES

"The Black Cat (Sabo-Tabby)." 2011. Chicago. IWW Historical Archives. https://www.iww.org/gu/history/icons/black_cat.

Clark, John, and Camille Martin. 2013. *Anarchy, Geography, Modernity: Selected Writings of Elisée Reclus*. Oakland, CA: PM Press.

Cornell, Andrew. 2017. *Unruly Equality: U.S. Anarchism in the 20th Century*. Oakland, CA: University of California Press.

Darroch, et al. 2015. "Biotic Replacement and Mass Extinction of the Ediacara Biota." *Proceedings of the Royal Society Biological Sciences* 282 (1814). doi:10.1098.

En Marcha. 2013. Documental Matapaco. Video. https://www.youtube.com/watch?v=wiEFhAAWCiw.

Gandhi, Leela. 2006. Affective Communities: Anticolonial Thought, Fin-De-Siècle Radicalism, And The Politics Of Friendship (Politics, History, And Culture). Durham: Duke University Press.

Haraway, Donna. 2016a. Manifestly Haraway. Minneapolis: University of Minnesota Press.

Haraway, Donna J. 2016b. Staying With The Trouble: Making Kin In The Chthulucene. Durham: Duke University Press.

Haraway, Donna. 2017. "Symbiogenesis, Sympoiesis, and Art Science Activisms for Staying with the Trouble." In Arts of Living On A Damaged Planet, 26–27. Minneapolis: University of Minnesota Press.

Kirksey, Eben. 2014. "Multispecies Communities." In The Multispecies Salon. Durham: Duke University Press. http://www.multispecies-salon.org/working/wp-content/uploads/2016/01/Multispecies-Communities-A-Recipe-for-Thneeds-Reseeds-byEben-Kirksey.pdf.

Kirksey, Eben. 2015. Emerging Ecologies. Durham: Duke University Press. (Kirksey 2015,)

Kives, Bartley. 2016. "'Ecosystem Engineers': Arctic Foxes Build Gardens on Tundra, Biologists Say." CBC News, May 26, 2017. http://www.cbc.ca/news/canada/manitoba/arctic-foxes-tundra-gardens-dens-1.3601477.

Kropotkin, Peter. 2006. *Mutual Aid: A Factor of Evolution*. Mineola, NY: Dover.

"'Matapaco,' El Perro Revolucionario Que No Se Pierde Una Protesta En Chile." 2013. RT En Español. https://actualidad.rt.com/actualidad/view/115493-perro-chile-estudiantes-matapacos-canino.

Mac Laughlin, Jim. 2016. *Kropotkin and the Anarchist Intellectual Tradition*. London: Pluto Press.

McFall-Ngai, Margaret. 2017. "Noticing Microbial Worlds: The Postmodern Synthesis in Biology." In Arts of Living On A Damaged Planet. Minneapolis: University of Minnesota Press.

"Meet Loukanikos, Athens Protest Dog." 2011. TIME, November 15, 2011. http://content.time.com/time/photogallery/0,29307,2102191_2327703,00.html.

Papadopoulos, Dimitris. 2010. "Insurgent Posthumanism." *Ephemera: Theory & Politics in Organization* 12 (2). http://www.ephemerajournal.org/contribution/insurgent-posthumanism.

Plackek, Kevin. 2012. "The Democratic Peace Theory." E-International Relations. http://www.e-ir.info/2012/02/18/the-democratic-peace-theory/.

Reclus, Élisée. 1866. "The Feeling For Nature In Modern Society." *La Revue Des Deux Mondes* 63 (May–June).

Reclus, Élisée. 2010. "On Vegetarianism" and "The Kinship of Humans and Fauna." Montreal: Kersplebedeb. 4. Originally published in *Humane Review*, January 1901.

Stengers, Isabelle. 2004. "The Cosmopolitical Proposal." https://balkanexpresss.files.wordpress.com/2013/09/stengersthe-cosmopolitcal-proposal.pdf.

Struthers, David. 2017. "'The Boss Has No Color Line': Race, Solidarity, and a Culture of Afinity in Los Angeles and the Borderlands, 1907–1915." Accessed October 13.

Zournazi, Mary. 2015. "In Search of Greece's Protest Dog, Loukanikos." Radio-tonic, October 15, 2015. http://www.abc.net.au/radionational/programs/radiotonic/in-search-of-greeces-protest-dog-loukanikos/6854042.

Chapter 9

"Street Dogs" of Istanbul: An Exemplary Case for the Construction and Contestation of Human Domination over Urban Animals

Ali Bilgin and Kiraz Özdoğan

INTRODUCTION

Political ecology is a trans-disciplinary research field addressing relations of domination and power in nature–society interrelations (Karlsson 2015). With a critical approach toward the eco-politics of governments and enterprises, political ecology often aligns with local struggles against the exploitation of nature. While this field of research frequently involves animals, they are mainly treated as "static components of a thoroughly human sociality" within the existing literature (Hobson 2007, 250 quoted by Collard, 2015: 131). This "anthroparchal" understanding (Cudworth 2014, 28) of the human–nature relations has been implicitly shared by most political ecologists and hasn't been duly problematized, nor criticized within the conceptual framework of the political ecology. Recently though, an effort to create a non-anthropocentric or "more-than-human" political ecology is beginning to emerge (Srinivasan 2015). This emergent work intends to treat non-humans as "actants" or living "subjects," who, in an *Umwelt*[1] of their own, are to be considered as capable of establishing social bonds within a culture (Lestel 2016), whereby they should be recognized as *creators* of significations (Delfour 2015, 87) and *authors* of premeditated actions.

The *Animal Liberation Movement*, along with *Critical Animal Studies* (CAS) (Taylor and Twine 2014), which has given rise to this new approach criticizing the human domination over other species, provides us with rich perspectives and a conceptual framework to be used in the rejection of all forms of ontological and structural hierarchy, as well as relations of domination, exploitation, or possession between humans and non-humans

(Best, 2009, 189). Whereas researches in CAS or *Animal Studies* problema-tize mostly the construction of human domination over working animals, eaten animals, pet animals, and wild animals,[2] very little attention has been placed on free-roaming urban animals.[3]

We argue that street dogs of Istanbul could offer a particular case of a non-speciesist relationship to other-than-human living beings that are not consid-ered as items of property, not working animals in the service of humans, nor "wild" (which we understand to mean living outside of regular contact zones with humans). In fact, for centuries, Istanbul has been a city where dogs in the streets could live without any specific owner[4] and establish independent links with humans as part of the city's social life. In their everyday relations with humans, they are to be considered as "actants" within their *Umwelt* that involves humans and the urban space as well. They are socialized beings living in the urban habitat. They maintain mutual aid relations with humans (Kropotkin, 2008), accomplishing specific functions in the city. However, this relation was forced to change under administrative measures and inter-ventions during the modernization process in Istanbul. The physical bodies of dogs, as well as their relationships with other species, including humans, began to be controlled, regulated, and manipulated by legal measures, institu-tionalized scientific/medical discourse, and modernist urban policies.

This chapter focuses on the relations between humans and street dogs in Istanbul from the 16th century to the present time, and seeks to problematize the construction of human domination over street dogs by illustrating the means of struggle around the issue and highlighting common life experience both historically and into the present. Our work is based on participant obser-vation combined with primary and secondary source material. We identify two significant turns in the formulation of the discourse and practice of gov-ernmental interventions. The institutionalization of modernist urban policies and medical discourse in the mid-19th century, which aimed at eradicating the dogs; and of the catch, neuter, release (CNR) program and the Dog Population Management (DPM) approach in the wake of the 21st century, which still pro-ceeds to govern the interspecies relations through a *let live* discourse, creating a market around the issue. Each displays more or less the same characteristics in the construction of anthroparchal discrimination: they are based on the repro-duction and modulation of a predominant scientific-political discourse that fundamentally denies all other-than-humans a meaningful, valuable, social, and individual "existence." Each turn challenges the common living space of humans and other species; implements a species-based spatial segregation; and produces scientifically "justified" pretexts to segregate these "others" from the "human" social life. In each turn against these governmental interventions, we observe new means of resistance and struggle led by both dog and human inhabitants of Istanbul that shape the urban political ecology of the city.

First, by the mid-nineteenth century, along with the institutionalization of modern medical discourse, and with the adoption of a new governmental approach over the urban space, street dogs of Istanbul emerged as a public health issue and became a "hygienic" problem of concern for the municipality. Like in many other cities in Western Europe, the first governmental measure was to attempt a "decaninization" of the urban "common" spaces. Dogs were allowed to live only as tamed, owned, and *petified*. This roughly meant the extermination of all the "unowned" dogs living in the urban sphere, where the *petified* ones were placed under the tutorial of a "rational animal," who would (and should) take care of their well-being by vaccinating them and supervising their breeding.

However, this policy did not entirely succeed throughout the roughly one hundred years that it was adopted, and a new approach called "population management" was put in place in the wake of the twenty-first century. This change in street dog policies, from extermination attempts of the 19th century to the DPM supported by the World Health Organization (WHO), portrays the transformations and continuities in the management of interspecies relations. The extermination attempts aimed at destroying this relationship, whereas the DPM became a means to govern it. At each turn, inhabitants of Istanbul developed strategies against the governmental street dog policies; humans and dogs displayed an amazing sense of cooperation and managed to continue their common life in the urban arena.

We believe that this struggle for liberty of the dogs of Istanbul to live without "masters," serves as an inspiration for a non-speciesist common life imagination that extends political ecology beyond its typical anthropocentric frame, as it displays spontaneous, creative interspecies cooperation and the creation of discourse and practice focused on the "here and now" (Springer, 2016).

I. A Long-Term Common Life Experience:
Before Governmental Interventions

The relations of Istanbul citizens with the non-human inhabitants of the city have a long and peculiar history, which constitutes quite a unique local urban culture. Some even consider street dogs of Istanbul to be a constitutive part of the city's character (Işın 2016).

Although the existence of street dogs in the byzantine period was reported in certain sources, we have no testimony on their relations to humans (Schick 2010). It's generally acknowledged that the socialized dogs were brought to Istanbul during the siege of Umayyads (Remlinger 1932) or with the Turkish conquest (Loti 1921; Schick 2010). Dogs of Istanbul found their place in travelogues of occidentals as exotic figures throughout the centuries that followed the conquest, and their relations with humans there were described in quite subtle detail.[5]

Street dogs, for quite a long period, were not subjected to legal regulations or governmental measures. Inhabitants of Istanbul established non-governmental organizations like foundations, charities, and hospitals for the care of street animals (Montaigne 1580; Rycaut 1670; Thévenot 1687, 1727; Tournefort 1727; Guer 1747; Nerval 1843; Amicis 1896; Remlinger 1932). In everyday life, they used to build huts especially in the winter for their protection (Tournefort 1727; Pardoe 1836; Remlinger 1932). Upon their death, some rich people used to bequeath money to locals to feed the dogs of the street (Rycaut 1670; Thévenot 1687, 1727; Guer 1747; Nerval 1843). Travelogues from the 16th century on provide numerous depictions of these cases. Thévenot, a traveler of the seventeenth century, who found this custom quite weird, offers a testimony:

> I could hear give an hundred instances of the charity of the Turks towards Beasts; I have seen them often practice such as to us would seem very *ridiculous*: I have seen several Men in good garb, stop in a street, stand round a Bitch that had newly puppied, and all go and gather stones to make a little wall about her, lest some heedless person might tread upon her; and many such like Examples; but it is not my design to trouble the Reader with such trifles. (Thévenot 1687, 51; emphasis added)

Thévenot, as an occidental traveler coming from an already capitalized world, beside considering this caring attitude toward the beasts as somehow "ridiculous," reports what he observes as one of the particularities of a cultural texture, and even a slight envy can be detected in his descriptions. Thévenot associates this "charity" with that for poor people and beggars, connecting all to the imperatives of Islam religion.

Jean-Antoine Guer, merely a century after Thévenot, promotes this impression from "ridiculous" to "madness" and relates all these customs to superstitious beliefs:[6]

> One sees some of the Muslims mad enough to extend their charity to pay an artisan for that he take care to water a merely dead tree, fearing that the drought might kill them. Many buy birds only to give them freedom. (Guer 1747)

This urban social life of Istanbul street dogs that seemed so weird to the travelers was shaped, according to Ekrem Işın, within the intersection of religious-symbolic life and the socio-economic structure. Işın argues that outside of the three places considered to be sacred according to the Islamic religion (the house, which assures the sacred life of the family; the mosque, which assures the sacred life of the community; and the marketplace, which transforms fair labor into a sacred "halal" gain), streets had been inhabited by anonymous homeless people and dogs as their genuine habitat until the 19th century. The streets of ottoman Istanbul, strictly speaking, created the street dogs with their peculiar manners and their links to humans (Işın 2016). Travelers also report that dogs living without human masters used to fulfil certain functions in the urban social life. Dogs controlled passers-by, providing security; they also sorted out the waste, thus collaborating in keeping the city clean (Busbecq 1881; Olivier 1801; Amicis 1896; Remlinger 1932).

Indeed, the Ottoman imperial capital in the early modern period was not a non-anthroparchal paradise. The precepts of social bonds in everyday life semiotics, and the onto-theologic framework of the overall imperial culture, were primarily based on anthropocentric and anthroparchal religious conceptions. Nonetheless, the dogs in the streets were obviously part of the urban ecology, and they were not denied to be autonomous "actants" in interspecies social relations.

Exiles, Extermination Attempts, and Resistances: Common
Life Turning into a Matter of Dominance and Struggle

The attitude of the Ottoman government toward dogs changes from the mid-eighteenth century onward, as part of the transformations in governmental, institutional, and cultural spheres taking place in the Ottoman Empire, along with the crisis of the trade and production economy caused by long-term wars and substantial territory losses. A subsequent loss of the global market share led the Ottoman economy to be rapidly invaded by Western capital flows (Faroqhi, 1993, 1998; Reyhan, 2008). Streets were gradually losing their "no man's land" status and becoming "public spaces" under the responsibility of the municipality, and dogs appeared as "heimatlos" vagabonds, or even residual parasites, in the modern urban panorama.

The first exile of the dogs took place in the seventeenth century, by an initiative of the Grand-vizier Nasuh Pasha (1611–1614), who deported the dogs in the Istanbul city center on barques to a suburb on the other side of the sea, Scutari (Üsküdar). He was not duly understood by his contemporaries though, since they interpreted this measure (incomprehensible for its time) merely as a result of some obscure superstitious beliefs, rather than a pro-modernist urban policy (d'Ohsson 1788).

However this avant la lettre "decaninization policy" has proven to be far beyond an issue of personal superstition, since it was pursued in the following centuries, and continued parallel to the modernization of the urban life in Istanbul. Hence, the second exile of the dogs took place under the reign of Mahmud II (1808–1839) who is renowned for substantially reforming the state institutions of the classical Ottoman period. After some street dogs attacked a British citizen (he had beaten them while drunk), all the street dogs were to be exiled onto a barren island Oxia (Sivriada) off the city. However, a storm erupted just then preventing the barques to reach the island, so under loud protests of the citizens, the Sultan had to withdraw his order (Işın 2016; Pinguet 2009; Schick 2010). This protest might be considered as a first massive resistance against the "modern dog policy." A third exile attempt under Sultan Abdülaziz (1861–1876) was successful. Soon after that, a fire ravaged the city, and the Crimean War led the Empire to a prompt defeat, so the people of Istanbul came to believe that all these tragedies happened because of the unjust treatments and torments imposed on innocent animals. Unrest spreading among citizens once again led the monarch to withdraw his order and bring back those dogs that remained alive (Schick 2010). These urban legends may be considered as signs of a first discursive resistance act (though myth-making) against the decaninization policies.

The organization of Istanbul as a municipality was inaugurated in 1855, initiating reforms to comply with the emerging urban needs in a new governmental approach. Urban planning, construction, and maintenance of public roads as well as keeping the city clean were henceforth among the duties of the municipality. The compartmented urban structure of the classical Ottoman period began to be pierced by the increasing circulation and mobility between the quarters; thus traditional habitats of the dogs were invaded and transformed by new urban policies and capital flow (Schick 2010), for example, dogs living on the new tramline route were transported (again) to Scutary in 1871 (Topçuoğlu 2010, 52).

Travelers visiting the city from the mid-19th century on describe it as consisting of traditional quarters that preserved most of their pre-modern texture (South of Golden Horn) and those where the production and the use of urban space were significantly transformed (North of Golden Horn). In these new quarters, the social organization of time, as well as relations between humans and other species were no longer in compliance with traditional attitudes and their respective world of meaning, which began to be reshaped according to new cultural references (Nerval 1843; Amicis 1896; Remlinger 1932). Travelers tell us how relations to street dogs change dramatically between two sides of the city. Interesting to note, on the relatively "occidentalized" side namely, attitude toward street dogs is quite rough as compared with old city quarters, preserving more or less the pre-modern texture. In modern quarters dogs fled humans as they were often beaten or maltreated by foreigners as well as local Levantines. Foreigners became upset when dogs did not move and let them pass (Craven 1799; Amicis 1896; Remlinger 1932). "I never saw such utterly wretched, starving, sad-visaged, broken-hearted looking curs in my life," writes Mark Twain who stayed in Pera, the occidentalized side of the city (Twain 1869). Dogs were systematically poisoned in these emerging modern quarters, where the howling of perishing dogs in the middle of the night was part of everyday life (Amicis 1896; Remlinger 1932).

The street dogs of Istanbul were finally declared as a "public health issue," officially considered as a hygienic problem, vectors of zoonotic diseases,[7] following the new medical paradigm, which was roughly anthropocentric. This new approach was institutionalized in the Ottoman capital toward the end of the 19th century[8] (Ülman 2007, 175–186; Ülman 2010, 105).

Around the beginning of the 20th century, the dogs of Istanbul, as their autonomous social existence was "scientifically" and politically denied, began to be used in medical experiments on rabies, as randomly chosen guinea pigs (Remlinger 1932).[9] Campaigns in the press denouncing dogs as dirty animals and source of disease started as early as 1890s so that the public opinion was prepared for the final extermination of the dogs (Pinguet 2016). Dogs, these centuries-old socialized inhabitants of Istanbul, created by the very streets of the old city and a vibrant urban ecology in the course of five centuries, were declared as "stray animals" thanks to the collaboration between the official urban policy and the scientific medical discourse. They became persona non gratae in the "sterilized" anthroparchal urban landscape of the future.

The "Final Solution"

The Young Turks overthrowing the absolutist regime in 1908 and establishing the constitutional monarchy saw in the street dog a symbol of the *ancient regime* as well as social backwardness (Abdullah Cevdet 1909; Goursat 1910 cited in Sungurbey 1993; Loti 1921; Remlinger 1932; Işın 1995; Pinguet 2009). So, after the 1909 military coup d'état, deposing Abdülhamit II (1876–1909), the Young Turks also exiled the dogs in 1910, as an emblematic act of modernization, and this time irreversibly, to the Island of Oxia (Sivriada), where they tragically perished, howling day and night for weeks on end, devouring each other in hunger (Colomban 1910 cited in Pinguet 2016; Goursat 1910 cited in Sungurbey 1993; Işın 1995; Pinguet 2009; Schick 2010).

This traumatic exile of 1910 left a deep scar in the public imagination and urban memory, which is still kept vivid today.[10] Pierre Loti, as well as numerous newspapers of the time (Pinguet 2016), described these events as horrific scenes, citing examples of spontaneous resistance and civil disobedience, which actually resemble those to come in the twentieth century:

Extermination did not work so easily; no Turk wanted to take part at the infamous task . . . they had to recruit vagabonds, bohemians, bandits. These people operated with large iron jaw-grips, grabbed the poor victims by their necks, paws or tail, threw them pell-mell, skinned and bleeding, in boats that took them to the island of torture. For several days there were cries, tears, and battles in

Stamboul; the Turks were indignant and unwilling. Poor good dogs! They were hidden as much as possible in private households. One of my friends, the cavalry captain Tewfik Bey, . . . went so far as to commit an act of open rebellion; the seekers arrived in the yard of his military barracks with a population of good familiar dogs, and his soldiers shouted in despair; then and there he commanded to close the gates on the assassins, to disarm them, and to hold them with their own tongs to throw them out; he was punished with a month's imprisonment, but the brave animals, friends of his horsemen, were saved. (Loti 1921)[11]

Apart from the deep unrest this exile provoked among local people, it also caused indignation in the foreign press (Pinguet 2016). But government policies toward street dogs didn't seem to change, and although exile on this scale never took place again, extermination attempts remained to be the main official policy for the next hundred years.

The Turkish Society for Protection of Animals inaugurated in 1912, soon after the final exile, counts among its members Tevfik Bey, mayor of Istanbul during the incident. This association, although interrupted in its work during the Great War, was reinstated in 1924, after the declaration of the Republic, and is still operating today.

Measures throughout the 20th Century until the Late 1980s

For many years to come in the Republican era, after 1923, the culling policy continued to be contested and confronted by some rudimentary acts of resistance. During this period, The Turkish Society for Protection of Animals seemed to have assumed the role of taking cognizance of the sensibilities of both the municipality and the general public ("painless killing") in the application of the policies over street dogs, and served to neutralize the social opposition against the killing policies (Toklucu 2016). Thus, in 1927, the Association began to "painlessly" assassinate street dogs and cats using gas chambers imported from abroad. Toklucu states, according to the reports of the Association that 3,309 dogs in 1929 and 9,500 dogs in 1940–1941 were "humanely" killed (Toklucu 2016, 32–33).

As the only official recognition of street dogs remained to be as a public health problem, they are mainly mentioned in scientific research. Though, even these works contain some testimony on civil resistance. Dr. Tunçman, in his book *Kuduz ve Kuduzun Çoğalma Nedenleri* [*Rabies and Causes of its Propagation*] (Tunçman 1935, 44), mentions people who force the poisoned dogs to eat yogurt as an antidote.[12] Topçuoğlu quotes a report by the *Akşam* newspaper (July 29, 1949) about some people who opened the doors of the trucks of Turkish Society for Protection of Animals, releasing the cats and dogs, to save them from a certain death (Topçuoğlu 2010, 99). Newspapers from the 1950s to 1970s display numerous cases of poisoning or shooting street animals, as well as some examples of spontaneous acts of resistance (Pinguet 2009; Toklucu 2016).

The killing policy continued as the official program until the end of the 1980s. According to the 1984 report of the Veterinary Service of the Municipality of Istanbul, 88,153 dogs had been killed by means of the municipal veterinary teams in the past three years (Topçuoğlu 2010, 101). Mayor Bedrettin Dalan (1984–1989), who intended to buy a killing machine and who even declared that he would "import Koreans to eat the dogs," had to give up these attempts because of the popular protest that followed (Sungurbey 1993).

Toward the end of the 20th century, there were still street dogs, stray dogs, or free-roaming owned dogs in many countries (Greece, Italy, etc.). This was partly due to the local cultures and partly to organized resistance against such policies as we have seen in the case of Istanbul. The rise of discourse on animal rights in "Western" countries also played a significant role. Of important note is the fact that the "owned dog" (petification) policy reproduced the category of "unowned" or "disowned" dogs. A significant number of the dogs produced within pet farms are abandoned to the streets or forests and comprise the main part of the actual stray dog population. Thus, killing and *petification* policies did not eradicate the street dogs but transformed the dynamics of the fact.

II. A New Strategy to Govern in the Era of Neoliberalism: Dog Population Management (DPM)

From the early 1990s onward, a new worldwide dog policy paradigm was formulated: the DPM, which was proposed as a global norm by the World Health Organization (WHO). Similar to the biopolitics as described by Foucault (Keskin 2016, 16), this new strategy involves intervening in the lives of street dogs to manipulate their life potential, tame their bodies, shape their behaviors, and regulate their interrelations among each other as well as with humans. Instead of annihilating life, it reshapes it to govern.

Neoliberalism generally consists of adapting the operation of state power toward the needs and logic of the market (Foucault 2015, 111). Within this framework, DPM seeks to find "market-based solutions" for the street dog "problem." DPM is a procedure that involves institutional (shelters, veterinary clinics, etc.), discursive (on health, disease, right to live, etc.), and industrial (breeding, food and gadget production, etc.) fields that integrate into a global neoliberal economy, turning street dogs into "forced consumers" of the veterinary-pet industry. It also produces a neoliberal version of a speciesist approach within a persistently anthroparchal conception of society.

These new policies bring along new forms of resistance and a new discourse. Some of these resistances "share at the bottom the axioms and founding concepts in whose name the violence is exercised" (Derrida 2008, 89 quoted by McCance 2013, 65), but they nevertheless imply various forms of inter-species relations that are far from the logic of the market, from the relations of property and domination, and might serve as an inspiration for imagining a non-speciesist common life.

We intend to problematize the very principles and the physical implementation of DPM in Turkey in its social, political, and economic context. We will then try to depict some old and new forms of resistance against speciesist governmental policies along with everyday common life experiences that improvise new ways of inter-species relations.

The DPM Discourse

According to the *Guidelines for DPM* published in 1990, the street dogs, ignoring their local specificities, are summed in the general category of "stray dogs." They are not acknowledged as part of social life, where they have their proper names and are recognized as individuals. Instead, they are treated as a totality, a population; measured, summed in statistical analysis— sex, age, birth rate, rearing success, survival and mortality rates, etc. (*Guidelines* 1990, 9); and evaluated according to certain norms derived from these statistical data. They constitute a population that is meant to be managed and put in order.[13]

We could sum the DPM approach in four points. The first would be on the public health issue. The DPM inherits this conception from the 19th century. The "stray" dogs are unfailingly considered as potential vectors of zoonotic diseases (*Guidelines* 1990, 1). To reduce the health risks for humans, it is suggested to maintain them under medical surveillance. This point of view, indeed, provides the anthropocentric legitimacy for intervening in the street dogs' lives and manipulating their bodies. The second is derived from the "fact" that dogs in general, but especially the ownerless ones living in urban areas, are overpopulated. As a result of this anthropocentric observation, the long-term reduction of their population becomes a priority. The third point is one that appropriates notions from animal rights and animal welfare discourses (which emerged in the 1970s). The interventions in the lives of the street dogs (castration, vaccination, enclosure, etc.) are presented as suitable and even desirable for the well-being of the street dogs. Finally, the fourth point is a forced acceptance of the failure of the killing and displacing policies after two centuries, so instead one concentrates on collecting ethological data[14] regarding free-roaming dogs, in order to manage them. DPM is in fact based on the observation that when an area is cleared of dogs, others immediately replace them, and dogs tend to reproduce even more rapidly when they feel themselves in danger:

the dogs keep on living their lives in the same area and, because of pack mentality, they keep other, unneutered dogs from entering the territory. In this way, the number of animals decreases slowly at the rate of natural mortality. ("Stray Dogs and Means for Solving the Problem")

Consequently, the lives and bodies of street dogs, as well as the human-dog relations continue to be a matter of regulation. DPM prescribes some legal and institutional arrangements for treating and managing dogs as a population. This paradigm charges the state to produce and propagate appropriate discourse and practices, as well as to found necessary institutions for its application. According to the DPM, the street dogs are framed as a population, which may survive under the control of state power only in a proper manner predicted by DPM.

The program prescribed for "stray" dogs in the DPM approach is labeled CNR. As of the 1960s, the Animal Birth Control (ABC) program ("The Stray"), which was the predecessor of the CNR was applied as a method to control street dog populations in some developing countries like India. But in due course, the CNR program became a model for developing countries, supported by the WHO and World Society for the Protection of Animals (WSPA) as expressed in the *Guidelines for DPM*. To reduce unplanned breeding, it suggests systematic neutering, and regular vaccination to prevent any risk to public health. Street dogs are now captured, vaccinated and neutered by public institutions (municipalities in Turkey) or subcontractors. They are then released to the place where they were caught.

Thus, theoretically since ownership and controlled pet farms were meant to prevent dogs from being abandoned, consequently the dog population was expected to decrease gradually. But in fact, the ownership strategy incessantly produced ownerless dogs, and their care had to be shared between volunteers and state institutions. The latter was responsible for neutering and vaccinating, and the former aimed to feed the dogs and look after them in order to comply with the public health standards.

According to the CNR supporting literature, there should be no ownerless street dog left, and the fact that some of them remained, is considered to be an anomic and unexpected situation, which "could only be solved through education and legislation, where abandoning is harshly sanctioned" ("The Stray"). Nevertheless, the "problem to be solved" seems to arise from the very conceptualization of the fact. Just as capitalism tries to remedy its damages only by eliminating the results, or by constructing new markets about it, without changing its logic of functioning, it is worth asking whether or not the criterion of being "owned" and "tamed" for an animal is not at the source of this problem. Do the dogs need to be owned? Do any animals (the definition of the term remains unclear, since humans are animals as well) need to be taken care of by a human tutor? Both more-than-human political ecology and animal liberation discourse, considering the animals as "actants" and criticizing animals as property, lead us to problematize this logic based on solving "the street dog question" within an animals as property system.

In this approach, the main problem may lie in the reproduction of the speciesist and anthroparchal conception within the contemporary neoliberal era. Both the CNR program and the DPM approach treat the street dogs as a population within a conceptual framework built on the evaluation of quantitative data, hence denying the individuality and the social being of the dogs, which is an explicitly "speciesist" approach. This discourse helps to organize and justify interventions into the dogs' lives, as well as the manipulation of their bodies. We will try to display these aspects through its implementation in Turkey.

Pioneering Practices of DPM in Turkey in the Era of the Neoliberal Turn

The earliest versions of the CNR program in Turkey appeared in the late 1980s and early 1990s, right when the neoliberal transformation was occurring (Özkazanç 2011). At this period we observe the first animal rights movement in Turkey (which would be institutionalized in the following years) emerging against the killing policies. Some animal rights associations were supporters of the CNR program. They were calling to the authorities to stop the killing policies, since it was not a "civilized" way of addressing the issue; affirming that to neuter as well as to vaccinate were more civilized and "more economical" than killing the animals. Eventually they claim both public health and the dogs' rights to live would be preserved by this CNR program.

Municipalities in turn, as from the mid-1990s on, promised to shift to these new programs. These animals' rights associations[15] collaborated with certain municipalities, which allocated them free space to set up their clinics or shelters (Bakırköy, Sarıyer, and Şişli [Sungurbey 1993, 568–574]). In turn, they also supported animal hospitals of the municipalities. The first shelters[16] established by municipalities—for the sake of image rather than genuine compassion—were founded in this period (Sungurbey 1993, 572; Topçuoğlu 2010, 105–106). However, the sanitary conditions of the shelters were so poor that many volunteers and animals' rights associations had to work voluntarily to improve them. Some of the shelters were even managed exclusively and directly by volunteers.[17]

This change in the discourse and practice regarding street dogs was not yet the predominant policy and had no legal ground; under the pretext of protecting "public health" or "EU access," killing (Ergu 2001), enclosure ("Köpekland kuruluyor" 1999), and displacement (Güven 1998) of the street dogs were still quite common,[18] although they were losing their moral legitimacy. From the early 2000s onward there were still people who defended street dogs, occasionally managing to prevent their capture, organizing public campaigns and demonstrations,[19] so the municipalities were ordered to create "animal rehabilitation centres" (Ergu 2001).

Legalization of the DPM and Building of Its Substructure

The legal regulation for the DPM program[20] was introduced during the first governmental period of the Justice and Development Party (AKP), as part of the adoption of neoliberal policies, in line with the EU integration process. The law for Animal Protection (law no: 5199), after being held in suspense for nine years, was accepted in 2004, and complementary regulations came into effect in 2006. This law and its associated regulations define street dogs as "ownerless animals," and prohibit—under certain conditions—killing, displacement, and enclosure of the dogs. Although The Animal Protection Law defines violence toward animals as misdemeanour, it at least categorizes it as illegal. According to the law, Ministry of Forestry and Water Management and local municipalities are named as official authorities to take care of the street dogs. Municipalities, authorized and financed by the ministry (Eroğlu 2016), are responsible for the implementation of the CNR program.

The Metropolitan Municipality of Istanbul, as well as the majority of the district municipalities in this city have established veterinary departments, specialized on street animals. But in some district municipalities (Pendik, Üsküdar, Sultangazi, Zeytinburnu, etc.), street animals remain under the responsibility of the unit for urban health and environment (Arslan 2016, 14). Nearly half of the district municipalities have built shelters or nursing homes for ill, elderly or presumably dangerous street animals, as well as several rehabilitation centers. Apart from the shelters of the district municipalities, Istanbul Metropolitan Municipality built a vast complex named *Kısırkaya Animal Shelter and Rehabilitation Centre*[21] in 2015, which is criticized by animal activists. So the technical and bureaucratic infrastructure of the CNR program seemed to be established only on paper. Before describing in detail the implications of this new law, let us first emphasize its economic dimensions that would allow us to expose its connection with the neoliberal reconstruction of State apparatus according to the market needs and principles that were mentioned above.

The Economic Aspect: A Neoliberal Solution to "Ownerless Dog" Problem

CNR's implementation also has a significant economic dimension, which involves suppliers, undertakers, and the pet industry. As the street dogs were positioned as "forced consumers" in this new market, municipalities and the ministry opened bids for the purchase of services or equipment (food, tools, etc.).

Municipalities work mainly with precarious subcontractors, which is also the case for veterinary experts. Ministry[22] and municipalities have to purchase the necessary equipment from commercial enterprises. Thus by implementing the CNR program, the government promotes the pet industry and a large market. In fact, since the first period of AKP government, the pet market in Turkey grew by about eight percent ("Kedi köpek maması . . ." 2015; "Evcil hayvanlara büyük destek" 2017). From microchips to dog food for the shelters, municipalities are the primary buyers within this market. The increasing demand for equipment and food affect the development of the national pet industry.[23]

CNR's legal adoption coincides with the institutionalization of neoliberal policies in Turkey, where the local pet industry has grown meteorically. The link between the pet industry, the *petification* discourse, and the WHO supported CNR program is well worth exploring in future research. But it exceeds the limits of our present study.

CNR Implementation: Silent Violence in Everyday Life

The theoretical framework of the CNR comprises a basis for implicit violence against not only street dogs but also their friends, as we frequently witness in the implementation process of this program. We would like to expose this underlying violence in practices, from both the side of the dogs and from those who love them.

For a dog living in the streets, "displacement" is undoubtedly a traumatic incident. The dog is suddenly shot by a pin, runs for his life, and tries to hide. When it loses consciousness, the dog is pulled on the ground to the service vehicle and locked in a cage. The dog opens his eyes—only if he can survive the anaesthesia, as the dosage is only rarely adapted to the dog's size—finding himself in a cage or an unfamiliar environment if he is left in a forest, far from human settlement.[24] He is marked, neutralized[25] and vaccinated. Although he has to be released where he has been taken from, he is usually enclosed in a large shelter similar to a concentration camp. It was also emphasized in the press that several dogs died due to the violent acts of caretakers in shelters (e.g., Birgün 2016).

The CNR program means violence toward local people who want to share their life with street dogs as well. One day they find out that the dogs of their street with whom they have long established personal relations suddenly disappear. Their search continues for days on end to find out about the dogs' fate. They try to understand whether or not the municipality has caught the dogs. And if so, they then experience the careless and reckless face of the "Kafkaesque" municipal bureaucracy. If they find out somehow that the dogs were in one of the shelters, people are forced to become "owners" to rescue the dogs (Özdoğan 2018).

Considering that the CNR program is based on the "let live" approach, with all the institutional and legal infrastructure provided, it is challenging to explain the violence and practice of killing. In fact, the physical violence, displacement, and killing are carried out in compliance if not with the theoretical frame of CNR in appearance, and may comply with its very reason to be. Again, the DPM is an approach to governing the other-than-humans and their relations with humans. It treats the dogs primarily as a population, as a totality, as passive subjects to be governed. It denies the dogs being "actants" in their bonds to the environment. It denies them to be sensible beings, existing as individuals. It denies their world to be meaningful and valuable. Hence, as a fundamentally anthropocentric discourse to govern "other species," the DPM aims essentially to ensure human domination over the dogs. Like other neoliberal solutions to environmental problems, it implies the creation of a market around the issue, and offers market-based solutions to it. It doesn't care about other-than-human beings as an end in their own right. If an accidental killing occurs, it doesn't have any substantial contradiction with the "spirit" of the CNR program.

Living with Dogs in the Streets of Istanbul

Daily life with dogs in the street is shaped under this neoliberal version of speciesism. Nevertheless, neither street dogs nor humans who wish to share life are passive subjects. As a political ecological perspective in conjunction with CAS emphasizes, they have an active role in resisting it. They improvise the "here and now" common life experiences with "free" dogs. Creating the necessary conditions for street dogs to live freely in the streets (building huts, installing water pots, feeding them regularly, assuring elementary health care, etc.), establishing mutual friendships with them, and helping to reshape the common space for an inter-species common life. Yet, this still remains to be a matter of hard work and struggle. Here, we would like to highlight various modes of conflicts and practices in this issue, as well as some self-defense strategies developed by dogs.

As explained in the first part of this chapter, since Ottoman times, practices for creating elementary conditions like feeding, sheltering and medical aid to facilitate or enable life with urban animals continue in Istanbul. However, Istanbul today is a megacity where neoliberal policies largely shape the urban space, with massive highways in the middle of habitation areas, newly built gated communities, great shopping malls, future mega-projects, and nearly twenty million inhabitants (Asu 2014, 31). That's why free-living conditions for street dogs become more and more precarious. Street dogs are not admitted in gated communities or shopping malls where it is nearly impossible to see a sleeping dog in a shop window. But in many neighbourhoods (especially in the old quarters) street dogs are still an essential part of social life: they have names, known stories, and are recognized as individuals. Local people provide food, shelter, and attend to their medical needs. Thus common spaces are shaped differently than those prescribed by national planning, for the official urban plans do not include dogs. Nevertheless, municipalities often interrupt common life experience, and this also provokes local, spontaneous, or organized resistance. Local people, witnessing an attempt to collect the dogs, disrupt it, save as many dogs as possible, record the event on video, publish it on social media, and follow the captured dogs. In spite of the direct intervention[26] of municipal authorities, urban spaces are still co-shaped by dogs and humans: there are feeding areas, dogs sleeping on the pavement, and so forth.

The assistance of dogs that are exiled into uninhabited areas and forests outside of the urban area, requires different coordination, mostly on social media. It requires schedule, a means to get there, and to account for feeding and health care needs. This is why most people who take care of the dogs released in the periphery begin to use social media more actively,[27] forming spontaneous horizontal solidarity networks.

Local friendships established with street dogs may establish awareness for how neoliberal strategies shape urban spaces by excluding non-humans. In fact, urban policies are against street dogs: roads expand, green areas diminish, and so forth. Thus the struggle of the street dogs opens a new critical perspective on urban ecology and policies, as well as governmental responses to interspecies relations. Many volunteers, though, supporting the adoption of ownerless dogs, are faced with a dilemma: the impossibility of adopting every one. Under these circumstances, they defend the conditions that enable dogs to live free in the streets. And they struggle to provide a legal status for it. This struggle also creates close friendships among dog lovers collaborating for their cause, regardless of their political perspective, religious beliefs, or social classes.

Besides the daily experience, many institutional organizations have emerged. In the 2000s, these grew to form platforms and confederations (HAYTAP [Animal Right Federation], HAYKONFED, Commission for Animal Rights of the Bar of Istanbul). Some of them[28] defend the CNR, in principle, and even practice it in clinics they founded; but they criticize the application of the governmental institutions. Some of these associations participate in the Provincial Animal Councils (İl Hayvan Kurulu) and in the parliamentary debates on the animal act. Among the anarchist movements in Istanbul, the Freedom to the Earth Association (Yeryüzüne Özgürlük Derneği) and the Independent Animal Liberation Activists are also interested in street dogs. They criticize the DPM explicitly for institutionalizing the criteria of ownership, and claim that this program aims primarily at exterminating the street dogs under the pretext of "public health and social order" (Yeryüzüne Özgürlük Platformu 2015).

In common life, dogs are not passive, but active subjects. Street dogs in Istanbul, in general, are very open to developing close bonds of friendship with humans. They notice persons who are sensitive to them, and they show their interest, stroll around and play with them, or from time to time visit them. This relationship, unlike "petified" relations, allows dogs to choose their fellows. Dogs, in these relationships are not properties and are not enclosed. This intimate common life experience is as much emancipatory for humans as it is for dogs. Love without possession, mutual care without concession.

Street dogs also develop strategies for survival vis-à-vis the violence of governmental institutions. More experienced dogs recognize the catching-cars and staff. They run and hide somewhere when they see them or find people who will take care of them. Pack leaders will help other dogs to escape. Although very rare, some manage to return from distant areas where they are caught and released in the forest.[29] They tend to move from areas or neighbourhoods that they, for some reason, find insecure, to more safe environments (not all these voluntary displacements are related to human behaviour, they might also be a result of the dogs' internal conflicts).

Street dogs are actors in the reshaping of the common urban space. Dogs, with humans, challenge the institutionalization of the "stray dog" category of the DPM and prevent the "petification" to become the predominant mode of human–dog relationship. Dogs, with humans, may incarnate a possession-free, exploitation-free, and domination-free interspecies relation.

CONCLUSION: EVERYTHING WILL BEGIN BY LOVING A STREET DOG

The history of common life with the street dogs in Istanbul displays the continuous transformation of the interspecies relations in the urban space under the influence of progressing capitalism. Until the nineteenth century, as we learn from the travelers' testimonies, dogs were a part of the social texture of the city. They had social functions like alerting people to fires or thieves, sorting the waste, and so forth; though they were not primarily meant to work, and importantly they were not property. The modernization paradigm, while restructuring the city and the state, also intervened in this relationship. Dogs were exiled or killed; certain businessmen, early in the past century even offered to export them to South America to use their bones and skins as raw material after being killed (Remlinger 1932). By administrative measures, they were forced to exist only as property items: controlled, tamed, vaccinated, and owned as pets. All through the twentieth century, this "decaninization" policy continued to be the effective governmental measure. But owing to some local people who protected dogs, and to those dogs who developed strategies not to leave their fellows, and also to the main change in the global approach to dog "population" at the dawn of the twenty-first century, Istanbul could not be decaninized. By the 2000s, municipalities in Istanbul began to apply the CNR program, supported and standardized by the WHO, under a new approach called DPM. This approach treats dogs merely as a population and doesn't take into account their specific social links as individuals. As the DPM approach was derived from the same logic as the extermination policy of the nineteenth and twentieth century, that is, taking all animals living with humans under medical, spatial, discursive, and tutorial control, the transition from "let live" to "let die" was quite smooth.

Is it possible for humans to live with other species, without dominating, exploiting or possessing them? Struggles for the street dogs' right to live in Istanbul may offer an example of an affirmative answer. It contains many thought-provoking experiences. But the invasion of the urban space by shopping malls, highways, and gated communities restrain the space for the development of this sort of relationship. Therefore people who wish to live with street dogs or other species usually find themselves debating political issues. Contact with street dogs forces even less politicized people to think about law, public measures, shopping malls, civil solidarity, and so forth. And despite the isolating, alienating effects of modern urban life, a relationship with street dogs creates bonds and solidary among people who share this feeling.

Dogs were the first domesticated species. They evolved together with humans in a mutually dependent relationship (Jouventin, Christen, and Dobson 2016). Humans created various dog breeds, while dogs, for their part, helped with the social life (assuming guard, transport, flock, or herd holding functions). According to a seemingly general agreement among biologists, the natural environment of dogs is the ecological niche created by humans (Miklósi 2015), outside of which they either cannot exist or must endure poor conditions of living. A political ecological question arises when we think about abolishing all domination in interspecies relations. How would one situate these domestic animals that are neither property, nor working or exploited as raw materials in an anarchist imagination? Would a choice have to be made for them between being an object of property or returning to the "natural" wildlife as wolves? (Donaldson and Kymlicka 2016). There is a distinct political ecology at play in the case of street dogs, and one that invites an anarchist imagination. We hope that the relationship with the street dogs of Istanbul that differentiates them from other captives, eaten, working, and liminal animals (Donaldson and Kymlicka 2016) might inspire anarchists in discussing and creating other possibilities for a common life.

NOTES

1. *Umwelt* is a term proposed by J. v. Uexküll, which emphasize the irreducibility of perceptual experience of each species to another. Yet Uexküll's conception denies all communicability between *umwelts* of different species and privileges the human *umwelt* as the unique which enables the individuals of this species to relate to the *objects as objects*, and shares therefore some of the age-old scholastic precepts on human's distinction among other species. Agamben asserts that this might even find echoes in Heidegger's conceptualization of the *Dasein* (Agamben 2004, 49). We think, however, that this conception might be updated by admitting transitivity of *umwelts* and questioning the prevalence and the very uniqueness of this so-called disinterested relation to *objects as objects*. Furthermore, we think that by doing so, we would be able to overturn the congenital anthropocentrism of the concept, and even use it in the very definition of the speciesism, that roughly means the imposition of the space-time experience of one species over all others as a universally shared base of existence, on which the privileged species develops technics and knowledge to rule the rest.

2. Cudworth 2011; Marvin and Mchugh 2014; Animal Studies G. 2006; Taylor and Twine 2014; Taylor and Signal 2011; Porcher 2017; Guillo 2009.

3. Exceptions like Baratay (2012) and Few and Tortorici (2013) do not address the free-roaming urban animal as a specific case study, but nonetheless mention their importance.

4. M. N. COŞKUN, director of veterinary service of the Municipality of Istanbul declared that the number of Street dogs in Istanbul is up to 130,000 ("İBB Veteriner Hizmetleri Müdürü Çoşkun . . .", 2017).

5. Dernschwam 1992; Busbecq 1881; Rycaut 1670; Thévenot 1687 and 1727; Tournefort 1727; Guer 1747; Craven 1799; Olivier 1801; Chateaubriand 1806; Pardoe 1836; Nerval 1843; Amicis 1896; Loti 1921; Remlinger 1932). Street animals, especially the dogs are also seen in engravings of the city as from 17th century (Merian 1638; Le Hay 1714; Thévenot 1727; d'Ohsson 1788; Melling 1819; Allom 1839).

6. Guer, merely two years later, will write a book on the nature of the animal soul, where he criticized the Arab-Muslim tradition for having seen in all the living beings the expression of the same and unique soul, thus considering beasts as equal to man. He namely asserts that philosophy is not for the taste of these crude and brutal people (Guer 1749, 4–6). See also Rycaut (1670, 167).

7. Guillaume-Antoine Olivier who came to Istanbul as a professional medical doctor in the late eighteenth century considered them also as potential vectors of zoonotic diseases (Olivier 1801). And Paul Rycaut, the British Ambassador, who had no medical formation, states some time earlier, that "Dogs of their street, . . . are fit for nothing but to breed Infection" (Rycaut 1670); which is translated in French (in the same year) with a slight emphasis: "vn vilain chien qui court les ruës, & qui ne

sert qu'à corrompre l'air & empester vne Ville" [a villain dog which serves only to *corrupt* the air and to *infect* the city] (Ricaut 1670).

8. The *Mekteb-i Tıbbiye-i Şahane* [Sultanate Medical School] inaugurated in the mid-nineteenth century was annexed by a laboratory of bacteriology following the cholera epidemic in 1893. This laboratory founded by the collaboration of *Pasteur Institute* in Paris, worked for some time as its branch office in Istanbul and was subsequently transformed into a centre for rabies researches (Pinguet 2009).

9. Remlinger also reports on the determined resistance and protests of local people against these experiments.

10. Our grandmothers' generation used to tell us that the howling reached the city at nights.

11. Brummett states that some coteries petitioned for the annulation of the extermination attempts (Brummet 2003, 424).

12. Remlinger reports very similar scenes from early 1900s (Remlinger 1932).

13. Some of the countries in which CNR is carried out: Bosnia-Herzegovina, Bulgaria, Greece, Italy, Moldova, Slovenia, Spain (Tasker 2006–2007, 13–14).

14. Beck's *The Ecology of Stray Dogs* (1973) and Nesbitt's "Ecology of a Feral Dog Pack on a Wildlife Refuge" (1975) (*Guidelines* 1990, 13–14) are the rare ethological research on street dogs in this epoch.

15. Animal Friends Association (*Hayvan Dostları Derneği*), Istanbul Animal Lovers Association (*İstanbul Hayvanseverler Derneği*), and so forth.

16. The first municipal shelter was established at Alibeyköy in 1994 by Istanbul Metropolitan Municipality (IBB). This building was an old slaughterhouse (Topçuoğlu 2010, 106). In February 2001, this number reached at 22 (Ergu 2001).

17. Between 1999 and 2006 Sarıyer (district) Kocataş Shelter had been organized by Society for Homeless Animals and Protecting the Nature (*Evsiz Hayvanlar ve Doğayı Koruma Derneği*) (Topçuoğlu 2010, 131–132; Yedikule Shelter of Fatih (district) Municipality has been organized since 2001 by volunteers ("Yedikule Hayvan Barınağı Kurucusu Mimar Meral Olcay ile röportaj" 2017).

18. We could mention two major massacres in this period: Just before the Habitat II Conference in 1996, street dogs of Istanbul were massively killed. Throughout the summer of 1999, under the pretext of rabies, dogs in 85 quarters under quarantine were killed (Topçuoğlu 2010, 107–122).

19. In 2000, demonstrations were organized against the extermination of street dogs (Topçuoğlu 2010, 122). In 2001, campaigns were launched against poisoning by meat containing strychnine (Ergu 2001).

20. In 2004, there were 38 shelters held by the Metropolitan Municipality of Istanbul, although they did not have any legal regulation. Municipalities vaccinated, neutered, and marked much fewer animals than they do today. They also re-homed a few dogs (İstanbul Çevre Durum Raporu 2004, 128–129).

21. It has the aspect of a huge jail situated in the north limits of the city, far from the center, with a capacity of 20,000 dogs, in 720 hectares. It has an isolation system of cages on cement floors that could barely admit an average-sized dog (Yıldırım 2015).

22. Between 2009 and 2011, 4,311,000 TL were given to municipalities for neutering street dogs; in 2014, 350 microchip readers, 122,500 microchips and implanters, 132,279 numbered earrings and 250 pliers for earrings that worth 1,000,000 TL for marking ownless dogs in the urban space granted them by the ministry. Between 2009 and 2015, 18,983,715 TL were granted for the construction of provisory carehouses, and in 2016, to build care houses and to buy microchips and earrings 5,310,000 TLs were granted to the municipalities (Eroğlu 2016).

23. As an example, Ayvetsan, a farming enterprise founded in 1995, has begun to produce marking earrings for street dogs, almost simultaneously with the 2004 Act. It has also started the production of microchips in Turkey, and the Ministry of Forestry and Water Affairs is its main customer (Ayvetsan 2017).

24. M. Yıldırım has pointed that between 2010 and 2015, over a 100,000 street dogs were caught and killed by the municipality, or informally displaced causing serious injuries or death cases (2015).

25. The president of HAYKONFED claims that medical operations are performed by non-specialists (Çıtırık 2016, 32).

26. Feeding or water pots and even huts for cats and dogs installed by local people are removed or demolished. There have been deadly assaults toward volunteers who feed the street animals. A friend of the authors who was feeding dogs in Istanbul forests was threatened with a knife (2016). President of the Animal Rights Commission, of Istanbul Bar Association, Yalçın, stated that women working with the street animals were subject to sexist attacks, that there are a number of cases reported to the Istanbul Bar Association (Yalçın 2009, 84).

27. As an example of feeding in Kemerburgaz forest, see "Ölüme terk edilen sokak köpeklerinin yardımına koşuyor," 2016.

28. President of the commission is criticizing the neutering measure of the CNR program, for it violates the right to reproduce (Şiddet Mağdurları 2009).

29. Shelters and release areas are in more distant areas as compared with those in the 1990s, so this practice is quite rare.

REFERENCES

Abdullah Cevdet. 1909. "İstanbul'da Köpekler" *İctihad Mecmuası*. Istanbul.

Agamben, Giorgio. 2004. *The Open: Man and Animal*. Palo Alto, CA: Stanford University Press.

Akşit, Merve. 2017. "Yeni Hayvan Hakları Yasa Tasarısının İçeriği ve Tuzak Maddeler." April 28. http://listelist.com/hayvan-haklari-tasarisi/.

Aksoy, Asu. 2014. "İstanbul'un Neoliberalizmle İmtihanı." In *Yeni İstanbul Çalışmaları*, edited by Ayfer Candan Bartu and Cenk Özbay. 26–46. Istanbul: Metis Yayınları.

Allom, Thomas. 1839. *Constantinople and the Scenery of the Seven Churches of Asia Minor*. London: Fisher Son & Co.

Amicis, Edmondo de. 1896. *Constantinople*. trans. M. H. Landsdale. Philadelphia, PA: H. T. Coates & Co.

Animal Studies Group. 2006. *Killing Animals*. Urbana and Chicago: University of Illinois Press.

Arslan, Murat. 2016. "İstanbul'da Sokak Hayvanları Sorunlarına Farklı Bakış açıları." In *I. Sokak Hayvanları Refahı Kongresi: May 10–11*, organized by Ataşehir Belediyesi. 14. Istanbul.

Baratay, Eric. 2012. *Le Point de vue animal*. Paris: Seuil.

Baştakar, Şenol. 1999. "Köpekland kuruluyor." *Sabah Newspaper*. Istanbul. October 30: 1.

Beck, Allan. 1973. *The Ecology of Stray Dogs: A Study of Free-Ranging Urban Animals*. West Lafayette, IN: Purdue University Press e-books OLD. Paper 4. http://docs.lib.purdue.edu/press_ebooks/4.

Best, Steve. 2009. "Rethinking Revolution: Total Liberation, Alliance Politics, and a Prolegomena to Resistance Movements in Twenty-First Century." In *Contemporary Anarchist Studies*, edited by Randall Amster, Abraham Deleon, and others. 189–199. London and New York: Routledge.

Birgün. 2016. "Kısırkayada kafası kırılan köpek kurtarıldı . . ." *Birgün Gazetesi*. April 11. https://www.birgun.net/haber-detay/kisirkaya-da-kafasi-kirilan-kopek-kurtarildi-merkezin-kapatilmasi-icin-kampanya-baslatildi-108778.html.

Brummett, Palmira. 2003. *İkinci Meşrutiyet Basınında İmge ve Emperyalizm 1908–1911*, translated by Ayşen Anadol. İstanbul: İletişim Yayınları.

Busbecq, Ogier Ghiselin. 1881. *Life and Letters*. London: C. K. Paul.

Chateaubriand. 1861. *Œuvres complètes*. Tome 5. Paris: Garnier.

Çıtırık, Nesrin. 2016. "Sokak Hayvanlarının Hakları ve Sorunların Çözümü." I. *Sokak Hayvanları Refahı Kongresi: Mayıs 10–11*, organized by Ataşehir Belediyesi, 30–33. Istanbul.

Collard, Rosemary-Claire. 2015. "Ethics in Research beyond the Human." In *The Routledge Handbook of Political Ecology*, edited by Tom Perreault, Gavin Birdge, and James McCarthy, 127–139. London and New York: Routledge.

Craven, Elizabeth. 1789. *A Journey through Crimea to Constantinople*. London: G.G.J. & J. Robinson.

Cudworth, Erika. 2011. *Social Lives with Other Animals*. London: Palgrave Macmillan.

Cudworth, Erika. 2014. "Beyond Speciesism: Intersectionality, Critical Sociology and the Human Domination of Other Animals." In *The Rise of Critical Animal Studies*, edited by Nick Taylor and Richard Twine. 19–35. London and New York: Routledge.

Dernschwam, H. 1992. *İstanbul ve Anadolu'ya Seyahat Günlüğü*, translated by Yaşar Önen, İstanbul, 1992.

Donaldson, Sue, and Kymlicka, Will. 2016. *Zoopolis*, translated by Mine Yıldırım. İstanbul: Koç Üniversitesi Yayınları.

Ergu, Elif. 2001. "Köpeklerin Katili Meçhul." *Sabah Newspaper*. February 24: 3.

Eroğlu, Veysel (Ministry of Forestry and Water Affairs). 2016. "Bütün Yaratılanı Yaradandan Ötürü Seviyorum," interviewed by Birgül Taşdemir. Mars 24. http://www.ajanimo.com/butun-yaratilani-yaratandan-oturu-seviyorum/.

Faroqhi, Suraiya. 1993. *Osmanlı'da Kentler ve Kentliler (1550–1650)*, translated by Neyyir Kalaycıoğlu. İstanbul: Tarih Vakfı Yurt Yayınları.

————. 1998. *Osmanlı Kültürü ve Gündelik Yaşam*, translated by Kılıç E. İstanbul: Tarih Vakfı Yurt Yayınları.

Ferriol and Le Hay. 1714. *Recueil de Cent Estampes Représentant Différents Nations du Levant*. Paris: Chez Basan Graveur.

Few, Martha, and Tortorici, Zeb. 2013. *Centering Animals in Latin American History*. Durham, NC, and London: Duke University Press.

Food and Agriculture Organization of the United Nations. 2011. *Dog Population Management Meeting*. org. by WSPA, FAO, IZSAM. Banna, Italy, March 14–19. http://www.fao.org/3/a-i4081e.pdf.

Foucault, Michel. 2015. Biyopolitikanın Doğuşu, College de France Dersleri, translated by Alican Tayla. İstanbul: İstanbul Bilgi Üniv. Yay.

Fuar Tv. *Ayvetsan*. https://www.youtube.com/watch?v=U8N9d0do0g8.

Guer, Jean Antoine. 1747. *Les mœurs et usages des Turcs*. tome premier. Paris: Pierre Mortier.

————. 1749. *L'histoire critique de l'âme des bêtes*. Amsterdam: François Changuion.

Guillo, Dominique. 2009. *Des Chiens et des Humains*. Paris: Le Pommier.

Güven, Zeynep. 1999. "İstanbul'un köpek çöplüğü." *Hürriyet Newspaper* (July 17): 6.

Haberler. 2016. "Ölüme terk edilen sokak köpeklerinin yardımına koşuyor." Mars 8 https://www.haberler.com/olume-terk-edilen-sokak-kopeklerin-yardimina-8235950-haberi/.

————. 2017. "İBB Veteriner Hizmetleri Müdürü Çoşkun: İstanbul Genelinde Sahipsiz 130 bin köpek, 125 bin de kedi . . ." April 27. https://www.haberler.com/ibb-veteriner-hizmetleri-muduru-coskun-istanbul-9550037-haberi/.

Howell, Philip. 2012. "The Dog Fancy at War: Breeds, Breeding and Britishness, 1914–1918." *Society & Animals* 20. doi: 10.1163/15685306–12341258, http://www.animalsandsociety.org/wp-content/uploads/2016/05/howell.pdf.

İBB. 2016. *1. Sahipsiz Hayvan Rehabilitasyon Çalıştayı*. Mars 30. Istanbul Hotel. Istanbul.

İhlas Haber Ajansı. 2009. "Sokak hayvanları ciplerle takip ediliyor." February 6. http://www.iha.com.tr/haber-sokak-hayvanlari-ciplerle-takip-ediliyor-55040/.

Illouz, Tiphaine. 2009. *Les animaux dans les villes*. Mémoire. Cycle urbanisme de Sciences Po.

Işın, E. 2016. "Sunuş [Foreword]." In *Dört Ayaklı Belediye*. Istanbul: Istanbul Araştırmaları Enstitüsü.

Jouventin, Christen, and Dobson, Stephen. 2016. "Altruism in Wolves Explains the Coevolution of Dogs and Humans." *Ideas in Ecology and Evolution* 9: 4–11.

Keskin, Ferda. 2016. "Sunuş: Özne ve İktidar." In *Özne ve İktidar, Michel Foucault*. Istanbul: Ayrıntı Yayınları.

Kropotkin, Pyotr Alekseyeviç. 2008. *Karşılıklı Yardımlaşma*. Istanbul: Kaos Yayınları.

Kurumsal Haberler. 2015. "Kedi köpek maması üreticilerinde teşvik beklentisi sürüyor." January 22. http://www.kurumsalhaberler.com/tropikalpet/bultenler/kedi-ve-kopek-mamasi-ureticilerinde-tesvik-beklentisi-buyuyor.

Lestel, Dominique. 2016. *Les origines animales de la culture*. Paris: Flammarion Champs Essais.

Loti, Pierre. 1921. *Suprêmes visions d'Orient*. Paris: Calmann-Lévi.

Marvin, Garry, and Mchugh, Susan. 2014. *Routledge Handbook of Human-Animal Studies*. London and New York: Routledge.

Matthäus Merian. 1638. *Constantinopolitanae urbis effigies ad vivum expressa, quam Turcae Stampoldam vocant*. A^D MDCXXXV.

McCance, Dawne. 2013. *Critical Animal Studies: An Introduction*. New York: Suny Press.

Melling, Antoine Ignace.1819. *Voyage pittoresque de Constantinople et des rives du Bosphore*. Paris: Chez les Editeurs Rue de Bourbon.

Miklósi, Ádám. 2015. *Dog Behaviour, Evolution, and Cognition*. Oxford: Oxford University Press. iBooks, 114–115.

Montaigne, Michel de. 1965. *Essais: De la cruauté*. Livre II. Paris: Puf.

Nerval, Gérard de. 1843. *Constantinople: Heureux qui comme . . . Gérard de Nerval*. 3^é. Paris: Magellan & Cie Éditions.

Nocelle II, Antony J., Richard J. White, and Erika Cudworth, eds. 2015. *Anarchism and Animal Liberation*. Jefferson, NC: McFarland and Company, Inc., Publishers.

Occupy for Animals. "The Stray." http://www.occupyforanimals.net/trap-neuter-release.html.

Ohsson, Ignatius Mouradgea d'. 1788. *Tableau général de l'empire Othoman*. Tome I. Paris: Monsieur.

Özdoğan, Kiraz. 2017. "Yasadışı Köpek Toplama Hikayesi." October 11. https://yesi lofke.org/yasadisi-kopek-toplama-hikayesi-otorite-sayi-coklugu-beyaz-kahraman/.

Özdoğan, Kiraz. 2018. "Yulaf Kısırkaya Ölüm Kampından Kurtuldu, ya Diğerleri." June 6 http://siyasihaber3.org/yulaf-kisirkaya-olum-kampindan-kurtuldu-ya-digerleri.

Özkazanç, Alev. 2011. "Neo-liberal Tezhürler: Vatandaşlık, Suç, Eğitim." *Dipnot*: 11–58.

Pardoe, Julia. 1837. *The City of the Sultan and the Manners of the Turks in 1836*. London: Henry Coburn Publisher.

Pativer. 2017. "Yedikule Hayvan Barınağı Kurucusu Mimar Meral Olcay ile röpor-taj." https://www.pativer.net/yedikule-hayvan-barinagi-kurucusu-mimar-meral-olcay-ile-roportaj/.

Pinguet, Catherine. 2009. *İstanbul'un Köpekleri*, translated by Saadet Özen. Istanbul: Yapı Kredi Yayınları.

———. (2016). "Street Dogs of Istanbul." In *Dört Ayaklı Belediye*. İstanbul: İstanbul Araştırmaları Enstitüsü.

Porcher, Jocelyn. 2017. *The Ethics of Animal Labor*. Palgrave Macmillan.

Remlinger. 1932. "Les chiens de Constantinople. Leur Vie. Leur Mort." *Mercure de France*, 817: 24–70. Juillet 1.

Resmi Gazete. 2006. "Hayvanların korunmasına dair uygulama yönetmeliği." http://www.resmigazete.gov.tr/eskiler/2006/05/20060512-7.htm.

Reyhan, Cenk. 2008. *Osmanlı'da Kapitalizmin Kökenleri*. İstanbul: Tarih Vakfı Yurt Yayınları.

Ricaut, Paul. 1670. *Histoire de l'état présent de l'Empire Ottoman*. Translated by Mr. Briot. Paris: Chez Sébastien Mabre-Cramoisy.

Rycaut, Paul. 1670. *The Present State of Ottoman Empire*. London: J. Starkey & H. Brome.

Schick, İrvin Cemil. 2010. "İstanbul'da 1910'da Gerçekleşen Büyük Köpek İtlafı: Bir Mekân Üzerinde Çekişme Vakası." *Toplumsal Tarih Dergisi*, 200 (August): 22–33.

Sönmez, Edda. 2017. "İstanbul'dan korkunç görüntüler! 300 Köpek ölü bulundu." *Sözcü*. October 21. http://www.sozcu.com.tr/2017/gundem/istanbuldan-korkunc-goruntuler-300-kopek-ormanda-olduruldu-2058504/?utm_source=szc&utm_medium=free&utm_campaign=ilgilihaber.

Springer, Simon. 2016. "Radikal bir coğrafya neden anarşist olmalıdır?" *Cogito* (Fall): 74–110.

Srinivasan, Krithika. 2015. "CFP for Conference Session on More than Human Political Ecology." https://networks.h-net.org/node/16560/discussions/98981/cfp-conference-session-more-human-political-ecologies.

Sungurbey, İsmet. 1993. *Hayvan Hakları*. İstanbul: İ.Ü.

Tasker, Louisa. 2006–2007. *Stray Animal Control Practices (Europe)*. with WSPA and RSPCA Int. http://www.stray-afp.org/nl/wp-content/uploads/2012/09/WSPA-RSPCA-International-stray-control-practices-in-Europe-2006-2007.pdf.

Taylor, Nick, and Signal, Tania. 2011. *Theorizing Animals*. Leiden and Boston: Brill.

Taylor, Nick, and Twine, Richard. 2014. *The Rise of Critical Animal Studies*. London and New York: Routledge.

TBMM. 2004. "Hayvanları Koruma Kanunu." https://www.tbmm.gov.tr/kanunlar/k5199.html.

TC İstanbul Valiliği İl Çevre ve Orman Müdürlüğü. 2004. *İstanbul Çevre Durum Raporu*. No:3. İstanbul: İstanbul Çevre ve Orman Müdürlüğü Yayınları.

Thévenot, Jean de. 1687. *The Travels of Monsieur de Thevenot into the Levant*, translated by A. Lovell. Printed by H. Clark, for H. Faithorne, J. Adamson, C. Skegnes, and T. Newborough, Book sellers in St. Paul's Church-Yard, London, Book I, Chap. XXXVIII.

———. 1727. *Voyages de M. de Thévenot en Europe, Asie et Afrique, première partie, contenant le Voyage du Levant*. 3ᵉ. Amsterdam: Charles le Céne.

Toklucu, Murat. 2016. "Sokak Hayvanları için en kötü yüzyıl." *Bugünü Anlamak için Tarih*. No: 31 (December): 30–35.

Topçuoğlu, Ümit Sinan. 2010. *İstanbul ve Sokak Köpekleri*. İstanbul: Sepya.

Tournefort, Joseph Pitton de. 1727. *Relation d'un Voyage du Levant*. Tome second. Lyon: Frères Bruyset.

Tunçman, Zekai Muammer. 1935. *Kuduz ve Kuduzun Çoğalma Nedenleri*. Istanbul: Marifet Basımevi.

Ülgen, Celal, and Ongun, Coşkun, ed. 2008. *Şiddet Mağdurları*, organized by İstanbul Barosu Hayvan Hakları Komisyonu, Istanbul: Istanbul Barosu Yayınları.

Ülman, Yeşim Işıl. 2007. "Türkiye'de 19. ve 20 yüzyıllarda Tıp Tarihinin Ana Hatları (1827–1923)." *Tıp Tarihi ve Tıp Etiği Ders Kitabı*. İ.Ü. Cerrahpasa Tıp Fakültesi, No.4711, Fakülte yay.no.00249.

———. 2010. "Medical Modernization in 19th Century Ottoman Empire With Special Reference to the Introduction of Roentgen Rays in Turkey." *Perilous Modernity, History of Medicine in the Ottoman Empire and the Middle East From the 19th Century Onwards*. edited by Anne Marie Moulin,. and Yeşim Işıl Ülman. Istanbul: The Isis Press.

Wolf, Silvia Ilonka. 2015. *"We Are All Animals": The Emergence Of The Grassroots Nonhuman Animal Rights Movement In Istanbul*. Master Thesis. Istanbul: Sabanci University August, Supervisor: Prof. Dr. Ayşe Öncü.

World Health Organization. 1990. *Guidlines for Dog Population Management*. Geneva: WHO. http://apps.who.int/iris/bitstream/10665/61417/1/WHO_ZOON_90.166.pdf.

Yeryüzüne Özgürlük Platformu. 2015. "ICAM- Bakanlık-IBB Katliam İttifakına Hayır!" Mars 7. https://yeryuzuneozgurluk.wordpress.com/2015/03/07/icam-bakanlik-ibb-katliam-ittifakina-hayir/.

Yıldırım, Mine. 2015. "Dört Ayaklı Şehrin İmhasında Son Durak: İBB, Kısırkaya hayvan ecrit ve itlaf merkezi." *Birikim*. January 29. http://www.birikimdergisi.com/guncel-yazilar/1162/dort-ayakli-sehrin-imhasinda-son-durak-ibb-kisirkaya-hayvan-tecrit-ve-itlaf-merkezi#.WeRg2K2B3_Q.

Chapter 10

Total Liberation Ecology: Integral Anarchism, Anthroparchy, and the Violence of Indifference

Simon Springer

INTRODUCTION

Speciesism. Anthropocentrism. Human supremacy. Anthroparchy. Whatever label you want to apply to this myopic and profoundly violent worldview, it represents nothing less than a planetary atrocity. Given the intensity of the malevolence that humans unleash against other animals in the name of science, industry, labor, and food, it is astonishing that discussions of the problematic legitimization of violence against animals haven't factored more prominently into the discourse of contemporary political ecology. As a loosely defined area of inquiry (Robbins 2012), debates have touched upon global warming, declines in air and water quality, soil degradation, deforestation, intensifying greenhouse gasses, species extinctions, and global population growth (Clark 2012; Peet et al. 2011). Yet the general outlook of political ecology remains decidedly anthropocentric. Above all else, these destructive processes are lamented for their impacts on human societies, where attention to the well-being of the Gaia itself is relegated to a secondary concern or externalized to the domain of "deep ecology." Meanwhile the deaths of non-human animals are usually framed in terms of the loss of biodiversity and the implications that this has for humans insofar as it represents a disappearance of potential future utility. Scant attention is paid to how factory farming plays a key role in environmental ruination (Emel and Neo 2011), and even those few studies that do take note seem to downplay or discount the unintelligible mass murder of sentient beings and what this means for the development of a greater planetary consciousness that may be able to turn the tides against ecocide.

In demanding a politicization of environmental issues, most political ecologists have been oddly apolitical in terms of their reflections on the agency and sentience of non-human animals and particularly the othering that underpins the very idea of dismembered and decapitated bodies being euphemized as "meat." Not to lay blame entirely at the foot of political ecology, this unreflexive stance is predominant within the whole of academia. While one might expect to see greater awareness and reflection among progressive scholars in particular, I find myself routinely bewildered and dismayed by anarchist academics and critical geographers who engage in fallacy and cognitive dissonance to excuse their own embeddedness in this cycle of profound and inexcusable violence. How is it that those who hold anti-racist, decolonial, environmentalist, feminist, autonomist, post-structuralist, queer, anarchist, and otherwise critical perspectives continue to ignore the horrors perpetuated against the non-human animal "other"? How can they actively participate in the continuation of such massacre and misery, knowing that it means actually suspending and contradicting the essence of the critical theory that they hold so dear? As critical scholars we collectively contemplate how such cognitive dissonance works with respect to race, gender, sexuality, age, and other categories of difference, mystified that anyone could believe that marginalizing and committing violence against others is permissible. Yet so few take a moment to pause and consider how they themselves perpetuate such brutality and butchery through their food choices, largely for the inexcusable sake of taste and convenience.

In this chapter, I aim to bring political ecology into direct conversation with the violence of indifference that surrounds non-human animals, insisting that we must go beyond the confines of a mere "liberation ecology" (Peet and Watts 1996), with its narrow Marxian focus on class and anthropocentric worldview, to embrace a much wider sense of what I will call "total liberation ecology." The idea of "total liberation," which has been widely taken up within the animal liberation movement, can be understood as an intersectional ethos that seeks to contest all forms of inequality and domination. Following Pellow (2014), I view total liberation as being comprised of four pillars: "(1) an ethic of justice and anti-oppression inclusive of humans, nonhuman animals, and ecosystems; (2) anarchism; (3) anti-capitalism; and (4) an embrace of direct action tactics." If political ecology is, at least in part, about questioning the organizational, discursive, physical, and symbolic forms of violence and how it becomes normalized as a habitus (Watts and Peet 2004), then how is it that the question of violence against non-human animals has been so routinely ignored within the political ecology literature? This is where the qualifier of "total" becomes necessary, as it offers a deeper reflexive questioning of the integral mechanisms of domination. It demonstrates why a Marxist approach to political ecology is not enough. To fulfil its promise as a politicization of ecological concerns I am convinced that political ecology must begin to embrace an anarchist current.

I begin this paper with a discussion of why liberation ecology is insufficient, advocating for an anarchist political ecology to embrace total liberation as part of its integral perspective. By recognizing the intersections between various forms of oppression we don't dilute an environmental focus, but instead actually shine greater light on possibilities for reconstructive, communal, and ethical approaches to environmental justice (Bookchin 1982). Next I argue that the state, capitalism, and the domination of non-human animals are interrelated processes, a recognition that forces us to acknowledge how practices of othering underpin ideas not only of gender and race, but of human supremacy more broadly. As a result of this malignant dominion, I argue that anarchism must focus its energies on undermining anthroparchy as much as it does on any other system of oppression. In the final section before the conclusion I turn my attention toward the apathy that pervades among critical academics, rebuking those scholars who lack the courage to think critically about their own complacency in speciesism and violence based on their food choices. In part this detachment stems from political ecology having been largely content to focus its energies on advocating for policy change, rather than an introspective commitment to implementing changes through the praxis of our lived experience. I contend that an ethos of direct action rooted in the everydayness of anarchism has greater possibilities for meaningful change vis-à-vis the abhorrent apathy that presently informs responses to widespread animal slaughter and suffering. In this contemporary moment of industrial agriculture and factory farms, I argue that veganism is the only ethical position to adopt against the holocaust that defines the lives of farmed animals.[1]

FROM MARXIST SPECIES IMPERIALISM
TO ANARCHIST POLITICAL ECOLOGY

Political ecology has its limitations, most notably the confusion about what the term even means. In the second edition of his critical introduction to the field, Robbins (2012) recognized just how vast the literature had become, growing in such a multitude of directions that some might consider the concept of political ecology to be too encompassing to be useful. Yet he insists that the world continues to produce scenarios that demand a political ecology perspective, which he maintains is a "characteristic of a text" inasmuch as it "examines winners and losers, is narrated using dialectics, begins and/or ends in a contradiction, and surveys both the status of nature and stories about the status of nature" (Robbins 2012, viii). Not a theory or a method, but instead a community of practice, political ecology allows us "to understand the complex relations between nature and society through a careful analysis of what one might call the forms of access and control over resources and their implications for environmental health and sustainable livelihoods" (Watts 2000, 257). The principle dialectic at play in a political ecological perspective is that of human —non-human, which for Robbins (2012, 3), help us "break from an image of the world where human and non-human are disconnected, a fiction that remains so stubborn a part of our modern reasoning that it is as difficult to unimagine as it is to picture a world without patriarchy or class." This stunted imagination represents the problem of the bulk of political ecology to date. For anarchists, picturing a world without patriarchy or class is not a difficult proposition, for indeed, it is something that anarchists are continually engaged in prefiguring. So to reconnect the human and the non-human world it seems all to appropriate to look to the prefigurative practices of anarchism as a mode to achieve a more critical and capable political ecology. Long ago Reclus (1894) recognized the integral relationship between the human and non-nonhuman world as a co-constituted "social geography," where for him anarchism was a conduit to recognizing that "humanity is nature becoming self-conscious."

In an effort "to mark the potential liberatory or emancipatory potential of current political activity around environment and resources," Watts and Peet (2004, 5) articulate what they call "liberation ecology." Their rational was to produce "a more robust political ecology which integrates politics more centrally" by highlighting "new theoretical entanglements between political ecology, Marxism and social theory on the one hand, and a practical political engagement with new movements, organizations, and institutions of civil society challenging conventional notions of development, politics, democracy, and sustainability on the other" (Watts and Peet 2004, 6). There can be little doubt that this argument made an important intervention that pushed political ecology forward at that time. Yet there are absences and invisibilities that deserve greater attention if we are to move more demonstratively toward emancipation. Liberation ecology is not enough, precisely because it is fundamentally Marxist in its outlook. What this means is that it fails to take an integral look at the patterns of oppression and the intersectionality that defines domination, instead falling back on the limited analysis of class. Certainly it is important to consider class politics, but to focus on this line of difference alone defines liberation only in the narrowest of terms. The recent (re)turn toward anarchist geographies provides an indication of where, how, and why Marxism has failed to transform the world, and indeed, contemporary social movements increasingly point toward an embrace of anarchist praxis, where a recognition of a plurality of subject positions coming together in solidarity is key. It is not the Vanguardist approach and party politics of Marxism that define the current moment of social struggle and it is for this reason that we should move beyond liberation ecology toward an embrace of total liberation ecology. How can a perspective account of social change that confines our analysis to a limited set of parameters and fails to take account of the intersectionality of identity politics and the integral patterns of domination be liberatory rather than yet another set of chains?

Given the objective of political ecology as recognition for the intersection between politics, society, and nature, a Marxist perspective is actually self-defeating in achieving this purpose from the outset. Bookchin's notion of "dialectical naturalism" helps us to understand why. In identifying the complex interplay between social problems and ecological destruction, dialectical naturalism stands in contrast to the "empyrean, basically antinaturalistic dialectical idealism" of Hegel, and "the wooden, often scientistic dialectical materialism of orthodox Marxists" (Bookchin 1995). So while Marx (1867/1990, 290) recognized "the metabolic interaction between man and nature," he did so through an explicitly anthropocentric view of labor as "the everlasting nature-imposed condition of human existence," failing to consider the labor of non-humans, or the broader relations of exploitation that shape the intersections between human societies and the natural world. Indeed, for Marx, "humans really begin to distinguish themselves from other animals when they begin to produce their means of subsistence. In other words focusing on consciousness or even language leaves us with the problem of understanding exactly what is going on when animals really think or communicate verbally, whereas the difference in our capacities to produce is tangible" (Wilde 2000, 39). This perspective is of course nonsense, as we can recognize a dizzying number of ways in which non-human animals labor to transform the landscape to their own benefit, from the world of microbes feeding on nutrients released by weathering to transform the soil, to the interactive relations between fluvial environments and fish as geomorphological agents, to the even more obvious examples revealed by the impressive array of non-human architectural structures like beaver dams, termite mounds, bee hives, spider webs, bird nests, and gopher towns. We can also see the extensive use of tools by numerous animals including, elephants, dolphins, sea otters, and a variety of primates and birds, which is entirely ignored within the anthropocentrism of Marxists like Neil Smith (2010), who wants to establish the development of the human hand as proof that only humankind is capable of labour. Yet the entire process of evolution denotes a sophisticated assemblage of labor relations, making it anything but a passive process of change.

There is, as Wilde freely admits, very little evidence to suggest that Marx was ever a champion of animal liberation. It's not surprising then that more contemporary Marxists like David Harvey (1996), Noel Castree (2005), and Neil Smith (2010), have likewise failed to take into serious consideration the plight of non-human animals within the matrix of capitalism's violence. Like Marx himself, his progeny embrace a Cartesian-mechanistic view of animals as unintelligent creatures, supposedly lacking the complex consciousness or social life of humans. It is this speciesist outlook that makes them unable "to grasp that human and nonhuman animals have equal interests in freedom, happiness, and life over captivity, suffering, and death" (Best 2014, 95). While a Marxist like Erik Swyngedouw (1999, 447) has done better by developing a hybridization approach of "perpetual metabolism" whereby the "natural" world is not only inflected with social creation through a myriad of chemical, physical, social, economic, and political inputs, he never extends his thought explicitly to the lives of animals. So although hinting that a boarder sense of agency is at play, and despite recent movements in political ecology to incorporate a more comprehensive view of ethics into its trajectory (Jarosz 2004), Marxism remains a philosophical domain that scarcely considers animal beings. It is for good reason then that Benton (1993, 42) identifies Marx's thought as a form of "species imperialism," as the non-human animal falls quickly out of view in most Marxist analyses. While Kowalczyk's (2014) attempt to make a case for why Critical Animal Studies needs Marx is commendable, one still wonders why she would expend so much effort in twisting an outmoded theory to fit her objectives when the building blocks for a more emancipatory lens on animals have long been available in the form of anarchism?

THERE IS NO EXCUSE FOR HUMAN
SUPREMACIST VALUES

At the same time that Marx was content to ignore the question of the animal other, Élisée Reclus (1901, n.p.) was demonstrating how anarchism and concern for nonhuman animals were intertwined: "Is there then so much difference between the dead body of a bullock and that of a man? The dissevered limbs, the entrails mingling one with the other, are very much alike: the slaughter of the first makes easy the murder of the second, especially when a leader's order rings out, or from afar comes the word of the crowned master, 'Be pitiless.'" Bookchin (2004: 4) clearly took inspiration from Reclus when he wrote that "the notion that man must dominate nature emerges directly from the domination of man by man," lamenting how capitalism, owing to its inherently competitive nature, "not only pits humans against each other, it also pits the mass of humanity against the natural world." But while Bookchin condemned the industrialization of agriculture owing to the widespread degradation it wrought, his focus never extended to the appalling systems of suffering and ruthless production methods that marked the lives of animals. Bookchin failed to internalize the depth of Reclus's message, for as clearly as he saw the social ecology connection, "he missed the profound relevance of veganism and animal liberation to a liberatory future" (Best 2014, 95). None-theless, in the articulation of his views on social ecology, Bookchin called for a "prudent rescaling of man's hubris," rejecting the notion of humans being situated at the apex of the food chain, placing them instead as an unfolding biological process entwined within the multiplicity of all organic life forms and dependent upon the biosphere. Here too an earlier anarchist thinker antic-ipated Bookchin's ideas. Peter Kropotkin's (1902/2008) notion of mutual aid, often presented as a theory about community reciprocity, was never confined to the social world.

Kropotkin was a geographer, and owing to his integrative view of the world, he understood the social and natural worlds as inseparable, where mutual aid was equally about the symbiotic relations between peoples, plants, and animals. Mutual aid interprets humanity though its enmeshment within the web of life, which is precisely what Bookchin (1995) meant when he spoke of "dialectical naturalism." Yet it was Reclus who developed these ideas to their fullest, compelling humanity to take ethical responsibility of our place in nature by transforming our social practices and unmaking the ideologies that distort it. In this pursuit Reclus sought "to explain the development of human society in its dialectical interaction with the rest of the natural world, expound[ing] a theory of social progress in which human self-realization and the flourishing of the planet as a whole can be reconciled with one another" (Clark 1997, 119). In these goals, Reclus established the foundations of contemporary political ecology over a century before such an analysis began to devise its radical critique against the apolitical perspectives of mainstream environmental theory. At the same time, Reclus had also laid the groundwork for the recent interest in "more-than-human geography," even as this emergent field has strangely and without exception completely ignored his work. Nonetheless, in seeking to trace a relational ethics that extends beyond the human subject as the sole container of value, and by attending to the immanent possibilities of an ecological complex based on a nonessentialist respect for the difference of the nonhuman (Lorimer 2009), more-than-human geographers (Whatmore 2006) and posthumanists (Har-away 2008) alike unknowingly retrace the path set forth by Reclus. "We are," Reclus writes, "the children of the 'beneficent mother,' like the trees of the forest and the reeds of the rivers. She it is from whom we derive our substance; she nourishes us with her mother's milk, she furnishes air to our lungs, and, in fact, supplies us with that wherein we live and move and have our being" (quoted in Clark and Martin 2013, 17). In short, we are all of the Earth, and the Earth is all of us. There is no separation. No exceptionalism. No apogee of life. Only synergy and symbiosis.

So whereas both the modernity of capitalism and the labor theory of Marx would have humans assume that they live rarified and distinct lives, a total liberation ecology would instead seek to demonstrate that humans are part of an intricate planetary assemblage of interdependencies, where we are entirely dependent upon the biodiversity of the planet and the "crucial role nonhuman animals play in maintaining and enriching nature" (Best 2014, 119). If the first principle of political ecology "is a metaphysics that places humans in nature not above it" (Merchant 2005, 92), then speciesism surely should be as big of a concern as class, ethnicity, gender, or any other category of difference. Since the political ecological status of humans is clearly not above, but within nature, "one cannot fully grasp the foundations of racism, classism, sexism, patriarchy, ageism, and ableism without also understanding speciesism . . . because they are all ideologies and practices rooted in hierarchy and the creation of oppositional superior and inferior subjects" (Pellow 2014, 2). Such a thoroughly intersectional approach demonstrates the weakness of Watts and Peet's (1996, 38–39) liberation ecology, which seeks to unleash a process of "broadening environmental issues into a movement for livelihood entitlements and social justice." On first glance this sounds all well and good, but upon closer examination it is simply not enough. It reflects the same anthropocentric framing that guides the bulk of Marxist thought, thereby representing a continuation of Marx's species imperialism inasmuch as its dialectic fails to consider how certain forms of oppression remain intact, particularly when livelihoods are built on the back of animal exploitation and justice is confined to the social affairs of humans. For Hegel, a dialectical life reaches truth "only by *looking the negative in the face, and tarrying with it*," which as Clark (2008, n.p.) explains, means that a "radical dialectic holds that change and transformation take place through negation, contradiction, and unexpected reversals of the course that conventional thinking quite reasonably and incorrectly expects."

It is common sense that animals are excluded from thinking about emancipation, precisely because their othering is so foundational to human supremacist thought. Taking pictures of oneself posing and smiling next to a dead body at Thanksgiving, for example, would be horrifying, if not for the othering that is perpetuated in advance of that gruesome performance. But think for a minute how appalling that scenario would be if the category of the "Other" was shifted from non-human animal to another marginalized group, for example, women, children, LGBTQ+, or an ethnic minority group? Who among us would post a picture to Facebook of yourself smiling beside the decapitated corpse of a Muslim child? If you're horrified by the analogy, responding by shaking your head and consoling yourself by saying "It's just a turkey, it's completely different," that is your prejudice speaking. You've just identified the problem. This is the face of anthroparchy and you've just acknowledged your own adherence to human supremacist thinking. Tarry with it for a moment. Don't allow yourself to rationalize the violence of your eating habits, as such post hoc thinking is the exact same thought process that white supremacists have engaged in when making "sense" of their own bigotry and loathing. Look the negative in the face. A radical dialectic demands more of us. It requires that we break with conventional thinking, and insofar as political ecology is concerned, it means that we must move from liberation to total liberation, so that the animal other is brought permanently into view. A total liberation framework goes beyond existing models of intersectionality and extends political ecology by insisting on a comprehensive politicization of its content by linking oppression and privileges across species, ecosystems, and human populations, suggesting a theory and path toward freedom. For Pellow (2014: 3), this means that the concept of total liberation "reveals both the complexity of various systems of hierarchy while also suggesting points of intervention, transformative change, solidarity and coalition building across myriad boundaries."

THE SHARED STRUGGLE

The power of a total liberation approach is to be found in the boldness of its vision. It is unapologetic in the way that it makes people uncomfortable when they have to confront the banality of evil, the malevolence that is unfurled through their own eating habits, and the blackness of their heart when they refuse to change. "The darkness of ecological awareness is the darkness of noir," Morton (2016, 9) muses, and in the case of total liberation ecology it represents a Möbius strip, where in positioning ourselves as having dominion over the Earth and its inhabitants, we have become nothing less than the agent of its execution. In the moribund drama of the Anthropocene, we have assumed the role of both redeemer, by promising that we can stop the fall, and betrayer, by refusing to recognize that animal agriculture represents a key driver of environmental ruination in the form of increasing deforestation, methane and ammonia emissions, overuse of antibiotics, and contamination of the water table with waste. As if the horror of this twisted tragedy weren't already obvious enough, it is culminated by murder and the consumption of dead bodies, where the stench of putrefaction is greeted with pleasure. The prevailing ideology of carnism, or the paradox between people's values and actions with respect to eating animals, transforms the misery of this massacre into a process that is ostensibly "necessary" (vegan diets are deficient), "normal" (most people do it), "natural" (humans are carnivores), and "nice" (it tastes good) (Piazza et al. 2015). As a series of defense mechanisms, psychic numbing, and cognitive dissonance used to shield oneself from taking responsibility for their apathetic participation and unthinking involvement in the torture, suffering and killing of nonhuman animal others, one of the most important elements of carnism is how only certain species are considered "food" and accepting treatment of those animals in ways that would be rejected as unacceptable cruelty if applied to other species. The process of othering along with its intersectional implications are clear, as indeed these same exact apologia have been used to justify racism in the form of slavery and sexism in the form of denying women's suffrage (Joy 2010). The other is always treated to an exceptionalism that depoliticizes their bodies and gives license to ferocious and abominable violence. The rationalization of this carnage follows a fallacious circular logic where animals categorized as food are viewed as having diminished mental faculties, and owing to this perceived inferiority their place as food is reinforced.

In short, human supremacy works the same way as white supremacy, gender supremacy, or any other form of domination, that is, through normative assumptions that situate preeminence in the self, while attributing deficiencies to the other. Sadly such thinking prevails even among those tasked with being the social conscious of society. Within the academy veganism remains marginalized and when the issue is raised, scholars often respond with ambivalence, disregard, or attempts to assuage their guilt. At an "Anarchist Geographies" session at a recent meeting of the American Association of Geographers in 2016, two critical scholars I admire and respect, responded as discussants to papers that brought veganism into view by speaking to their frailties. The first recounted his "bacon" cravings, while the other pointed to the supposed inconvenience of veganism. There is a conceptual thoughtlessness to these sentiments that must be challenged. So for example, white privilege is convenient for white people, just as anthroprivilege is convenient for humans. Does mere convenience make one's own apathy justified? How many critical scholars are making defenses of white privilege or male privilege? I would hope none. So why then are so many willing to make defenses of anthropriviledge, whether in thought or deed? For the first speaker, his craving to consume the flesh of a murdered pig was deflected by saying that while he wished he could be vegan, he admitted he was "weak." There is much to be said about dependency and addiction to particular foods, and particularly meat and dairy, but when refracted through an intersectional lens a justification of weakness is clearly revealed as absurd. Satiating a sexual appetite with an unwilling participant is undeniably an act of domination, where the "weakness" of the perpetrator is no defense for such action. While there are significant differences between each of these behaviours, whereby sexual assault and eating animals cannot be reduced to moral equivalents, I do nonetheless want to highlight the similarity insofar as each functions to objectify the victim in a similar way (Adams 2002). The abused is reduced to an inanimate thing that serves only to yield pleasure to the perpetrator and death (physical or emotional) for the victim. Critical scholars need to be called to account for these disturbing sorts of rationalizations with respect to non-human animals and their indifference. Given that the emancipation of one is premised on the liberation of all, we can't be quiet any longer. A total liberation ecology demands that we grapple with these inconsistencies in our praxis vis-à-vis marginalized others.

Along these lines, the fact that academic gatherings at conferences and various university functions continue to serve decaying animal tissue, skin, and bones is a testament to just how devoid of critical thought on this matter academia is. Eating the torsos and limbs of slaughtered victims around vegans is one the most disrespectful and abhorrent practices. For someone who has taken an ethical stance against the murder of another sentient being, consuming that being in their presence is to ask that individual to sanction an act of violence, to give license to a sense of indifference they struggle against. Every bite into the decomposing corpse is scaring and painful reminder of the absolution of culpability that is made in the name of "taste." It wouldn't kill anyone to abstain from meat for a single meal, and yet it always kills somebody when meat is consumed. And that's just it, a sentient being, a body, a *somebody* has their life taken to satisfy a craving. There are other things to eat, and consequently nothing could be more horrifying, more cruel, and more violent than taking another's life for this selfish reason. Yet as the animal is othered by the rending of its flesh between your teeth, its murder somehow doesn't count. In this process, so too is the vegan othered as their emotional response to this ghastly performance of butchery that is played out before their eyes is not considered. It is the equivalent of asking someone suffering post-traumatic stress to sit down with an oppressor and bear witness to them exacting their violence on another individual, to allow them to desecrate their body and commit the ultimate act of abhorrence by swallowing their flesh. If political ecology is to be understood as a "theoretical commitment to critical social theory and a post-positivist understanding of nature and the productions of knowledge about it" (Bridge et al. 2015, 7), then the unfolding violence of the capitalism demands greater scrutiny of how animals are situated within its production. Since capitalism is a social order that seeks to recreate the world in its own image as "second nature" (Smith 2010), then just as trees become "timber" for milling and bitumen becomes "oil" for refining, so too do the bodies of animals become "food" for consumption. Their independent worth is torn from of them, limb from limb, as their being is rendered only in terms of its utility with respect to human purposes.

A life, precious and irreplaceable, is snuffed out of existence in the obscene satisfaction of something as arbitrary and adaptable as taste. As the cadaver is consumed, sentience is denied. The intrinsically precious lives of animals are literally and figuratively dismembered into a functional role in the satiation of human desire. The very idea of "meat," as a socially produced euphemism for mangled and mutilated body parts, is consequently a key signifier of anthroparchy, where a relation of domination becomes explicit through the wider violence of capitalism. Much of the cognitive dissonance surrounding the slaughter of animals is rooted in the binary production of "human" versus "nature" that is made possible through a capitalist lens, where the latter is continually produced as a site for exploitation and extraction by the former. When humans and animals are instead imagined as being co-constituted within the elegant symmetry of existence, and the Earth itself is considered as an integral whole (Clark and Martin 2013), such violence disappears. It is for this reason that many vegans see no issue with the relationship between some Indigenous peoples and non-human animals, as the bond is one of mutual aid. Rather than a hierarchy with humans situated at the pinnacle, each expression of life is but a single drop of dew, cast within the infinite connections and interdependences of Indra's net. When grinders, captive bolt pistols, veal crates, and battery cages are replaced with a deep humility and profound respect, human supremacy breaks down. Since the whole of non-human nature, ranging from climate to cows and bacteria to broccoli, has agency that entwines itself within human struggles, resistance emerges through human/non-human alliances. The soil will revolt when stressed through monoculture, and as livelihoods are threatened from poor crop yields, so too will the people. There is a shared struggle here. So to the question of the animal, we should start to appreciate how, as Said argued, the "other" is inevitably implicated in the construction of the "self." Any separation is always and only artificial.

THE INTEGRAL FREEDOM OF VEGANARCHISM

Michael Watts (quoted in Walker 2006: 389) has argued that political ecology should celebrate its diversity, and "let the flowers of openness and dialogue bloom." But what are we to make of those who can't engage in dialog? How does a cow that has had her throat slit communicate post-mortem that her execution was anything but compassionate and that she didn't want to die? How do so-called free range chickens convey the torment of being so crowded in huge warehouses that they cannot spread their wings or the torture of having their beaks seared off? How can any flowers bloom next to the rivers of blood and excrement that flow from factory farms, poisoning the soils, polluting the waterways, and choking the skies? Surely openness in political ecology should consider that eighty percent of the antibiotics used in the United States are fed to livestock. Certainly it would have to give attention to the fact that pneumonia is endemic among hogs in factory farms due to being kept in small concrete cages and left to wallow in their own manure. And obviously the fact that methane from the animal agriculture industry remains largely unregulated, despite the fact that livestock production accounts for approximately thirty-five percent of all anthropogenic methane emissions would be taken into account. If, as Walker (2006, 388) argues, "it is probably fair to say that political ecology that does not focus on power as it shapes human-environmental relations would not be political ecology as most recognize it today," then one wonders how political ecology is recognizable at all when there remains such a profound blind spot at the center of its analysis. For political ecology to function in the critical capacity it claims, relations of power—including those between human and non-human, must be foregrounded. More-than-human and hybrid geographies have opened considerable space for reflection on the centering of humans (Whatmore 2008), rejecting a priori distinctions of separate worlds such as human/animal, or nature/culture. In this way they seek to afford animals a position that isn't reducible to human attributed qualities or the mindset of instrumentalism. Such an outlook can work to transform sensibilities, signaling a potential to promote a renewed sense of connectedness to the Earth as a whole in a way that political ecology has heretofore been unable to do.

While hybrid and more-than-human geographies might lead us down a path than begins to converge with the "bioethics" of Arne Naess (1989) in the articulation of his deep ecology, the intersection isn't assured and there are obstacles that might yet trip us up. In particular, animals are seemingly stripped of agency and inherent qualities cannot be envisaged, which raises concerns for the corporeality of animal bodies as they become "lost among a miasma of stretched out subjects made and remade in complex intra-actions with myriad other things" (Wilber 2009). The infusion of anarchism into political ecology and reading them both alongside more-than-human and hybrid geographies offers promise for a more liberatory outlook, whereby "a truly humble, empathic, animal-respecting stance" can begin to emerge (Dominik 2015, 23). Total liberation ecology would accordingly bring the radical potential of these various perspectives together. The result would be a centering of the place of veganism and the formulation of "vegan geographies," precisely because the refusal of the commodity status that animals have been assigned draws attention to a broader set of power relations at the heart of capitalism and its inherently human supremacist values. While Marxist political ecology, like Marxism more generally, has failed to challenge to the "anthropocentric, speciesist, and humanist dogmas entrenched in radical and progressive traditions" (Best 2014, 79), aligning anarchism with political ecology offers a greater chance for a holistic emancipatory theory. Most of the components of a total liberation perspective mesh very well with the intended focus of contemporary political ecology. Within the dialectical approach to human–nonhuman natures, we can appreciate how an anti-oppression ethic vis-à-vis ecosystems, nonhuman animals, and humans coincides with such an outlook. Similarly we can also recognize how anti-capitalist perspectives have been folded very thoroughly into political ecology. Yet when it comes to anarchism and the use of direct action tactics, which are also constitutive of a total liberation approach, political ecology has been slow to respond.

One of the reasons for this is that political ecology has been advanced as a scholarly exercise and has not embraced praxis in the same way that feminists, participatory geographies, and other forms of scholar-activism have. Again we can point to the prioritization of Marxism within political ecology as a key to this failure. There are distinct limits of the radical imagination of Marxists, which Walker (2006, 388) demonstrates when he argues that "For political ecologists who desire to engage policy and still work with Marxian analytical methods, the question arises whether a degree of compromise and even subterfuge is justified to get the camel's nose of radical critique under the tent of mainstream policy." For Walker the point is still to contribute to the formulation of policy in the hierarchical halls of government, rather than taking direct action in the here and now to create the kinds of changes we'd like to see in the world through a prefigurative political ecology. Is policy ever going to stop pipelines from being built when the political system is thoroughly corrupted by the promise of economic growth? Is it going to undo the arsenal of law that seeks to silence those who seek to lift the veil on what goes on in factory farms and incarcerate those who would open a cage when presented with a confined victim of torture and abuse? Moreover, the failure is reflected in the fact that "the overriding concern of the Left is with fisheries, not fish; with forests, not its nonhuman inhabitants; with 'resources' for human use, not animals with inherent value" (Best 2016, 97). Marxist political ecology was not devised as a biocentric respect for the innate value of all life, and its anthroprocentrism can only serve to stifle the possibility of total liberation. Enter anarchist political ecology, appropriately attuned to an integral sensibility that places all forms of domination, including human supremacy, at the center of its concern.

The local community center in my neighborhoods recently organized a message board for children to pin up messages of hope and social justice. My daughter's message, which stated very simply "go vegan," was defaced by what was clearly an adult, who wrote, "if you can; but don't feel guilty if it's just not for you." Whether one is vegan or not, the childism on display here should be immediately obvious (Young-Bruehl 2012). The introduction of this caveat was just as much an attempt to speak over, discredit, and silence the voice of a child, as it was a rejection of the ethics of veganism. Consequently, it serves as a reminder that oppression is always intersectional. In other words, it is the same process of domination that sees a child as an illegitimate voice that condones the killing of non-human animals as "food." The child and the animal are both constructed as "other," and in this fabrication "our" agency is elevated above "them," where violence becomes easily rationalized. Small wonder then that childhood is so frequently marred by the domination of adults, where "adulthood is privileged as the space of agency and freedom—deliberative and principled—in contradistinction to the slavish capitulation to impulse that characterizes childhood" (Rollo 2015). This insightful rejection of misopedy could also be read through the lens of anthroparchy: humanity is privileged as the space of agency and freedom—deliberative and principled—in contradistinction to the slavish capitulation to impulse that characterizes animality. When we eat animals, we objectify their bodies as objects for our consumption, presenting them in ways, such as the removal of head and hooves, intended to make us forget about the body that was (Joy 2010). Try as we might to disavow the agency of the other, a body in pain, a threatened body, a body in the midst of torture as death seems assured will always reveals its agency through piercing screams and flailing limbs. Veganism isn't a fashion that can be "just not for you." It is an ethical response to the senseless and unnecessary mass murder of sentient beings caught up in the violent machinery of contemporary capitalism. It is a commitment to the defiance of human supremacy, which represents the same reprehensible scourge as all forms of supremacy, whether in support of race, gender, sexuality, age, or any other identity category. The implication of such an integral approach to violence is that none are free until all are free.

CONCLUSION

As Nochella et al. (2015, 12) aptly summarizes, "Total liberation is intersectionality in action." Yet one of the key points of weakness in a political ecology perspective to date is the way that non-human animals continue to be depoliticized and assigned to the category of environment. While being draw back into the frame, the lives of animals remain marginalized as they continue to be conceptualized largely in terms of utility to human livelihoods and well-being, rather than considered as having intrinsic and inalienable value in their own right. Insofar as political ecology is concerned, there is consequently a profound importance to adopting the thoroughly integrative approach of a total liberation perspective. For political ecology to succeed as a worthwhile approach, "it must become as radically dialectical as possible," at once ruthless in its outlook on capitalism and destructive in its response to the blinkeredness of anthropocentricism, while also caring for the well-being of the biosphere as a whole and creative in its placing of humans back within the web of nature (Clark 2001, 2). The thoroughly hybrid and relational ethics of total liberation avoids the limited morality of the animal rights discourse, which problematically ignores the nonhuman majority in elevating small groups of species (for example dogs in America and cows in India) to ethical parity with humans and therefore frames the question of animals once more through an anthropocentric lens.

What is at stake in political ecology is nothing less than the very fate of the planet. A burden that we often assume must be shouldered alone. Yet thinking this to be the case is to once more assume a position of human supremacy, renewing the hubris that has long underpinned everything from Marxism to modernization theory. Such anthroparchy also rests at the rotten core of capitalism, a form of domination that much of the Left is not well equipped to transcend given the class-centric outlook that has defined much of its formulation. In contrast, the intersectional spaces of feminism and the integral geography of anarchism offer significant promise for the disavowal of such speciesism (Harcourt and Nelson 2015; Springer 2016). Reconvening the oneness that has been lost in human civilization's forward march is the only path of hope, and it is irrefutable that the fates of humans, animals, and the earth are inextricably tied together. "Progress can no longer entail the zero sum game of human 'gain' at the expense of animals and the environment," Best (2012, 158) argues, "Rather, a deeper concept of progress must emerge that eliminates the opposition between human and animals and society and nature. Most fundamentally, it would understand the profound interrelatedness of all aspects of planetary ecology." Total liberation ecology allows us to realize that the future will not be decided solely through human intervention. The providence of the Earth is collective, unavoidably bound in unison by the intersections and evolution of all life forms, identities, and processes. As our land bleeds from the lacerations that come with the clearing of its trees, as our oceans choke from being fed with effluence from rivers of shit, and as our skies converge with greenhouse gases that will eventually suffocate the life out of the planet, hope is difficult to find. We've been consumed in the throes of a global bloodbath called capitalism, and as with all great noirs, only in the final revelation do we finally recognize that the enemy is inside. In that final scene all moral ambiguity is stripped away, and we see our own selves reflected in this fatalist mirror. We are the criminals. The antagonists. The executioners.

Yet in the grace of humility there exists the potential for a radical transformation of planetary consciousness. Looking within, attuning ourselves to the affective lives of the animal other, and finding the current that flows through all life on this planet is to realize that "what is human and what is natural is always the effect, rather than the grounds for politics" (Lorimer 2009). When we become aware that human interests blend with that of nature, binding us together as a single idea, we can begin to think quite differently. We repair the damages incurred by our predecessors and in this process of having become the consciousness of the earth (Reclus 1894), we see the beauty of harmony and recognize that love and life are indivisible. Love is the preeminent condition, temporarily shattered only through the falsity of separation. The reflexivity that veganism implies is an attempt to reconnect with this vital frequency and realize the other of nature as self. When we establish our politics as a total liberation ecology, the human/nature binary breaks down allowing everything to transform from the assumed fixity of partition to an inherently shared processes of symbiosis and mutual becoming. This unfolding dance has never been choreographed, and the sequence has no beginning and no end. It is a geopoetics traced in air, a bending of the light of existence, a realization of mutual aid through the process of evolution (Kropotkin 1902). So it is not our actions as "humans" that will determine the fate of the world but paradoxically the abandonment of our humanity. By letting go of our ego we might yet come to learn that love, planetary well-being, and the immanence of connection are all one and the same.

NOTE

1. The term *holocaust* is derived from the Ancient Greek *holokaustos*, and originally referred to animal sacrifice, only later being applied as a metaphor to describe the atrocities in Nazi Germany.

REFERENCES

Adams, C. 2002. *The Sexual Politics of Meat: A Feminist-Vegetarian Critical Theory*. New York, NY: The Continuum Publishing Company.

Benton, T. 1993. *Ecology, Animal Rights, and Social Justice*. London: Verso.

Best, S. 2012. "Total liberation and moral progress: The struggle for human evolution." In: *Animal Ethics: Past and Present Perspectives*. Ed. Protopapadakis, E. D. Berlin: Logos Verlag, pp. 233–256.

Best, S. 2014. *The Politics of Total Liberation: Revolution for the 21st Century*. New York: Palgrave MacMillan.

Bookchin, M. 1982. *The Ecology of Freedom: The Emergence and Dissolution of Hierarchy*. Palo Alto, CA: Cheshire Books.

Bookchin, M. 1995. *The Philosophy of Social Ecology: Essays on Dialectical Naturalism*. 2nd Ed. Montreal: Black Rose Books.

Bookchin, M. 2004. *Post-Scarcity Anarchism*. Oakland, CA: AK Press.

Bridge, G., McCarthy, J., and Perreault, T. 2015. "Editor's introduction." In: *The Routledge Handbook of Political Ecology*. Eds. Perreault, T., Bridge, G., and McCarthy, J. London: Routledge, pp. 3–18.

Castree, N. 2005. *Nature*. London: Routledge.

252 *Simon Springer*

Clark, J. 1997. "The dialectical social geography of Elisée Reclus." In: *Philosophy and Geography I: Space, Place, and Environmental Ethics.* Eds. Light, A., and Smith, J. M. London: Rowman & Littlefield. pp. 117–142.

Clark, J. 2001. "Contributions to the critique of political ecology." *Capitalism Nature Socialism 12* (3), 29–36.

Clark, J. 2008. *Dialectical Political Ecology.* Presented at Colby College, Waterville, Maine, October 6, 2008. https://www.academia.edu/2937823/_Dialectical_Political_Ecology_.

Clark, J. 2012. "Political ecology." In: *Encyclopedia of Applied Ethics.* 2nd Ed., Vol. 3. Ed. Chadwick, R. San Diego: Academic Press, pp. 505–516.

Clark J., and Martin, C. 2013. *Anarchy, Geography, Modernity: Selected Writings of Elisée Reclus.* Oakland, CA: PM Press.

Dominik, B. 2015. Anarcho-veganism revisited. In: *Anarchism and Animal Liberation: Essays on Complementary Elements of Total Liberation.* Eds. Nocella, A. J., White, R. J., and Cudworth, E. Jefferson, NC: McFarland & Company. pp. 23–39.

Emel, J., and Neo, H. 2011. *Political Ecologies of Meat.* New York: Routledge.

Haraway, D. 2008. *When Species Meet.* Minneapolis: University of Minnesota Press.

Harcourt, W., and Nelson, I. L. 2015. *Practising Feminist Political Ecologies: Moving beyond the "Green Economy."* London: Zed Books.

Harvey, D. 1996. *Justice, Nature and the Geography of Difference.* London: Blackwell.

Jarosz, L., 2004. "Political ecology as ethical practice." *Political Geography 23* (7), pp. 917–927.

Joy, M. 2010. *Why We Love Dogs, Eat Pigs and Wear Cows: An Introduction to Carnism.* San Francisco, CA: Conari Press.

Kowalczyk, A. 2014. "Mapping non-human resistance in an age of biocapital." In: *The Rise of Critical Animal Studies: From the Margins to the Centre.* Eds. Taylor, N., and Twine R. New York: Routledge, pp. 183–200.

Kropotkn, P. 1902/2008. *Mutual Aid: A Factor in Evolution.* Charleston, SC: Forgotten.

Lorimer, J. 2009. "Posthumanism/Posthumanistic Geographies." *International Encyclopedia of Human Geography.* Eds. Kitchen, R., and Thrift, N., pp. 344–354.

Marx, K. 1867/1990. *Capital V. 1: A Critique of Political Economy.* New York: Penguin Classics.

Merchant, C. 2005. *Radical Ecology: The Search for a Liveable World.* London: Routledge.

Morton, T. (2016). *Dark Ecology: For a Logic of Future Coexistence.* New York: Columbia University Press.

Naess, A. 1989. *Ecology, Community and Lifestyle: Outline of an Ecosophy.* Cambridge: Cambridge University Press.

Nocella, A. J., White, R. J., and Cudworth, E. 2015. Introduction: The Intersections of Critical Animal Studies and Anarchist Studies for Liberation. In: *Anarchism and Animal Liberation: Essays on Complementary Elements of Total Liberation.* Eds. Nocella, A. J., White, R. J., and Cudworth, E. Jefferson, NC: McFarland & Company. pp. 7–20.

Peet, R., Robbins, P., and Watts, M. 2011. *Global Political Ecology*. London: Routledge.

Peet, R., and Watts, M. eds. 1996. "Liberation ecology: Development, sustainability, and environment in an age of market triumphalism." *Liberation Ecologies: Environment, Development, Social Movements*. First Edition. London: Routledge, pp. 1–45.

Pellow, D. N. 2014. *Total Liberation: The Power and Promise of Animal Rights and the Radical Earth Movement*. Minneapolis: University of Minnesota Press.

Piazza, J., Ruby, M. B., Loughnan, S., Luong, M., Kulik, J., Watkins, H. M., and Seigerman, M., 2015. "Rationalizing meat consumption. The 4Ns." *Appetite 91*, pp. 114–128.

Reclus, E. 1894. *The Earth and Its Inhabitants: The Universal Geography*. London: J. S. Virtue.

Reclus, E. 1901. "On Vegetarianism." *Humane Review*. http://dwardmac.pitzer.edu/Anarchist_Archives/bright/reclus/onvegetarianism.html.

Robbins, P. 2012. *Political Ecology: A Critical Introduction*. Oxford: Wiley-Blackwell.

Rollo, T. 2015. *The Age of Empire: Development, Modernity, and the Nightmare of Childhood*. Unpublished.

Smith, N. 2010. *Uneven Development: Nature, Capital and the Production of Space*. London: Verso.

Springer, S. 2016. *The Anarchist Roots of Geography: Toward Spatial Emancipation*. Minneapolis: University of Minnesota Press.

Swyngedouw, E. 1999. "Modernity and hybridity: Nature, regeneracionismo, and the production of the Spanish waterscape, 1890–1930." *Annals of the Association of American Geographers 89* (3), pp. 443–465.

Walker, R. 2006. "Political ecology: Where is the policy?" *Progress in Human Geography 30* (2), pp. 382–395.

Watts, M. 2000. "Political ecology." In: *A Companion to Economic Geography*. Eds. Barnes, T. and Sheppard, E. Oxford: Blackwell, pp. 257–274.

Watts, M., and Peet, R. 2004. "Liberating Political ecology." In *Liberation Ecologies: Environment, Development, Social Movements*. Second Edition. Eds. Peet, R., and Watts, M. London: Routledge, pp. 3–43.

Whatmore, S., 2006. "Materialist returns: Practising cultural geography in and for a more-than-human world." *Cultural Geographies, 13* (4), pp. 600–609.

Whatmore, S., 2017. "Hybrid geographies: rethinking the 'human' in human geography." In: *Environment: Critical Essays in Human Geography*. Eds. Anderson, K., and Braun, B. London: Routledge. pp. 411–428.

Wilber, C. 2009. "Posthumanism/Posthumanistic Geographies." *International Encyclopedia of Human Geography*. Eds. Kitchen, R., and Thrift, N. pp. 122–126.

Wilde, L., 2000. "'The creatures, too, must become free': Marx and the Animal/Human Distinction." *Capital & Class, 24* (3), pp. 37–53.

Young-Bruehl, E. 2012. *Childism: Confronting Prejudice against Children*. New Haven, CT: Yale University Press.

Index

Note: Page numbers in *italics* refer to figures.

About the Editors and Contributors

Maleea Acker teaches Geography and Canadian Studies at the University of Victoria. Her work takes multiple forms, from scholarly to journalistic, literary to artistic. She serves on the editorial board of the Malahat Review. Her book of essays, *Gardens Aflame: Garry Oak Meadows of BC's South Coast*, charts the Indigenous history and restoration of an endangered Vancouver Island ecosystem; her third poetry collection is forthcoming in 2022 from Nightwood Editions.

Randall Amster, J.D., Ph.D., is Co-Director and Teaching Professor of Environmental Studies at Georgetown University. He teaches and publishes on subjects including peace and nonviolence, social and environmental justice, political theory, and emerging technologies. His most recent book is *Peace Ecology* (Routledge, 2015).

Ali Bilgin was born in Istanbul, studied philosophy at Galatasaray University, and took philosophy courses at Saint-Denis and Paris-Sorbonne Universities. Ali worked on a master thesis project on Decartes's conception of living being and currently works as archivist and editor at Tek-Esin Foundation in Istanbul. Ali is co-editor of *Human, Animal and Beyond* (İnsan, Hayvan ve Ötesi, 2021), a collection of texts on animal studies, with Kiraz Özdoğan and Fatih Tatari.

John Clark is an eco-communitarian anarchist writer, activist, and educator. He lives and works in New Orleans, where his family has been for twelve generations, and at Bayou La Terre, in the forest of the Mississippi Gulf Coast. His most recent book is *Between Earth and Empire: From the Necrocene to the Beloved Community*.

Martin Locret-Collet is a Paris-based geographer, urban designer and political ecologist who holds a PhD from the University of Birmingham (UK). His interests lay in community planning, governance, open democracy and the commons. Martin is either a hands-on, very practical researcher or a rather thoughtful and daydreaming practitioner, depending on who you ask!

Patrik Gažo is a doctoral student at the Department of Environmental Studies at Masaryk University, dealing with society's socio-ecological transformation in terms of industrial work, just transition of production, and (auto) mobility. He focuses on contradictions and relationships between the interests of the working class and nature and how it relates to efforts to address the environmental and climate crisis. Specifically, he examines the role of production workers in the process of transition of the automotive industry to electromobility and also automobile workers´ opportunities and obstacles to be a part of the larger socio-ecological transformation of the society.

Jennifer Mateer is an Adjunct Professor in the Department of Geography at the University of Victoria, Canada. She is also a SSHRC-funded Post-Doctoral Research Fellow at the University of British Columbia, Canada. Her research focuses on the intersections of environmental justice, political ecology, animal geographies, and participatory action research. These projects have allowed Jennifer to live and work across Turtle Island (Canada, the USA and Mexico) as well as India and Rwanda.

Shane Mc Donnell is a vegan and a political activist in the Republic of Ireland. In 2014 he received a bachelor's degree in Philosophy and Theology from All Hallows College, a sister college of Dublin City University (DCU) and his master's degree in Philosophy and Public Affairs from University College Dublin (UCD) in 2015. Shane campaigned successfully as a member of the Abortion Rights Campaign (ARC) to remove an article from the Irish constitution criminalising abortion. Shane's main philosophical interest is Nietzsche. Other research interests include, but are not limited to, the environment, restorative justice and the rise of the far right.

Ben O'Heran is an activist scholar living in the country currently known as "Canada". They investigate multispecies relationships, explore anarchism's ecological past, and theorize more egalitarian relationships between humans, other-than-human animals, and plants. Ben is also the host of the Crittercism Podcast.

H. Kiraz Özdoğan is graduated from Sociology Department at Mimar Sinan Fine Art University with a thesis named *Collective Ecoagriculture, Human Self- Management and Management of Non-Human Living Beings in Longo Maï*. Currently a visiting scholar in Anthropology in Yeditepe University (Turkey), she lectures on Ecology and Anthropology, and Quantitative Methods. Her research centers on relations between human and non-human beings encompassing different occurrences of human centered power relations. She is the co-editor (with Fatih Tatari and Ali Bilgin) of *Human, Animal and Beyond* (İnsan, Hayvan ve Ötesi, 2021). She is currently working on the archive of her grand-grandfather (Sedat Aziz Erim), who was a bureaucrat in the early Turkish Republic.

R.D. is a communist with an interest in struggles over animality, dehumanization, racialization, and colonization.

Friederike Schmitz studied philosophy and German literature and received her PhD from Heidelberg University, Germany, with a thesis on the nature and methods of philosophy. She's the author of two books and a number of papers on animal ethics and political theory of human-animal relations. After several years of research and teaching at various universities, she is now an independent scholar, speaker and activist in the animal liberation and climate justice movement in Germany.

Marcelo Lopes de Souza is a professor of environmental geography and political ecology at the Department of Geography of the Federal University of Rio de Janeiro (UFRJ), Brazil. He acted as an academic visitor or visiting professor at several universities in Europe (Germany, United Kingdom and Spain) and Latin America (Mexico). He has published seventeen books (thirteen monographs and four edited volumes) and about one hundred and forty papers and book chapters in several languages, covering subjects such as the spatial dimension of social movements, political ecology (focusing especially on environmental justice) and the epistemology of geography.

Simon Springer is an Earthling and one of the approximately 117 billion humans who have ever lived.

Ophélie Véron works as a Leverhulme Early Career Fellow at the Department of Geography of the University of Sheffield. She is also associate researcher at the Marc Bloch Center, Berlin, and international fellow at the Centre for Metropolitan Studies of the Technische Universität Berlin. Her work focuses on urban divisions, socio-ecological transformation and social justice, animal rights activism and anarchist geographies. In 2022, she will join the TU Berlin as a Marie Skłodowska-Curie fellow.

Richard J. White is a Reader in Human Geography at Sheffield Hallam University, UK. Greatly influenced by anarchist praxis, his work explores a range of ethical, economic and activist landscapes rooted in questions of social and spatial justice. Richard has published his research widely, including contributions to *A Historical Scholarly Collection of Writings on the Earth Liberation Front* (2019); *Education for Total Liberation* (2019); *Animal Oppression and Capitalism* (2017); *Critical Animal Geographies* (2014) and *Defining Critical Animal Studies* (2014).

www.ingramcontent.com/pod-product-compliance
Lightning Source LLC
Chambersburg PA
CBHW050632280326
41932CB00015B/2611